# EARLY CHILDHOOD EDUCATION 92/93

**Thirteenth Edition**

## Editor

### Karen Menke Paciorek
**Eastern Michigan University**

Karen Menke Paciorek is an assistant professor of Early Childhood Education at Eastern Michigan University. Her professional training is in Early Childhood Education with a B.S. from the University of Pittsburgh, an M.A. from George Washington University, and a Ph.D. from Peabody College of Vanderbilt University. She is the vice president of the Michigan Association for the Education of Young Children, and she serves on the advisory board for many community groups. Her workshops and presentations focus on quality programming, teacher training, and curriculum development.

## Editor

### Joyce Huth Munro
**Centenary College**

Joyce Huth Munro is Chair of the Education Division at Centenary College. She received her Ph.D. from Peabody College of Vanderbilt University. In addition to administration and teaching, she directs the Children's Center at Centenary College. Regionally and nationally, she presents seminars on curriculum design and teacher education. Currently, she is coordinator of a research project on case studies in teacher education for the National Association for Early Childhood Teacher Educators.

Cover illustration by Mike Eagle

Annual Editions
*A Library of Information from the Public Press*

**The Dushkin Publishing Group, Inc.**
**Sluice Dock, Guilford, Connecticut 06437**

# The Annual Editions Series

Annual Editions is a series of over 55 volumes designed to provide the reader with convenient, low-cost access to a wide range of current, carefully selected articles from some of the most important magazines, newspapers, and journals published today. Annual Editions are updated on an annual basis through a continuous monitoring of over 300 periodical sources. All Annual Editions have a number of features designed to make them particularly useful, including topic guides, annotated tables of contents, unit overviews, and indexes. For the teacher using Annual Editions in the classroom, an Instructor's Resource Guide with test questions is available for each volume.

## VOLUMES AVAILABLE

Africa
Aging
American Government
American History, Pre-Civil War
American History, Post-Civil War
Anthropology
Biology
Business and Management
Business Ethics
Canadian Politics
China
Commonwealth of Independent States and Central/Eastern Europe (Soviet Union)
Comparative Politics
Computers in Education
Computers in Business
Computers in Society
Criminal Justice
Drugs, Society, and Behavior
Early Childhood Education
Economics
Educating Exceptional Children
Education
Educational Psychology
Environment
Geography
Global Issues
Health
Human Development
Human Resources
Human Sexuality

International Business
Japan
Latin America
Life Management
Macroeconomics
Management
Marketing
Marriage and Family
Microeconomics
Middle East and the Islamic World
Money and Banking
Nutrition
Personal Growth and Behavior
Physical Anthropology
Psychology
Public Administration
Race and Ethnic Relations
Social Problems
Sociology
State and Local Government
Third World
Urban Society
Violence and Terrorism
Western Civilization, Pre-Reformation
Western Civilization, Post-Reformation
Western Europe
World History, Pre-Modern
World History, Modern
World Politics

Library of Congress Cataloging in Publication Data
Main entry under title: Annual Editions: Early Childhood Education. 1992/93.
    1. Education, Preschool—Periodicals. 2. Child development—Periodicals. 3. Child rearing—United States—Periodicals. I. Paciorek, Karen Menke, *comp.*; Munro, Joyce Huth, *comp.* II. Title: Early Childhood Education.
ISBN 1–56134–084–7          372.21'05          77–640114
HQ777.A7A

Thirteenth Edition

Manufactured by The Banta Company, Harrisonburg, Virginia 22801

# Editors/Advisory Board

# To the Reader

In publishing ANNUAL EDITIONS we recognize the enormous role played by the magazines, newspapers, and journals of the *public press* in providing current, first-rate educational information in a broad spectrum of interest areas. Within the articles, the best scientists, practitioners, researchers, and commentators draw issues into new perspective as accepted theories and viewpoints are called into account by new events, recent discoveries change old facts, and fresh debate breaks out over important controversies.

Many of the articles resulting from this enormous editorial effort are appropriate for students, researchers, and professionals seeking accurate, current material to help bridge the gap between principles and theories and the real world. These articles, however, become more useful for study when those of lasting value are carefully *collected, organized, indexed,* and *reproduced* in a *low-cost format,* which provides easy and permanent access when the material is needed. That is the role played by *Annual Editions.* Under the direction of each volume's *Editor,* who is an expert in the subject area, and with the guidance of an *Advisory Board,* we seek each year to provide in each ANNUAL EDITION a current, well-balanced, carefully selected collection of the best of the public press for your study and enjoyment. We think you'll find this volume useful, and we hope you'll take a moment to let us know what you think.

How has the professional of early childhood education weathered the past year? How are young children and their families faring in our country today? As teachers, we know it is good practice to communicate a negative comment about a child's behavior or performance to a parent sandwiched between two positives. We would prefer to start this *Annual Editions: Early Childhood Education* with a positive, upbeat article on young children; unfortunately, they are few and far between. Professional journals and magazines are filled with doom and gloom articles on the state of America's children and families. Articles 2–5 in this edition are not good news, but they do contain suggestions for professionals who are highly motivated to make changes and are ready to act.

A major purpose of the thirteenth edition of *Annual Editions: Early Childhood Education 92/93* is to highlight the progress made on issues facing young children and their families and to plan the hard work that lies ahead. We are hearing a great deal about the family and children during 1992, this being an election year. Many groups have drafted position papers or documents outlining proposals to improve the lives of children and families. The issues of family leave, national health insurance, revised tax laws for dependent deductions, the availability and quality of child care, and divorce laws focusing first on the children are discussed in many of the statements. As citizens concerned with the care and education of children and the quality of life for their families, the most important step we can take during this election year is to educate others on what is needed and to work diligently to make life better for all our children. Become involved and make your voice heard.

After a long and often frustrating battle lasting more than twenty years, the Child Care and Development Block Grant was passed by Congress and signed by President Bush in 1990. In the final hours of the budget negotiations, there was cause for a major celebration as the United States finally had legislation and funding to assist in providing for quality education and care for young children. Families, child care professionals, and children will definitely benefit, but, as with all new legislation and appropriations, it takes time for the funds to be distributed and decisions to be made at the state level.

Given the diversity of topics included in the volume, it may be used with several audiences: with parents as an available resource in an early childhood center; with undergraduate or graduate students studying early childhood education; or with professionals pursuing further development. It is also useful in many ways as an anthology of primary and secondary sources; as supplementary readings correlated with textbooks in developmental or child psychology, human development, special education, family life, pediatrics, or child care; as a source book for individual term papers, oral presentations, or projects; or for class discussions, group work, panel discussions, or debates.

The selection of articles for this edition has been a cooperative venture between the two editors, the members of the advisory board, and other professionals. We would especially like to thank the advisory board who share with us in the selection process. Your comments on this edition are welcomed and will serve to modify future anthologies. Please fill out and return the article rating form on the last page. Continue to work diligently for young children, their families, and teachers. Our future depends on it.

Karen Menke Paciorek

Joyce Huth Munro
*Editors*

# Contents

## Unit 1

## Perspectives

Nine selections consider both the national and international development of early childhood education.

**To the Reader** iv
**Topic Guide** 2
**Overview** 4

*A. NATIONAL PERSPECTIVES*

1. **A New Code of Ethics for Early Childhood Educators!** 6
   Stephanie Feeney and Kenneth Kipnis, *Young Children,*
   November 1989.
   Starting in 1984, a National Association for the Education of Young Children (NAEYC) board-established Ethics Commission began a process to clarify the early childhood education profession's understanding of its own ethics. The final document was approved by the NAEYC governing board in July 1989 and was given the name *Code of Ethical Conduct and Statement of Commitment.*

2. **Children in Peril,** Geoffrey Cowley, *Newsweek,* Special 12
   Issue, Summer 1991.
   Being a child in America today is a difficult task. Children under five suffer from *poverty* more than any other age group. *Children are at risk* of facing the effects of abuse, *homelessness, drugs,* and *poverty.* The *federal government* has set goals to assist children and families, but it may be too little, too late. We need strong *advocates* to be the voice for children.

3. **The Shadow Children: Preparing for the Arrival of** 15
   **Crack Babies in School,** Marilee C. Rist, *Research Bulletin,* July 1990.
   Almost overnight, children born exposed to crack cocaine started arriving in schools. The way this *drug* attacks one's body and overall *health* is powerful and relentless. The *special needs* of these children and their families have left *teachers* scrambling for answers to new questions. These *children are at risk* of not being able to function, and their future is in peril. The author ends with five suggestions for those who are ready to act now to help these children.

4. **I Couldn't Afford My Job,** Elizabeth Ritchie Johnson, 20
   *Redbook,* April 1991.
   What would it take to make *dual-income families,* mainly working mothers, happy? The answer from many is more support both financially and emotionally from *employers,* the *federal government,* and others. The *child care* dilemma will be solved through *collaborative efforts,* flexibility, financial support, and a realization that this is not a woman's issue, but an issue that has grave consequences for the entire nation if it continues on a haphazard makeshift track.

5. **When Parents Accept the Unacceptable,** Michael Hoyt 24
   and Mary Ellen Schoonmaker, *Family Circle,* October 15, 1991.
   According to Dr. Edward Zigler of Yale University, "At least one-third of the children in America are having *child-care* experiences that will compromise their development. . . ." The fact that so many children are receiving poor care is compounded by the acceptance of this inadequate care by their *parents.* Professionals need to work diligently to educate parents and to lobby for *health and safety* standards and *quality programming* for all children.

6. **Head Start: The Nation's Pride, A Nation's Challenge,** 29
   Joan Lombardi, *Young Children,* September 1990.
   *Head Start* has developed a set of recommendations for its future based on the first 25 years of service for children living in *poverty.* Services for *children at risk* and *minorities* are still of primary concern, but some new areas are being explored. Recommendations include expanded parent involvement along with program enrollment options, full-day child care, and more *collaborative efforts* among community agencies.

The concepts in bold italics are developed in the article. For further expansion please refer to the Topic Guide and the Index.

### B. INTERNATIONAL PERSPECTIVES

7. **A Global Collage of Impressions: Preschools Abroad,** 36
Leah D. Adams, *Day Care and Early Education,* Spring 1991.
This well-traveled early childhood educator shares with us a glimpse of programs for young children in six countries. As the author points out, having an ***international perspective*** often helps us in developing programs that meet the needs of our own children.

8. **Excellent Early Education: A City in Italy Has It,** 40
Rebecca New, *Young Children,* September 1990.
The early childhood program of the Reggio Emilla preschools in northern Italy has been named the best in the world. The community has formed a unique system of ***high-quality child care programs*** for preschool children and the recent nation-wide tour of an exhibit has increased awareness of this program.

9. **A Glimpse of Kindergarten—Chinese Style,** Geraldine 47
Beaty Shepherd, *Young Children,* November 1991.
The author gives us an informal tour of a Beijing ***kindergarten*** that differs greatly in setting and materials available in Western kindergartens. By becoming familiar with programs in other countries, we can more closely examine how we interact and establish a learning environment for our own children.

**Overview** 52

### A. CHILD DEVELOPMENT

10. **First Year Milestones,** Jenny Friedman, *American Baby,* 54
August 1989.
Researchers have been unable to find a way to evaluate ***infants*** that will accurately predict how well they will do later in life. ***Development*** varies so much that it is difficult to assess children based solely on age. Developmental charts have merit when used correctly by parents and ***infant educators***; they alert adults to possible future difficulties, encouraging early action to solve them.

11. **Easing Separation: A Talk With T. Berry Brazelton,** 59
**M.D.,** *Scholastic Pre-K Today,* August/September 1991.
Everyone's favorite pediatrician and spokesperson for families and children talks about the difficult process of ***separation.*** T. Berry Brazelton discusses ways ***parents*** and children are affected by separation and how ***teachers*** and parents can work together to ease difficult situations that may arise.

12. **Guns and Dolls,** Laura Shapiro, *Newsweek,* May 28, 1990. 62
The author presents new facts along with some often-debated issues related to ***sex differences*** in young children and how they affect ***children's development. Parents,*** often unknowingly, perpetuate traditional sex differences among children through toy purchases, verbal interactions, and parental responsibility around the home. ***Affective development*** is related to the experiences one encounters in his or her environment.

### B. FAMILY LIFE

13. **What Birth Order Means,** Jean Marzollo, *Parents,* 67
December 1990.
How come firstborns have higher IQs than younger siblings? Why do only children have a very positive self-esteem? Do ***parents*** really spoil the baby of the family? How are our ***personality*** and ***temperament*** affected by our birth order? These and other issues relating to a child's birth order in a ***family*** are explored by Jean Marzollo.

# Unit 2

## Child Development and Families

Eight selections consider the effects of family life on the growing child and the importance of parent education.

14. **How Schools Perpetuate Illiteracy,** La Vergne Rosow, 71
*Educational Leadership,* September 1991.
The main focus of this article is to assist teachers who work with children from homes where **illiteracy** is prevelant. Suggestions are given to assist teachers in making home/school connections with all families. La Vergne Rosow does an excellent job of providing an emotional look at the real problem of illiteracy, and how it affects children and the ways in which we teach them.

15. **Children of Divorce,** Candy Carlile, *Childhood Education,* 74
Summer 1991.
In this article, the author lists some effects of **divorce** on children and gives specific suggestions for **teachers.** Included are a list of books that will help relieve some of the stress and assist children and **families** in the healing process.

16. **Single-Parent Families: How Bad for the Children?** 77
K. Alison Clarke-Stewart, *NEA Today,* January 1989.
Children in families undergoing a **divorce** often experience **stress** and turmoil. School need not be another source of stress. Suggestions are given for **parents,** and especially **teachers,** for assisting children and their parents in handling divorce and the transition to life in **single-parent families.** An annotated bibliography is included.

17. **Where Are the Parents?** John McCormick, *Newsweek,* 82
Special Issue, Summer/Fall 1990.
**Teachers** are now responsible for teaching subjects as varied as sex education, moral development, and self-concept. Children come to school not knowing basic rules of health and safety, and they are not encouraged to take schoolwork seriously. **Parent involvement has reached an all-time low** in many areas and teachers are becoming increasingly frustrated. School personnel are sending the message to families, "Help us help your children."

**Overview** 84

A. *PRESCHOOL AND SCHOOL-AGE PROGRAMS*

18. **Guidelines for Appropriate Curriculum Content and** 86
**Assessment in Programs Serving Children Ages 3**
**Through 8,** *Young Children,* March 1991.
What young children should learn and how they should learn it is the heart of **curriculum** development. Two important national associations concerned with young children have designed guidelines to integrate curricular content with educationally and **developmentally appropriate practice.** The guidelines are intended to assist **teachers** in their role as curriculum decision-makers.

19. **Synthesis of Research on Grade Retention,** Lorrie A. 95
Shepard and Mary Lee Smith, *Educational Leadership,* May 1990.
Conclusions from research on children retained in **primary grades** show negative effects on behavior and academic achievement, yet schools continue to use **retention.** Solutions other than retention may be costly, yet are proving more effective. These include individualizing instruction, extra teaching aides, and curriculum support.

Unit

3

# Appropriate Educational Practices

Thirteen selections examine various educational programs, assess the effectiveness of some teaching methods, and consider some of the problems faced by students with special needs.

The concepts in bold italics are developed in the article. For further expansion please refer to the Topic Guide and the Index.

20. **Understanding Bilingual/Bicultural Young Children,** 100
Lourdes Diaz Soto, *Young Children,* January 1991.
The growing number of **bilingual/bicultural** young children in
America requires **teachers** to address the needs of these children
of other languages and cultures. It is also helpful to know and use
**developmentally appropriate** strategies for enhancing the children's second language and bilingual education.

21. **Structure Time & Space To Promote Pursuit of Learn-** 105
**ing in the Primary Grades,** Marianne Gareau and Colleen
Kennedy, *Young Children,* May 1991.
It is important for **teachers** in the **primary grades** to support
children engaged in meaningful learning experiences. They do
this by structuring the classroom day to increase children's task-
orientation time. They provide a variety of **equipment and mate-**
**rials** that foster children's learning in different ways.

22. **Why Not Academic Preschool? (Part 1),** Polly Green- 110
berg, *Young Children,* January 1990.
Polly Greenberg describes, in practical terms, the contrast between choice, discovery, and construction of **developmentally**
**appropriate practice** and direct instruction, seatwork, and com-
pilance of basic **academic** programs. She evaluates the effects of
these two approaches on the growth of **self-esteem** and self-
discipline in young children.

23. **What's Missing in Children's TV,** Peggy Charren, *World* 119
*Monitor,* December 1990.
The founder and president of Action for Children's Television is
not convinced children's programming is the quality it should be.
As more toy manufacturers use half-hour programs to advertise
their products and as classroom newscasts are interrupted by
ads, the concern is that commercialism interferes with even the
best of children's **television**.

24. **School-Age Child Care: A Review of Five Common** 123
**Arguments,** Mick Coleman, Bryan E. Robinson, and Bobbie H. Rowland, *Day Care and Early Education,* Summer
1991.
The authors provide clear information on the importance of
**school-age child care.** They address issues of **quality pro-**
**gramming,** costs, and **curriculum.** A thorough bibliography of
curricular and staff training sources is included.

**B.  ASSESSMENT**

25. **Tests, Independence, and Whole Language,** Brian Cut- 128
ting, *Teaching K-8,* May 1991.
New Zealand's well-known proponent of whole language argues
for an alternative to standardized testing in **language arts** and
reading. He believes that an individualized approach to **assess-**
**ment** is more appropriate to the developmental nature of whole
language. The basis for evaluating children would be **observa-**
**tion** and running records.

26. **Tracking Progress Toward the School Readiness Goal,** 131
Penelope Engel, *Educational Leadership,* February 1991.
In keeping with the national goals for education **readiness** established by the National Governors' Association, an alternative to
the usual paper-and-pencil readiness tests is described. **Assess-**
**ment** for readiness should be determined from teachers' cumulative **observations** of children. The article includes assessment
suggestions for **teachers** from research on readiness.

27. **Project Spectrum: An Innovative Assessment Alterna-** 135
**tive,** Mara Krechevsky, *Educational Leadership,* February
1991.
This preschool **assessment** program is based on the multi-
intelligence theory of Howard Gardner. It emphasizes many areas
of **cognition, creativity,** and styles of learning. Through careful
**observation** of children engaged in the **curriculum,** these domains are assessed by the Spectrum approach. It is a flexible
program, linking children's real-world activity to assessment of
their strengths.

The concepts in bold italics are developed in the article. For further expansion please refer to the Topic Guide and the Index.

**C. SPECIAL NEEDS**

28. **Identification of Preschool Children With Mild Handicaps: The Importance of Cooperative Effort,** Ronald L. Taylor, Paula Willits, and Nancy Lieberman, *Childhood Education,* Fall 1990.    139

Information important to the screening and evaluating of **special needs children** is given in an organized and detailed format. A sample model for evaluating preschool special education children is included. This article will prove helpful to any school personnel now working with mildly handicapped children and their families as a result of the passage of Public Law 99-457.

29. **Preschool Classroom Environments That Promote Communication,** Michaelene M. Ostrosky and Ann P. Kaiser, *Teaching Exceptional Children,* Summer 1991.    145

To enhance use of language by **special needs** children, the physical and social environment should be considered as an occasion for **language development.** Placement and availability of learning materials create opportunities for conversation. Teachers can prompt **emergent literacy** by making minor adjustments in **equipment and materials.**

30. **Parental Feelings: The Forgotten Component When Working with Parents of Handicapped Preschool Children,** Richard M. Gargiulo and Stephen B. Graves, *Childhood Education,* Spring 1991.    149

The newest federal laws regarding preschool children with **special needs** recognize the importance of **parental involvement.** The **teacher** and parents have the responsibility of establishing a **collaborative** relationship, one that is based on empathy and respect. The article concludes with helpful suggestions for working with parents.

**Overview**    152

31. **How Well Do We Respect the Children in Our Care?**    154
Stacie G. Goffin, *Childhood Education,* Winter 1989.

**Respect** is an issue of quality that relates directly with children's well-being. Stacie G. Goffin proposes twelve ways to actively respect children, including being sensitive to individuality, facilitating their growth, and organizing an interesting curriculum. Respectful educators are also trained professionals in the field who are **advocates** for young children.

32. **Nurturing Success,** Patricia H. Berne with Eve Berne, *Scholastic Pre-K Today,* August/September 1988.    161

A successful environment for young children is based on supportive relationships that build **self-esteem.** Children's confidence grows as their teachers help them deal with strong emotions and fears. The authors provide specific suggestions for teachers to weave throughout the **curriculum.**

33. **Children's Self-Esteem: The Verbal Environment,** Marjorie J. Kostelnik, Laura C. Stein, and Alice P. Whiren, *Childhood Education,* Fall 1988.    165

Caregivers and teachers play a vital role in enhancing or damaging young children's self-esteem. The words teachers use establish either a negative or positive verbal environment that ultimately influences **affective development.** Steps for achieving a positive environment are described, along with specific attributes of positive verbal exchanges with children.

34. **Solving Problems Together,** Susanne Wichert, *Scholastic Pre-K Today,* March 1991.    170

Young children need guidance from their **teachers** in developing **social skills** of cooperation and conflict resolution. When children are taught to communicate with each other, to hear and be heard, their **self-esteem** is enhanced. The process of negotiating problems helps children gain **self-control** as well.

# Unit 4

## Guiding Behavior

Six selections examine the importance of establishing self-esteem in the child and consider the effects of stressors and stress reduction on behavior.

# Unit 5

## Curricular Applications

Eight selections consider various curricular choices. The areas covered include creating, inventing, emergent literacy, motor development, and conceptualizing curriculum.

35. **The Tasks of Early Childhood: The Development of Self-Control—Part II,** Alice Sterling Honig and Therese Lansburgh, *Day Care and Early Education,* Summer 1991. 174
Mature emotional behavior is based on **self-control.** Young children need careful guidance from **teachers** in learning what emotions need to be controlled and when and how to control them. Factors influencing self-control are discussed from research in **affective development.** Suggestions for teachers emphasize prevention and bibliotherapy.

36. **A Is for Apple, P Is for Pressure—Preschool Stress Management,** Janai Lowenstein, *Journal of Physical Education, Recreation, and Dance,* February 1991. 180
Janai Lowenstein describes the signs of emotional **stress** in young children and urges teachers to guide children in recognizing stress signs. Role-playing and demonstration activities are given for use with children. The goal is for children to communicate their anxiety and tension in order to gain **self-control** in stressful situations.

**Overview** 184

A. *CREATING AND INVENTING*

37. **Learning to Play: Playing to Learn,** Pauline Davey Zeece and Susan K. Graul, *Day Care and Early Education,* Fall 1990. 186
For the beginning early childhood student, or an experienced teacher who wants a refresher, this article contains a great deal of information on **stages of play,** types of play, and the role of the adult in encouraging play.

38. **"Put Your Name on Your Painting, But . . . the Blocks Go Back on the Shelves,"** David Kuschner, *Young Children,* November 1989. 191
The clear message to **teachers** and **parents** in this article is to value all types of creative endeavors by children, not just ones that will grace the doors of refrigerators. Parents should receive tangible evidence of their children's work in many areas of development. **Creative play,** block building, story telling, physical abilities, and musical endeavors can all be recorded through print, tape, or pictures and shared with visitors to the school and families at home.

39. **The State of American Preschool Playgrounds,** Joe L. Frost, Louis E. Bowers, and Sue C. Wortham, *Journal of Physical Education, Recreation, and Dance,* October 1990. 196
As the staff of many preschool programs strive to provide an environment that is safe, challenging, and developmentally appropriate, they often concentrate on the inside and neglect to plan for learning and playing on the outside area. The authors present facts from a recently published study on the state of America's **playgrounds,** focusing on the **play** value and **safety** of the **equipment** and environment. Suggestions for providing an appropriate outside play space are given.

40. **Emergent Literacy: How Young Children Learn to Read and Write,** Dorothy S. Strickland, *Educational Leadership,* March 1990. 201
Understanding the process called emergent literacy, through which young children go as they become literate, can enable teachers and parents to provide the necessary ingredients for a successful experience. Learning to read and write, just like learning to talk, evolves over time with support from family and teachers. **Developmentally appropriate practices** include providing a print-rich environment, putting spoken language on paper, and supporting children in their attempts to communicate.

The concepts in bold italics are developed in the article. For further expansion please refer to the Topic Guide and the Index.

**B. CONTENT AND PROCESS**

41. **The Many Faces of Child Planning,** Mary Hohmann, 206
*High/Scope ReSource,* Spring/Summer 1991.
By allowing children time to *plan* how they will spend their time, which materials they will use, and with whom they will play, we are giving them a very valuable gift: a sense of control over their actions and trust in themselves. There are many types of children's plans, verbal and nonverbal, and they are expressed at different levels of complexity. The role of the *teacher* in faciliating the planning process is described.

42. **Writing in Kindergarten: Helping Parents Understand** 211
**the Process,** Kathleen A. Dailey, *Childhood Education,*
Spring 1991.
Kathleen A. Dailey provides answers to questions on *emergent literacy* commonly asked by *parents* of *kindergarten*-aged children. How does my child learn to read and write? How can I encourage my child to write at home? Should I correct my child's written work? What should I look for in my child's writing program? Answers to these questions and others, along with charts showing stages in the writing process, are included.

43. **Science-Centered Curriculum in Elementary School,** 217
Lynda C. Greene, *Educational Leadership,* October 1991.
A creative approach to *teaching science* in the *primary grades* is being used in many California schools. It incorporates thematic webbing to bring science to life and integrate the total *curriculum.*

44. **Creating a Reading/Writing Environment,** Beverly D. 221
Stratton and Martha C. Grindler, *Journal of Computing in Childhood Education,* Summer 1991.
The authors describe a pilot program where children in the *primary grades* were encouraged to expand their *creative* thinking and writing skills through the use of *computers* and photography. Motivation and comprehension improved, as did the self-concept of the children.

**Overview** 224
45. **The Day Care Generation,** Pat Wingert and Barbara 226
Kantrowitz, *Newsweek,* Special Issue, Winter/Spring 1990.
Serious and disturbing questions are being raised about the long-term effects on young children of spending their early years in the care of an adult other than their parent. The research on *child care* is inconclusive and contradictory, and the issues of quality, continuity, child-adult ratios, staff training, and regulation of programs remain. The authors discuss child care staff turnover, controversial research findings, and health risks.

46. **The Costs of *Not* Providing Quality Early Childhood** 229
**Programs,** Ellen Galinsky, from *Reaching the Full Cost of Quality in Early Childhood Programs,* NAEYC 1990.
The solution to the child care dilemma will require collaboration from many groups at all levels. We know what constitutes *quality programming* for young children and under what conditions children flourish. Ellen Galinsky challenges individuals to become involved in their community to educate parents and community and business leaders on the costs of not providing quality programs. The time is now and momentum is on our side since the passage of *federal child care legislation.*

47. **Reaching for the Year 2000,** Katie Haycock, *Childhood* 237
*Education,* Annual Theme, 1991.
America 2000 includes ambitious educational goals for increasing the productivity of citizens. At the same time, the achievement gap widens between students from *poverty* and *minority* backgrounds and those from more privileged backgrounds. Teachers and administrators must work together to select better approaches for ensuring that *children at risk* achieve.

**Index** 241
**Article Review Form** 244
**Article Rating Form** 245

**Unit 6**

## Reflections

Three selections consider the present and future of early childhood education.

The concepts in bold italics are developed in the article. For further expansion please refer to the Topic Guide and the Index.

# Topic Guide

This topic guide suggests how the selections in this book relate to topics of traditional concern to students and professionals involved with early childhood education. It is useful for locating articles that relate to each other for reading and research. The guide is arranged alphabetically according to topic. Articles may, of course, treat topics that do not appear in the topic guide. In turn, entries in the topic guide do not necessarily constitute a comprehensive listing of all the contents of each selection.

| TOPIC AREA | TREATED IN: | TOPIC AREA | TREATED IN: |
|---|---|---|---|
| Academics | 22. Why Not Academic Preschool? | Developmentally Appropriate Practice | 8. Excellent Early Education |
| Advocacy | 2. Children in Peril | | 18. Guidelines for Appropriate Curriculum Content and Assessment |
| | 31. How Well Do We Respect the Children in Our Care? | | 20. Understanding Bilingual/Bicultural Young Children |
| Affective Development | 12. Guns and Dolls | | 22. Why Not Academic Preschool? |
| | 35. Tasks of Early Childhood | | 40. Emergent Literacy |
| Assessing | 18. Guidelines for Appropriate Curriculum Content and Assessment | Divorce | 15. Children of Divorce |
| | 25. Tests, Independence, and Whole Language | | 16. Single-Parent Families |
| | 26. Tracking Progress Toward the School Readiness Goal | Drugs | 2. Children in Peril |
| | 27. Project Spectrum | | 3. Shadow Children |
| Bilingual/Bicultural | 20. Understanding Bilingual/Bicultural Young Children | Dual-Income Families | 4. I Couldn't Afford My Job |
| | | | 5. When Parents Accept the Unacceptable |
| Child Care: Full Day/Half Day | 4. I Couldn't Afford My Job | Emergent Literacy | 14. How Schools Perpetuate Illiteracy |
| | 5. When Parents Accept the Unacceptable | | 29. Preschool Classroom Environments That Promote Communication |
| | 8. Excellent Early Education | | 40. Emergent Literacy |
| | 45. Day Care Generation | | 42. Writing in Kindergarten |
| | 46. Costs of *Not* Providing Quality Early Childhood Programs | Employer Sponsored Child Care | 4. I Couldn't Afford My Job |
| Child Development | 10. First Year Milestones | Equipment/ Materials | 21. Structure Time & Space to Promote Pursuit of Learning |
| | 12. Guns and Dolls | | 29. Preschool Classroom Environments That Promote Communication |
| Children at Risk | 2. Children in Peril | | 39. State of American Preschool Playgrounds |
| | 3. Shadow Children | | |
| | 6. Head Start | Ethics | 1. New Code of Ethics for Early Childhood Educators! |
| | 47. Reaching for the Year 2000 | | |
| Cognitive Development | 27. Project Spectrum | Families | 13. What Birth Order Means |
| | | | 15. Children of Divorce |
| Collaboration | 4. I Couldn't Afford My Job | | 16. Single-Parent Families |
| | 6. Head Start | | 17. Where Are the Parents? |
| | 28. Preschool Children With Mild Handicaps | Federal Government's Role | 2. Children in Peril |
| | 30. Parental Feelings | | 4. I Couldn't Afford My Job |
| Computers | 44. Creating a Reading/Writing Environment | | 46. Costs of *Not* Providing Quality Early Childhood Programs |
| Creativity | 27. Project Spectrum | Guiding Behavior | 34. Solving Problems Together |
| | 38. "Put Your Name on Your Painting, But . . . the Blocks Go Back on the Shelves" | | 35. Tasks of Early Childhood |
| | 44. Creating a Reading/Writing Environment | Head Start | 6. Head Start |
| | | Health and Safety | 3. Shadow Children |
| Curriculum | 18. Guidelines for Appropriate Curriculum Content and Assessment | | 5. When Parents Accept the Unacceptable |
| | 24. School-Age Child Care | | 39. State of American Preschool Playgrounds |
| | 27. Project Spectrum | | |
| | 43. Science-Centered Curriculum in Elementary School | Homelessness | 2. Children in Peril |
| | | Illiteracy | 14. How Schools Perpetuate Illiteracy |
| | | Infants and Infant Care | 10. First Year Milestones |

| TOPIC AREA | TREATED IN: | TOPIC AREA | TREATED IN: |
|---|---|---|---|
| **International Perspectives** | 7. Global Collage of Impressions<br>8. Excellent Early Education<br>9. Glimpse of Kindergarten—Chinese Style | **Readiness** | 26. Tracking Progress Toward the School Readiness Goal<br>42. Writing in Kindergarten |
| **Kindergarten** | 9. Glimpse of Kindergarten—Chinese Style<br>42. Writing in Kindergarten | **Respect** | 31. How Well Do We Respect the Children in Our Care? |
| **Language Development/ Language Arts** | 25. Tests, Independence, and Whole Language<br>29. Preschool Classroom Environments That Promote Communication<br>40. Emergent Literacy | **Retention** | 19. Synthesis of Research on Grade Retention |
| | | **School-Age Child Care** | 24. School-Age Child Care |
| **Minority Children** | 2. Children in Peril<br>6. Head Start<br>47. Reaching for the Year 2000 | **Science** | 43. Science-Centered Curriculum in Elementary School |
| **Observation** | 25. Tests, Independence, and Whole Language<br>26. Tracking Progress Toward the School Readiness Goal<br>27. Project Spectrum | **Self-Control** | 34. Solving Problems Together<br>35. Tasks of Early Childhood<br>36. A Is for Apple, P Is for Pressure |
| **Parents/Parent Involvement** | 5. When Parents Accept the Unacceptable<br>11. Easing Separation<br>12. Guns and Dolls<br>13. What Birth Order Means<br>14. How Schools Perpetuate Illiteracy<br>16. Single-Parent Families<br>17. Where Are the Parents?<br>30. Parental Feelings<br>42. Writing in Kindergarten | **Self-Esteem** | 22. Why Not Academic Preschool?<br>32. Nurturing Success<br>33. Children's Self-Esteem<br>34. Solving Problems Together |
| | | **Separation** | 11. Easing Separation |
| | | **Sex Differences** | 12. Guns and Dolls |
| **Personality** | 13. What Birth Order Means | **Single-Parent Families** | 15. Children of Divorce<br>16. Single-Parent Families |
| **Play** | 37. Learning to Play<br>38. "Put Your Name on Your Painting, But . . . the Blocks Go Back on the Shelves"<br>39. State of American Preschool Playgrounds | **Social Development** | 34. Solving Problems Together |
| | | **Special Needs** | 3. Shadow Children<br>28. Preschool Children With Mild Handicaps<br>29. Preschool Classroom Environments That Promote Communication<br>30. Parental Feelings |
| **Playgrounds** | 39. State of American Preschool Playgrounds | | |
| **Position Statement** | 18. Guidelines for Appropriate Curriculum Content and Assessment | **Stress** | 16. Single-Parent Families<br>36. A Is for Apple, P Is for Pressure |
| **Poverty** | 2. Children In Peril<br>6. Head Start<br>47. Reaching for the Year 2000 | **Teachers/Teaching** | 3. Shadow Children<br>14. How Schools Perpetuate Illiteracy<br>16. Single-Parent Families<br>17. Where Are the Parents?<br>18. Guidelines for Appropriate Curriculum Content and Assessment<br>20. Understanding Bilingual/Bicultural Young Children<br>21. Structure Time & Space to Promote Pursuit of Learning<br>40. Emergent Literacy<br>42. Writing in Kindergarten<br>43. Science-Centered Curriculum in Elementary School |
| **Primary Grades** | 19. Synthesis of Research on Grade Retention<br>21. Structure Time & Space to Promote Pursuit of Learning<br>24. School-Age Child Care<br>43. Science-Centered Curriculum in Elementary School<br>44. Creating a Reading/Writing Environment | | |
| | | **Television** | 23. What's Missing in Children's TV |
| | | **Temperament** | 13. What Birth Order Means |
| **Quality Programming** | 5. When Parents Accept the Unacceptable<br>8. Excellent Early Education<br>18. Guidelines for Appropriate Curriculum Content and Assessment<br>46. Costs of *Not* Providing Quality Early Childhood Programs | | |

# Perspectives

- **National Perspectives (Articles 1–6)**
- **International Perspectives (Articles 7–9)**

There is a storm brewing on the near horizon and we know that it is going to hit with intense ferocity. We are talking about the vast numbers of young children being born into, and raised in, environments where poverty, drugs, abuse, homelessness, and lack of medical care are prevalent.

The President's National Drug Control Strategy Report estimates 100,000 cocaine-exposed children are born each year. After their birth, these children live in environments where drugs are an everyday part of their lives. Within a few years they enter preschool and public school settings, but very few professionals are ready to meet the special needs of these children and their families. "The Shadow Children: Preparing for the Arrival of Crack Babies in School" contains steps school personnel can take to better prepare themselves and the learning environment to meet the desperate needs of these children.

Of continuing concern are the 13.4 million young children who live in poverty—which translates into a child poverty rate of 20.6 percent (Children's Defense Fund Reports, 1991). These children do not receive health care,

proper nutrition, shelter, or educational opportunities necessary for survival in America today. Families living in poverty are faced with a multitude of concerns, but few resources. They must find a safe place to sleep for the night or a church offering a meal and a box of used clothing. Their children receive so little of quality.

Head Start, one of the few government-funded programs for young children and their families, has been praised for the progress made by the children. It has also received criticism because the program does not serve more children. Less than 20 percent of the children eligible are actually enrolled in a Head Start Program. The program is now being embraced by many as the best avenue to take as we look to the twenty-first century. Head Start celebrated its 25th anniversary in 1990 and a Silver Ribbon Panel comprised of prominent educators has detailed ideas and plans to lead the program into the future.

In 1990 Congress passed the long awaited Child Care and Development Block Grant. For years legislators and business leaders had been joining ranks with early child-

hood professionals in calling for greater funding and the establishment of partnerships among varied constituencies to ensure high quality programs for America's young children. The reasons for these collaborative efforts were inadequate support from the federal government during the 1980s, greater numbers of families living in poverty, and an increase in the percentage of working mothers and dual-income families who need affordable quality child care. Successful government, business, and educational collaboration has occurred in the past—during the Depression, World War II, and Head Start. The lessons learned from those interagency efforts have clearly shown both the necessity and effectiveness of early childhood programs that are comprehensive and high quality.

Public perceptions about society's investment in young children in general and at-risk and minority children in particular are gradually changing. Today, millions of working parents need quality child-care programs that are consistently and adequately funded, comprehensive in nature to meet the basic needs of children and families, and operated by dedicated and specially educated professional staffs. The day-to-day stresses that parents face in their jobs have become more intense and complex, and they often have to cope with them alone due to lack of support from employers, colleagues, family, and friends. This is where alliances formed among home, school, and business can be extremely helpful and comforting.

Still, the majority of child-care centers struggle to be self-supporting, receive only a fraction of their operating budget from outside sources, pay low wages to their staff and cannot provide comprehensive services to children and families. Consequently, millions of young children under six years of age are inadequately cared for by untrained, uncaring, or indifferent persons.

Many children are cared for in three or more settings during the day—shuffled between relatives, friends, and neighbors. Uncounted numbers of children are left to fend for themselves. This patchwork of ineffective child-care arrangements is having significant developmental effects on today's young children who will be tomorrow's adolescents. Questions must be raised about what these vulnerable young children are experiencing in these varied settings during their formative years. According to Dr. Edward Zigler of Yale University, five years of inadequate care will affect the child and his or her learning ability when it is time to start kindergarten.

For some Americans, domestic issues and problems surrounding early childhood are overwhelming, and it is difficult to look beyond our own country. Yet what is happening internationally will affect us and the ways we interact with children. By studying others, we can often learn more about ourselves. The world is changing rapidly, and the increase of children from other cultures into our country occurs daily. In this unit, we have included three articles on education in other countries. In "A Global Collage of Impressions: Preschools Abroad," Leah D. Adams states, "What makes for a good preschool or kindergarten program depends in part upon the culture in which the program is located." Teachers in the United States depend on local customs, climate, and populations to develop curricula to meet the needs and interests of their children, and the same happens in other countries. We cannot judge quality based solely on our standards, but need to take into account the local setting, population, and life-style of the country.

As we examine the living and learning conditions for children today, we see many problems. There are, however, educators, parents, and community groups ready to assist children and their families. Unfortunately, the number of people requiring assistance is growing at a rapid pace. Preventing problems from occurring in the first place seems to be the one key to ensuring a safe, nurturing, and successful educational experience for all our country's children.

## Looking Ahead: Challenge Questions

How are children from families headed by young, poor, and single parents at jeopardy for failure in school and society in general? What steps can be taken to assist these children who face poverty every day of their lives?

What can schools do to assist children and their families as they struggle to walk the thin line between economic disaster and a safe and secure life?

What steps need to be taken if the recommendations made by the Silver Ribbon Panel addressing the achievements and challenges of Head Start are followed? What recommendations do you see as achievable in your community?

What steps are considered more "user friendly" for families with young children?

What steps could employers take to assist families as they struggle to meet the demands of child care? How well are employers currently meeting these needs?

Why do parents continue to use a child-care setting deemed unacceptable?

What can we learn by studying preschool settings in other countries?

# A New Code of Ethics for Early Childhood Educators!

## Code of Ethical Conduct and Statement of Commitment

### Stephanie Feeney and Kenneth Kipnis

**Stephanie Feeney,** Ph.D., is Professor and Early Childhood Education Specialist at the University of Hawaii at Manoa. She is a former member of NAEYC's Governing Board.

**Kenneth Kipnis,** Ph.D., Professor of Philosophy at the University of Hawaii at Manoa, has written on legal philosophy and ethical issues in law, medicine, engineering, and other professions.

### Editor's Note:

*Under the leadership of Stephanie Feeney, appointed by the Governing Board in 1984, and a Board-established Ethics Commission, NAEYC began a process in which members would explore and clarify the early childhood profession's understanding of its own ethics. This process has entailed*

*• a survey of members to learn concerns* (Young Children *March 1985),*

*• numerous workshops in various locations with early childhood educators to identify and explore dilemmas, and*

*• another survey of members to help formu-*

*Financial assistance for this project was provided by NAEYC, the Wallace Alexander Gerbode Foundation, and the University of Hawaii.*

*late principles of ethical action* (Young Children *May 1987).*

*Written reports summarizing readers' contributions served as the basis for three more articles published in* Young Children: *"The Working Mother" November 1987 with commentary by Lilian Katz; "The Aggressive Child" January 1988 with commentary by Bettye Caldwell; and "The Divorced Parents" March 1988 with commentary by Sue Spayth Riley. Kenneth Kipnis wrote a commentary from the philosopher's perspective to all three articles.*

*With the additional resources of ethicists and relevant codes of ethics developed by other groups, the process next produced a "Draft Code of Ethics and Statement of Commitment." That was presented to the membership at the NAEYC Conference in November 1988, resulting in further refinements.*

*The final document, presented below, was approved by NAEYC's Governing Board in July 1989.*

*The Statement of Commitment accompanying the Code is a recognition that the ultimate strength of the Code rests in the adherence of individual educators.*

# The National Association for the Education of Young Children
# Code of Ethical Conduct

## Preamble

NAEYC recognizes that many daily decisions required of those who work with young children are of a moral and ethical nature. The NAEYC Code of Ethical Conduct offers guidelines for responsible behavior and sets forth a common basis for resolving the principal ethical dilemmas encountered in early childhood education. The primary focus is on daily practice with children and their families in programs for children from birth to 8 years of age: preschools, child care centers, family day care homes, kindergartens, and primary classrooms. Many of the provisions also apply to specialists who do not work directly with children, including program administrators, parent educators, college professors, and child care licensing specialists.

Standards of ethical behavior in early childhood education are based on commitment to core values that are deeply rooted in the history of our field. We have committed ourselves to:

● Appreciating childhood as a unique and valuable stage of the human life cycle

● Basing our work with children on knowledge of child development

● Appreciating and supporting the close ties between the child and family

● Recognizing that children are best understood in the context of family, culture, and society

● Respecting the dignity, worth, and uniqueness of each individual (child, family member, and colleague)

● Helping children and adults achieve their full poten-

tial in the context of relationships that are based on trust, respect, and positive regard

The Code sets forth a conception of our professional responsibilities in four sections, each addressing an arena of professional relationships: 1) children, 2) families, 3) colleagues, and 4) community and society. Each section includes an introduction to the primary responsibilities of the early childhood practitioner in that arena, a set of ideals pointing in the direction of exemplary professional practice, and a set of principles defining practices that are required, prohibited, and permitted.

The ideals reflect the aspirations of practitioners. The principles are intended to guide conduct and assist practitioners in resolving ethical dilemmas encountered in the field. There is not necessarily a corresponding principle for each ideal. Both ideals and principles are intended to direct practitioners to those questions which, when responsibly answered, will provide the basis for conscientious decision making. While the Code provides specific direction for addressing some ethical dilemmas, many others will require the practitioner to combine the guidance of the Code with sound professional judgment.

The ideals and principles in this Code present a shared conception of professional responsibility that affirms our commitment to the core values of our field. The Code publicly acknowledges the responsibilities that we in the field have assumed and in so doing supports ethical behavior in our work. Practitioners who face ethical dilemmas are urged to seek guidance in the applicable parts of this Code and in the spirit that informs the whole.

This Code of Ethical Conduct and Statement of Commitment was prepared under the auspices of the Ethics Commission of the National Association for the Education of Young Children. The Commission members were Stephanie Feeney (Chairperson), Bettye Caldwell, Sally Cartwright, Carrie Cheek, Josué Cruz, Jr., Anne G. Dorsey, Dorothy M. Hill, Lilian G. Katz, Pamm Mattick, Shirley A. Norris, and Sue Spayth Riley.

## Section I: Ethical responsibilities to children

Childhood is a unique and valuable stage in the life cycle. Our paramount responsibility is to provide safe, healthy, nurturing, and responsive settings for children. We are committed to supporting children's development by cherishing individual differences, by helping them learn to live and work cooperatively, and by promoting their self-esteem.

### Ideals:

**I-1.1**—To be familiar with the knowledge base of early childhood education and to keep current through continuing education and in-service training.

**I-1.2**—To base program practices upon current knowledge in the field of child development and related disciplines and upon particular knowledge of each child.

**I-1.3**—To recognize and respect the uniqueness and the potential of each child.

**I-1.4**—To appreciate the special vulnerability of children.

**I-1.5**—To create and maintain safe and healthy settings that foster children's social, emotional, intellectual, and physical development and that respect their dignity and their contributions.

**I-1.6**—To support the right of children with special needs to participate, consistent with their ability, in regular early childhood programs.

### Principles:

**P-1.1**—Above all, we shall not harm children. We shall not participate in practices that are disrespectful, degrading, dangerous, exploitative, intimidating, psychologically damaging, or physically harmful to children. *This principle has precedence over all others in this Code.*

**P-1.2**—We shall not participate in practices that discriminate against children by denying benefits, giving special advantages, or excluding them from programs or activities on the basis of their race, religion, sex, national origin, or the status, behavior, or beliefs of their parents. (This principle does not apply to programs that have a lawful mandate to provide services to a particular population of children.)

**P-1.3**—We shall involve all of those with relevant knowledge (including staff and parents) in decisions concerning a child.

**P-1.4**—When, after appropriate efforts have been made with a child and the family, the child still does not appear to be benefitting from a program, we shall communicate our concern to the family in a positive way and offer them assistance in finding a more suitable setting.

**P-1.5**—We shall be familiar with the symptoms of child abuse and neglect and know community procedures for addressing them.

**P-1.6**—When we have evidence of child abuse or neglect, we shall report the evidence to the appropriate community agency and follow up to ensure that appropriate action has been taken. When possible, parents will be informed that the referral has been made.

**P-1.7**—When another person tells us of their suspicion that a child is being abused or neglected but we lack evidence, we shall assist that person in taking appropriate action to protect the child.

**P-1.8**—When a child protective agency fails to provide adequate protection for abused or neglected children, we acknowledge a collective ethical responsibility to work toward improvement of these services.

## Section II: Ethical responsibilities to families

Families are of primary importance in children's development. (The term *family* may include others, besides parents, who are responsibly involved with the child.) Because the family and the early childhood educator have a common interest in the child's welfare, we acknowledge a primary responsibility to bring about collaboration between the home and school in ways that enhance the child's development.

### Ideals:

**I-2.1**—To develop relationships of mutual trust with the families we serve.

**I-2.2**—To acknowledge and build upon strengths and competencies as we support families in their task of nurturing children.

**I-2.3**—To respect the dignity of each family and its culture, customs, and beliefs.

**I-2.4**—To respect families' childrearing values and their right to make decisions for their children.

**I-2.5**—To interpret each child's progress to parents within the framework of a developmental perspective and to help families understand and appreciate the value of developmentally appropriate early childhood programs.

**I-2.6**—To help family members improve their understanding of their children and to enhance their skills as parents.

**I-2.7**—To participate in building support networks for families by providing them with opportunities to interact with program staff and families.

### Principles:

**P-2.1**—We shall not deny family members access to their child's classroom or program setting.

**P-2.2**—We shall inform families of program philosophy, policies, and personnel qualifications, and explain why we teach as we do.

**P-2.3**—We shall inform families of and, when appropriate, involve them in policy decisions.

**P-2.4**—We shall inform families of and, when appropriate, involve them in significant decisions affecting their child.

**P-2.5**—We shall inform the family of accidents involving their child, of risks such as exposures to contagious disease that may result in infection, and of events that might result in psychological damage.

**P-2.6**—We shall not permit or participate in research that could in any way hinder the education or development of the children in our programs. Families shall be fully informed of any proposed research projects involving their children and shall have the opportunity to give or withhold consent.

**P-2.7**—We shall not engage in or support exploitation of families. We shall not use our relationship with a family for private advantage or personal gain, or enter into relationships with family members that might impair our effectiveness in working with children.

**P-2.8**—We shall develop written policies for the protection of confidentiality and the disclosure of children's records. The policy documents shall be made available to all program personnel and families. Disclosure of children's records beyond family members, program personnel, and consultants having an obligation of confidentiality shall require familial consent (except in cases of abuse or neglect).

**P-2.9**—We shall maintain confidentiality and shall respect the family's right to privacy, refraining from disclosure of confidential information and intrusion into family life. However, when we are concerned about a child's welfare, it is permissible to reveal confidential information to agencies and individuals who may be able to act in the child's interest.

**P-2.10**—In cases where family members are in conflict we shall work openly, sharing our observations of the child, to help all parties involved make informed decisions. We shall refrain from becoming an advocate for one party.

**P-2.11**—We shall be familiar with and appropriately use community resources and professional services that support families. After a referral has been made, we shall follow up to ensure that services have been adequately provided.

## Section III: Ethical responsibilities to colleagues

In a caring, cooperative work place human dignity is respected, professional satisfaction is promoted, and positive relationships are modeled. Our primary responsibility in this arena is to establish and maintain settings and relationships that support productive work and meet professional needs.

## A—*Responsibilities to co-workers*

### Ideals:

**I-3A.1**—To establish and maintain relationships of trust and cooperation with co-workers.

**I-3A.2**—To share resources and information with co-workers.

**I-3A.3**—To support co-workers in meeting their professional needs and in their professional development.

**I-3A.4**—To accord co-workers due recognition of professional achievement.

### Principles:

**P-3A.1**—When we have concern about the professional behavior of a co-worker, we shall first let that person know of our concern and attempt to resolve the matter collegially.

**P-3A.2**—We shall exercise care in expressing views regarding the personal attributes or professional conduct of co-workers. Statements should be based on firsthand knowledge and relevant to the interests of children and programs.

## B—*Responsibilities to employers*

### Ideals:

**I-3B.1**—To assist the program in providing the highest quality of service.

**I-3B.2**—To maintain loyalty to the program and uphold its reputation.

### Principles:

**P-3B.1**—When we do not agree with program policies, we shall first attempt to effect change through constructive action within the organization.

**P-3B.2**—We shall speak or act on behalf of an organization only when authorized. We shall take care to note when we are speaking for the organization and when we are expressing a personal judgment.

## C—*Responsibilities to employees*

### Ideals:

**I-3C.1**—To promote policies and working conditions that foster competence, well-being, and self-esteem in staff members.

I-3C.2—To create a climate of trust and candor that will enable staff to speak and act in the best interests of children, families, and the field of early childhood education.

I-3C.3—To strive to secure an adequate livelihood for those who work with or on behalf of young children.

## Principles:

P-3C.1—In decisions concerning children and programs, we shall appropriately utilize the training, experience, and expertise of staff members.

P-3C.2—We shall provide staff members with working conditions that permit them to carry out their responsibilities, timely and nonthreatening evaluation procedures, written grievance procedures, constructive feedback, and opportunities for continuing professional development and advancement.

P-3C.3—We shall develop and maintain comprehensive written personnel policies that define program standards and, when applicable, that specify the extent to which employees are accountable for their conduct outside the work place. These policies shall be given to new staff members and shall be available for review by all staff members.

P-3C.4—Employees who do not meet program standards shall be informed of areas of concern and, when possible, assisted in improving their performance.

P-3C.5—Employees who are dismissed shall be informed of the reasons for their termination. When a dismissal is for cause, justification must be based on evidence of inadequate or inappropriate behavior that is accurately documented, current, and available for the employee to review.

P-3C.6—In making evaluations and recommendations, judgments shall be based on fact and relevant to the interests of children and programs.

P-3C.7—Hiring and promotion shall be based solely on a person's record of accomplishment and ability to carry out the responsibilities of the position.

P-3C.8—In hiring, promotion, and provision of training, we shall not participate in any form of discrimination based on race, religion, sex, national origin, handicap, age, or sexual preference. We shall be familiar with laws and regulations that pertain to employment discrimination.

## Section IV: Ethical responsibilities to community and society

Early childhood programs operate within a context of an immediate community made up of families and other institutions concerned with children's welfare. Our responsibilities to the community are to provide programs that meet its needs and to cooperate with agencies and professions that share responsibility for children. Because the larger society has a measure of responsibility for the welfare and protection of children, and because of our specialized expertise in child development, we acknowledge an obligation to serve as a voice for children everywhere.

## Ideals:

I-4.1—To provide the community with high-quality, culturally sensitive programs and services.

I-4.2—To promote cooperation among agencies and professions concerned with the welfare of young children, their families, and their teachers.

I-4.3—To work, through education, research, and advocacy, toward an environmentally safe world in which all children are adequately fed, sheltered, and nurtured.

I-4.4—To work, through education, research, and advocacy, toward a society in which all young children have access to quality programs.

I-4.5—To promote knowledge and understanding of young children and their needs. To work toward greater social acknowledgment of children's rights and greater social acceptance of responsibility for their well-being.

I-4.6—To support policies and laws that promote the well-being of children and families. To oppose those that impair their well-being. To cooperate with other individuals and groups in these efforts.

I-4.7—To further the professional development of the field of early childhood education and to strengthen its commitment to realizing its core values as reflected in this Code.

## Principles:

P-4.1—We shall communicate openly and truthfully about the nature and extent of services that we provide.

P-4.2—We shall not accept or continue to work in positions for which we are personally unsuited or professionally unqualified. We shall not offer services that we do not have the competence, qualifications, or resources to provide.

P-4.3—We shall be objective and accurate in reporting the knowledge upon which we base our program practices.

P-4.4—We shall cooperate with other professionals who work with children and their families.

P-4.5—We shall not hire or recommend for employment any person who is unsuited for a position with respect to competence, qualifications, or character.

P-4.6—We shall report the unethical or incompetent behavior of a colleague to a supervisor when informal resolution is not effective.

**P-4.7**—We shall be familiar with laws and regulations that serve to protect the children in our programs.

**P-4.8**—We shall not participate in practices which are in violation of laws and regulations that protect the children in our programs.

**P-4.9**—When we have evidence that an early childhood program is violating laws or regulations protecting children, we shall report it to persons responsible for the program. If compliance is not accomplished within a reasonable time, we will report the violation to appropriate authorities who can be expected to remedy the situation.

**P-4.10**—When we have evidence that an agency or a professional charged with providing services to children, families, or teachers is failing to meet its obligations, we acknowledge a collective ethical responsibility to report the problem to appropriate authorities or to the public.

**P-4.11**—When a program violates or requires its employees to violate this Code, it is permissible, after fair assessment of the evidence, to disclose the identity of that program.

# CHILDREN *in* PERIL

## GEOFFREY COWLEY

**American kids remain the most neglected in the developed world**

Children have never had it easy. A fair proportion have always been beaten, starved, raped or abandoned, and until quite recently even the loved ones faced daunting obstacles. At the beginning of this century, one American child in 10 didn't live to see a first birthday. Today, thanks to major strides in nutrition, sanitation and medical care, 99 out of 100 survive infancy. Yet astonishing numbers continue to die or suffer needlessly. Nearly one child in four is born into poverty, a formidable predictor of lifelong ill health, and a growing number lack such basic advantages as a home, two parents and regular access to a doctor. Every year thousands die violently, from abuse or preventable accidents. Millions go unvaccinated against common childhood diseases. Millions more are poisoned by cigarette smoke or household lead.

Decrying the situation has become a national pastime. Panels are assembled, studies conducted, articles written, speeches made. Yet by vital measures, American children remain the most neglected in the developed world. Their health and welfare are simply "not high on the agenda of this country," laments Dr. Reed Tuckson, a former Washington, D.C., health commissioner and now a vice president at the March of Dimes Birth Defects Foundation. "The federal government doesn't think this is as important as the savings and loan crisis." Here's proof.

### Infant mortality

According to newly released government figures, 9.1 out of every 1,000 American babies died during infancy last year (down from 9.7 per 1,000 in 1989). Such rates are a far cry from India's 97 deaths per 1,000 or Guinea's 143, but they're among the highest in the industrialized world—and they don't apply equally to all Americans. The death rate for black infants (17.6 per 1,000 births as of 1988) is more than twice

that for whites (8.5 per 1,000). And some regions remain what the National Commission to Prevent Infant Mortality calls "disaster areas." Washington, Detroit and Philadelphia suffer higher infant-death rates than Jamaica or Costa Rica. Parts of the rural South fare even worse. "What we have here in the Mississippi delta is a Third World situation," says Mike Gibbs of Mississippi's Sharkey-Issaquena Health Alliance. Indeed, a baby born in Sharkey or Issaquena county is less likely to survive infancy than one born in Chile.

The main reason children die during infancy is that they're born too soon or too small. Babies with low birth weights (under 5.5 pounds) are 40 times more likely than others to die during their first month, and 20 times more likely to die within a year. Those who survive often grow up deaf, blind or mentally retarded. The problem has eminently preventable causes, including drug and alcohol abuse, smoking, poor nutrition and a lack of prenatal care. Yet low birth weight is as common today as it was a decade ago. Nearly 7 percent of all U.S. babies—a quarter million a year—are born too small. The rate is far higher, and rising, among minorities. In 1988 fully 13 percent of all black children came into the world dangerously underweight.

### Substance abuse

Low birth weight is not the only effect of parental substance abuse. Fetal alcohol exposure is the nation's leading known cause of mental retardation, surpassing both Down syndrome and spina bifida. Cigarette smoke not only poisons developing fetuses—causing a quarter of all low birth weights and a tenth of all infant deaths—but disables children who breathe it growing up. Smokers' kids are at increased risk for many respiratory diseases, including asthma. And babies born to cocaine users suffer devastating neurological problems.

The number of fetuses exposed to tobacco and alcohol hasn't changed much lately; America produces 5,000 to 10,000 children with full-blown fetal alcohol syndrome each year, and 10 times that number may suffer the similar but less severe symptoms of fetal alcohol effect. By contrast, cocaine use rose ominously among young women during the 1980s. Though recent findings suggest the problem has peaked, experts guess that a million women of childbearing age use the drug and that 30,000 to 100,000 deliver cocaine-exposed babies each year. At New York's Harlem Hospital, the frequency of cocaine use among expectant mothers jumped from 1 percent in 1980 to 20 percent in 1988. A 1989 survey suggested that 17 percent of Philadelphia's babies were born exposed.

## Contagion

Syphilis, gonorrhea and AIDS may sound like adult afflictions, but children are paying dearly for the surge in sexually transmitted diseases over the past decade. They're paying, too, for the decline of childhood immunization efforts. For less than $100 a child can gain immunity against polio, whooping cough, diphtheria, tetanus, measles, mumps and rubella. Virtually all America's kids receive these basic vaccines by the time they start school. Yet vast and growing numbers of 1- to 4-year-olds remain unvaccinated, especially in poor areas. Dr. Antoinette Eaton, president of the American Academy of Pediatrics (AAP), calls the situation "disastrous."

The government stopped tracking early-childhood immunization rates six years ago, but signs of trouble abound. As of 1985 the proportion of preschoolers receiving particular vaccines was 23 percent to 67 percent lower in this country than in Europe. Only half of America's 1- to 4-year-olds were being immunized against polio, according to the AAP, and a quarter received no vaccinations. Recent studies have identified inner-city neighborhoods where 50 to 70 percent of preschool children are unvaccinated. Not surprisingly, these lapses have triggered a major resurgence of once rare childhood diseases. Whooping cough is twice as common today as it was in 1970. Measles cases rose from 1,500 in 1983 to an astounding 25,000 last year.

## Lead poisoning

This summer federal health officials are expected to acknowledge formally what researchers and activists have long maintained: that 3 million youngsters—one in six children under 7—have dangerous levels of lead in their blood. A standard ingredient in wall paint until the late 1970s, lead still pervades many households, and mounting evidence suggests that blood levels once considered safe can cause neurological damage. Many experts now consider it the nation's foremost environmental hazard.

Children don't have to eat paint chips to be poisoned; a more common source is the dust that falls from old walls and window panes. Experts are also wary of water systems, lead crystal and imported cans and ceramics. Babies exposed to low doses of lead in the womb tend to be underweight and underdeveloped at birth. During grade school, lead-exposed kids exhibit behavioral problems, low IQ and deficiencies in speech and language. And research has shown that teenagers with histories of lead exposure drop out of school seven times as often as their peers.

Lead poisoning is most prevalent among the least privileged—a 1988 study suggested that more than half of low-income black children are afflicted—yet the hazard extends far beyond the ghetto. The study found that in the group with the *lowest* risk—whites living outside central cities—one of every 11 children had high levels of lead in his blood. Officials at the federal Centers for Disease Control in Atlanta have recommended lead screening for all children under 6, yet only one in 10 receives it. If the agency redefines lead poisoning as expected, the demand for a national testing program will surely grow.

## Injuries

No disease, drug or environmental hazard rivals traumatic injuries as a killer of children. Every year mishaps claim the lives of 8,000 American youngsters and permanently disable 50,000. Car and bicycle accidents are the main menace, with a death toll of 3,400. Burn injuries kill 1,300—and 1,200 drown. Others die from choking or falls or gunshot wounds. Though most of these injuries are unintentional, child advocates resist calling them accidents. "Our contention," says former surgeon general C. Everett Koop, now chairman of the national Safe Kids Campaign, "is that 90 percent of permanent childhood injuries can be prevented."

The challenge is simply to make parents more vigilant. Koop's campaign stresses such basic precautions as installing smoke alarms (9 out of 10 fire deaths occur in houses that lack them), keeping toddlers away from swimming pools, turning pot handles toward the back of the stove where kids can't reach them and getting children to wear bicycle helmets. According to the National Center for Health Statistics, nearly 70 percent of all hospitalized bicyclists are treated for head trauma. Helmets reduce the risk of brain injury by almost 90 percent—yet only 5 percent of young bike riders wear them.

Injury would seem an equal-opportunity hazard, yet black children die from injuries at nearly twice the rate of others. Koop blames inadequate supervision and a lack of medical care—which is to say he blames poverty. "When I look back on my years in office," he says, "the things I banged my head against were all poverty."

## Poverty

Kids under 5 suffer more poverty than any other age group in America. Roughly one in four is poor, versus one in eight adults, and the consequences are manifold. Poor children are more likely to suffer from low birth weight, more likely to die during the first year of life, more likely to suffer hunger or abuse while growing up and less likely to benefit from immunizations or adequate medical care. Moreover, notes Dr. Peter Boelens of the Sharkey-Issaquena Health Alliance, poor kids grow up without ever "understanding what is necessary for healthy living."

## Infant Mortality Rates

**A**s of 1988, infant death was twice as common in the U.S. as in Japan. American black children were dying at twice the rate of whites. Selected rankings:

| Country | Deaths per 1,000 live births |
|---|---|
| Japan | 5.0 |
| Switzerland | 6.8 |
| Singapore | 7.0 |
| Canada | 7.3 |
| France | 7.7 |
| East Germany | 8.1 |
| U.S. Whites | 8.5 |
| United Kingdom | 8.8 |
| All U.S. | 10.0 |
| Czechoslovakia | 11.9 |
| China | 12.0 |
| Nigeria | 13.8 |
| U.S. Blacks | 17.6 |

SOURCES: STATISTICAL OFFICE OF THE UNITED NATIONS; NATIONAL CENTER FOR HEALTH STATISTICS

## The First to Suffer

**Y**oung children endure more poverty than any other age group in the population.

Percent of children under 6 years who are poor

Percent of all people in U.S. who are poor

SOURCE: NATIONAL CENTER FOR CHILDREN IN POVERTY

Healthy People 2000, the federal government's public-health blueprint for the rest of the decade, seeks to reduce the nation's infant mortality rate to 7 deaths per 1,000 (from today's 9.1), to reduce the frequency of low birth weight to 5 percent (from today's 7 percent) and to ensure that 9 out of 10 (instead of 3 out of 4) expectant mothers get early prenatal care. Modest goals, yet few children's advocates expect them to be met. Too many better-armed interests are competing for the available federal dollars. "Children don't vote," says Florida Gov. Lawton Chiles, chairman of the National Commission to Prevent Infant Mortality, "and they do not contribute to political campaigns."

There are glimmers of hope. The Bush administration recently proposed a five-year, $171 million initiative to reduce infant mortality by half in 10 hard-hit cities—but proposed paying for it by taking money away from existing maternal and child-health programs. Congress blocked that move and has appropriated $25 million to fund the 10-city effort next year. No one is complaining, but the effort is only a start. "We want to encourage and celebrate Mr. Bush's initiative," says Tuckson, of the March of Dimes. "But if we recognize that reducing infant mortality is important, why not 20 cities?"

Or 40? There is no economy in neglecting children's health. Kids born underweight end up in intensive-care units, often at state expense. Many remain lifelong burdens to society. "Forget the humane reasons for providing prenatal health care," says Jennifer Howse, president of the March of Dimes. "There is a cold, hard business reason. It saves money."

*With* LARRY WILSON *in New York,*
MARY HAGER *and* STEVEN WALDMAN *in Washington*
*and* JOE DELANEY *in Carey, Miss.*

# THE SHADOW CHILDREN

## Preparing for the arrival of crack babies in school

Marilee C. Rist

*MARILEE C. RIST is senior editor of The American School Board Journal.*

## The Shadow Children

The initial wave of crack babies, born after crack cocaine hit the streets in the mid-1980s, are kindergarten age today. The arrival of those first afflicted youngsters in public schools marks the beginning of a struggle that will deplete educational resources and test the compassion of public school educators. Perhaps the only chance of being equal to the task is to appreciate it now and begin at once to prepare schools.

Children prenatally exposed to crack cocaine, says one psychologist, are kids wired for 110 volts, living in a 220-volt world. According to available evidence, many of these children will not be easy to teach.

What cocaine-exposed newborns go through during the days and weeks after birth is a rocky start on life: Some have birth defects — deformed hearts, lungs, digestive systems, or limbs — attributed to cocaine exposure in the uterus. Most are small and underweight. Crack babies are irritable, tremulous, and difficult to soothe for at least the first three months. They also have a significantly higher rate of Sudden Infant Death Syndrome than babies not prenatally exposed. Many suffer neurological damage from prenatal drug exposure. For them, coping with the normal activities and stimuli of daily life will be difficult.

The victimization continues when these infants are ready to go home. Many are being abandoned in hospitals by their crack-smoking mothers. The majority (from 50% to 75%, according to a recent survey by the U.S. Department of Health and Human Services[1]) go home with their mother or a relative. If the mother is drug-dependent, and takes the child home to an environment characterized by deep poverty and little physical or emotional nurturing, the already-victimized crack baby is at high risk for further neglect and abuse.

Douglas Besharov, former director of the National Center on Child Abuse and currently a scholar at the American Enterprise Institute, has dubbed these children a potential "bio-underclass" — a cohort of children whose combined physiological damage and extreme socioeconomic disadvantage could foredoom them to a life of permanent inferiority.[2] Child development experts who try to paint a more hopeful picture say these children need special attention right from birth to overcome difficulties ranging from congenital problems to learning disabilities.

For educators, the question of how to handle cocaine-exposed children cannot be ignored for long. From 48 to 60 months after these babies enter the world, public schools face the compounded result of their multiple layers of problems. Although, at first glance, drug-exposed children might not look much different from other youngsters, the long-term effects of fetal drug exposure emerge as the children begin interacting in the larger world. In the typical classroom environment — where noises, voices, instructions, questions, interactions, and distractions crowd one upon the other — cocaine-exposed children tend to react in one of two ways. They withdraw completely, or they become wild and difficult to control. Like fuses when a burst of current pulses through and overloads them, these children are prone to short-circuit or burn out with too much stimulation.

The question facing public school educators right now is how to prepare schools to serve these youngsters — to enable this growing population of innocent victims to be the best they can be.

## Crack Cross-Country

Like an Old Testament plague, crack has hurled devastating destruction on society with terrifying suddenness. This potent, crystallized, smokable derivative of cocaine (so named for the crackling sound it makes while burning) has been on the streets for only four or five years. Yet, in big cities, suburbs, even rural areas, the rate of crack use is skyrocketing — and with it, the number of newborns showing effects of prenatal exposure.

To the user, crack produces an intensely pleasurable, almost instantaneous high by stimulating the brain's pleasure receptors. So powerful is the sensation — report authorities such as Dr. Thomas R. Kosten, acting director of the Substance Abuse Treatment Center at the Yale School of Medicine — that the events and sensations that normally give a person pleasure no longer satisfy.[3] And because each high lasts only from six to 10 minutes and is immediately followed by a deep letdown, the user is sucked into an endless cycle of getting high, then acquiring the next piece of crack for the next high. Although each plastic bag of crack might cost only a few dollars, crack abusers can spend upwards of several hundred dollars a day to stay high.

Crack users become addicted quickly — some reports say within a month or two; others claim in just one or two uses of the drug. Among pregnant crack users, the drug's potency is devastating — in its effects on the developing child and by the sheer numbers of women and infants involved. (The National Institute on Drug Abuse estimates that more than 5 million women of childbearing age are using illegal substances; one million of these are using cocaine.)

No one knows for sure how many cocaine-exposed children are being born each year. The President's National Drug Control Strategy report estimates 100,000. Other estimates run upwards of 200,000. A more realistic estimate, says Douglas Besharov, runs between 30,000 and 50,000 — or between 1% and 2% of all babies born in the U.S. In New York City, Besharov says, approximately 7,000 such births occur annually—and in Washington, D.C., some 1,500.

The statistics are most stark in big cities and among minorities. A recent survey of hospitals conducted by the National Association for Perinatal Addiction Research and Education (NAPARE) found that 15% of newborns in New York City's Harlem Hospital showed traces of cocaine in their urine, 16% of newborns in Chicago Osteopathic Hospital, and 10% of newborns in San Francisco General Hospital.[4]

In Washington, D.C., city health authorities can track the crack explosion in the city by the growing proportion of mothers using drugs at the time of delivery at D.C. General Hospital: In 1987, the ratio was one in 10; in 1989, it had grown to one in five.[5]

Elizabeth Graham, New York City's assistant health commissioner, told the New York Times that cocaine abuse among the city's pregnant women has increased "3,000% over the last 10 years." In 1985, just as crack became available, she said, five of every 1,000 childbearing women identified themselves as cocaine users. Last year, the figure was 21 — a 320% increase in just four years.[6]

Although urban areas show the most severe effects of crack abuse, suburban and even rural areas are not immune. Two years ago, crack babies were "a problem we didn't see," says pediatric social worker Forrest Ehmke, who works in the newborn intensive care unit of St. Joseph's Medical Center in Wichita.[7] Now, says Ehmke, the problem is "becoming more and more commonplace." And it's not limited to the cities of Kansas: Crack-using mothers are brought to St. Joseph's from all over the state's rural areas, he says.

As Ehmke puts it, "Crack is everywhere."

Like alcohol and other addictive substances, crack is proving itself an equal-opportunity drug, reaching well beyond poor, high-minority populations of U.S. inner cities. A recent NA-

PARE study of pregnant mothers at public and private clinics in Pinellas County, Florida, found no significant difference in the rates of substance exposure in private or public patients.[8]

The study found that a minority woman who uses drugs or alcohol during pregnancy is almost 10 times more likely to be reported to child abuse authorities than is a white woman. White middle-class mothers — along with other white middle-class cocaine users — find it easier to hide their substance abuse than do poor, minority women.

Hiding the problem, though, serves to compound its effects, says NAPARE President Dr. Ira J. Chasnoff, a pediatrician at Northwestern University Hospital and a noted authority on prenatal cocaine exposure.[9] The key to the greatest success with cocaine-exposed children, says Chasnoff, is early identification of the mother's cocaine abuse and early treatment of the child. But the vast majority of drug-exposed children, he says, are getting no special attention.

## Crack In The Cradle

The need for early intervention and treatment is clear to those who work with infants born suffering the effects of cocaine exposure. And even though experts such as Chasnoff aren't sure what prenatal exposure to the drug will mean for children over the long run, the evidence is mounting.

The danger to the child begins in the womb. Early in pregnancy, a woman who takes cocaine is at risk for spontaneous abortion (health authorities say some women deliberately take cocaine to terminate their pregnancies). If spontaneous abortion does not occur, the fetus is subjected to a diminished oxygen supply during development — caused by cocaine's constriction of the blood vessels in the placenta. This can result in physical malformations and can damage the infant's central nervous system. A pregnant mother's use of cocaine also can bring on a stroke in the unborn child.[10]

Because cocaine causes the mother's uterus to contract spasmodically, a high percentage of cocaine-exposed babies — some 30% in Harlem, for example — are born extremely prematurely. Wichita's Forrest Ehmke says one baby born at home last year to a mother high on cocaine weighed just over a pound at birth — the smallest infant to survive in the state that year.

The cost of bringing these extremely premature infants to a normal birth weight is high. Each day in intensive care at St. Joseph's Medical Center costs from $1,500 to $2,000, says Ehmke. An infant born after 32 weeks of gestation (eight weeks premature) needs two months of intensive care — at a cost upwards of $100,000. And the earlier an infant is born, the longer and more complicated — and more expensive — is the care that child needs.

Along with the physical complications of being born prematurely, many cocaine-exposed newborns show signs of extremely disturbed behavior. According to NAPARE's Dr. Chasnoff, who runs a clinic at Northwestern Memorial Hospital for drug-abusing mothers and their prenatally exposed children, crack babies are typically hypersensitive. Just trying to pick the child up brings on uncontrollable tremors and crying. The infant cries when awake and doesn't sleep well. Crack babies also typically exhibit "gaze aversion" — that is, the infant avoids eye contact.

This tendency to withdraw from intimacy and stimulation doesn't disappear, says Dan Griffith, a developmental psychologist who works with Chasnoff.[11] From birth onward, the cocaine-exposed child typically has difficulty forming attachments and appears emotionally flat—a type of behavior that Griffith says is likely to jeopardize the child's later ability to learn and adapt to a classroom.

Even while still a newborn, though, the child begins suffering the combined effects of its own inability to form an emotional bond and of the mother's drug dependence. Difficult to handle, care for, and soothe even by experienced professionals in the best of situations, crack babies go home with mothers who are, at best, ill-equipped to care for their children. In the worst cases, when the mother is abusing crack, she does not respond to her infant's needs at all, driven instead by her craving for the next high. The mother's need to feed, clothe, and nurture her child—commonly thought to be instinctive—is overwhelmed by her need for drugs.

This breakdown in the basic mother-child bond is reflected in two direct measures of crack abuse among women: rising infant mortality rates and increasing numbers of infants being abandoned in hospitals by drug-dependent mothers.

In Washington, D.C., where the use of crack has exploded in the past three or four years, the infant mortality rate — that is, the rate of infants who died before their first birthdays — surged to 32.3 deaths per 1,000 live births during the first half of 1989.[12] That means babies in the nation's capital are dying at a rate more than triple the 1988 national average of 9.9 deaths per 1,000 — and nearly 50% more than the city's 1988 rate of 23.2 deaths per 1,000. City health officials attribute the startling hike to the increase in babies born to cocaine-addicted women.

Mothers abandoning infants in hospital nurseries was virtually unknown before the crack explosion. To find out more about these so-called "boarder babies," the Child Welfare League of America conducted a survey of hospitals in five U.S. cities one day in June 1989. On that one day in those five cities, the survey tallied 304 babies who had been medically cleared for discharge and simply left in the hospitals. At least 69% of these infants showed signs of impairment attributed to their mothers' drug use (especially cocaine). Most had been in the hospital since birth; some had been returned once or more because of neglect, abuse, failure to thrive, or other health problems.[13]

As disturbing as it is that infants are spending, in some cases, the first year or more of their lives in the impersonal environment of hospital nurseries, boarder babies — unlike those at home with crack-addicted mothers — at least receive nourish-ment, medical care, and a modicum of attention and affection from hospital staff members.

Carol Cole, a teacher and child development specialist in the Los Angeles Unified School District who works with cocaine and other drug-exposed preschoolers, tells what happens to the majority of crack babies: The typical three-year-old entering the pilot program in which Cole teaches has lived in three different situations — handed, for example, from mother to grandmother or another family member and then into foster care.[14]

A negative cycle develops, says Cole: Unable to satisfy or soothe the cocaine-exposed infant, the caretaker becomes frustrated and interacts negatively with the child or simply gives up and turns the baby over to someone else. For a child who has trouble forming attachments, being passed on to new caretakers simply compounds the problem.

## Crack In The Classroom

It's difficult to say exactly what behavioral and learning problems a crack-exposed child will bring to school. No one knows for certain whether the effects of prenatal cocaine exposure will follow youngsters beyond early childhood (the oldest cocaine-exposed children being systematically studied are just turning age three). The luckiest ones, say child development specialists, might not show any lasting damage. But evidence accumulated so far suggests the others will not have an easy time in school.

The most severely damaged children are likely to be diagnosed in need of special education. As for the rest, the severity and scope of their problems will vary. What's clear is that schools need to prepare for a potentially significant influx of children who will have difficulty learning in traditional school settings.

Teachers in Los Angeles Unified's pilot program for drug-exposed children, says Carol Cole, are dealing with the same types of behavior in cocaine-exposed preschoolers that's typically seen in cocaine-exposed infants: the difficulty in developing human attachments, the inability to deal with many different stimuli at once, the tendency to act overly aggressive or to withdraw completely when overstimulated.

L.A. Unified's program accepts only children of a normal intelligence range. Even so, Cole says, "these babies have had a double whammy" — first, prenatal drug exposure and, later, social and environmental insults. The combination, she says, makes them unlikely to fit well into the typical classroom.

Northwestern's Dan Griffith concurs: "These children have a low tolerance for frustration," he says. "They have difficulty structuring information, and they're easily overwhelmed by information coming in."

Even though the children Griffith works with perform in the normal range on standard development tests by age two, the tests take place in one-on-one situations, he notes, with children asked to carry out one specific task at a time. As soon as the youngsters are distracted by more than one instruction or given more than one toy or apparatus to handle, they withdraw or become hyperactive.

Cocaine-exposed children seem unable to engage in free play, reports Dr. Judith Howard, director of the Suspected Child Abuse and Neglect Team at the University of California, Los Angeles.[15] Crack babies typically lack the skills and characteristics necessary for free play — self-organization, initiative, and follow-through without adult guidance. According to Howard, cocaine-exposed toddlers in an unstructured play situation hardly know what to do. They scatter and bat toys, pick toys up and put them down, without purpose and with seeming uninvolvement. Like Griffith and Cole, Howard says these children will need lots of structure and individual attention, both at home and in school.

The problem is not that cocaine-exposed children are brain-damaged and can't learn at all, emphasize these experts. It's that they can't learn in the typical classroom environment. Given the proper supportive, structured environment — with a low adult/child ratio, strong emotional support, and conscious efforts by teachers to form emotionally satisfying attachments with children — the youngsters respond, says Cole. Gradually, some seem to do better in a more typical classroom environment.

Cole and Griffith both caution, however, that the drug-exposed children in their programs are not typical of the thousands of cocaine-exposed children across the U.S.: Unlike the vast majority, the children in these programs are receiving early treatment and intense developmental attention.

Indeed, says Griffith, the youngsters in the Northwestern clinic are marked exceptions to the rule: Unlike most crack-using pregnant women, the mothers of these babies were motivated enough to seek help; they received proper nutrition and medical attention during their pregnancies, and are getting treatment and developmental followup for their babies. This is the best of situations for crack babies, says Griffith. Even so, the children "will have difficulty adapting to a normal school environment."

The educational environment cocaine-exposed children need is intensive, say these experts. The Northwestern clinic works directly with mothers and babies, providing medical care, nutritional counseling, training in parental skills, and developmental followup. The L.A. Unified preschool program puts two- and three-year-olds in groups with an adult/child ratio of 3:8.

The cost to public schools of providing such structured, supportive learning environments — like the cost of giving hospital intensive care to crack-exposed newborns — is bound to be high. But waiting to identify and treat drug-exposed children when they're enrolled in kindergarten is a mistake that could add substantially to the overall cost, warn Cole and Griffith. Early intervention is the key to success.

Here's why: The overt aggression and extreme withdrawal characteristic of these children begin developing immediate-ly after birth. In chaotic, nonsupportive home environments, these types of behavior are necessary coping mechanisms for crack babies. Over time, explains Griffith, these types of behavior become firmly entrenched and increasingly difficult to change. Working with the children before these problems become ingrained is critical, says Griffith, "to make them the best they can be."

A day-care center in St. Petersburg, Fla. — funded by the federal government and run by Operation Par, a drug abuse treatment service — offers a model for doing just that. Three teachers and three aides work with 25 cocaine-exposed children from two months to age five — patiently teaching them how to play, how to concentrate on a task or a toy for longer than a few seconds. Essential to the program is to give the children lots of attention, structure, and emotional support.[16]

## Where to Begin

Educators face the immediate question of where to begin in preparing for drug-exposed children in the classroom. The following suggestions, culled from conversations with people already working with cocaine-exposed children, can help.

1. *Develop means of early identification.* Work with child-welfare services in the community to identify crack-affected children. Contact state and local health departments, hospital administrators, and juvenile authorities. Form alliances with child-protective service agencies. These organizations can function as early-warning systems and important allies. If these agencies are keeping accurate records of the numbers of drug-exposed infants being born annually in the community, schools will have an estimate of how many may be enrolling in kindergarten in the coming years.

Unfortunately, the quality of available data ranges from excellent to unreliable. In 1987, Florida passed a law requiring hospitals and clinics to report to county health departments all cases in which a newborn shows signs of substance abuse by the mother or in which the mother reports having used controlled substances during pregnancy. In other states, though, statistics are less complete or even nonexistent. A recent hospital survey conducted by NAPARE found that some hospitals conduct no substance-abuse assessment—either by history or by urine toxicology—during or after pregnancy. Other hospitals, by policy, ask all women about substance abuse. The most thorough data, the study found, are collected by hospitals with established procedures for assessing every pregnant woman or every newborn for substance abuse or exposure through medical history and urine toxicology.[17]

Child-protective service agencies and juvenile justice divisions can help schools identify children who are likely to need special education services. In urban centers where crack use has exploded in recent years, child welfare and foster care systems are finding their resources overwhelmed by the num-

> **"Using drugs while pregnant is wrong. It cripples and sometimes kills babies."**
>
> Douglas Besharov
> American Enterprise Institute
> for Public Policy Research

bers of drug-affected children. Schools stand next in line to have their resources stretched to the limit.

2. *Lobby for funds to develop programs for drug-exposed infants from birth to age three and beyond.* Providing the low teacher-child ratio to serve prenatally exposed children will be expensive. Make state and federal legislators aware of the problem.

3. *Educate students.* Schools need drug education and prevention programs that include teaching students the skills they need to resist drug use, advises Herbert D. Kleber, Deputy Director for Demand Reduction at the federal Office of National Drug Control Policy.[18]

Douglas Besharov says that because approximately a million teenage girls become pregnant each year — and because these girls often don't believe crack is bad for their babies — it's important to get the message out that drugs and parenthood do not mix. The message needs to be blunt, he says: "Using drugs while pregnant is wrong. It cripples and sometimes kills babies."

4. *Prepare to provide appropriate classroom environments for cocaine-exposed youngsters.* Stability and security are essential for drug-exposed children, says L.A. Unified's Carol Cole. Schools might consider allowing children to remain with the same teacher for longer than one school year. Rethinking the structure of the school day also is important — reducing fragmentation, cutting down on interruptions and outside intrusions, and emphasizing routine, rituals, and schedules. Cole's program permits class visitors only one day a week for a short period.

Teachers will have to give special consideration to the psychosocial and emotional needs of these children. Cole says it's not enough for teachers just to pass information to children, refer an ill-behaved child to a psychologist, or assume parents will deal with their child's classroom behavior. Teachers may have to cross traditional boundaries, developing warm, strong relationships with children. Cole's advice: Find ways to make schools less stressful, less demanding, more predictable.

5. *Call for research.* Little data exist—especially at the national level—on the extent or the long-term effects of prenatal cocaine exposure. The problem, though, will not wait. Crack babies already are arriving in public school classrooms. The time to begin intensive study—on a wide scale—is now.

It's clear that meeting the needs of cocaine-exposed children will be expensive. And it won't be easy to compel legislatures and communities to act soon enough for treatment programs to be the most effective. Without immediate and aggressive attempts to intervene, though, crack promises to extract a toll far more dear to the society than money spent on programs. Like the Angel of Death descending on the firstborn in Egypt, crack has just begun to do its deadly work, producing tens of thousands of blameless children each year who, by biology and environment, are cast into a world devoid of nearly every hope but one — that educators and other leaders of our society will take the actions now that ultimately might redeem their lives.

1. Office of the Inspector General's draft recommendations for the final report, "Crack Babies," U.S. Department of Health and Human Services, February 1990, p. 9.
2. Besharov, Douglas J., American Enterprise Institute for Public Policy Research, Washington, D.C., telephone conversation, September 28, 1989.
3. Kosten, Thomas R., M.D., Acting Director of Research, Substance Abuse Treatment Unit, Yale University School of Medicine, New Haven, Conn., telephone conversation, October 2, 1989.
4. Pat O'Keefe, spokesperson, National Association for Perinatal Addiction Research and Education, Chicago, Ill., telephone conversation, October 2, 1989.
5. Marcia Slacum Greene, "Abuse, Neglect Rising in D.C.," *Washington Post*, September 10, 1989.
6. French, Howard W., "For Pregnant Addicts, a Clinic of Hope," *New York Times*, September 29, 1989.
7. Ehmke, Forrest, Pediatric Social Worker, Newborn Intensive Care Unit, St. Joseph's Medical Center, Wichita, Kan., telephone conversation, September 27, 1989.
8. Press release, National Association for Perinatal Addiction Research and Education, Chicago, Ill., September 18, 1989.
9. Press release, National Association for Perinatal Addiction Research and Education, Chicago, Ill., September 17, 1989.
10. Andrew C. Revkin, "Crack in the Cradle," *Discover*, September 1989, p. 67.
11. Griffith, Dan, Developmental Psychologist, Northwestern University, telephone conversation, September 29, 1989.
12. Abramowitz, Michael, "Infant Mortality Soars Here," *Washington Post*, September 30, 1989.
13. Munns, Joyce Matthews, "The Youngest of the Homeless: Characteristics of Hospital Boarder Babies in Five Cities," Child Welfare League of America, August 2, 1989, p. 8.
14. Cole, Carol, Teacher and Child Development Specialist, Salvin Special Education Center, Los Angeles Unified School District, telephone conversation, September 29, 1989.
15. Blakeslee, Sandra, "Crack's Toll Among Babies: A Joyless View, Even of Toys," *New York Times*, September 17, 1989.
16. Ibid.
17. Pat O'Keefe, op. cit.
18. Kleber, Herbert D., M.D., Deputy Director for Demand Reduction, Office of National Drug Control Policy, "Prevention and Treatment in the National Drug Control Strategy," lecture delivered at Yale University, September 26, 1989.

# "I couldn't afford my job"

## Hard times ahead for working mothers... but who cares?

*Redbook does. We know it isn't easy juggling a job and family. We know you're not getting the help you need—not from the people who employ you or the politicians who are supposed to represent you. Here, a working mom who's mad as hell says she's not going to take it anymore, and offers some good advice.*

### Elizabeth Ritchie Johnson

After nearly ten years in the workplace and more than a year back at my job following maternity leave, I found myself invited to a goodbye party I hadn't expected to attend—my own. I liked my job and my coworkers; I had a sympathetic boss, a trustworthy babysitter, a happy baby and a supportive husband. So why the farewells? I had to quit because I couldn't afford my job.

A visit to our accountant a few months earlier had graphically spelled out what I had reluctantly begun to suspect—we were *losing* money, even though we were both working full-time. Our babysitter received the equivalent of two-thirds of my take-home pay, and after shelling out funds for transportation, lunches, office attire and higher-priced, time-saving foods, the one-third left was quickly reduced to about thirty dollars a week. Of course, the higher tax bracket we, as a two-income couple, fell into took care of that, and then some.

After that meeting it became extremely difficult for me to justify my job, no matter how gratifying I found it, when it took me away from my daughter fifty hours a week *and* made no improvement in our financial situation.

**Parental leave**
Percentage of companies providing leave for both male and female employees:

YES 26.9%
NO 73.1%

I debated the options. Should I try to find a higher-paying job? Even if I could, it would probably mean more responsibility and longer hours, and I'd end up spending even less time with my daughter. That didn't strike me as an acceptable solution.

More economical child-care approaches, such as a live-in *au pair*, were also dismissed because, while the weekly salary would be less than what we were paying our current baby-sitter, having an *au pair* would require an extra room in a bigger (and therefore more expensive) apartment. We considered enrolling our daughter in a day-care center, but in our city, quality day care costs almost as much as at-home sit-

ters do. No wonder every Friday night found me with a huge migraine.

Why did *I* quit and not my husband? In the three years since we had both started our respective jobs (I as a magazine researcher, he as a cable television account representative) at the same salary, he had received two promotions and a 100 percent pay increase, while I had received two promotions and a 16 percent increase. On top of that, I had a career that offered the possibility of doing freelance work at home. The discussion of who should stay home was obviously brief.

Once I finally made the decision to leave my job, I felt a mixture of great excitement—I would be home with my baby—

and great anxiety. It had always been important to me to contribute my equal share financially. But now I worried that my financial contribution was about to be reduced, making me less independent than I liked. Still, I was lucky that, given my profession, I had the option to work from home.

I'm far from alone in my dilemma. Of the 21 million children under the age of six in this country, about half have mothers who hold paying jobs. And by 1995, it's predicted that two-thirds of children in this age group (nearly 15 million) will have mothers who are employed.

In spite of these facts, the United States remains the only industrialized country other than South Africa without a "national family policy," according to the Child Care Action Campaign (CCAC). What this means is that there are not only not enough spaces in daycare centers to go around, the cost is exorbitant, and the quality of such care is often unpredictable, since there are no Federally mandated standards.

### Unequal pay

No matter what level of education they completed, men, on average, earn more than women do. Worse, women with a high school diploma make less than men with only an elementary-school education. These are the average annual earnings based on level of education for men and women:

| | |
|---|---|
| $16,016 | **men** |
| $11,128 | **women** |
| **elementary school** | |
| $19,656 | |
| $12,636 | |
| **1–3 years high school** | |
| $23,400 | |
| $15,808 | |
| **4 years high school** | |
| $26,884 | |
| $19,708 | |
| **1–3 years college** | |
| $36,660 | |
| $24,336 | |
| **4 years college** | |
| $40,716 | |
| $30,576 | |
| **postgraduate study** | |

And while the Child Care and Development Block Grant, signed into law with the budget last November, is considered by the Children's Defense Fund "the most significant pro-family, antipoverty legislation ever enacted," it is debatable whether this can be considered a national child-care bill. It will, over the next five years, provide up to $6 billion in child-care assistance to low-income working families who desperately need it. Yet millions of middle-class families who don't meet the requirements—but have difficulty affording quality child care nonetheless—will still be left out in the cold. How are we women supposed to give our best at the office if we're constantly worried about how well our children are being taken care of elsewhere?

Compounding the problem, women still earn only 72 cents to a man's dollar for comparable work, which further reduces a family's total income and ability to pay for quality child care. No one feels this financial squeeze more than single mothers. Their need for reliable, affordable child care is even more acute, since there are fewer support systems for these families.

Frankly, I'm shocked that children are *still* given such low priority by our government. It took four years to hammer out last year's child-care legislation and scrape together the funds for it—and yet, at a moment's notice, the government has had no trouble committing to $500 million a day to wage war in the Persian Gulf. Obviously, the White House is sending a clear message to working mothers everywhere—we can get lots of money very fast when it *really* matters, but the welfare of your children just doesn't matter enough.

As for me, I've come up with an arrangement that works most of the time. After three years of freelancing from home, I'm earning almost what I did when I left the office. But my need for child care hasn't ended: Try sounding professional on the phone with a client while a three-year-old is playfully attempting to wrestle the receiver away from you.

Of course, my home-based work arrangement *does* mean I no longer have to make apologetic phone calls to my boss when my sitter is late, but I'm still caught in the catch-22 of many working parents: I need to work more hours in order to pay for child care and other bills, but the more work I get, the more child care I need and the more hours I need to work.

The truth is that many mothers today must work to make ends meet, whether they want to or not. Those mothers require decent care for their children, and their children deserve it. There are millions of American families struggling to support themselves and provide satisfactory care for their children. How much longer can politicians close their eyes to this reality?

# what working moms want and need

Although there is still a long way to go, there is no question that some American companies have begun to respond to the needs of working parents. Management is slowly beginning to realize that family-oriented benefits are not only a great recruiting tool, they are also an efficient means of fostering employee job satisfaction, productivity and loyalty. But for every company that helps (most of them

**Don't companies care?**

Percentage of companies (over 250 employees) that provide the following work options and benefits:

**34.9%**
Flex-time

**26.1%**
Voluntary part-time

**15.7%**
Job-sharing

**14.0%**
Child-care information and referral services

**8.9%**
Child-care vouchers

**5.2%**
On- or near-site day-care centers

**3.8%**
Work at home

the extremely large Fortune 500), there are thousands more that do not.

Of the nation's six million employers, roughly 5,500, or .09 percent, currently offer some form of child-care assistance, according to studies by the Families and Work Institute (FWI) in New York City. While this percentage is small, it *is* a vast improvement when you consider that, in 1978, a mere 110 employers offered *any* kind of child-care assistance.

What are the benefits that working mothers really want? Here is the wish-list mentioned again and again in surveys conducted by various family organizations, as well as examples of how some companies are meeting those needs.

### 1. FLEXIBLE WORK SCHEDULES

"Time flexibility is always first on the list of what parents want," says Ellen Galinsky, cofounder of FWI. "It's important for parents to be able to leave work an hour earlier to take a child to the doctor or attend the school play without having to lie about it."

Typically, families' varying needs, often determined by their children's ages and school schedules, are best addressed by a *variety* of flexible work options. These options include part-time work, flex-time (employees determine their own work hours and days within a given range), job sharing (two people divide one job by alternating shifts or days) and telecommuting (working from home on a computer and transmitting work via telephone lines).

For instance, at Oracle Systems, a computer software firm in Redwood Shores, California, 15 percent of the staff telecommutes. And at Steelcase Inc., an office furniture manufacturing company in Grand Rapids, 94 employees share 47 jobs.

Flex-time is a given for the entire staff of the Phoenix Mutual Life Insurance Company in Hartford, Connecticut. Employees can start work any time between 7:15 and 9 A.M., and leave after working 7¼ hours. Indeed, flex-time for all may be the wave of the future. According to FWI's Ellen Galinsky, approximately 13 percent of all firms now offer flexible work schedules, with more and more companies adopting the plan.

### 2. GOOD, AFFORDABLE CHILD CARE

According to the Children's Defense Fund in Washington, D.C., unless mothers get free babysitting from relatives, child-care costs are comparable to housing and taxes in terms of the bite they take out of the family budget. There is also the question of quality. Regulation of day-care facilities varies widely from state to state, and being licensed is no guarantee of quality (just as a restaurant's being licensed to serve food provides no assurance of a tasty meal). As a result, parents must cope with the prob-

lem of locating affordable child care, along with the equally pressing issue of how well their children will be tended. Here are the ways companies can help:

• *On- or near-site child-care centers.* There are approximately 1,300 on- or near-site child-care centers sponsored and, in many cases, subsidized by employers nationwide. For families with small children, such centers are a godsend. The SAS Institute Inc., a software firm in Cary, North Carolina, goes a step further and provides free, on-site care for infants and preschoolers. Other companies reserve spaces for employees' children in nearby community day-care centers.

• *After-school programs.* The need for child care doesn't end once a child reaches school age, and yet older-child care can be even harder to find than programs for preschoolers. As a result, many parents are left with no choice but to allow their children to return home alone after school. Until government and business recognize this need, however, it is unlikely that the number of latchkey children, currently estimated at up to 7 million, will subside.

Only a handful of employers offer any kind of care for school-age children. One notable exception is G.T. Water Products, Inc., in Moorpark, California, which offers its 32 employees a fully subsidized, on-site Montessori school (K-12). The school is open year-round and offers care both before and after regular school hours.

• *Sick or emergency child care.* The best-laid plans of a working mother fall apart quickly when a child is sick and can't go to day care or school, or when a caregiver is a no-show. To help employees caught in this bind, Fel-Pro Incorporated, an auto-parts supplier in Skokie, Illinois, provides emergency and sick care to children in their own homes, charging workers a nominal fee. And Home Box Office, Inc., in New York City provides free emergency child care up to 10 hours a day for three consecutive days.

• *Financial assistance.* The majority of companies assisting employees with dependent-care cost do so through benefit options such as a Flexible Spending Account. Using this program, employees can have up to 5,000 pretax dollars deducted from their paychecks and put into an account from which they are reimbursed as they pay for child care. Other methods include the voucher system, in which the employer picks up part or all of the cost of child care either by making payments directly to a provider or by reimbursing the employee.

### 3. SYMPATHETIC SUPERVISORS

Supervisors who are most valued by working parents—and are more likely to win their loyalty—are those who are sensitive to family issues, especially as they affect job performance; supervisors who are up-to-date on the firm's family policies and

---

## Your Friends and Enemies

Who can help working mothers most? Those legislators who actively support the pro-family bills that come before Congress. Two recent bills—the Family and Medical Leave Act (FMLA), which was vetoed by President Bush, and the Comprehensive Childcare Bill (CCB), which was signed into law, offer a way to measure just how much our representatives are willing to help beleaguered families. Here, in alphabetical order, the lawmakers who have done the most—and least—on behalf of family and child-care issues.

### Friends in the Senate
**Senator Christopher Dodd (D-CT)** Author of the Senate version of both the Comprehensive Childcare Bill and the Family and Medical Leave Act. He plans to reintroduce the FMLA in Congress this year.
**Senator Edward Kennedy (D-MA)** Has long championed bills in favor of women, families and education, including the CCB and FMLA.
**Senator Barbara Mikulski (D-MD)** Was instrumental in winning Senator Hatch's (R-UT) support for the CCB which, in turn, created a groundswell of Republican support in the Senate.

### Friends in the House
**Rep. Dale Kildee (D-MI)** Introduced the CCB in the House, and, as a member of the Budget Committee, played a key role in getting funding for it.
**Rep. Patricia Schroeder (D-CO)** A cosponsor of the FMLA, she has worked tirelessly on behalf of child-care issues since 1973.

### Enemies in the Senate
According to the Congressional voting records compiled by the nonpartisan Children's Defense Fund, six members of the Senate scored a zero rating in 1989 for voting against *every* pro-family bill. They are, in alphabetical order: **Senator Jake Garn (R-UT); Senator Slade Gorton (R-WA); Senator Don Nickles (R-OK); Senator William Roth (R-DE); Senator Steve Symms (R-ID); Senator Malcolm Wallop (R-WY).**

If you want to know how your representatives rate, contact the Children's Defense Fund, 122 C Street, N.W., Washington, D.C. 20001; 202-628-8787.
—E.R.J.

put them into practice; and supervisors who are not only flexible when work/family issues arise, but handle any such problems fairly.

While it's difficult to measure how many such supervisors exist, parents unanimously agree that a sympathetic supervisor is key to efficiently handling work/family conflicts when they arise during work hours.

## 4. CHILD-CARE INFORMATION AND REFERRALS

Parents may find it difficult to obtain child care due to long waiting lists, high fees, inconvenient locations or unsatisfactory choices, according to a 1988 study conducted by the staff of FWI. In fact, 65 percent of working mothers with infants reported trouble finding suitable care, which affected their decision to return to work. Approximately 2,500 companies now contract with agencies to counsel and provide referrals to their workers.

For over ten years Steelcase Inc. has offered an in-house referral service for everything from at-home care to summer camps. And Home Box Office, Inc., has an Employee Assistance Program that offers child-care referrals.

## 5. PARENTAL LEAVE POLICIES

Working women received their latest slap in the face last July when President Bush, buckling under pressure from big business, vetoed the Family and Medical Leave Bill. Had this legislation taken effect, American women working for companies with more than 50 employees would have received a three-month guaranteed unpaid maternity leave. As it stands, mothers of newborns tend to fashion their own severely limited maternity leave by taking whatever disability leave they're entitled to, then using up their sick days and vacation days after childbirth. An appalling 40 percent of the working women in this country receive no maternity leave at all.

The leave policies considered most important by working parents include a period of parenting leave following disability; the option of a job-protected, extended leave of absence; some wage replacement; and continued health insurance coverage.

For many women, such benefits are only a pipe dream. But some employers do offer their workers sane—and humane—maternity leaves and other benefits. For instance, Indeeco, an industrial engineering company in St. Louis, offers 26 weeks of paid maternity leave to salaried workers and 13 weeks of paid maternity leave to unionized factory workers. Additional unpaid leave is negotiable. And Lost Arrow Corporation, a clothing manufacturer in Ventura, California, gives new mothers *and* fathers a two-month paid leave after the mother's disability leave runs out.　　　　　—E.R.J.

## The Day-Care Delusion

# When Parents Accept the Unacceptable

Michael Hoyt and
Mary Ellen Schoonmaker

*Michael Hoyt is associate editor of "Columbia Journalism Review" in New York City. Mary Ellen Schoonmaker is an editor at "The Record" in Hackensack, New Jersey.*

When the police arrived at her neat brick house in Oxon Hill, Maryland—a middle-class suburb of Washington, D.C.—Nannie Marie Pressley was not at home. The operator of a family day-care business, she was out with six of the children in her care, unaware that a parent had called in a complaint. The police found 22 children, ages 2 to 11, sitting quietly on rows of benches in the basement, and 12 others, 3- to 7-year-olds, lying on a sheet in another room, where an infant was propped on a sofa. Upstairs, in a dark room that reeked of urine, the officers discovered eight infants strapped into car seats, and one lying face down on the floor. In another room were two infants sharing a crib. Pressley had left her teenage stepdaughter in charge of the children—all 46 of them.

• On a recent hot day in a wealthy suburb in New Jersey, police found an 18-month-old boy locked in a car. He was sweating and screaming by the time a passerby noticed. According to the baby's father, a New York-area writer, the child's sitter had developed a serious toothache and driven to her dentist's. Not knowing what to do with the baby, she left him locked in the car.

• Last year, at Wil-lo Haven Day Care Center, a city-run facility that serves working parents in the Crown Heights section of Brooklyn, New York, a tile from the ceiling fell and hit the center's director on the shoulder, leaving a bad bruise. Given the center's condition—broken windows, no heat, dirty plastic sheeting for window shades—the accident was not a surprise. The director was just thankful that the tile hadn't hit her head. Or a child's.

Child-care conditions like these could easily lead to tragedy. But what is more troubling is the reaction of many of the parents involved. For example, at Pressley's family day-care home, some mothers and fathers, even after learning of the overcrowded conditions there, did not object. "I'd take my kids back today except that she was shut down," one father told a reporter for *The Washington Post*. "I saw children there, but I never took the time to count them. She was a very good baby sitter, and that's all I cared about," said the mother of a 7-year-old.

"Fire her? Are you kidding?" said the New York writer of the sitter who left his infant son in a hot locked car. Although he told her never to do such a thing again, he still believes, "She's great with the kids."

> "If we just provide vouchers for every crummy day-care situation, we're accomplishing nothing."
> Rep. George Miller
> (D.-California)

The Brooklyn parents, afraid budget cuts would cause Wil-lo Haven to close defended even that crumbling facility. "I depend on it to help me keep working and stay off welfare," the mother of a 3-year-old explained.

Often, parents do not see what is right in front of their eyes. They tell themselves that the day-care situation they have found is good, even when down deep they may know better. If you criticize it, they get defensive.

Call it the Day-Care Delusion: The mind rationalizes so that the body can go to work. "Some parents have a

## Day-Care Checklist | Name of Program _____

**Use this list of questions as a scorecard. Make several copies and fill one out for each program you are considering. Answer each question using a scale of 1 through 5 (5 is the highest rating; 1, the lowest). Total each sheet so that you have a score for each facility you visit. (Questions are not listed in order of importance.)**

### How Do You Feel About:

1. The cleanliness and safety of the day-care environment? ____
2. The safety of the neighborhood? ____
3. The quality of the toys? ____
4. The amount of space available per child? ____
5. The meals and snacks served? ____
6. The procedures at mealtime and the diapering routines? ____
7. The time spent on physical activities? The amount of quiet time? ____
8. The gender and racial balance (both staff and children)? ____
9. The way rules are enforced? ____
10. The opportunities for family involvement? ____
11. The degree to which staff members are prepared to teach children? ____
12. The amount of one-to-one attention children get from the staff? ____
13. The amount of affection children get from staff? ____
14. The ratio of staff to children? ____
15. The availability of the program to parents—can you make unannounced visits? ____
16. The distance of the site from your home? Your workplace? ____
17. The hours of operation? ____
18. The cost of enrollment? ____
19. The overall philosophy? ____
20. The overall quality of the program? ____

**Total score for this program**

### Other considerations:
Many other matters are important when choosing day care. Among them:

☐ In addition to low adult/child ratios, look for small group sizes.

☐ Sit in for a morning or drop in unexpectedly and watch how the children relate to the care provider and how she relates to them.

☐ Check the program for current license and liability insurance.

☐ Inquire about the history of the facility—how long has it been in operation, how much turnover has there been among children and staff?

☐ If the program rents or leases space, what is the duration of the rental agreement or lease?

—*Angela Browne Miller*

---

need not to see because they feel so desperate," says Mary Babula, executive director of the Wisconsin Early Childhood Association. "They have to choose what they can afford. Or maybe there's only one center that's open at 7:30 A.M., when they need child care."

Are these parents—the same people who fire off letters of complaint if a box of cereal doesn't have enough raisins—just lousy consumers of child care?

"Some of us go to more trouble in buying a car than in choosing child care," says Angela Browne Miller, who holds master's degrees in social welfare and public health and a Ph.D. in both social welfare and education. For her book, *The Day Care Dilemma,* Dr. Miller recently studied hundreds of different day-care settings and found that parents did not know how to evaluate the quality of the programs; nor did they take the time to find out. Whether from desperation or a lack of knowledge or money, parents are accepting the unacceptable.

To many, child care is still consid-ered to be a woman's issue. But it's not. If all the working mothers in the United States suddenly quit their jobs to care for their children full time, the economy would crumble. Deprived of that income, hundreds of thousands of families would fall right out of the middle class, some to the poverty level.

With more than 10 million children in day care today, someone must take responsibility for lowering the risk to their well-being and raising the standards of care. Some say it should be the parents; others say it should be the Government. And the battle lines are drawn. Many people—including some mothers who choose to stay home with their children, senior citizens and childless couples—don't want their tax dollars spent on raising other people's kids. But with the growing number of single parents and women who work outside the home, it's clear that day care is here to stay.

Although the Federal Government sets standards for everything from food labels to nursing homes, it plays a minor role in child care, leaving regulation up to the states. As a re-sult, there is a tremendous variety in the laws and enforcement of rules governing child care.

One of the leading proponents of Federal involvement, Congressman George Mill (D.-Calif.), points out that children are our most valuable asset, our future: "Government must take an active role, to make sure children's needs are met and their safety protected while in child care. There's no evidence that the marketplace will perform that function."

While there is a need for financial assistance, like tax credits and the new child-care vouchers the states are now offering, Miller says money is not enough: "If we just provide vouchers for every crummy day-care situation, we're accomplishing nothing. We have to go to the issue of quality. We have to have skilled, trained people who are properly paid, so we don't get massive turnover rates."

Congresswoman Patricia Schroeder (D.-Colo.) also calls for Federal action. If Government would see to it that child-care workers were better paid, she says, many of the problems concerning quality would clear up: "A lot of good people want to go into child care, but they also like to eat."

Miller and Schroeder would like to see the Federal Government establish national child-care standards that would address such issues as safety, child-developmental needs and training of care providers.

But quality child care is expensive, leaving some parents with little choice but to conclude that the kind of care they're able to buy is all right because it has to be.

After Jessica McClure fell into a backyard well and was trapped for 58 hours in Midland, Texas, in October 1987, it was clear there had been a safety hazard at the family day-care center run by Jessica's aunt and mother. If the Government had set minimum safety standards, that accident might have been prevented. (Other regulations are needed to insure that wastebaskets, cleaning supplies and medicines are covered and out of children's reach, and that all day-care providers frequently wash their hands, particularly after changing diapers or wiping runny noses, to prevent the spread of infection.)

Yet the dangers of inadequate care are usually not so obvious as open wells, falling tiles or one teenager left in charge of scores of children. The dangers may be more subtle, more psychological than physical. But they are real.

"The average quality of child care in this country is poor," says Edward Zigler, Ph.D., Sterling Professor of Psychology at Yale University and co-author, with Mary E. Lang, of *Child Care Choices* (The Free Press, 1991). Dr. Zigler has been visiting day-care centers and studying children for 35 years, and his findings are alarming: "My feeling is that at least one-third of the children in America are having child-care experiences that will compromise their development, by inhibiting their ability to trust, to relate to other children and adults, and to learn." If a child has had five years of inadequate child care, Dr. Zigler believes—ignored for long periods of time, lost in the crowd of other infants and toddlers, or left in a crib or playpen for hours on end—that child may not be ready to learn when it comes time to start school.

"We can tell by 9 months of age which kids are on a failure line or on the success line," says T. Berry Brazelton, M.D., FAMILY CIRCLE contributing editor and professor emeritus of pediatrics at Harvard Medical School. "So what we have to do is get to children early—get them feeling good about themselves, feeling self-confident—then they'll be ready to learn."

"Children learn for the same reasons birds fly—they are learning machines," Dr. Zigler says. One way we turn off that machine is by failing to provide early nurturing. Yet evidence is mounting that many American parents are settling for care that is just not good enough and fooling themselves into believing everything is O.K.

> One father found his family day-care provider's teenage son watching *Dawn of the Dead* on TV as toddlers ambled by the screen.

In her research, Dr. Miller focused on six day-care centers in California. She found programs that ranged from poor to mediocre; only one was rated "good." What is remarkable about Dr. Miller's study, however, is that the 241 parents she interviewed uniformly judged their programs as "excellent," despite Miller's much poorer ratings. Her findings exemplify the Day-Care Delusion.

In his book *Working and Caring* (Addison Wesley, 1985), Dr. Brazelton explains that a parent who shares a small child with another caregiver may grieve, feel guilty, inadequate, hopeless, helpless and even angry at having to give up the child. The parent pulls out emotionally—not because he or she doesn't care, but because it hurts so much to care. As a New Jersey mother of two laments, "Nothing is harder than leaving a baby. Even if you know you have to, and even if you know she's in good hands."

Day-care providers often report

that parents at all income levels rush out the door when they drop their kids off in the morning, and rush out again after picking them up in the afternoon. They ask few questions beyond "Did everything go O.K.?" They don't want to know any more, to be reminded that the child spent all day without them.

And in fact, not many parents will admit to having doubts about the place where they leave their child. One Brooklyn couple remembers leaving their 2-year-old daughter with a neighborhood woman who ran a family day-care home, despite having doubts from the beginning. "But we figured if other people like us liked her, she must be O.K.," the father remembers. Yet when he dropped his daughter off one morning and found the woman's teenage son watching the graphic horror movie *Dawn of the Dead* as the toddlers ambled past the TV screen, that was the end of the line. Other neighborhood parents, however, continued to rave about the woman.

Parents need to learn how to find all the child-care options available to them in their communities, and how to choose among them. This means knowing how to evaluate a child-care situation instead of relying on word-of-mouth references from other parents in the neighborhood, what questions to ask and what to look for, and their own rights and responsibilities. (*See "Day-Care Checklist."*)

One stumbling block for parents is that even in the worst situations, they find it hard to be critical of people to whom they have entrusted their children. Meryl Frank, who analyzed and spoke on child-care issues for five years while doing graduate work at Yale, came to know this dilemma well, but only after she had children of her own. "You rationalize," she says. "Parents are busy, harassed. They don't want to know what's wrong. It's a defense mechanism. You say, 'My children are not going to become mass murderers just because they go to this day-care center.'"

"The problem is that it's a provider's market," says Marilyn Ward, executive director of Everywoman's Resource Center, which handles child-care referrals in Topeka, Kansas. For many parents, the simple dearth of quality day care is the problem. "Parents have to work so hard to find something, they want to believe what they've found is a good program," Ward continues. "They don't want to start all over again."

Consider the situation faced last year by families on Orcas Island, a small community near Seattle, Washington, where instances of alleged sexual abuse of toddlers were reported at two local child-care facilities, one a day-care center and the other a family day-care home. When the day-care center in question was closed as a result, six parents wrote a letter to state officials asking that it be relicensed and reopened. Its closing left more than a dozen parents with nowhere to leave their children. They said the state had overreacted in shutting the center down.

In "Variations in Early Child Care: Do They Predict Subsequent Social, Emotional and Cognitive Differences?" Deborah Lowe Vandell of the University of Wisconsin and Mary Anne Corasaniti of the University of Texas at Dallas studied 236 Texas 8-year-olds, all white and mostly from middle-class families. The idea was to trace their early child-care histories and determine the effects of day care on them. The disturbing result was that children with more extensive day care were rated by teachers and parents as harder to discipline. They had poorer work habits, poorer peer relationships, and poorer emotional health than other children.

Vandell points to a similar study of 8-year-olds recently completed in Sweden, a study that came up with nearly opposite findings. In the Swedish study, children with extensive day-care histories were found to be less anxious, more independent and persistent; they also had better verbal skills than home-reared children.

Vandell suspects the difference in the two studies can be found in the quality of care. Sweden has some of the highest standards for child care in the world, with specialized training for caregivers and low child-to-adult ratios. Texas, on the other hand, has no educational requirements for family day-care providers and minimal requirements for caregivers at centers. In Texas, a single family day-care provider may be responsible for up to 12 children; in center-based care, one caregiver may have to watch as many as six infants, or up to 18 toddlers (4-year-olds).

Experts agree that the most important factor for all children is having a stable relationship with warm and skilled caregivers who have enough time to give them the attention they crave.

"If children don't have a relationship

## BY THE NUMBERS

More than 10 million children under the age of 6 have mothers in the work force, according to the U.S. Department of Labor. Latest figures from the Census Bureau show that 29.9 percent are cared for in their own homes by a relative or sitter; 35.6 percent are in family day care or are cared for in a relative's or sitter's home; 24.3 percent are in organized child-care programs.*

The Children's Defense Fund reports:
• *Of the more than 6 million children who spend part or all of their day in child care outside their own home, nearly half—2.6 million—are not protected by any state regulations at all.* For example, 22 states do not require even minimal standards in family day care if fewer than five children are involved. Fourteen states do not regulate, or only partially regulate, child-care centers run by religious institutions, even though one-third of all child-care centers are run by religious groups.
• *When child care is regulated by the state, the standards are often inadequate to insure the safety and health of small children.* Nineteen states, for example, allow child-care centers to have a ratio of five or more infants to one adult. In Idaho, it's legal to have one adult for every 12 infants. Louisiana does not regulate family day-care homes serving fewer than eight children. Amazingly, 22 states have no group size limits whatsoever. As for basic health requirements: 13 states do not even require children in licensed or registered family day-care homes to be immunized against such preventable diseases as measles, polio, rubella, or mumps.
• *Regardless of regulations a state may have on its books, many fail to enforce them or to monitor child-care facilities.* Licensing officials in 18 states admit they lack the enforcement staff to see that their laws are being followed. Thus, a license on the wall can give parents a false sense of security. Sometimes complaints are not acted upon. Eight states report that they are unable to respond to all complaints. Do you think you have the unqualified right to visit your child's family day-care facility unannounced? Better check. Parents in 29 states currently do not have that right spelled out in law; yet it is crucial to insuring a child's safety and well-being. (Experts agree that more states are now beginning to pay attention to this issue.)

*The remaining 10.2 percent of children are either in kindergarten or in other forms of child care.

FAMILY CIRCLE evaluated each state based on statistics from "Who Knows How Safe?"—a report by the Children's Defense Fund on state policies as of April 1990. The five categories reviewed were regulation and inspection standards, child-to-staff ratio, group size, parental access, and staff training requirements. We also spoke with Gina Adams of the Children's Defense Fund, Gwen Morgan of Work Family Directions and Barbara Reisman of the Child Care Action Campaign—all experts on the states' role in child care. Their comments plus the results of our evaluation indicate that most states mandate mediocre child care at best.

The following ratings tell which states are doing well and which should be doing better. It should be noted that our rating system is based on an evaluation of laws currently on the books; it does not take into consideration the degree to which they are enforced, the amount of money the states are putting toward child care, or how recent budget cutbacks may have affected states' ability to insure quality programs.

### GOOD
Calif., Colo., Conn., Del., Hawaii, Ill., Kan., Md., Mass., Maine, Minn., Mo., Utah, Vermont, Wash., Wis.

### FAIR
Ala., Ark., Alaska, Ariz., Wash. D.C., Ind., Iowa, Ky., Mich., Miss., Mont., Neb., Nev., N.H., N.J., N.M., N.D., N.Y., Ohio, Okla., Oreg., Pa., R.I., S.Dak., Tenn., Tex., Va., Wyo.

### POOR
Fla., Ga., Ind., La., N.C., S.C., W.Va.

Some states listed as fair or poor are doing well in other categories not addressed in these ratings.

### FOR MORE INFORMATION . . .
To help you in choosing the best day care for your child, send for: "How to Choose a Good Early Childhood Program" or "Finding the Best Care for Your Infant or Toddler"—two free booklets from the National Association for the Education of Young Children, 1834 Connecticut Ave. N.W., Dept. HC/FB, Washington, DC 20009 (include a self-addressed stamped envelope with your request). • The National Association of Child Care Resource and Referral Agencies will refer you to local resource and referral programs. Write: 2116 Campus Dr., S.E., Rochester, MN 55904; 507-287-2220.

[with a caregiver], they feel very insecure. They feel abandoned by their own parents," says Dr. Albert J. Solnit, Sterling Professor Emeritus in pediatrics and psychiatry at Yale and senior research scientist at the university's Child Study Center.

The number of children per caregiver is another important factor. The younger the children, the lower the ratio ought to be. (The National Association for the Education of Young Children recommends the following child-to-staff ratios: • From 0 to 24 months, 3 to 1; maximum group size, 6. • From 25 to 30 months, 4 to 1; maximum group size, 8. • From 31 to 35 months, 5 to 1; maximum group size, 10. • For 3-year-olds, 7 to 1; maximum group size, 14. • For 4-year-olds, 8 to 1; maximum group size, 16.) Also, the smaller the size of the group the better, since children tend to feel lost in groups that make them compete for attention.

The results of too-high ratios and too-large group sizes are predictable. The National Child Care Staffing Study, a major study published by the Child Care Employee Project in 1990, observed a typical day-care situation in Atlanta, Georgia, a state that allows very high ratios and group sizes. The researchers found that preschoolers spent close to one-fourth of their time in aimless wandering and were ignored by caregivers for more than three-quarters of the observation period. Less than one in 10 of the preschoolers observed could engage in the complex pretending games that children of that age should be able to play.

"It all fits together," Dr. Solnit says. "Good care produces something attractive. With poor care, the child functions as if everything is an effort—eating, relating to adults or to playmates. They are like little ghosts."

If child-care conditions are to improve, parents must realize that no government agency or state licensing inspector can be as vigilant as they themselves can be. Maryland's child-care regulations are better than many others. Yet despite the fact that Nannie Marie Pressley flouted state rules in caring for 52 children by herself in an unlicensed day-care home, her only punishment was a $175 fine. Her facility was closed, but no charges were filed against her.

Parents need to ask specific questions when checking out child care: How many children are cared for? What activities are provided? How much weight is given to parents' wishes and their requests for time to talk about how the child is doing? Is the caregiver genuinely interested in both child and parents, and forthcoming with information?

"Look for a place where the care provider wants to know more about you," says Dr. Brazelton, "and where you can stop in at unexpected times. Be sure the provider will sit down with you—at least once a week, but even every day—to talk about your child."

Dr. Edward Zigler believes he has a solution to the Day-Care Delusion, a plan to insure that parents no longer have to accept the unacceptable. He envisions what he calls the "School of the 21st Century," built around the local public school (programs are currently under way in Missouri, Colorado, Wyoming, Kansas and Connecticut; sites in the works include Kentucky, Arkansas, Iowa and Oklahoma). It includes all-day, year-round, on-site child care for all preschoolers from age 3 to prekindergarten, as well as before- and after-school and summer care for children from kindergarten through at least sixth grade. The school offers a network of family day-care providers, training and support, gives referrals to parents, and helps find substitutes when an individual caregiver is sick or on vacation. Dr. Zigler's program would benefit children of stay-at-home mothers too, because he calls for the Federal government to provide cash allowances for new parents so they can either stay home or use the money to pay for quality day care.

Right now, parents in many parts of the country can only dream about such a program. "Finding [any kind of] child care is a struggle," says a mother with two boys in day care since infancy. "You feel you have to reinvent the wheel." And so parents continue to grapple with real problems, hoping to be able to convince themselves that they're doing their best for their children. *(See preceding page for day-care statistics and for additional sources of information.)*

*Recommendations for Head Start
in the 1990s*

# Head Start:
## The Nation's Pride, A Nation's Challenge

**Joan Lombardi**

A Report on the Silver Ribbon Panel
sponsored by
The National Head Start Association

*Joan Lombardi, Ph.D., served as the Project Director of the Silver Ribbon Panel for the National Head Start Association. She is a member of NAEYC's Governing Board.*

Head Start celebrates its 25th anniversary with an impressive record of achievement and a new set of challenges. Over the years Head Start has proven to be a significant and sound investment in our nation's future. It has received widespread support from parents, policymakers, and the business community.

Since 1965 however, the world has changed dramatically. Over the past 25 years the percentage of children living in poverty has escalated at an alarming rate. Today, American children are much more likely to have families in which both parents are working away from home, or which are headed by single parents. Child care needs

and educational reform have resulted in an increased supply and demand for early childhood programs. At the same time, problems such as substance abuse and homelessness pose serious threats to child development and family life. These changes, coupled with the demands on limited funds, have created a new social context within which the Head Start of the 21st century will emerge.

To help meet these new challenges, as part of the 25th Anniversary the National Head Start Association (NHSA) convened a panel of experts to develop policy recommendations for the future of the program. This article, based on the Silver Ribbon Panel report released in May 1990, provides background on the panel, summarizes Head Start's successes and challenges, outlines the panel's recommendations, and discusses implications of the panel report.

## Background

NHSA is a membership organization that represents the parents, staff, directors and friends of Head Start programs across the country. In the Fall of 1989, NHSA convened a panel of distinguished advisors to examine what has made Head Start a success and how the program should be expanded and improved. The panel was composed of leaders with expertise in Head Start, other early childhood programs, health services, policy and business (see Members of the Silver Ribbon Panel).

The panel met to hear expert opinion and to review various task force reports and relevant policy documents. The panel process was based on the Head Start philosophy which values the opinions of those most directly affected by the program. Panel members therefore reached out and listened to the concerns expressed by the Head Start community.

More than 70 witnesses, including Head Start parents, staff and other early childhood experts, testified at three hearings held in Washington, D.C., Atlanta and Phoenix. More than 1,400 people (including 900 Head Start parents

From *Young Children*, Vol. 45, No. 6, September 1990, pp. 22-29. Copyright © 1990, NAEYC, National Association for the Education of Young Children, 1834 Connecticut Avenue, N.W., Washington, D.C. 20009.

and 500 staff) responded to an open-ended questionnaire soliciting their opinion on program success and future issues. Finally, a score of national organizations provided material and input to the panel's deliberations.

## Celebrating 25 years of success

Head Start enjoys a long list of accomplishments. Over the years Head Start has provided comprehensive services including health, education, and social services to more than 11 million children and extensive involvement opportunities for parents and families. It has provided a model of parent participation by including parents in key roles as decision makers and as staff. It has served as a national laboratory for early childhood innovation by launching such efforts as Parent and Child Centers, Child and Family Resource Programs, and the Child Development Associate Program. It has provided critical leadership in bilingual/multicultural programming, parent education, and the mainstreaming of children with special needs.

Research has provided abundant evidence that Head Start is an investment, not an expense. Organizations calling for the expansion of Head Start and other effective early childhood programs include the National Governors' Association, the National Conference of State Legislatures, and the Committee on Economic Development.

Data collected by the Silver Ribbon panel confirm Head Start's success. Testifying before the panel and responding to the panel survey, parents expressed overwhelming satisfaction with the program. In the survey, ninety percent of the parents spontaneously indicated a positive program effect on their children, and many spoke of improvements in the parent-child relationship. One parent put it this way:

Head Start has helped build my family's

### Members of the Silver Ribbon Panel

Eugenia Boggus, Silver Ribbon Panel Chair and President, National Head Start Association

Susan S. Aronson, M.D. F.A.A.P., American Academy of Pediatrics

Mattie Brown, Utica Head Start

Gail Christopher, Gail C. Christopher Enterprises

Raul Cruz, Head Start Parent

Marian Wright Edelman, Children's Defense Fund

Sandra Kessler Hamburg, Committee for Economic Development

Betty L. Hutchison, Chicago City-Wide College

Sharon Lynn Kagan, Bush Center in Child Development and Social Policy, Yale University

Sister Geraldine O'Brian, East Coast Migrant Head Start

Katie Ong, National Alliance of Business

Shelby Miller, Ford Foundation

Evelyn Moore, National Black Child Development Institute

Roszeta Norris, Total Community Action, Inc.

Mary Tom Riley, Texas Tech University

Winona Sample, Consultant Early Education and American Indian Programs

Tom Schultz, National Association of State Boards of Education

Jule Sugarman, Special Olympics International

self–esteem. It has given my children the opportunity and experience that I could never afford to give them. It has helped me learn better ways to use and acquire resources available in the community. After being a Head Start parent for 3 years, I have learned that I am just as good as anybody else; my opinion does matter, and if I apply myself and work toward a goal, I can make it.

In a world in which people are poor not only in material goods, but often lack critical social supports as well, Head Start helps establish important relationships. Head Start directors and staff

# "Head Start has helped build my family's self-esteem."

spoke about the many ways that the program helps to build the self–esteem of children, parents and staff. Testifying before the panel in Atlanta, Arvern Moore, a Head Start Director from Mississippi, expressed the sentiment of many when he said:

Once Head Start touches the lives of people, it makes you a new person and that impacts the family and community in which one lives.

Parents and staff attributed Head Start's success to the involvement of parents, parent–staff relations, the comprehensive nature of the services, and the commitment of the staff.

## Facing new challenges

Addressing the Head Start Conference in 1977, Dr. Edward F. Zigler said:

This basically positive view of Head Start does not mean that we should rest on our laurels. I prefer to think of Head Start not as a static program but as an evolving concept, an effort that must continue to grow and develop (1978, p. 6).

This statement is more timely today than ever before. Head Start's record of achievement and experience makes it an ideal program to address the challenges of rising poverty and the increasing changes in the family, provide critical comprehensive services to children and supports for families, and serve as a model for the entire early childhood field. However, in order to meet the challenges of a changing world, the panel identified three conditions that must be addressed: the need to protect quality, to expand enrollment and service delivery, and to encourage collaboration and research.

## Quality

To be effective in the future, Head Start must continue to provide good early childhood services. Yet the panel heard repeated concerns about Head Start's ability to provide quality services, due to inadequate funding, at a time when demands on program effectiveness are increasing. The National Head Start Association (1990) reports that even with moderate inflation rates, funding per child in constant dollars has declined during the 1980's.

Like most early childhood programs, Head Start faces increased difficulty attracting and retaining qualified staff due to inadequate salaries. According to a 1988 survey by the Administration for Children, Youth and Families (ACYF), 47% of Head Start teachers earn less than $10,000 per year (National Head Start Association, 1989). The overall average salary of a Head Start teacher was $12,074. Furthermore, salaries are low for staff working in all aspects of the program. Inadequate salaries often force Head Start staff (many of whom are former Head Start parents) to live in or near poverty, affecting overall program morale.

At the same time, Head Start must respond to increasing numbers of multiple-problem families. However, programs report that they lack sufficient numbers of qualified staff to provide family support. In addition, despite the demands for additional training to respond to new issues, Head Start training funds have not kept up with program expansion (NHSA, 1990).

Along with staffing needs, Head Start parents and directors talked about the need to improve facilities and transportation. Head Start programs reported that they have had to vacate space due to increased rents and the rising cost of renovations. Lack of adequate space often affects the program's ability to

expand services. Similarly, the rising costs of purchasing and maintaining vehicles has caused cutbacks in transportation services. Head Start parents mentioned lack of transportation as a disincentive to parent involvement and a barrier to obtaining both medical services and job training.

## Expansion

The panel heard stories of long waiting lists for Head Start programs, especially where no other services exist. They heard concerns about recent policies which

hours and days of operation. At a time of increasing employment among parents, Head Start has been moving away from directly using Head Start dollars to meet the extended-day needs of working families. Only 6% of Head Start programs use Head Start funds to provide full-day services that run nine hours or more (Congressional Research Service, 1990). Although many programs use other funds to supplement Head Start dollars and extend the day, the panel heard reports that outside funds are often inadequate to meet Head Start needs and directors often face conflicting regulations and fiscal requirements.

**Head Start has provided comprehensive services including health, education, and social services to more than 11 million children, and extensive involvement opportunities for parents and families.**

target four-year-olds and appear to limit multiple years of service. Parents and staff spoke of the critical need to serve children three years old and younger, particularly to provide continuity of services and to respond to family needs.

In addition to the need to expand Head Start to include programs for younger children, many Head Start staff and parents raised issues regarding the income guidelines for eligibility. Head Start eligibility guidelines are more stringent than many other federal programs. In fact, local costs of living and family circumstances put many families at risk who are above the federal poverty level.

Finally in the area of expansion, the panel heard a repeated need to expand service delivery, particularly to provide full-day services. Responding to the Silver Ribbon Panel questionnaire on improvement and expansion, parents most often listed the need for extended

### Collaboration and research

As the importance of early childhood programs has grown and the funding has become more diversified, there is a need for federal leadership to establish a more cohesive and effective early childhood system by promoting collaboration and new research. New programs such as those provided by recent state early childhood initiatives, the Education of the Handicapped Act and the Family Support Act, provide new challenges for coordination. The panel found that additional incentives are needed to promote collaboration between Head Start and other early childhood and human service programs, to ensure continuity with the public schools, and to provide linkages with new funding sources and with the business community. In addition, new research efforts are needed to influence practice and inform policy.

The panel survey and testimony

revealed that although many Head Start programs are making tremendous progress towards collaboration, they often lack incentives due to limited public awareness of Head Start, barriers to launching creative funding initiatives with other programs already serving low-income children, the need for more flexibility in programming and limited paid time for collaboration. When collaboration does not occur, programs may compete for children, space and staff (Goodman and Brady, 1988).

have been few systematic efforts to disseminate promising practices both within Head Start and to the larger early childhood and human service field.

## A renewed vision: Silver ribbon panel recommendations

The Silver Ribbon Panel provides a renewed vision of Head Start. Its recommendations are based on the founding principles that Head Start should be a model of compre-

to protect program quality in seven key areas.

*Staff compensation.* Immediate steps should be taken to provide equitable salaries to all staff and a responsive portion of all new funds should be earmarked for such increases. Furthermore, new initiatives should be explored to supply health benefit packages and retirement funds to all staff. In addition, working with the Head Start community and appropriate professional organizations, a career ladder should be developed and implemented.

---

# Head Start's record of achievement and experience makes it an ideal program to address the challenges of rising poverty and the increasing changes in the family, provide critical comprehensive services to children and supports for families, and serve as a model for the entire early childhood field.

---

There is also increasing concern that as Head Start children move on to pubic schools, their progress may be lost if there is not a continuation of comprehensive services for them and appropriate support for their families. The panel found that there is a need for better collaboration between Head Start and federal education programs serving low-income children such as Chapter I.

In the area of research, the panel found that the percentage of the Head Start budget devoted to research, demonstration and evaluation has decreased over the past 15 years (NHSA, 1990). Furthermore, new research is needed to explore the ingredients for delivering effective services for various types of children and families. Finally, the panel found that although Head Start has been a leader in launching local innovations, there

hensive services, should be flexible enough to meet emerging local needs and should provide leadership in serving low-income children and their families. To build on Head Start's success, the panel made three recommendations to federal policymakers.

## Investments should be made in the quality of Head Start to ensure that the program provides effective comprehensive services to children and families.

The panel recommended that the protection of quality be the top priority. They warned that program expansion should never occur at the expense of quality. They urged Congress to establish a quality set aside as an integral part of any new funds. Below are some of the strategies suggested by the panel

*Training and technical assistance.* Additional funds should be earmarked for training and technical assistance to adequately reflect program expansion. Further guidance should be provided to promote training which is long-term, competency-based, supervised and focused on staff/child and staff/parent interaction. College credit should be provided.

*Developmentally and culturally responsive practice.* A formal Education Coordinators Task Force should be convened to identify issues facing the education component and to develop recommendations for improvements. Efforts should be made to upgrade the Head Start Program Performance Standards to reflect new knowledge, younger children and new settings. In addition, new materials and training should be provided on multicultural/bilingual programming and on developmentally appropriate practice.

*Parent involvement.* New initiatives should be launched to provide more extensive training to parents, to establish clearer policies on parent involvement and to develop new approaches that reflect the current life circumstances of individual families. For example, further training should be provided to parents for their role as both volunteer and decisionmaker in the program and new innovations

# Funding per child in constant dollars declined during the 1980s . . . members of the early childhood community must join together to increase funding for Head Start and the other early childhood programs struggling with similar issues.

should focus on parent involvement for different types of families (teens, fathers, working parents, hard-to-reach families, etc).

*Family support and health services.* There should be an increase in the number of family support staff and new efforts to provide case management and service integration. Furthermore, a national symposium should be convened on new directions for family support and additional strategies should be developed to respond to children and families affected by substance abuse.

*Facilities and transportation.* New funding should include a targeted amount to improve facilities and transportation. In addition, the feasability of building permanent multi-use Head Start facilities should be explored.

*Program oversight.* Additional qualified staff, training and travel funds should be made available to the national and regional offices. New efforts should be made to improve the collection and reporting of Head Start program information.

## Funds should be increased so that all eligible children who need Head Start can participate and local programs can provide services that meet the needs of today's families.

The panel envisioned a Head Start expansion that allows much more flexibility for local programs to meet the specific needs of the children and families in a particular community. This view of expansion calls for increased enrollment and for allowing programs to decide the age and scope of services provided. Below are some of the strategies suggested by the panel in three key areas.

*Enrollment and program options.* The panel recommended two enrollment targets. By 1994, quality programs should be provided to all eligible three- to five-year-olds in need of Head Start services. By the year 2000, substantial progress should be made to build the capacity and serve children in need younger than age three. Expanded enrollment should be accompanied by the implementation of new program options such as Parent and Child Centers, Family Resource Centers, and Head Start Family Day Care.

*Full-day services.* Head Start programs should be encouraged to provide full-day services for those families in need. Clearer policies should be established for the use of Head Start funds for full-day services. While supporting the use of non–Head Start funds to supplement Head Start operations, the panel urged that such policies should be implemented in a way that provides continuous developmental services across a child's day rather than promoting a false distinction between care and education.

*Flexibility in income criteria.* While the panel strongly recom-

mended that Head Start give priority to families with greatest need, it suggested that a working group and demonstration effort be launched to explore issues related to flexibility of income guidelines.

## Leadership should be provided to build a more coordinated and effective system of services for children and families through collaboration and research.

The panel believes that the Head Start Bureau, ACYF, as the administrator of the largest early childhood system in the country, should reaffirm its leadership role, not only by ensuring that Head Start is a model of quality, but also by continuing to promote collaboration efforts and new research. Below are some of the strategies in each of these two areas.

*Collaboration.* The panel recommended that collaboration accomplish four goals: encouraging the continuation of quality comprehensive services to children as they move on to public schools, fostering linkages with other early childhood programs, encouraging the development and utilization of services for low-income children, and securing stronger commitments from the business community. The panel applauded recent efforts by ACYF to promote collaboration and suggested several new initiatives including, among others:

● materials and support to help establish state and local early childhood councils to foster continuity among programs and to serve as a coordinating and planning body;
● additional projects with Head Start feeder schools to continue comprehensive services;
● a high-level summit on the future relationship of Head Start and

state-funded early childhood programs;

• a new demonstration effort to promote linkages at the state level between the Head Start community and other state programs serving young children and families;

• a study to explore the feasibility of establishing State Resource Centers to network the Head Start and early childhood community and encourage collaborative training;

• new and ongoing initiatives to encourage the business community to invest in Head Start and other early childhood programs and to advocate for comprehensive services for young children.

*Research.* The panel commended ACYF for recent efforts to launch a new wave of research. They suggested that future research efforts explore such issues as the effects of quality variables, particularly those related to staffing; the impact of Head Start on the whole family; and the effects of more than one year of participation. They also suggested new demonstration and evaluation efforts to explore such areas as Head Start public school linkages, family day care, and economic integration of Head Start eligible and middle–class children. Finally they recommended new initiatives to disseminate information on local innovations.

## Implications and conclusions

The Silver Ribbon Panel Report was released in the midst of unprecedented attention and support of the program by both Congress and the Administration. In early 1990, President Bush demonstrated a strong commitment to Head Start by requesting a $500 million increase. Throughout the spring and summer of 1990, Congress moved forward on a Head Start reauthorization bill that called for more than seven billion dollars by 1994 to serve all eligible children

ages three to five (Human Services Reauthorization Act of 1990).

Along with the strong voice of the Head Start community and the many longstanding supporters in the early childhood field and in Congress, the Silver Ribbon Panel Report lent support to the movement to ensure that expansion will be accompanied by the protection of program quality. The new Head Start reauthorization bill provides that funds be set aside for salaries, training, facilities and transportation. It also includes some limited expansion to younger children and

exciting new initiatives for Head Start research and demonstration.

The implications of the Silver Ribbon Panel Report, however, go beyond any contribution to the current Head Start debate. Even after this reauthorization is passed, Congress and the Administration face important issues on how best to spend limited federal Head Start dollars and how Head Start relates to other programs. At the same time, state and local policymakers will continue to plan new early childhood initiatives that will often serve Head Start eligible children.

## Summary of Recommendations for Head Start in the 1990s

**I.** Investments should be made in the quality of Head Start to ensure the program provides effective comprehensive services to children and families. Specifically, investments should

• provide equitable salaries for all staff

• increase funds for training and technical assistance

• improve the education component to ensure that it is developmentally appropriate and culturally responsive

• enhance parent involvement

• increase family support

• improve facilities and transportation

• support program supervision

**II.** Funds should be increased so that all eligible children who need Head Start may participate, and local programs can provide services that meet the needs of today's families. Specifically, funds should

• provide, by 1994, programs for all eligible three- to five-year-olds in need, and provide programs for children younger than three years by the year 2000

• encourage full-day programs for those in need

• consider flexibility in income guidelines

**III.** Leadership should be provided to build a more coordinated and effective system of services for children and families through collaboration and research. Specifically, leadership should

• focus collaboration efforts to encourage continuation of comprehensive services in elementary grades, to foster linkages with other ECE programs, to encourage more services for young children and their families, and to secure commitments from the business community

• increase research, demonstration, evaluation, and dissemination efforts.

To influence decisionmaking, partnerships among the various segments of the early childhood community are becoming more important than ever. Below are some of the implications of the panel report for each of these groups.

## Congress

As the reauthorization process draws to a close, the critical issue facing Congress is the appropriation of sufficient funds to meet the goals for expansion and improvement. The Silver Ribbon Panel recommended that Head Start become a priority in the national budget and that expenditures be adequate enough to provide quality. Bipartisan program support must be translated into new dollars. Head Start must not become a victim of looming budget problems.

At the same time, Congress must show support for other federal programs so critical to children and families. The Silver Ribbon Panel endorsed the principle that Head Start expansion must be accompanied by the continuation, improvement and expansion of other early childhood and human services needed by low-income families. Head Start's comprehensive services cannot fill in the gaps for a system plagued by inadequate housing, health, and other family supports.

## The Administration

As the Head Start program expands, the importance of its role in the early childhood community increases. Head Start policies and practice should be carefully designed to reflect important changes in the field and within families. Decisions about policies should include input from the Head Start community and other early childhood experts. The Silver Ribbon Panel therefore recommended an ongoing Head Start Advisory Panel to review and develop future Head Start policies.

## State and local policymakers

Although the Silver Ribbon Panel report was directed at federal policymakers, its message has important implications for policy planners at the state and local level. As early childhood programs move forward in the states and municipalities, they should be planned to ensure quality comprehensive services, to provide linkages with Head Start and other existing programs, and to respond to the needs of the total family. Inadequate and unrealistic costs per child and reliance on half-day programs that target only one age, are not responsive to these needs.

## The early childhood community

The early childhood community faces new challenges as the supply and demand for our services grow. No one segment of this community can meet all the needs of today's families. In order to be effective advocates, we must join together to increase funding for Head Start and the other early childhood programs struggling with similar issues.

The many voices of the early childhood community are critical to the policy process. The stories collected by the panel make the statistics on Head Start come alive. In order to ensure that program expansion is broadly defined, that local programs have the flexibility to tailor services to their particular communities, that quality is protected, and that other critical human services are available to low-income families, advocates for Head Start and other early childhood programs must continue to share their wisdom with policymakers at all levels.

Head Start has made significant contributions to our country and our field. Upon releasing the Silver Ribbon Panel Report on May 18, 1990, the official day of the 25th anniversary, Eugenia Boggus, President of the National Head Start Association and Chair of the panel, called Head Start "an American success story for millions of children and their families." The panel report sets forth ways to sustain and extend this success in an increasingly challenging environment.

## References

Congressional Research Service. (1990). *Head Start program: Background information and issues.* Washington, DC: Author.

Goodman, I. & Brady, J. (1988). *The challenge of coordination.* Newton, MA: Education Development Center.

Human Services Reauthorization Act of 1990. (H.R. 4151). *Congressional Conference Report of the 101st Congress.* Committee on Education and Labor. Washington, DC: U. S. Government Printing Office.

National Head Start Association. (1990). Draft paper on the full cost of Head Start. Alexandria, VA: Author.

National Head Start Association. (1989). Highlights from Part I of the 1988 ACYF Head Start Salary Study. *NHSA Newsletter, 7*(4), 22.

Zigler, E. F. (1978). America's Head Start program: An agenda for its second decade. *Young Children, 33*(5), 4–11.

**Copies of *Head Start: The nation's pride, a nation's challenge, the final report of the silver ribbon panel* may be obtained from NHSA (1220 King Street, Alexandria, VA 22314) for $6 a copy, prepaid.**

# A Global Collage of Impressions: Preschools Abroad

### Leah D. Adams

"What do you think of European preschools?" "Do they have good schools in Yemen?" "What are Chinese child care centers like?" I am always taken aback when asked such questions. Of course, I'm always taken aback when someone asks what I think of kindergarten education in the United States; I never know how to answer that either. Does the question refer to kindergarten classes in the school near my home? Or kindergartens across the United States? Even if the inquirer expected an answer based on the schools which I visit regularly to supervise student teachers I would have to give a general statement, followed by some qualifying statements related to different teachers, different schools, and different school districts — all within *one* county! The old adage that "All generalizations are dangerous, including this one" always comes to mind.

It is also impossible to make simple comparisons between our schools and child care centers and those in other nations. People in every culture tend to think that their way of doing things is the best and the most natural. Many factors, such as cultural traditions, a country's needs and available resources, and the frequency with which children assume all or part of the responsibility as family wage-earners, must be taken into account when examining the educational system of any nation. We must steer clear of the temptation to look at other nations's efforts as good or bad, according to our own views of education and child rearing.

*Leah D. Adams is Professor of Early Childhood Education, Eastern Michigan University, Ypsilanti, MI.*

I have been fortunate to visit schools and child care centers and talk with educators in many parts of the world, and while keeping the above cautions in mind, there are some generalizations which I feel are reasonable: (1) The teacher is the most important ingredient in any classroom. Bertrand Russell said that teachers are, more than any other class, the guardians of civilization. This appears to be true, regardless of extent to which a system's goals and curriculum are standardized. There are outstanding teachers and poor teachers in every nation. (2) Good physical facilities are always preferred, but facilities alone do not determine program quality; mediocre programs can be found in excellent settings, and some good teaching goes on in woefully inadequate environments. (3) Throughout the world there is need for more child care and for better educational services; the wealthier nations could expand and improve services, and poorer nations need to offer more opportunity for education.

There are other well-founded generalizations which can be constructed, but individual experiences are more likely to offer small, limited insights. The impressions garnered are based on how the programs looked to me when I visited. These impressions are personal, not scientific nor penetrating. Each, however, has made an impact on my thinking. Travel with me through a collage of those experiences.

### North Yemen (Yemen Arab Republic)

We begin in Sana'a, the capital city

From *Day Care & Early Education*, Spring 1991, pp. 4-7. Published by Human Sciences Press, 72 Fifth Avenue, New York, NY 10011.

of the Muslim nation North Yemen, in the mountainous southwestern corner of the Arabian Peninsula. The UNESCO-funded program was housed in a single-story building, constructed of the sand-colored bricks used for most buildings there. The director, trained as a nurse, was dressed in white from head to toe, including a white veil across her face. I had talked earlier with the program's UNESCO consultant from Lebanon, who told me that she urges the staff to teach with their faces uncovered. That morning, because a male served as my interpreter, the veils remained in place.

The setting was clean and well furnished. Brightly colored murals decorated the walls, soft pillows were on the floor of the book corner, and blocks and manipulative toys were available. Fourteen four-year-old boys and girls sat at a rectangular table playing with wooden puzzles. They were given verbal encouragement and occasional help by the teachers wearing the traditional black sharshaf. The children, wearing blue and white checked smocks, appeared happy and relaxed, and the director showed us around with justifiable pride. This setting was far superior to the physical environment of a typical school in this poor nation, and staff had in-service training on how to run a developmentally appropriate program. The program seemed quite structured to my Western eyes, and the playground, in this desert setting, was nearly barren. The excitement which I felt during that visit was not because this was a program model which should be emulated elsewhere, but because it represented a beginning. At the end of the visit I left with the hope that the staff was becoming comfortable with this approach to education. It is not traditional in this part of the world for classrooms to have manipulative materials available. Nor is it traditional for children to work with their hands and create with clay and paint. It is giant step in a nation which has a long history of keeping females at home and a relatively short history of providing education much beyond the reading of the Koran. In Yemen, as in the rest of the world, more mothers have entered the work force, and more child care is needed. This program represented a positive step for a nation with many steps to take toward modernization.

For contrast, travel with me next to the capital of an Eastern European nation, Sofia, Bulgaria, to a program, called a kindergarten, which serves over two hundred children three to six years old.

## Bulgaria

The large building was built and designed as a child care center and included a spacious outdoor area, a teacher's lounge, a gymnasium and a swimming pool. The Bulgarian hosts explained that they had done research which showed that children who swam at least twice a week had less flu and fewer colds. Their goal was to have a swimming pool in every kindergarten in the city of Sofia. The children eat three meals a day at the center. All kindergartens in the city are under the same authority and serve the same food. The menus are planned not only for a balanced diet but also with an eye to the appropriate number of calories. I do not recall seeing an overweight child at that large center; they all looked rosy-cheeked and physically fit.

The visitors, a group of us attending a conference in Sofia which was sponsored by OMEP, the World Organization for Early Childhood Education, were entertained by five- and six-year-olds performing a series of traditional folk dances. The folk dances required a high degree of agility and coordination as well as considerable stamina. The children performed with grace and enthusiasm, displaying healthful vigor. A conference delegate from Switzerland remarked to the hosts: "Compared to yours, our children are elephants!" The physical fitness and coordination which the children displayed was concrete evidence of the program's concern for health, diet, and exercise. Ethnic identity and the preservation of cultural components such as folk dances are important parts of their curriculum.

The extensive use of the outdoor area was also impressive. It featured gross motor activity areas including a wheel-toy space for learning traffic rules and space for running and playing games. In addition, a wide variety of materials such as dramatic play props and art materials had been brought outside.

The classroom groups were large by our standards, with as many as thirty-five three-year-olds napping in one room under the supervision of two adults. The cots were placed too close together to pass fire inspection in many of our states, but the rooms were clean and attractive.

It was apparent that group participation and adherence to group rules receive more attention there than in our culture, where we put heavy emphasis on individuality. An accent on group behavior is often the most glaring difference we observe when visiting programs abroad. For example, in the People's Republic of China, I watched a class of twenty-five children play a circle game. The children patiently waited for their turns without being reminded by the teacher.

## England

There is a church-sponsored day care program in England which I have visited several times over a period of years. I get a good feeling every time I think about my recent visits there. The first time I visited, in 1977, I took a number of photographs. Those slides have served as good illustrations for graduate classes when I want to show how *not* to run a child care program but do not wish to show pictures of a center known to class members. The setting was bleak and underequipped, the staff appeared indifferent and poorly trained, and the children seemed bored and somewhat unruly. I went back nearly eight years later and found the center had undergone a complete restructuring, and I now have both "before" and "after" pictures. The difference could be attributed to the energetic, knowledgeable, and competent director/head teacher. The setting had been redecorated, and the huge room with its horrendously high ceiling no longer seemed dismal. The director had selected excellent staff and had purchased appropriate equipment. The circle time, in contrast to one which I had observed on the first visit, was interesting and fun and invited the children's involvement. It was a graphic example of the impact an administrator can have on a program. It also points out that we cannot make judgments about child care in any nation without a comprehensive analysis.

If I had rated the British center described above on a scale of 1 to 10 during my first visit in 1977, I would have awarded it a 3; but a different day care center which I visited that very same week, located only a few miles away in the same city, would have been given a 9½. While I have visited many wonderful child care centers in Scandinavia, one which would have drawn a rating of about 4 out of 10, at least on the day of my visit, sticks out in my mind. The numerous child care centers within a ten-mile radius of my home would also draw a wide range of scores on the same scale, and the ratings would fluctuate from year to year, possibly month to month, depending to a great extent on the quality of the staff and the volume of staff turnover.

While well-trained, long-term staff are more likely to be found in high-quality programs, volunteer efforts can also have a positive impact on children.

## Indonesia

One of my most memorable visits was to a preschool program in Jakarta, Indonesia, run by student volunteers. For this piece of our collage, imagine a small corrugated-steel building, half the size of our average classroom, crowded with preschoolers on long benches. The children sat still for long periods of time. During my visit, both the temperature and the humidity must have been hovering around 95, but as I stood there in that hot room, channels of perspiration running down

my back, I was thrilled by what I saw. That program was run by students from the Jakarta Campus of the Institute for Teacher Training and Education. The year before, some of the students had conducted a survey in some poor sections of the city to find out how many school-aged children were not enrolled in elementary school. The students were appalled by their findings and decided to take some action. They opened weekend preschool programs in several neighborhoods, volunteering their time and furnishing the materials for the activities. Their goals included helping the children prepare for school and taking steps to instill in the parents an appreciation of the value of education.

Parent cooperation was crucial to the endeavor. The benches had been built by the community members. The members of the community were pleased to show off their school to a visiting American, and many of them, and some of their chickens, came out to greet me as I walked down the dusty alley to the school that morning. I felt it was child advocacy at its finest.

## Ecuador

Non-industrialized nations have limited resources available for funding, equipping, and staffing educational systems. Ecuador is one of those nations. It is struggling to provide an adequate educational system for a diverse population of about ten million people.

I visited a preschool in Guayaquil which serves as a training center for the university there. The children, ages two to four, attend five mornings per week, and the university students serve as the classroom teachers. Two student teachers are assigned to each classroom, with twenty-five to thirty-five children, for a school year. A director handles all administrative functions, and university supervisors oversee the student teachers. Ecuador's mild climate enables the school to function very differently from schools in less tropical environments. There is no glass in the classroom windows facing the courtyard, and dramatic

play areas are out in the courtyard, protected by an overhang. The student teachers must furnish most of the teaching materials, including paper and crayons. This school shares a problem with schools I have visited in other developing nations: there is no on-site source of water. This contributes to the school's financial problems, as a large portion of the budget must be spent on the drums of water delivered each day.

Student teachers are required to keep extensive records on individual children and to do thorough planning for each day. The parent program is impressive also. I was shown some of the Christmas gifts, ranging from puzzles to beautifully made, fully clothed cloth dolls which parents had made during parent workshops at the center. The toys were age-appropriate, and it was obvious that much love and effort had gone into their construction.

## Australia

Australia's special programs for aborigine children are an example of the global efforts to meet the needs of minority populations. Every nation has diversity in its population, and care is needed to counteract biases and to balance the resources and opportunities available to all children. The Kindergarten Head Start program which I visited in Townsville, Queensland, offered a well-rounded, play-based curriculum to children from the aborigine community. The head teacher appeared to be very supportive of parents and their ethnicity and was creative in her ability to integrate community resources into the program. On the morning of my visit a group of adult male students from the local community college landscape architecture program was installing a new patio area, replacing the older paving blocks. The head teacher had arranged for the free labor to be carried out during the time the program was in session so the children could observe the men at work. She seized every opportunity for field trips and activities which would help the children to feel a part of the larger community, while at the same time instilling pride in their cultural heritage.

## Summary

The impressions in this collage are based on personal observations and, in many cases, a single day's visit. The programs described have probably changed. Some may no longer be in existence as this goes to print. Others may be dramatically different now.

The intent here is not to draw definitive conclusions or make stark comparisons. Instead, it is to reflect on how looking at other nations can aid us in better understanding ourselves. It helps to look in a mirror, to recognize the importance of meeting local needs and meshing programs with local values. What makes for good preschool or kindergarten program depends in part upon the culture in which the program is located. School classrooms and child care cen-

ters in other nations may look barren by our standards. In many nations there is little evidence of the consumable supplies, such as paint and paper, which we take so for granted, and teaching resources such as books and demonstration materials are sparse. The teaching methods are often more rigid than we are accustomed to or what our children would be able to adjust to, but the teachers may be enthusiastic and competent and the children may seem content and attentive.

There are aspects of some of the programs abroad which perhaps we should try harder to emulate: attention to physical fitness and nutrition, developing a sense of responsibility, and perpetuating cultural traditions and ethnic identities.

In our nation we want children to become independent, creative problem solvers. These qualities are not nurtured in programs with high emphasis on conformity. We should not

consider putting larger numbers of children together with few adults, even though that approach seems to "work" in other cultures. We know it is not best for children.

Whenever I visit other nations I am reminded that we do not have a monopoly on high-quality programs for children. When I visit schools in developing nations I come away with admiration of the resourcefulness and dedication of both teachers and students. They "make do" with very limited resources and with physical facilities which are far from satisfactory. Nonetheless, the teachers are trying to teach, and the students are trying to acquire an education. That is what is important.

All that we can ask of anyone, including those who run other nations' programs for young children, is that they do their best. We should ask no less of ourselves in our efforts for our own children.

# Excellent Early Education:

# A City In Italy Has It

## Rebecca New

*Rebecca New, Ed.D., is an Assistant Professor of Early Childhood Education at the University of New Hampshire. She has lived and worked in Italy, and has visited preschool and infant/toddler classrooms in Reggio Emilia on numerous occasions.*

Who knows what's best for children—their parents or their teachers? Can children's creative and intellectual potentials be maximized without sacrificing their need for play and exploration? How can we use available space to support our curriculum goals? For the past three decades, these questions have been part of discussions among parents, educators, and community members in Reggio Emilia, Italy—site of one of the most renowned examples of community-supported child care systems in Western Europe. This municipal preschool and infant/toddler day care program challenges notions of adverse effects of out-of-home care for young children and illuminates the potential of early childhood programs that are truly responsive to young children's interests and capabilities. To understand this unique and exciting program and its implications for early childhood education here in the United States, a brief description of the cultural setting is necessary.

The town of Reggio Emilia is in a wealthy region of northern Italy well known for its agricultural and industrial productivity as well as for its art and architecture. Child welfare is a major priority of Reggio Emilia's well-subsidized social services (Rankin, 1985), as evidenced by the community's response to child care needs of dual-earner families since the end of World War II. Well in advance of the 1968 national law that established funding of public preschools for *all* three- to six-year-old Italian children, the town council of Reggio Emilia established the first public preschools. Today, Reggio Emilia has 22 community preschools and 13 infant/toddler centers serving, respectively, 49% of all three- to six-year-old children and 37% of those under the age of three. (Virtually all preschool-aged children in Reggio Emilia attend *some* form of preschool; church-affiliated programs serve 33% of the population, private and state-run preschools the remaining 18%. Of the 42% of infants and toddlers in day care, 88% are in the municipal centers [Department of Education, 1989].)

This municipal early childhood program incorporates high-quality day care beginning in infancy with a preschool program built around a philosophy of education that has evolved over 25 years of intense collaboration, discussion, and work with young children. Classrooms are organized to support a problem-solving approach to learning, with extensive reliance on the arts as a natural form of expression and exploration; parents and teachers are mutually involved in observing and evaluating children's growth and development. Since 1979, the Reggio Emilia program has attracted thousands of visitors worldwide from countries as diverse as Sweden, West Germany, Argentina, Japan, and the United States. Two traveling exhibitions sponsored by the City Administration of the Municipality of Reggio Emilia—one for European, the other for English-speaking countries—were created to convey central themes and characteristics of the program. **The English version of *The Hundred Languages of Children* exhibit, on an extended tour of the United States, is scheduled for October 1 through December 1, 1990 at the Capital Children's Museum, Washington, D.C.**

Numerous aspects of the Reggio project are intriguing to American educators, including the level of community support for quality programs for children. (Twelve percent of the annual Town Council budget is allocated to the preschool and infant/toddler program. Program fees are assigned on a sliding scale, with a maximum fee for full-time infant care less than $150 per month U.S. equivalent.) While we continue to ponder the ways and means of reaching such a level of consensus *and* support in our own communities, other features may prove more immediately useful in our own efforts to provide high-quality early childhood

---

*Ongoing exchanges with Reggio Emilia personnel—including director Sergio Spaggiari, former director Loris Malaguzzi, and curriculum coordinators Tiziana Filippini and Carla Rinaldi—and with American early childhood educators Lella Gandini, Carolyn Pope Edwards, George Forman, and Baji Rankin—also serve as a basis for this discussion.*

# Virtually every three- to five-year-old attends some form of preschool. Outstanding programs in which parents are deeply involved make the "home is best" argument much less meaningful than in the United States.

programs. Three aspects are particularly relevant: the community of families and schools; the curriculum, based on projects and the arts; and the use of space to support curriculum goals.

## School is a community of exchange

The Reggio Emilia program reflects a long-standing commitment to cooperative and supportive home/school relationships, advocating a partnership among parents, teachers, and community members. A blending of beliefs about what is best for young children and their families facilitates this partnership in a number of ways. Contrary to prevalent perceptions in the United States, citizens of Reggio Emilia don't see day care as an issue of maternal substitution, even though a majority of children in the program are from dual-earner households with 75% of the mothers of the preschool children and 88% of the mothers of children in infant/toddler day care employed (Department of Education, 1988). From the outset, teachers acknowledge the critical role of both parents, emphasizing that the child is also capable, at a very young age, of developing other quality relationships. Because teachers and parents consider isolation from one another a hindrance to professional and child development, they have designed formal and informal strategies to establish a rich community of exchange.

## Groups are long-lasting, like families

Schools begin the process of collaboration by keeping the same group of children and teachers together for a three-year period, so that children who begin as infants remain together at the *asilo nido* ("nest" or day care) until the third birthday, at which time they move into preschool classrooms where they remain with a new preschool teacher for another three years. Each classroom of children, varying in number from 12 infants to 25 preschoolers, has two teachers, with occasional assistance from the school art teacher, the cook, and auxiliary staff. Besides creating a stable and secure environment for children, the three-year grouping provides a degree of continuity and familiarity that enables more effective relationships among parents and teachers, and results in a large community of adults around a group of children.

## Parents actively collaborate

Parents are initiated into the program as soon as a

child is enrolled. Teachers solicit information about each child's daily routines and sleeping and eating preferences, and urge parents to stay in the classroom for the first few weeks of school if their work schedules allow, until the child is comfortable without a family member. Albums are created for each child upon entry to a class, for family members and school personnel to fill with observations, photographs, and anecdotal records; by the time the child leaves for elementary school, there may be as many as three or four volumes. As one teacher notes, the notebooks (1) serve as a method of communication between parents and teachers, (2) document the child's progress relative to other children, and (3) provide evidence to the child of the importance attributed to this period of her life (Carlina Rinaldi, personal communication, June 13, 1989). Regular meetings with the cook to share favorite family and school recipes also foster a sense of shared responsibility.

These long-term home/school relationships have the flavor of the traditionally typical Italian extended family (New, 1988). Another advantage for parents is the opportunity to develop among themselves a stable network of families of young children. The strength of this

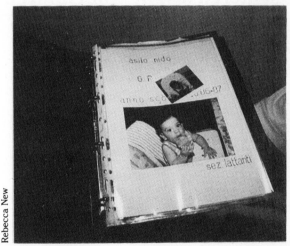

Notebook

network is apparent in the subsequent level of parent cooperation and participation in school projects. Field trips, for example, become major social events for the adults as well as the children. One preschool class of 25 children that was studying outer space took a field trip with 50 parents, two classroom teachers, an art teacher, the school custodian, and the cook to dinner at a local pizzeria followed by a late-night visit to the small observatory several miles outside town.

Parental involvement extends beyond individual classrooms to include decision making at the school and community levels. Each school has a Parent-Teacher Board made up of elected representatives of staff, parents, and citizens; parents consider this board important enough that 85% of eligible families participated in recent elections. To accommodate working parents, meetings are held in the evening, often beginning at 9:00 P.M. and running past midnight. The Board deals with problems specific to the school. It also elects one person for membership to *La Consulta,* a committee that includes representatives from the directorial staff, the town council, and the local Department of Education and asserts significant influence over local government policy.

This community of adults shares the understanding that no one has a monopoly on deciding what is best for the children. Reggio Emilia citizens acknowledge the difficulties of such a cooperative relationship; the process of maintaining a dialogue between parents and teachers has been described as one "which is and *should be* complicated" (Department of Education, 1989, p. 11).

Perhaps no topic has provoked more thought and discussion among these adults than what pedagogical approach to take in the Reggio Emilia classrooms. The resulting curriculum is a testimony to the virtues of ongoing staff development, parent involvement, and respect for children's interests and capabilities.

# Even a rain puddle is considered a "gift" for children.

## *Problems, projects, and the symbolic languages: A natural combination*

Reggio Emilia teachers believe that children's learning is facilitated by actively exploring problems that

Window drawing by four-year-old

children *and* teachers help determine. They also believe that art is inseparable from the rest of the curriculum, and in fact is central to the educational process as a form of both exploration and expression (Gandini & Edwards, 1988). Reflecting this centrality, children's efforts with various media are referred to as "symbolic representations" rather than "art."

Each school has an art teacher who is available to work with the children and their teachers throughout the day, and children are given many opportunities to discover the properties of artistic materials, in the belief that exploration is essential for emerging aesthetic awareness. More importantly, teachers believe in the need to nurture children's natural tendency to use the symbolic languages—including drawing, painting, constructing, and creative dramatics—as a way to make sense of their world.

Art

### Project-based teaching

**One strategy** that provides numerous reasons for symbolic representation and maximizes opportunities for shared problem solving is the use of short- and long-term projects. The "art" work that results from such projects astounds and delights most viewers, and conveys a broad interpretation of the typical preschool thematic approach, not to mention children's creative, communicative, and intellectual potentials.

Though some projects last only several days, others may continue for months, reflecting a belief in the need for long periods of time for both children and teachers to stay with an idea, to "enter inside a situation, to enjoy . . ., to discover . . ., and finally—to find one's own way out" (Filippini, 1989). Projects, which may involve the entire class or only a small group of children, are of three broadly defined types: those resulting from a child's natural encounter with the environment, those reflecting mutual interests on the part of the teacher and children, and those based on teacher concerns regarding specific cognitive and/or social concepts (Gandini & Edwards, 1988; Edwards, Forman, & Gandini, in preparation).

For example, a child's spontaneous play on a sunny day can turn into an extensive exploration of the properties and magic of *l'ombra,* or shadow. Observing such play, the teacher "captures" the event through a photograph, which leads to more elaborate attempts at variations in the forms shadows might take. As other children join in, they are encouraged to explain (by drawing) their understanding of shadows. Thus they must not only come to terms with their own beliefs about the event, but they must find a way to communicate those perceptions to others. Children and teachers then spend many more days, outside as well as inside the classroom, creating and observing shadows. As children begin to develop theories about the properties of light and the magical shadow, the teachers follow their lead by providing props and questions for additional experimentation. This sequence of events—playing, documenting, exploring, hypothesis building, and testing—characterizes most classroom projects.

**Another type of project** that involves more advance planning is based on the teachers' understanding of the keen interest young children display in themselves—their bodies, their feelings, their sense of being alive. Such a project also corresponds to a curriculum goal of helping children learn to appreciate themselves as unique individuals who are also contributing members of the class group. Children have repeated opportunities to contemplate the image they present to others, in mirrors and other reflective surfaces as well as in frequent photographs taken by the teacher. Children are encouraged to create images of themselves (through drawing, clay, wire sculptures). These activities and ensuing discussions are repeated throughout the time that children are in a particular class, providing multiple opportunities to increase observational and representational skills. Discussions of children's images often lead to other related problems, such as discovering how we communicate through body language, how our voices convey emotion, and exploring the variations in the human form associated with movement.

**The third type of project** is one that is initiated by the teacher(s) in response to an observed need on the part of some or all of the children. For example, teachers and parents were concerned about the major role that war toys, especially action figures based on popular television cartoons, were assuming in children's dramatic play. Rather than insisting that the action figures be left at home, parents and teachers decided to redirect the interest in war play, suggesting that the children create the space scene in which the typical battles took place. Children constructed several space vehicles out of cardboard boxes and recycled material, and previously uninvolved children were invited to assist in the creation of an "outer-space" atmosphere. Within a short time the action figures were put aside as new challenges and problems associated with the space project (including how to communicate with an alien being) took their place. Such an approach not only gave

**The curriculum is played out in projects that emerge from children's expressed interests, teachers' knowledge of what interests children, and teachers' observations of children's needs. Parents' concerns are also sources of curriculum.**

teachers the opportunity to gain a better understanding of children's fascination with war toys and war play in general, but also provided them with a more direct way to encourage prosocial values and foster critical thinking about such issues as conflict and negotiation (Edwards, 1986; Carlsson-Paige & Levin, 1990).

In these and other Reggio Emilia projects, children are given problems to solve, opportunities to explore and interact with each other, and materials and objects related to the quest. They are encouraged to reflect and reconsider their perceptions and understandings, and to share their ideas and experiences with parents and other children through one or more means of symbolic

Rebecca New

Outer space

representation. Throughout, teachers serve as the "memory" of the group, making photographs and tape recordings of children's activities and discussions. Other roles of the teacher include provoking theory building and engaging children in conversation of the sort that encourages "reflection, exchange and coordination of points of view" (Lay-Dopyera & Dopyera, 1989). Typically, such projects involve the use of "little money and a lot of fantasy."

# Children represent their understanding and learning in a great variety of ways—pictures, sculptures, constructions, collections, and creations fill the school.

## *The use of space supports the curriculum*

Visitors to Reggio Emilia are often astonished by the visual appeal of the preschool and infant/toddler classrooms. One Reggio Emilia parent, reflecting on her first impressions, remembers an ambience that was . . . *"molto luminoso, sereno e stimolante nello stresso tempo"* (luminous, serene, and stimulating at the same time) (Department of Education, 1986). While the furnishings are of good quality, what is compelling about the appearance of the schools and classrooms is the result *not* of a higher-than-average budget but of a creative, meticulous consideration of the potentials of the environment to meet program and curriculum goals.

## The environment informs and stimulates

What one sees upon entering any one of the community preschools includes the work of children (drawings, paintings, sculptures) and their teachers (photographs and displays of projects in process), often with the dramatic use of graphics. Such displays convey ongoing curriculum and research projects in a manner that keeps families informed about and interested in children's school activ-

ities and captures the interest of other children in the projects.

There is more to see, however, than evidence of children's thinking. Everywhere you turn, there is something else to ponder. Art supplies, including paints and clay as well as recycled or naturally found materials (leaves, bottle caps, fabric scraps) are pleasingly arranged, often by color, on shelves within children's reach. Groupings of found objects, including flower petals and plastic bags filled with "memories" from field trips, are carefully displayed so as to acknowledge the importance children attribute to the objects as well as the aesthetic qualities (shape, texture, color) of the objects themselves (Gandini, 1984). This attention to visual stimuli extends beyond the classroom walls. Doors, windows, and other translucent surfaces highlight children's image making. Lunchrooms are inviting and personal, and the daily menu is a vivid display of close-up color photos of the foods to be served that day, enticing children to comment on the shape of the pasta or the color of a vegetable.

Rebecca New

Lunchroom

## The environment fosters sustained working and a sense of community

When discussing the issue of space, teachers make reference to more than the physical plant, alluding to the social environment as well. Each classroom includes a large central area where all children and teachers can meet, in addition to smaller work spaces, and a *"mini atelier"* (small art room) where children can

# The environment and curriculum are inseparable. Rooms connect in ways that promote community, yet allow space for children's works-in-progress that require weeks of effort. Multiple mirrors and reflective surfaces constantly invite children to interact with themselves.

work on long-term projects. Schedules and supplies are flexibly arranged so that children hard at work on a project may continue in their efforts throughout the school day without the need to return things to their places before completing the activity. Each school also has a large central *atelier* (workroom) where the art teacher works with children as well as teachers.

Classrooms typically open to a large area that connects each individual classroom to the entire school. Kitchens, centrally located when possible, are often surrounded by glass windows so that the activities are always observable. Children are frequently invited to participate in the cooking process. Bathrooms, important centers of social exchange, are decorated with mobiles, paintings, and colorful arrangements of towels and toothbrushes. Mirrored-tile arrangements in the bathrooms and hallways encourage children to perform antics to the amusement of their peers, puzzle over the cognitive task presented by a missing piece, or simply contemplate their growing bodies. Gardens and courtyards also extend the classroom, and each school has rooms in which parents can meet and families can gather.

Such features are characteristic of renovated as well as modern facilities, each planned to support program goals, including facilitating social exchanges among and between adults and children and nurturing children's interests in problem solving and symbolic representation. This use of school space draws attention to unique aspects of the environment while making the everyday atmosphere more appealing.

### What are the implications of this Italian program for early childhood education in the United States?

While some features described certainly reflect Italian cultural values, and, as such, might not be applicable to American programs, there are many lessons to be learned from the teachers and children of Reggio Emilia. For example, given the strong Italian view that mothers should be the major influence with young children, perhaps the tight home-school relationship is natural. Yet even without this cultural view, there are ample theoretical grounds to support the development of cooperative home-school relations (Powell, 1989), particularly in the early years (Honig, 1979), despite the difficulties inherent in establishing such relations (Kontos & Wells, 1986). Teachers in Reggio Emilia emphasize the *value* of multiple points of view and reciprocal participation, as they purposely seek out diversity of opinion.

The significance of the environment as a source of opportunities for social exchanges among adults as well as children reflects a cultural appreciation of group *discussione* (Corsaro, 1988). Yet attention to a classroom's social climate is equally important in the United States if schools are to be places where children and adults can truly learn from and with each other (Bruner, 1985; Slavin, 1987).

Rebecca New

Bathroom

Rebecca New

Dramatic play space

The emphases on the arts and aesthetic sensibilities reflect an appreciation of detail and sensitivity to design consistent with the Italian cultural tradition of creative endeavors. Though Americans purportedly also value creativity and individual expression, we historically neglect the expressive arts in favor of competing demands within the curriculum. Yet the contribution of the arts, within a personally meaningful and intellectually stimulating environment, to developmentally appropriate early childhood curriculum is well acknowledged by American educators (Bredekamp, 1987; Hoffman & Lamme, 1989).

Katz and Chard (1989) have recently reminded us of the importance of providing for and enabling children's engagement in meaningful work. Extensions of children's experiences not only validate their interest in the world around them but afford children multiple opportunities to reflect on their understanding of the world—as we saw in their studies of shadows, self, conflict, and outer space. Yet American teachers too seldom provide children with the luxury of time to explore their ideas; our insistence on "clean-up time" even as a block structure begins to take shape routinely inhibits opportunities for growth within our classrooms.

### Our unrealized potential

Perhaps the greatest contribution the preschools of Reggio Emilia might make to American education is to reveal the potential for enhancing children's creative and intellectual development. The works produced by three-, four-, and five-year-old children in Reggio Emilia are the results of prolonged efforts on the part of children, fostered by a set of parent and teacher expectations about what children can do, which clearly exceeds the expectations of the average American parent and teacher. Such beliefs are based not only on cultural "folk wisdom" but also actual experiences with children (Edwards & Gandini, 1989). We have much to gain by providing ourselves and our children such opportunities for learning.

# References

Bredekamp, S. (Ed.). (1987). *Developmentally appropriate practice in early childhood programs serving children from birth through age 8.* Washington, DC: NAEYC.

Bruner, J. (1985). Vygotsky: A historical and conceptual perspective. In J. V. Wertsch (Ed.)., *Culture, communications, and cognition: Vygotskian perspectives,* (pp. 21-34). New York: Cambridge University Press.

Carlsson-Paige, N., & Levin, D. (1990). *Who's calling the shots? How to respond effectively to children's fascination with war play and war toys.* Santa Cruz, CA: New Society.

Corsaro, W. (1988). Routines in the peer culture of American and Italian nursery school children. *Sociology of Education, 61,* 1–14.

Department of Education. (1989). *A historical outline, data and information.* Reggio Emilia, Italy: Center for Educational Research.

Department of Education. (1988). *Scuole dell'infanzia e asili nido: Ieri e oggi.* Reggio Emilia, Italy: Center for Educational Research.

Department of Education. (1987). *I cento linguaggi dei bambini/The hundred languages of children.* Reggio Emilia, Italy: Center for Educational Research.

Department of Education. (1986). *Dieci anni di nido.* Reggio Emilia, Italy: Center for Educational Research.

Edwards, C. (1986). *Promoting social and moral development in young children: Creative approaches for the classroom.* New York: Teachers College Press, Columbia University.

Edwards, C., Forman, G., & Gandini, L. (Eds.). (in preparation). *Education for all the children: The multi-symbolic approach to early education in Reggio Emilia, Italy.*

Edwards, C. P., & Gandini, L. (1989). Teachers' expectations about the timing of developmental skills: A cross-cultural study. *Young Children, 44*(4), 15–19.

Filippini, Tiziana. (1989, June 12). Presentation to Syracuse University students, Reggio Emilia, Italy.

Gandini, L. (1984 Summer). Not just anywhere: Making child care centers into "particular" places. *Beginnings: The magazine for teachers of young children,* p. 17–20.

Gandini, L., & Edwards, C. P. (1988). Early childhood integration of the visual arts. *Gifted International, 5*(2), 14–18.

Hoffman, S., & Lamme, L. L. (1989). *Learning from the inside out: The expressive arts.* Wheaton, MD: Association for Childhood Education International.

Honig, A. (1979). *Parent involvement in early childhood education* (rev. ed.). Washington, DC: NAEYC.

Katz, L., & Chard, S. (1989). *Engaging children's minds: The project approach.* Norwood, NJ: Ablex.

Kontos, S., & Wells, W. (1986). Attitudes of caregivers and the day care experiences of families. *Early Childhood Research Quarterly, 1,* 46–67.

Lay-Dopyera, M., & Dopyera, J. (1989). The child-centered curriculum. In C. Seefeldt (Ed.), *Continuing issues in early childhood education* (pp. 207–222). Columbus, OH: Merrill.

New, R. (1988). Parental goals and Italian infant care. In R. A. LeVine, P. Miller, & M. West (eds.), Parental behavior in diverse societies (pp. 51–63). *New Directions for Child Development,* no. *40,* San Francisco, CA: Jossey-Bass.

Powell, D. R. (1989). *Families and early childhood programs.* Washington, DC: NAEYC.

Rankin, M. (1985). *An analysis of some aspects of schools and services for 0–6-year-olds in Italy with particular attention to Lombardy and Emilia-Romagna.* Unpublished master's thesis, Wheelock College, Boston.

Slavin, R. (1987). Developmental and motivational perspectives on cooperative learning. *Child Development, 58,* 1161–1167.

# A Glimpse of Kindergarten —Chinese Style

## Geraldine Beaty Shepherd

*Geraldine Beaty Shepherd is a member of the Broadoaks School Advisory Council, Whittier College. She has been very involved in community service, especially in the area of health.*

## About half of China's kindergartners attend boarding schools. This practice enables their parents to work full time.

Twenty screaming 5- and 6-year-olds may not be what most of us would choose to have on our hands, but here I was, in the center of a Beijing kindergarten classroom as these nearly hysterical Chinese boys and girls crowded around their "American friend." I knelt down among them. They pushed and elbowed each other to get close enough to touch me—my clothes, my hair, several times knocking me off balance, causing us all to laugh. They shouted and babbled at me and at each other. Their two teachers, visibly upset, stood off to one side with the school director. The director, however, smiled on and on. I could not read her chiseled features. Perhaps she was embarrassed, or perhaps she was just genuinely amused at the chaos I had caused. After all, it was her daughter, an interpreter and a teacher at Beijing University, who had brought me unannounced to the school.

I embraced the situation wholeheartedly. Beyond walking the Great Wall, my strongest desire while visiting China was to gain access to an ordinary kindergarten. This, I knew, was discouraged by the Chinese government. Visitors to China are taken to see only a select few of Beijing's primary schools. Or they are taken to the Children's Palace, a special school for unusually talented children. Children at these "model" schools are accustomed to foreign visitors and are groomed to behave accordingly. That my visit to China coincided with the Tiananmen Square student demonstrations was in my favor, for the mood in Beijing at this time was one of optimism and hope. Martial law had not yet been imposed. Had the atmosphere been different, I know my friend would not have risked taking me to the school.

In China one quickly learns that there are two sides to everything: the official and the unofficial. Officially I was not "registered" to visit the school. Because I was there unofficially, my host took certain precautions to prevent being reported for conduct against government policy. This included leaving the taxi and walking the last few blocks to the school and a rapid, conciliatory-sounding conversation between my host, the director's daughter, and the school's gatekeeper. The director personally greeted us at the gate and escorted us in. With a sweep of her arm she indicated we could go where we wished and discreetly disappeared. We did this two mornings in a row, spending a total of approximately six hours at the school. My mind hummed as I absorbed and contrasted my observations with my knowledge of our American kindergartens.

The facility I visited served children of workers from one of the government's large social ministries. The 1,000 children were housed at two separate facilities. Infants and toddlers were cared for in a large nursery in the basement of the ministry; this I did not visit. I attended the preschool, located about one mile away, which housed 300 4- to 6-year-olds. Both were boarding schools, as are approximately one-half of the 4,571 kindergartens in China. Most of the children lived there from Monday morning until Saturday afternoon when they joined their parents for the weekend. This system makes it possible for both men and women to fulfill their obligation of working for their country six days a week. The children eat breakfast, lunch, and dinner at their desks. They are cleaned, clothed, taught, and attended to by the teachers and caretakers. The staff of 80, which results in a ratio of approximately 12 adults to 1 child, includes teachers, aides, nurses, cooks, and maintenance people.

I imagine a Chinese teacher arriving at a typical American preschool would be overwhelmed with the wealth of color and material. I found myself struggling to suppress my reactions as I approached the school I was about to visit. It was obvious that what little resources there were did not go into furnishings, maintenance, paint for the brick and concrete block buildings, or grounds upkeep. The walled compound had various old, dirty, small, one-story brick buildings along one side of the perimeter, the administrative office, a kitchen and laundry building, and storage facility. As we entered the compound, we had to detour around the main walkway that skirts the back of the kitchen building because a huge pile of coal used for cooking and heating had been deposited adjacent to the kitchen door. The combination classrooms/sleeping rooms are contained in two long, one-story brick buildings parallel to each other and about thirty feet apart. It is in this area of sand and weeds that the children play.

Our first stop was at the one-room building that served as a classroom for 30 4-year-olds. This area was fenced separately from the rest of the compound with the building fronted by a play yard approximately 15′ x 30′. One jungle gym/slide, painted bright blue, constituted their playground equipment. Children's laundry hung from clotheslines on the playground and was also laid over the fence to dry.

As I approached the building, it was apparent that guests were expected, for I could hear the excited whispering of children as they quickly moved their chairs into a semicircle. Here were 29 preschoolers (19 boys and 10 girls, perhaps a validation of the importance the Chinese place on having male offspring when adhering to China's one-child policy) sitting quietly with hands folded in their laps. They greeted us in unison with "Hello American friend!" and, with some giggles and much staring, they sang several songs under the direction of their beaming teacher. The interpreter asked if they had any questions to ask me, but they responded with more giggles and stares. The atmosphere was polite and formal.

As they continued with their songs and dances, I had an opportunity to look around their classroom. There were no tables or desks for the children, perhaps because at this age they receive little formal instruction. Most of the day is spent playing outside. The wainscoting, doors, and window frames were painted pale green, whereas the remainder of the walls and the floor were unpainted plaster/concrete. An automatic washing machine occupied one corner of the room, whereas a wooden cabinet containing teaching materials was in the other. At the opposite end of the room was a wooden teacher's desk and chair with some shelves

Geraldine Beaty Shepherd

*I found myself struggling to suppress my reactions . . . it was obvious that what little resources there were did not go into furnishings, maintenance, or grounds upkeep. The rooms were almost colorless, but full of children's warmth and energy.*

for odds and ends. Children's aprons, one for each child, hung on a row of pegs along one wall above which was a wall heater connected to exposed pipes along the walls. Two large, colorful cardboard cutouts of Chinese children, one watering a sunflower garden and one dancing, constituted the room's decor. Some children's drawings were displayed, as in the other classrooms, depicting attempts to all make the same drawing.

This colorless room, in such contrast to our preschools filled with blocks and toys and children's art, vibrated with the warmth of the children. They exuded merriment, enthusiasm, and excitement. They were the focus, a point made all the clearer by the complete void of material wealth. We bowed and smiled our thanks and left amid squeals and giggles.

Next, I spent considerable time observing a kindergarten music lesson. Each classroom has its own adjoining sleeping room for the children. By entering this sleeping room, I was able to observe the 5-year-old children who sat in rows on benches behind small, rectangular tables. The children were learning a song about a cat's meow that they would perform for their parents at the upcoming June 1 spring festival. The teacher played the notes on an old, upright piano while the children sang in unison, over and over. For this 20-minute lesson the children sat quietly, hands in their laps or, as is more customary, behind their backs. A few squirmed, and occasionally the teacher gave a reprimand, but, according to my interpreter, most of the teacher's comments were praise and exhortations to do better and sing louder. One little boy could not behave. He would not sing a note, nor sit still, nor stop poking the children in front of him. As his behavior progressed from disinterest in the lesson to bothering the others, an aide moved to stand directly in back of him. When this did not bring compliance and he tried to get off his chair, the aide physically restrained him. When we left some 15 minutes later, the aide was still standing behind this child, her hands on his shoulders, encouraging him to stay seated.

I hoped he would learn his song, as he would be expected to learn a new song the next week and another new song each week of school. This, and the pianos I saw in each classroom, emphasized the importance the Chinese schools place on music as a vehicle of instruction. In this week's song, the cat was not only meowing but was teaching the children that it was not safe to be out alone at night. Although the subjects of other songs I heard varied, most of the themes centered around peer friendship and patriotism.

Communal living is another area that signaled to children the relative importance of their peer group. The sleeping room I was in contained 36 sturdy, wood-framed youth beds, with guard rails on both sides. Each had a thin mattress neatly covered by a clean sheet on which were printed Chinese abstractions of birds. At the head of each bed, in the same or-

*Thirty-six children slept together in this neat, bare room.*

Geraldine Beaty Shepherd

der, was a neatly folded pile containing a blanket (no pillow), a towel, and the child's clothes. I wondered where clothes were kept while the children slept. Except for a small cabinet and a wooden desk for the teacher, the room was empty. The room's only decor was two picture calendars above the desk, one in Chinese and one in English. The floors were bare concrete, as were the floors in all of the rooms I visited, including the director's office. How cold it must feel to the children tumbling out of bed on winter mornings!

As the director later described it, the children's regime is structured to group living throughout the day, beginning with their first morning activity. The children wake at 7:00 A.M., wash, dress with the help of "nurses" (usually high-school girls studying to become teachers), have a cup of hot chocolate (hot water and cocoa), and together take a half-hour walk outside the school compound. Upon their return, it is time for breakfast, which they eat at their desks in the classrooms. Next, they all visit the bathroom located at the back of the classroom—girls on one side of the room, boys on the other. I did not go inside the bathroom, but a glance showed an unpainted room with concrete floor, barren of any fixtures, partitions, or sinks. I understand that either the Chinese school bathrooms have a trough with running water or the children use individual chamber pots.

The school day begins at 9:00 A.M., with morning classes of math, language, music, and art, interspersed with recesses. Lunch is followed by naptime. Afternoons are unstructured. Children play outside until dinner or they may watch a video cartoon in the classroom, as they did on one of my visits. Bedtime is 7:00 P.M. I did not think to ask if an adult slept in proximity to the children, but I believe perhaps not. I saw no adult-size bed in the sleeping room nor anywhere else. An

## For most of the week, young children are living away from their families, in large groups. Still, they apparently thrive. Does this challenge our assumptions about what children require?

event relayed to me by the director, who lives with her husband in two rooms adjacent to her one-room office/conference room/teacher's lounge, validates this possibility. The week prior to my visit, two 5-year-old boys were discovered missing from their beds at 1:00 A.M. Searching the streets of Beijing, the director found one of the boys a few blocks from the school. The other child turned up several hours later at his parents' ministry, having walked the entire way. I understood the boys were not punished but were told they must never do such a thing again.

It is well known that China lags behind the industrialized nations. I saw much to substantiate this throughout my visit, including at the school. The television set, with its tiny curved green screen, reminded me of the 12-inch televisions we had in the early 1950s. The cartoon we watched had stilted animation that jerked from frame to frame. The hero was a Chinese version of Mickey Mouse, who was having to deal with a wolf lurking among the trees. The children, however, were enraptured and sat quietly, intently watching the video.

Observing the outdoor play area, I watched four boys using plastic badminton paddles to wield a small, partially deflated ball about the yard, each boy cooperating to keep the ball moving. Another boy, who had been playing alone with a ball, stood holding his ball and watching the children. Another boy tried to take the ball away, and a scuffle occurred, resulting in the child's losing his ball and crying. We were

not close enough to hear what the aide said when she tried to intervene and adjudicate, but through his tears we saw this boy yell at the aide and hit her with a full arm and fist swing. She turned and walked away without taking any action toward this child except to hold his arm mid-air for a moment when he tried to hit her again. Several girls comforted him. He joined a group of boys and was soon playing again.

There were few toys for outdoor use other than the jungle gym in the preschool section and a small, metal slide, painted bright blue. I saw one tricycle near the director's office, some distance from the play areas. A cardboard box held six or seven balls, all too deflated to bounce. I wondered if they were just old and had leaked or if they were kept deflated to limit play to tossing and rolling. Next to the box was a large metal washtub that held about 15 plastic paddles. A metal, tubular climbing apparatus shaped like a fish had been placed on the grounds near the kitchen's coal repository, some distance from the central play area. An adult-size wooden glider swing, also painted bright blue, was on the playground, but may have been broken because it was turned backwards and pushed up against a building so the children could not climb on it. There were long jump ropes, which the girls were using in groups. I did not see any boys playing with the ropes. Boys were playing roughhouse tag or ball games or were standing around. Except when the girls comforted the boy who cried, I saw no intermingling of boys and girls during the afternoon recess.

In another classroom, identical to the others except for some foil cutout garlands strung across the ceiling, the teacher conducted an English lesson. She would say a word—usually a noun—in Chinese, and the children would chorus an English word. They seemed proud of their vocabulary. I was told that the government chose English over Russian despite their closer economic ties to the Soviets, in recognition of the universality of the English language. As the teacher explained, the kindergartners were not expected to learn English phrases or sentences; they were merely introduced to English object words. At one recess the children had an English shouting match for my benefit. "Airport" seemed to be a favorite word. "American," "truck," "tree," "grass," "pants," "hand," and many others came pouring out as the children suddenly competed to impress me with their English.

Now it was my turn. We went into a classroom and I was seated on a chair facing the children at their tables. A quick count again indicated a predominance of boys—twice as many as girls. The interpreter stood ready. I wondered what they would ask, believing that at their age it would probably be referent to their own lives more than to their perception of me as a foreigner. The answer to the first question was listened to solemnly by all: "What did you eat for breakfast this morning?" There were a lot of "food" questions, but they also asked what work I did and where I lived. They had all heard of Disneyland. In fact, one of the boys was wearing a Mickey Mouse T-shirt. One child asked why I was visiting China. This was the only question that was not about my personal needs. After the first few questions, I found myself holding a questioner's hand or giving a hug

**Despite the lack of worldly goods, these children—well-fed and well-dressed, so open and full of enthusiasm, embracing life in an atmosphere so lacking in material things— promise a sturdy future for their country.**

as I answered the question. The children were very warm and seemed to like the physical contact. One little boy tried to sit in my lap but was gently chided by the interpreter when he asked his question. I sensed that he had said something wrong. She explained that he had asked an impolite question. I pressed for the question and we all laughed when I answered it: He wanted to know how old I was.

When it was my turn to ask questions, I learned that they liked playing the best and math the least. They liked to eat hot soup with vegetables (and indeed, these children, like the people I saw throughout Beijing, looked well-nourished). Being at school with their friends was the favorite activity of many of the children. Some said they wanted to be teachers, nurses, railroad men, taxi drivers (one of the higher paying jobs in China), and policemen. One beautiful, delicate little girl wanted to be a doctor like her father. The children answered questions readily, showing no self-consciousness nor any dependence on their teachers for approval of their answers. I thought, this conversation would have been similar in any country, in any language.

At times I was reminded of how old China's culture is, relative to ours. The children were going to dance for me. They were jumping up and down in their eagerness to be chosen to perform. While the teacher played the piano and the class sang, the selected children danced the routines with grace and

self-confidence. In one dance, four boys and four girls faced off and did an intricate minuet, never missing a beat. Four girls performed to a song about the importance of being kind to friends and helping others. To carry their "friends," they formed their arms into a cat's cradle chair, just as I had done as a child and had not seen done for forty years.

Everywhere I was reminded of the uneven qualities of this culture that the Chinese seem to handle with such aplomb: modern video machines hooked up to televisions designed 30 years ago; primitive sanitary conditions with immaculate sleeping rooms; coal and coal dust spilling freely onto the play area; a huge, open cauldron of enamel paint left in the corner of the playground, endangering the health of the children who figure so dearly in China's future; the teachers, who begin training in high school and continue for two years at the teachers college, earning one-third (100 Yuan, or approximately $30 per month) what a tour guide or a policeman earns.

I left the school feeling wonderfully uplifted. It seemed to me that, despite the lack of worldly goods, these children—well-fed and well-dressed, so open and full of enthusiasm, embracing life in an atmosphere so lacking in material things—promise a sturdy future for their country. The children of any culture, including our own, are its most precious resource.

# Child Development
# and Families

- Child Development (Articles 10–12)
- Family Life (Articles 13–17)

We cannot separate the child from his or her family or home environment, therefore, for professionals in early childhood education, much of what we do involves the child's family. We know families come in many different arrangements, and the more familiar we are with the people the child sees on a regular basis, the easier communication with those individuals will be.

Families and their child-rearing beliefs and strategies have changed in the last few decades, and so must parent education and the ways in which teachers communicate with families. More than one-half of all American children can be expected to spend part of their childhood in some type of nontraditional family. By the year 2000 it is estimated that 60 percent of children will spend some time before the age of eighteen in a single-parent family. These families need to be supported; moreover, they have special needs that require early childhood educators to be especially vigilant to potential complications and problems that may affect the children's learning processes.

This unit starts with a look at "First Year Milestones," and contains seven additional articles related to child development and family life. More and more research is being conducted that focuses on infants and toddlers. The capacity of infants to do and understand is far greater than was known even five years ago. This area of knowledge is quickly expanded as is the care of children under the age of three outside of the home.

The changes taking place in American families have been one of the reasons the field of early childhood education has grown so rapidly in the past decade. Along with more dual-income families and single-parent families in our communities comes the need for quality early childhood programs. Specially trained caregivers and teachers will enable the school setting to be a consistent force in the lives of young children and will provide them with a safe, exciting, and nurturing environment. The nuclear family can no longer depend on an extended family network to provide care, assistance, or daily support. Families frequently relocate and do not have direct access to family resources. Therefore, it is increasingly necessary for educators to assist children and their parents as they strive to work and learn together. Information we can pass on to parents, such as the reassuring, caring advice given by Dr. T. Berry Brazelton in "Easing Separation," can help parents and teachers solidify the team approach to education. Professionals who are aware of the enormously varied life circumstances children and parents experience today are mindful not to offer magic formulas, quick remedies, or simplistic suggestions to complicated, longstanding problems of living and growing together. What many parents do seem to appreciate is a sense that they are respected and given up-to-date objective information about their child. The problem educators face is that some families are neglecting their responsibility of assisting the schools in educating their children. Parents are not available to meet with school personnel, requests for materials from home are unanswered, and, most important, children are not coming to school prepared to learn. This lack of cooperation occurs at all socioeconomic levels.

The selection of "How Schools Perpetuate Illiteracy" by La Vergne Rosow was an instant decision. The suggestions for teachers are excellent and the message may encourage teachers to reevaluate the ways in which they share literature and reading with children and communicate with their families. Rosow and her mentor Steve Krashen send a powerful message with the statement, "Those who are rich in literacy fortify their children with good stories and beautiful books long before they enter school; the poor readers don't even understand that process and so perpetuate illiteracy from generation to generation . . . thus the poor get poorer" (Rosow, 1991).

Two articles in this unit address issues not traditionally found in education texts. The effects of birth order on social, academic, professional, and creative activities has captured the attention of scholars for over a century. Recognizing the unique personality differences in each child can assist parents in better relating to their children. The article "Guns and Dolls" also explores an issue often discussed by parents and teachers but always surrounded by controversy. The way teachers establish the environment and provide activities for students can affect the learning experiences of children. Much has been written concerning the ways in which teachers relate to girls and boys in the classroom, or the skills possessed by girls in math and science. Laura Shapiro's article reports on recent findings on gender research and assists parents and teachers in providing experiences for and communicating with girls and boys.

**Looking Ahead: Challenge Questions**

What are some normal developmental milestones for babies during their first year?

Do parents really treat girls and boys differently? What can parents do to ensure equal treatment for all their children?

Is being a firstborn in a family a burden many find hard to bear? Why is it important for teachers to be familiar with birth order characteristics?

What attitude changes have taken place among many parents in the past twenty years? How have these changes affected the ways in which parents and teachers relate?

What are the effects of divorce on children of different age levels? Why are boys especially vulnerable to divorce?

How is illiteracy perpetuated from generation to generation? What can teachers do to aid children and their families who live in print-poor homes?

What makes the separation process so difficult? Are there specific steps teachers can take to assist parents and children in this process? Give three examples.

# First Year Milestones

JENNY FRIEDMAN

*Jenny Friedman has a PhD in learning disabilities with a specialty in preschool language and cognitive development. She is the mother of two.*

## FIRST WEEK

- *Arm, leg, and hand movements controlled primarily by reflexes.*
- *Sleeps 70 to 80 percent of day, in about eight naps.*
- *Requires seven to eight feedings a day.*
- *Sensitive to location of sound.*
- *Focuses about eight inches away.*
- *Is individual in looks, feelings, activity level, and reaction to stimulation.*

Parenting books are meant to be encouraging, certainly to be helpful—but to cause despair? That's what one mother of a healthy eight-month-old girl recently felt after reading a popular book on child rearing. The author had written that by eight months most children were pulling up on furniture and crawling. Her child was doing neither. Although embarrassed to admit it, this mother worried that her daughter's development might be slow.

Babies don't come with instructions. So in the first one or two years of our baby's life, most of us are hungry for information. We want to know when and how to feed our child, how to get her to sleep, and how to comfort her when she cries. And we want to know that she's developing into a bright, happy child. To get some answers, parents turn to the many child-development books available. In them we may find a great deal of helpful information but encounter some pitfalls as well.

Many parenting books describe the stages of growth for the "average" baby and sometimes provide a chart, such as the one that accompanies this article, that lists when parents can expect developmental milestones, such as crawling, walking, and uttering a first word. But many times this information leads parents to believe that their child should conform to these norms.

Bob Brancale, director of the Minneapolis Early Childhood Family Education program, has heard such concerns many times. "Even though we believe development happens in a systematic fashion, it doesn't always happen when the book says it's going to," he says.

Most books caution parents about comparing their baby's development with the norms listed in the charts. For instance, Frank Caplan, in the popular book *The First Twelve Months of Life* (Bantam, 1984), writes, "Please do not regard this chart as a rigid timetable. Babies are unpredictable." In fact, the phrase "no two babies are alike" is common in these books, but it is human nature to want our offspring not only to meet developmental expectations but also to surpass them.

A deeper concern among some parents, however, is that their child's deviation from a norm may signal a real problem. Or—and this is something even the most self-assured parents experience—there is concern that if children are behind where the chart says they

## FIRST MONTH

- *Lifts head briefly*
- *Usually keeps hands fisted.*
- *Stares at faces and objects.*
- *Indicates response to human voice.*

- *Reflexes becoming more efficient.*
- *Daily patterns of sleeping, crying, and eating are very disorganized.*
- *Is alert about one out of every ten hours.*

should be, they will lag in that particular area their whole life.

A child who talks early is described by everyone as "very bright." The infant who's walking before her first birthday is dubbed "a track star." So when a child shows no interest in walking until well after her first birthday or says few words before her second birthday, what does that portend for her future? "At 13 months," one mother wrote to a popular

## SECOND MONTH

- *Reflex control begins to disappear as actions become voluntary.*
- *Can hold head at 45-degree angle for a few seconds.*
- *Coordinates senses: looks for sound; sucks at sight of bottle or breast.*

- *Studies own hand movements.*
- *Is able to express distress, excitement, or delight.*
- *Quiets in response to being held or to person's voice or face.*

newsletter for parents, "our first child said only three words. I was worried. Even if I subtracted one-and-a-half months for her prematurity, she was only 'average.' To me 'average' meant an IQ of 100—not likely to make it through college."

Is there a measure of truth in these predictions? Are the roots of intelligence apparent in the behavior of infants? Can a parent—or indeed a highly trained infant-behavior researcher with sophisticated tests

and measures—tell with any degree of certainty how bright a child will be or what talents she will possess as an adult by considering her rate of development in the early years?

## PREDICTING THEIR FUTURE

No, says Robert McCall, director of the University of Pittsburgh office of child development and author of *Infants* (Harvard University Press, 1979). He believes that the evidence indicates "unequivocally" that mental performance in the first 18 months does not predict later intelligence "to any practical extent." Furthermore, says McCall, "there is no evidence that a child who walks earlier runs faster at age eight."

Researchers measure "mental performance" in babies by administering infant-intelligence tests. These gauge many of the skills described in the familiar milestone charts—age of crawling, standing, walking, talking, build-

## THIRD MONTH

- *When on stomach, holds chest up and head erect for a few seconds.*
- *Begins to recognize and differentiate family members.*
- *Gurgles and coos.*

- *Visually follows a slowly moving object.*
- *Views fingers individually instead of in fisted position.*
- *Smiles easily and spontaneously.*

ing block towers, and so forth. What researchers have found is that infants who perform well at these tasks in their first two years are not necessarily those who do well on IQ tests as preschoolers or who do well in school in later years.

Also, development can be lopsided. The baby who toddles before a year is not necessarily the one who will be putting words together at 18 months. Furthermore, a child's "strengths" might shift. The child who talks late but walks early may be verbal and poorly coordinated by age three.

Although research continues, scientists have been unable to find a measurable behavior, manifested in the first two years, that accurately predicts how smart a child will be or what talents she will possess. No one is sure why intelligence, which tends to be fairly stable by the preschool years, predicts so little when measured in the first two years of life. Some think that infant-intelligence tests measure different behaviors (such as motor skills) than later tests do. Many believe, in fact, that the nature of infant intelligence is fundamentally different (i.e., sensorimotor) from childhood intelligence, which is symbolic in nature.

## KNOWLEDGE IS CRITICAL

The best way for parents to be reassured about their child is to gain a good understanding of the nature of development. "Parents who have little knowledge of child development are much more anxious about the rate [at which] their children develop skills," says Kate Horst, a Minneapolis parent educator and specialist in early-childhood development. "If their child isn't walking somewhat early, then they will really work hard to push

The first year of a child's life is full of exploration and a hunger for information. Developing the ability to walk is of enormous importance to the young child. (EPA Documerica)

### FOURTH MONTH

* When on stomach, rolls from side to side.
* Holds head steady and erect for a short time.
* Can now focus at different distances.

* Bats at objects.
* Follows source of sound.
* Laughs while socializing.
* Is interested in making new sounds and imitating others.

that child. They feel the child's rate of development is a reflection on them, and late walking means their child is not very smart." Parents with an understanding of development, she says, know children progress at different rates; these parents are not as likely to be concerned.

Ironically, reading those milestone charts can help. Although the rate of development has little predictive value in general, severe delays in skill development or unusual milestone patterns may indicate a problem. Parents who are aware of the general pattern of development are more likely to catch potential problems early. Although many such problems may not have a "cure," early detection may mean greater understanding—and less frustration—if and when the child encounters difficulties. "Once you know there are certain limitations," says McCall, "you can get about the business of coping by developing alternative strategies and not expecting as much."

Most experts agree that there is enormous variation in the age at which children acquire each stage of speech—babbling, using first words, and producing sentences. Even children in the same family may show remarkably different patterns of speech development. Jessica, now five years old, began talking before her first birthday and was putting

### FIFTH MONTH

* Rolls from back to stomach or vice versa.
* Reaches for objects with one or both hands.
* May transfer objects from hand to hand.
* Can squeal, grunt, blow "raspberries."

* Vocalizing takes on adult inflections and intonations.
* When seated or pulled to sit, head is balanced steadily and held erect.
* Smiles at faces and voices.

words together at 15 months. Her sister, Rachel, spoke few words until her second birthday. Yet by age three their verbal skills exhibited few differences. What researchers have discovered, however, is that a child's understanding of language is a more critical indicator of development than his expression of it.

### WARNING SIGNS

How can parents know at what point

### SIXTH MONTH

| | |
|---|---|
| • *Can roll from stomach to back.* | *thing he sees.* |
| • *Sits with support.* | • *Creeps, forward or backward, by propelling self with legs and steering with arms.* |
| • *Eyes now direct hands for reaching.* | |
| • *Reaches quickly and without jerkiness for any-* | • *May be disturbed by strangers.* |

developmental delays signal a serious problem that requires intervention? First, consider the warning signs described below. If you are still concerned, check with your pediatrician. He or she can refer your child to the appropriate specialist. In the end, trust your intuition. If it feels as though something might be wrong, have the child checked.

• Are your child's skills consistently delayed

### SEVENTH MONTH

| | |
|---|---|
| • *Sits alone steadily for several minutes or more.* | *lates, mouths, bangs objects.* |
| | • *Explores body with mouth and hands.* |
| • *Pushes up on hands and knees and rocks back and forth.* | • *Is more able to concentrate attention.* |
| • *Grasps, manipu-* | • *Understands first words.* |

in a *number* of areas—motor, language, and self-help?

• If your one-year-old has not started to *understand* some words, there may be a problem.

• Do you have any questions about your child's hearing? If so, act immediately. No

### EIGHTH MONTH

| | |
|---|---|
| • *Crawls, either forward or backward at first.* | • *Retains small series of immediate past events.* |
| • *Sits alone steadily for several minutes.* | • *Babbles with a variety of sounds.* |
| • *Is developing pincer grasp with thumb and forefinger.* | • *Enjoys games such as "peekaboo" and "so big."* |
| • *Claps and waves hands.* | |

child is too young for a hearing screening. Consider whether your child is awakened by loud noises, turns toward voices behind him, hears when you call from another room, and notices such things as the doorbell's ringing.

• Is your child's motor development significantly delayed in a *variety* of tasks, such as sitting, crawling, standing, and walking?

Knowledge of child development is important even for parents of children with no serious problems. A unique parent-education project in Missouri trained parents in the basics of child development. A subsequent evaluation found a strong correlation between a parent's knowledge of development and a child's achievement. "The more knowledgeable a parent was," researchers concluded, "the better the child performed on measures of intelligence, achievement, and language ability."

The awareness of what children are capable of at various ages allows parents to enhance

### NINTH MONTH

| | |
|---|---|
| • *May crawl up steps.* | *object with finger and thumb.* |
| • *May be able to stand, with or without support.* | • *Follows simple instructions.* |
| | • *Can keep a series of ideas in mind.* |
| • *Approaches small* | • *Initiates play.* |

their growth at each stage without rushing them into areas they are not ready for. Parents who know that children understand language long before they are able to speak are more likely to talk with their infant. Exposure to conversation will help the child develop expressive language skills.

At the same time, knowledge of child development assures parents that it is appropriate and healthy for a two-year-old to be more interested in playing with dolls, trucks, and blocks, for example, than reading flashcards. These parents can provide appropriate toys and make adjustments in the environ-

### TENTH MONTH

| | |
|---|---|
| • *Stands with little support.* | • *Is interested in fitting things together.* |
| • *Sidesteps along furniture (cruises).* | • *Searches for hidden object if she sees it hidden.* |
| • *Sits down from standing position.* | • *Understands and obeys some words and commands.* |
| • *Enjoys water play.* | |

## ELEVENTH MONTH

| | |
|---|---|
| • *Stands alone.* | *tions and some of* |
| • *Takes a step or two* | *their implications.* |
| *without holding on.* | • *Seeks approval* |
| • *Climbs up stairs.* | *and avoids* |
| • *Deliberately places* | *disapproval.* |
| *objects.* | • *Obeys commands;* |
| • *Aware of own ac-* | *understands "no."* |

ment as her skills develop. They realize that rushing a child into early academics not only is unproductive but often can be detrimental if it makes the child feel worth is based on performance.

### ENJOY, ENJOY

The most important reason for learning about development, says McCall, is that "it makes having children more fun." It is "more intellectually interesting and emotionally fulfilling," he says, when you understand the normal process of development. We live in a society in which parents are not content to let their children be merely average and certainly not to let them be below average. Thus children are often rushed into formal learning. Everything we know about development tells us that this is not appropriate. When parents understand the wonder and uniqueness of each child's development, they will relish each stage of childhood—whenever it occurs.

## TWELFTH MONTH

| | |
|---|---|
| • *Displays some combina-* | *together instead of just* |
| *tion of standing, walking,* | *taking them apart.* |
| *and cruising.* | • *Gives affection to hu-* |
| • *Can reach accurately* | *mans and favored ob-* |
| *for something as he looks* | *jects, such as toys.* |
| *away.* | • *Distinguishes self as* |
| • *Can put things back* | *separate from others.* |

PRE-K TODAY TALKS WITH

# T. BERRY BRAZELTON, M.D.

*T. Berry Brazelton is clinical professor emeritus of pediatrics at Harvard Medical School and founder of the Division of Child Development Unit at the Children's Hospital in Boston. Dr. Brazelton is the author of many books about childhood and parenting, a columnist for* The New York Times *and* Family Circle, *and an advocate for children.*

*This month, Pre-K Today's Dr. Adele M. Brodkin spoke with noted pediatrician and family advocate Dr. T. Berry Brazelton about his views and experiences in helping parents and children cope with separation.*

**Pre-K Today: Dr. Brazelton, for many years you have been helping children and their parents meet the challenges of growing up. You know an awful lot about their feelings. Is separation frequently difficult for parents as well as children?**

**Dr. Brazelton:** It's very difficult for parents, particularly in the earlier years. And, unfortunately, unless parents handle their side of it, any difficulties the child may have in separating are reinforced. You see, parents hate to give a baby up. The kind of love affair you get into with a baby is such an amazing surprise that I think it's almost frightening to share it with someone else.

**Are those feelings similar for parents of infants, toddlers, and preschoolers?**

They are different at each age, probably less each time. By toddlerhood you know that these children are going to benefit from peer interactions and learning about other people. And you know that, by preschool age, it's really time for children to have experiences with other kids.

**What sort of effect does separation have on the parent/child relationship?**

I think early separation causes a kind of grief reaction on the mother's part and probably, maybe to a lesser extent, the father's part. What I call grieving is a tendency to feel depressed, unhappy, a little bit helpless, and guilty. So you defend yourself in three ways: 1. *Denial*—this means denying that it matters. 2. *Projection*—Projecting on to the caregiver that his or her behavior and judgment are negative and the parent's are positive *or* vice versa. 3. *Detachment*—The parent detaching himself or herself, not because he doesn't care, but because it hurts. These defenses are unconscious but they are liable to exist when there are repeated separations, such as a working parent leaving a child at a center or school. We need to be ready for that with parents and help them.

**How can we do that?**

By helping parents understand that their feelings and reactions are normal and healthy; that this experience doesn't lead to real loss or permanent separation; and that the defenses that are surfacing are not necessarily mechanisms one needs to live with, because if they are aware of these defenses then they aren't at the mercy of them.

Some teachers and parents may feel competitive. If so, the person in charge at the center needs to take time to sit down with each and acknowledge that the feelings are normal and healthy.

**You have observed that teachers can feel resentful toward parents. How can we address that?**

I think many teachers feel mothers ought to be home with their kids and these feelings often reflect a deep-seated bias. But remember, a bias needs to be brought to light and talked about, so teachers can then say, "Hey, of course she has to go off to work. Thank goodness she's leaving that child with me — I can do a good job with her."

**Let's move up in the age scale a little bit to when children are toddlers or even preschoolers. What's your feeling about how separation should be handled. Should it be gradual?**

Yes, ideally. And it should be with people the children know and trust, particularly people who the parents know and trust, and who the child learns to know and trust—giving the child a chance to adjust at his or her own pace.

**Let's say that there's a program in which the parent is encouraged to stay for a period of time—days or weeks. When the time comes, how should the parent go about leaving?**

Saying goodbye means telling the child ahead of time about what is going to happen, preparing her at home, then saying, "I'm going and I'm staying away for ten minutes (or twenty minutes — a certain amount of time). Then I'll come right back."

The parent, then, comes back in just that amount of time, saying, "Remember, I said I'd be gone ten minutes and now here I am." Repeat this until a child is comfortable.

**Sometimes parents have let us know that when they are in an early childhood setting in those early days, they're not really sure what their roles should be. What can teachers do to help them?**

Give parents clues about what is acceptable and what isn't. Parents are there to help the child with separation, so whatever works best in that setting is the goal. Unless the program is a cooperative, and I think those are wonderful, I think the teacher should encourage what would help her manage the group.

**How else can a teacher, in the case of younger children, make it easier for the parents and the children during this time?**

By forming relationships. That's the first job of any center—seeing and forming relationships with the whole family, not just the child. NAEYC's philosophy about healthy early childhood development is really aimed at trying to focus on the family rather than just the child.

**Let's look at several common parent reactions to separating. How about the parent who leaves without saying goodbye?**

That's really deserting the child at a time when she needs the parent very much. The parent's inability to face his own grief may be influencing her actions.

**How can the teacher, then, avoid that situation?**

The teacher can say to the parent, "You don't need to leave without saying goodbye. It will be better for both of you to tell her you're leaving. Please come back."

**What about the parent who may drag out goodbyes?**

It's so hard for parents to make the separation. The teacher, at that point, could step aside with the parent and say, "One or two goodbyes is enough. More than that isn't fair to your child."

**Then there's the parent with the stiff-upper-lip approach who sees the quivering lip on the child and says, "You're fine. Mommy's got to go to work. This is your work." What can the teacher do in that case?**

The teacher can come over to the child and say reassuringly, "I'm going to be right here with you. I'll help you." We all need to remember that there's a lot to be learned, and a lot is learned from separation. Parents may need to be helped to see it this way. And kids, too, when they've made it for a short time. You can congratulate children and say, "Look what you did. You really did it."

The way a parent separates affects the way a child separates. When a parent is ambivalent, the child is bound to pick up on it, and play on it and get caught in a kind of morass of feeling sorry for herself, wondering if Mommy has put up a big enough fight, rather than turning to the coping systems that would help her get used to the new situation and learn that she can have fun with the other kids and caregivers. I think this is one reason that I would suggest that parents prepare their children at home so that when they get to the center, they can begin to look outward and see the things that would help them make it.

**And in preparing them at home, the parent would tell them all the wonderful things there are in school.**

A parent might say, "I'm going to miss you and you're going to miss me, but this is a pretty special time. You're going to have some kids to play with and a teacher who cares about you, and I'll come back to get you and you can tell me all about it when I do."

**I know that the infancy period is especially important to you. Do you want to say anything more about that time in a child's life?**

Yes. I think it's harder to separate in that period because you do feel the tendency and the need for that dependency much more acutely than you do when the child gets older and you know they have coping systems they can fall back on. In infancy, I don't think you ever quite think they do. In fact, you don't even want them to have them. Separating from an infant is very complex for both the parent and the child.

**What about that growing bond or relationship that they have? Is it impaired by this?**

It doesn't need to be. It can be enhanced by it. You learn to separate and learn how critical your relationship is, but also how strong it is. You can separate successfully and come back together, and the passion is still there, which is very reassuring.

**EDITOR'S NOTE:** *In 1989, T. Berry Brazelton and Bernice Weissbourd (founder of the Family Resource Coalition), helped to set up a national advocacy organization to represent the interests of parents and families. Officially titled Parent Action, the organization speaks out for parents "whenever Congress is considering action on tax policies, health care, child care, and employment regulations that affect America's families," and "links parents with other organizations and publications to build a network of support for those who have America's most important job: raising the next generations of American citizens." Find out more about this membership organization to share with the parents in your program by contacting Parent Action, P.O. Box 1719, Washington, DC 20013.*

# Guns and Dolls

Alas, our children don't exemplify equality any more than we did. Is biology to blame? Scientists say maybe—but parents can do better, too.

LAURA SHAPIRO

**M**eet Rebecca. She's 3 years old, and both her parents have full-time jobs. Every evening Rebecca's father makes dinner for the family—Rebecca's mother rarely cooks. But when it's dinner time in Rebecca's dollhouse, she invariably chooses the Mommy doll and puts her to work in the kitchen.

Now meet George. He's 4, and his parents are still loyal to the values of the '60s. He was never taught the word "gun," much less given a war toy of any sort. On his own, however, he picked up the word "shoot." Thereafter he would grab a stick from the park, brandish it about and call it his "shooter."

Are boys and girls *born* different? Does every infant really come into the world programmed for caretaking or war making? Or does culture get to work on our children earlier and more inexorably than even parents are aware? Today these questions have new urgency for a generation that once made sexual equality its cause and now finds itself shopping for Barbie

clothes and G.I. Joe paraphernalia. Parents may wonder if gender roles are immutable after all, give or take a Supreme Court justice. But burgeoning research indicates otherwise. No matter how stubborn the stereotype, individuals can challenge it; and they will if they're encouraged to try. Fathers and mothers should be relieved to hear that they do make a difference.

Biologists, psychologists, anthropologists and sociologists have been seeking the origin of gender differences for more than a century, debating the possibilities with increasing rancor ever since researchers were forced to question their favorite theory back in 1902. At that time many scientists believed that intelligence was a function of brain size and that males uniformly had larger brains than women—a fact that would nicely explain men's pre-eminence in art, science and letters. This treasured hypothesis began to disintegrate when a woman graduate student compared the cranial capacities of a group of male scientists with those of female college students; several women came out ahead of the men,

Girls' cribs have pink tags and boys' cribs have blue tags; mothers and . . .

## NEWBORNS

. . . fathers should be on the alert, for the gender-role juggernaut has begun

and one of the smallest skulls belonged to a famous male anthropologist.

Gender research has become a lot more sophisticated in the ensuing decades, and a lot more controversial. The touchiest question concerns sex hormones, especially testosterone, which circulates in both sexes but is more abundant in males and is a likely, though unproven, source of aggression. To postulate a biological determinant for behavior in an ostensibly egalitarian society like ours requires a thick skin. "For a while I didn't dare talk about hormones, because women would get up and leave the room," says Beatrice Whiting, professor emeritus of education and anthropology at Harvard. "Now they seem to have more self-confidence. But they're skeptical. The data's not in yet."

Some feminist social scientists are staying away from gender research entirely—"They're saying the results will be used against women," says Jean Berko Gleason, a professor of psychology at Boston University who works on gender differences in the acquisition of language. Others see no reason to shy away from the subject. "Let's say it were proven that there were biological foundations for the division of labor," says Cynthia Fuchs Epstein, professor of sociology at the City University of New York, who doesn't, in fact, believe in such a likelihood. "It doesn't mean we couldn't do anything about it. People can make from scientific findings whatever they want." But a glance at the way society treats those gender differences already on record is not very encouraging. Boys learn to read more slowly than girls, for instance, and suffer more reading disabilities such as dyslexia, while girls fall behind in math when they get to high school. "Society can amplify differences like these or cover them up," says Gleason. "We rush in reading teachers to do remedial reading, and their classes are almost all boys. We don't talk about it, we just scurry around getting them to catch up to the girls. But where are the remedial math teachers? Girls are *supposed* to be less good at math, so that difference is incorporated into the way we live."

No matter where they stand on the question of biology versus culture, social scientists agree that the sexes are much more alike than they are different, and that variations within each sex are far greater than variations between the sexes. Even differences long taken for granted have begun to disappear. Janet Shibley Hyde, a professor of psychology at the University of Wisconsin, analyzed hundreds of studies on verbal and math ability and found boys and girls alike in verbal ability. In math, boys have a moderate edge; but only among highly precocious math students is the disparity large. Most important, Hyde found that verbal and math studies dating from the '60s and '70s showed greater differences than more recent research. "Parents may be making more efforts to tone down the stereotypes," she says. There's also what academics call "the file-drawer effect." "If you do a study that shows no differences, you assume it won't be published," says Claire Etaugh, professor of psychology at Bradley University in Peoria, Ill. "And until recently, you'd be right. So you just file it away."

The most famous gender differences in academics show up in the annual SAT results,

which do continue to favor boys. Traditionally they have excelled on the math portion, and since 1972 they have slightly outperformed girls on the verbal side as well. Possible explanations range from bias to biology, but the socioeconomic profile of those taking the test may also play a role. "The SAT gets a lot of publicity every year, but nobody points out that there are more women taking it than men, and the women come from less advantaged backgrounds," says Hyde. "The men are a more highly selected sample: they're better off in terms of parental income, father's education and attendance at private school."

**Girls are encouraged to think about how their actions affect others . . .**

**2–3 YEARS**

**. . . boys often misbehave, get punished and then misbehave again**

Another longstanding assumption does hold true: boys tend to be somewhat more active, according to a recent study, and the difference may even start prenatally. But the most vivid distinctions between the sexes don't surface until well into the preschool years. "If I showed you a hundred kids aged 2, and you couldn't tell the sex by the haircuts, you couldn't tell if they were boys or girls," says Harvard professor of psychology Jerome Kagan. Staff members at the Children's Museum in Boston say that the boys and girls racing through the exhibits are similarly active, similarly rambunctious and similarly interested in model cars and model kitchens, until they reach first grade or so. And at New York's Bank Street preschool, most of the 3-year-olds clustered around the cooking table to make banana bread one recent morning were boys. (It was a girl who gathered up three briefcases from the costume box and announced, "Let's go to work.")

By the age of 4 or 5, however, children start to embrace gender stereotypes with a determination that makes liberal-minded parents groan in despair. No matter how careful they may have been to correct the disparities in "Pat the Bunny" ("Paul isn't the *only* one who can play peekaboo, *Judy* can play peekaboo"), their children will delight in the traditional male/female distinctions preserved everywhere else: on television, in books, at day care and preschool, in the park and with friends. "One of the

things that is very helpful to children is to learn what their identity is," says Kyle Pruett, a psychiatrist at the Yale Child Study Center. "There are rules about being feminine and there are rules about being masculine. You can argue until the cows come home about whether those are good or bad societal influences, but when you look at the children, they love to know the differences. It solidifies who they are."

**Water pistols:** So girls play dolls, boys play Ghostbusters. Girls take turns at hopscotch, boys compete at football. Girls help Mommy, boys aim their water pistols at guests and shout, "You're dead!" For boys, notes Pruett, guns are an inevitable part of this developmental process, at least in a television-driven culture like our own. "It can be a cardboard paper towelholder, it doesn't have to be a miniature Uzi, but it serves as the focus for fantasies about the way he is going to make himself powerful in the world," he says. "Little girls have their aggressive side, too, but by the time they're socialized it takes a different form. The kinds of things boys work out with guns, girls work out in terms of relationships—with put-downs and social cruelty." As if to underscore his point, a 4-year-old at a recent Manhattan party turned to her young hostess as a small stranger toddled up to them. "Tell her we don't want to play with her," she commanded. "Tell her we don't like her."

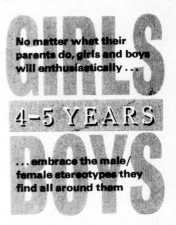

**No matter what their parents do, girls and boys will enthusiastically . . .**

**4–5 YEARS**

**. . . embrace the male/ female stereotypes they find all around them**

Once the girls know they're female and the boys know they're male, the powerful stereotypes that guided them don't just disappear. Whether they're bred into our chromosomes or ingested with our cornflakes, images of the aggressive male and the nurturant female are with us for the rest of our lives. "When we see a man with a child, we say, 'They're playing'," says Epstein. "We never say, 'He's nurturant'."

The case for biologically based gender differences is building up slowly, amid a great deal of academic dispute. The theory is that male and female brains, as well as bodies, develop differently according to the amount of testosterone circulating around the time of birth. Much of the evidence rests on animal studies showing, for instance, that brain cells from newborn mice change their shape when treated with testosterone. The male sex hormone may also account for the different reactions of male and female rhesus monkeys, raised in isolation, when an infant monkey is placed in the cage. The males are more likely to strike at the infant, the females to nurture it. Scientists disagree—vehemently—on whether animal behavior has human parallels. The most convincing human evidence comes from anthropology, where cross-cultural studies consistently find that while societies differ in their predilection toward violence, the males in any given society will act more aggressively than the females. "But it's very important to emphasize that by aggression we mean only physical violence," says Melvin Konner, a physician and anthropologist at Emory University in Atlanta. "With competitive, verbal or any other form of aggression, the evidence for gender differences doesn't hold." Empirical findings (i.e., look around you) indicate that women in positions of corporate, academic or political power can learn to wield it as aggressively as any man.

Apart from the fact that women everywhere give birth and care for children, there is surprisingly little evidence to support the notion that their biology makes women kinder, gentler people or even equips them specifically for motherhood. Philosophers—and mothers, too—have taken for granted the existence of a maternal "instinct" that research in female hormones has not conclusively proven. At most there may be a temporary hormonal response associated with childbirth that prompts females to nurture their young, but that doesn't explain women's near monopoly on changing diapers. Nor is it likely that a similar hormonal surge is responsible for women's tendency to organize the family's social life or take up the traditionally underpaid "helping" professions—nursing, teaching, social work.

Studies have shown that female newborns cry more readily than males in response to the cry of another infant, and that small girls try more often than boys to comfort or help their mothers when they appear distressed. But in general the results of most research into such traits as empathy and altruism do not consistently favor one sex or the other. There is one major exception: females of all ages seem better able to "read" people, to discern their emotions, without the help of verbal cues. (Typically researchers will display a picture of someone expressing a strong reaction and ask test-takers to identify the emotion.) Perhaps this skill—which in evolutionary terms would have helped females survive and protect their young—is

the sole biological foundation for our unshakable faith in female selflessness.

**Infant ties:** Those who explore the unconscious have had more success than other researchers in trying to account for male aggression and female nurturance, perhaps because their theories cannot be tested in a laboratory but are deemed "true" if they suit our intuitions. According to Nancy J. Chodorow, professor of sociology at Berkeley and the author of the influential book "The Reproduction of Mothering," the fact that both boys and girls are primarily raised by women has crucial effects on gender roles. Girls, who start out as infants identifying with their mothers and continue to do so, grow up defining themselves in relation to other people. Maintaining human connections remains vital to them. Boys eventually turn to their fathers for self-definition, but in order to do so must repress those powerful infant ties to mother and womanhood. Human connections thus become more problematic for them than for women. Chodorow's book, published in 1978, received national attention despite a dense, academic prose style; clearly, her perspective rang true to many.

Harvard's Kagan, who has been studying young children for 35 years, sees a different constellation of influences at work. He speculates that women's propensity for caretaking can be traced back to an early awareness of their role in nature. "Every girl knows, somewhere between the ages of 5 and 10, that she is different from boys and that she will have a child—something that everyone, including children, understands as quintessentially natural," he says. "If, in our society, nature stands for the giving of life, nurturance, help, affection, then the girl will conclude unconsciously that those are the qualities she should strive to attain. And the boy won't. And that's exactly what happens."

Kagan calls such gender differences "inevitable but not genetic," and he emphasizes—as does Chodorow—that they need have no implications for women's status, legally or occupationally. In the real world, of course, they have enormous implications. Even feminists who see gender differences as cultural artifacts agree that, if not inevitable, they're hard to shake. "The most emancipated families, who really feel they want to engage in gender-free behavior toward their kids, will still encourage boys to be boys and girls to be girls," says Epstein of CUNY. "Cultural constraints are acting on you all the time. If I go to buy a toy for a friend's little girl, I think to myself, why don't I buy her a truck? Well, I'm afraid the parents wouldn't like it. A makeup set would really go against my ideology, but maybe I'll buy some blocks. It's very hard. You have to be on the alert every second."

In fact, emancipated parents have to be on

All children have to deal with aggression; girls wield relationships as . . .

## 6-7 YEARS

. . . weapons, while boys prefer to brandish water pistols.

the alert from the moment their child is born. Beginning with the pink and blue name tags for newborns in the hospital nursery—I'M A GIRL/I'M A BOY—the gender-role juggernaut is overwhelming. Carol Z. Malatesta, associate professor of psychology at Long Island University in New York, notes that baby girls' eyebrows are higher above their eyes and that girls raise their eyebrows more than boys do, giving the girls "a more appealing, socially responsive look." Malatesta and her colleagues, who videotaped and coded the facial expressions on mothers and infants as they played, found that mothers displayed a wider range of emotional responses to girls than to boys. When the baby girls displayed anger, however, they met what seemed to be greater disapproval from their mothers than the boys did. These patterns, Malatesta suggests, may be among the reasons why baby girls grow up to smile more, to seem more sociable than males, and to possess the skill noted earlier in "reading" emotions.

The way parents discipline their toddlers also has an effect on social behavior later on. Judith G. Smetana, associate professor of education, psychology and pediatrics at the University of Rochester, found that mothers were more likely to deal differently with similar kinds of misbehavior depending on the sex of the child. If a little girl bit her friend and snatched a toy, for instance, the mother would explain why biting and snatching were unacceptable. If a boy did the same thing, his mother would be more likely to stop him, punish him and leave it at that. Misbehavior such as hitting in both sexes peaks around the age of 2; after that, little boys go on to misbehave more than girls.

Psychologists have known for years that boys are punished more than girls. Some have conjectured that boys simply drive their parents to distraction more quickly; but as Carolyn Zahn-Waxler, a psychologist at the National Institute of Mental Health, points out, the difference in parental treatment starts even before the difference in behavior shows up. "Girls receive very different messages than boys," she says. "Girls are encouraged to care about the problems of others, beginning very early. By elementary school, they're showing more caregiver behavior, and they have a wider social network."

Children also pick up gender cues in the process of learning to talk. "We compared fathers and mothers reading books to children," says Boston University's Gleason. "Both parents used more inner-state words, words about feelings and emotions, to girls than to boys. And by the age of 2, girls are using more emotion words than boys." According to Gleason, fathers tend to use more directives ("Bring that over here") and more threatening language with their sons than their daughters, while mothers' directives take more polite forms ("Could you bring that to me, please?"). The 4-year-old boys and girls in one study were duly imitating their fathers and mothers in that very conversational pattern. Studies of slightly older children found that boys talking among themselves use more threatening, commanding, dominating language than girls, while girls emphasize agreement and mutuality. Polite or not, however, girls get interrupted by their parents more often than boys, according to language studies—and women get interrupted more often than men.

Despite the ever-increasing complexity and detail of research on gender differences, the not-so-secret agenda governing the discussion hasn't changed in a century: how to understand women. Whether the question is brain size, activity levels or modes of punishing children, the traditional implication is that the standard of life is male, while the entity that needs explaining is female. (Or as an editor put it, suggesting possible titles for this article: "Why Girls Are Different.") Perhaps the time has finally come for a new agenda. Women, after all, are not a big problem. Our society does not suffer from burdensome amounts of empathy and altruism, or a plague of nurturance. The problem is men—or more accurately, maleness.

"There's one set of sex differences that's ineluctable, and that's the death statistics," says Gleason. "Men are killing themselves doing all the things that our society wants them to do. At every age they're dying in accidents, they're being

## GIRLS

When girls talk among themselves, they tend to emphasize mutuality . . .

## 9–10 YEARS

## BOYS

. . . and agreement, while boys often try to command and dominate

# Where Little Boys Can Play With Nail Polish

For 60 years, America's children have been raised on the handiwork of Fisher-Price, makers of the bright plastic cottages, school buses, stacking rings and little, smiley people that can be found scattered across the nation's living rooms. Children are a familiar sight at corporate headquarters in East Aurora, N.Y., where a nursery known as the Playlab is the company's on-site testing center. From a waiting list of 4,000, local children are invited to spend a few hours a week for six weeks at a time playing with new and prototype toys. Staff members watch from behind a one-way mirror, getting an education in sales potential and gender tastes.

According to Kathleen Alfano, manager of the Child Research Department at Fisher-Price, kids will play with everything from train sets to miniature vacuum cleaners until the age of 3 or 4; after that they go straight for the stereotypes. And the toy business meets them more than halfway. "You see it in stores," says Alfano. "Toys for children 5 and up will be in either the girls' aisles or the boys' aisles. For girls it's jewelry, glitter, dolls, and arts and crafts. For boys it's model kits, construction toys and action figures like G.I. Joe. Sports toys, like basketballs, will be near the boys' end."

The company's own recent venture into gender stereotypes has not been successful. Fisher-Price has long specialized in what Alfano calls "open gender" toys, aimed at boys and girls alike, ages 2 to 7. The colors are vivid and the themes are often from daily life: music, banking, a post office. But three years ago the company set out to increase profits by tackling a risky category known in the industry as "promotional" toys. Developed along strict sex-role lines and heavily promoted on children's television programs, these toys for ages 5 and up are meant to capture kids' fads and fashions as well as their preconceptions about masculinity and femininity. At Fisher-Price they included an elaborate Victorian dollhouse village in shades of rose and lavender, a line of beauty products including real makeup and nail polish, a set of battery-operated racing cars and a game table outfitted for pool, Ping-Pong and glide hockey. "The performance of these products has been very mixed," says Ellen Duggan, a spokesperson for Fisher-Price. "We're now refocusing on toys with the traditional Fisher-Price image." (The company is also independent for the first time in 21 years. Last month longtime owner Quaker Oats divested itself of Fisher-Price.)

Even where no stereotypes are intended, the company has found that some parents will conjure them up. At a recent session for 3-year-olds in the Playlab, the most sought-after toy of the morning was the fire pumper, a push toy that squirts real water. "It's for both boys and girls, but parents are buying it for boys," says Alfano. Similarly, "Fun with Food," a line of kitchen toys including child-size stove, sink, toaster oven and groceries, was a Playlab hit; boys lingered over the stove even longer than girls. "Mothers are buying it for their daughters," says Alfano.

Children tend to cross gender boundaries more freely at the Playlab than they do elsewhere, Alfano has noticed. "When 7-year-olds were testing the nail polish, we left it out after the girls were finished and the boys came and played with it," she says. "They spent the longest time painting their nails and drying them. This is a safe environment. It's not the same as the outside world."

LAURA SHAPIRO *in East Aurora*

shot, they drive cars badly, they ride the tops of elevators, they're two-fisted hard drinkers. And violence against women is incredibly pervasive. Maybe it's men's raging hormones, but I think it's because they're trying to be a *man*. If I were the mother of a boy, I would be very concerned about societal pressures that idolize behaviors like that."

Studies of other cultures show that male behavior, while characteristically aggressive, need not be characteristically deadly. Harvard's Whiting, who has been analyzing children cross-culturally for half a century, found that in societies where boys as well as girls take care of younger siblings, boys as well as girls show nurturant, sociable behavior. "I'm convinced that infants elicit positive behavior from people," says Whiting. "If you have to take care of somebody who can't talk, you have to learn empathy. Of course there can be all kinds of experiences that make you extinguish that eliciting power, so that you no longer respond positively. But on the basis of our data, boys make very good baby tenders."

In our own society, evidence is emerging that fathers who actively participate in raising their children will be steering both sons and daughters toward healthier gender roles. For the last eight years Yale's Pruett has been conducting a groundbreaking longitudinal study of 16 families, representing a range of socioeconomic circumstances, in which the fathers take primary responsibility for child care while the mothers work full time. The children are now between 8 and 10 years old, and Pruett has watched subtle but important differences develop between them and their peers. "It's not that they have conflicts about their gender identity—the boys

are masculine and the girls are feminine, they're all interested in the same things their friends are," he says. "But when they were 4 or 5, for instance, the stage at preschool when the boys leave the doll corner and the girls leave the block corner, these children didn't give up one or the other. The boys spent time playing with the girls in the doll corner, and the girls were building things with blocks, taking pride in their accomplishments."

**Little footballs:** Traditionally, Pruett notes, fathers have enforced sex stereotypes more strongly than mothers, engaging the boys in active play and complimenting the girls on their pretty dresses. "Not these fathers," says Pruett. "That went by the boards. They weren't interested in bringing home little footballs for their sons or little tutus for the girls. They dealt with the kids according to the individual. I even saw a couple of the mothers begin to take over those issues— one of them brought home a Dallas Cowboys sleeper for her 18-month-old. Her husband said, 'Honey, I thought we weren't going to do this, remember?' She said, 'Do what?' So that may be more a function of being in the second tier of parenting rather than the first."

As a result of this loosening up of stereotypes, the children are more relaxed about gender roles. "I saw the boys really enjoy their nurturing skills," says Pruett. "They knew what to do with a baby, they didn't see that as a girl's job, they saw it as a human job. I saw the girls have very active images of the outside world and what their mothers were doing in the workplace—things that become interesting to most girls when they're 8 or 10, but these girls were interested when they were 4 or 5."

Pruett doesn't argue that fathers are better at mothering than mothers, simply that two involved parents are better than "one and a lump." And it's hardly necessary for fathers to quit their jobs in order to become more involved. A 1965-66 study showed that working mothers spent 50 minutes a day engaged primarily with their children, while the fathers spent 12 minutes. Later studies have found fathers in two-career households spending only about a third as much time with their children as mothers. What's more, Pruett predicts that fathers would benefit as much as children from the increased responsibility. "The more involved father tends to feel differently about his own life," he says. "A lot of men, if they're on the fast track, know a lot about competitive relationships, but they don't know much about intimate relationships. Children are experts in intimacy. After a while the wives in my study would say, 'He's just a nicer guy'."

Pruett's study is too small in scope to support major claims for personality development; he emphasizes that his findings are chiefly theoretical until more research can be undertaken. But right now he's watching a motif that fascinates him. "Every single one of these kids is growing something," he says. "They don't just plant a watermelon seed and let it die. They're really propagating things, they're doing salad-bowl starts in the backyard, they're breeding guinea pigs. That says worlds about what they think matters. Generativity is valued a great deal, when both your mother and your father say it's OK." Scientists may never agree on what divides the sexes; but someday, perhaps, our children will learn to relish what unites them.

# What Birth Order Means

A child's place in the family can't explain
everything about him, but it
can yield important clues to his personality.

## Jean Marzollo

**Jean Marzollo** is the author of many books for children and adults, including *Your Maternity Leave: How to Leave Work, Have a Baby, and Go Back to Work Without Getting Lost, Trapped, or Sandbagged Along the Way* (Poseidon).

I have two teenage sons. My older son has many of the characteristics researchers attribute to firstborns. He is organized, is a serious list maker, and is driven in accomplishing the goals that he sets for himself. On the other hand, when it comes to his schoolwork, "driven" hardly describes him. He's one of the most laid-back people I know. And believe me, if he's supposed to be a perfectionist, you wouldn't know it by looking in his closet.

My second child, and last-born, is, typically, a real charmer. When it's said that the baby of the family tends to get away with murder, I can relate. My younger son can talk me out of punishments and into privileges much too easily. Yet like his older brother, he's driven to accomplishment. At one point in their lives, the older one was quiet and responsible, as a firstborn is wont to be, while the younger one was chatty and irre-

sponsible. But as my sons have grown older, these distinctions have blurred or largely disappeared. The older one talks more; the younger one is more responsible. In fact, although my sons have many of the characteristics attributed to first-born and second- or last-born children, it has become clearer that while their personalities are surely influenced by their position in the family, there's more to it than that.

### Where birth order fits in.

In 1923, the renowned psychiatrist Alfred Adler, M.D., wrote that a person's "position in the family leaves an indelible stamp" on his or her "style of life." Subsequent research has shown that although birth order does affect a child, it does not automatically shape personality. If it did, life would be much more predictable and a good deal less interesting. Along with other critical factors—including heredity, family size, the spacing and sex of siblings, education, and upbringing—birth order provides clues about our children that we can use to help them feel good about who they are. "The point is not to put people in boxes but to

add to our general understanding of them," says Kevin Leman, Ph.D., author of *Were You Born for Each Other?* (Delacorte) and *The Birth Order Book* (Dell).

The danger of putting too much stock in birth-order analysis is that we may stereotype our children solely on the basis of their position in the family. We expect our firstborn to be John Glenn and our baby to be Paul Newman. "Our negative expectations can turn out to be self-fulfilling prophecies," warns psychologist Linda Musun-Miller, Ph.D., associate professor of psychology at the University of Arkansas at Little Rock. If we expect our last-born to be manipulative, we may unconsciously encourage that trait. If we expect our middle child to be insecure, we may treat her as an insecure person regardless of her true nature. Also, depending on the size of the family and the spacing of siblings, birth-order descriptions may not really apply. For example, according to Leman, if there are more than five years between a child and his closest brother or sister, he may be more like an only child than like a sibling. And in very large families, everything changes.

## Your One and Only

"Only children may have high self-esteem and be more self-sufficient than all other children except those with one sibling," says Norval D. Glenn, Ph.D., professor of sociology at the University of Texas at Austin.

In many ways the only child is like the firstborn child. He benefits greatly from his parents' enthusiastic attention, as long as it isn't too critical and invasive. Because of their isolation, only children often develop agreeable ways of relating to adults—their parents and their parents' friends. They may also develop admirable skills for entertaining themselves when they are alone. "Because only children never have to compete with siblings for parental affection, they can develop a deep sense of security and self-worth," says Glenn.

On the downside, only children miss out on forming bonds and alliances with siblings. They may not have much opportunity at home to learn how to compete, negotiate, and compromise. As a result, they may have trouble sharing with other children and will have to wait until they're in school to learn to lead, cooperate, and follow.

Raising an only child is similar to bringing up a firstborn. In addition, though, it's important to make the most of your child's freedom to be himself by encouraging individual pursuits at home. Make sure you have art materials, books, records, tapes, and toys for him to explore. Take time to share in these activities with him.

Be patient if your child has problems making friends at school. Realize that your child is learning the people skills that children with siblings get a head start on at home. Help your child solve problems with friends just as you would help him learn any set of skills. —J.M.

"In families with four or more kids, there is a change in dynamics," explains Leman. "Large families tend to divide the children into two 'families'—the big ones and the little ones. And each of these 'families' will have its own firstborn, middle child, and baby."

We need to keep birth-order research in perspective. As Leman explains, each position in a family has its advantages and disadvantages, and knowing this gives parents some important guidance for maximizing their children's strengths and minimizing their problems.

### The first child: the achiever.

"Firstborn," says Leman, can be used to describe either the first child or the first male or female child. These kids are typically the ones "who [as adults] are driven toward success and stardom in their given fields." Many choose a demanding career in science, engineering, medicine, or law. Of the first 23 astronauts, 21 were firstborn or only children.

In general, firstborn children have higher IQs than younger siblings have—not because they're innately more intelligent but, say researchers, because of the amount of attention eager new parents pay to their first child. The firstborn's audience of parents and caregivers is enthusiastic, so she takes pride in her accomplishments and develops a deep sense of self-worth. Because the first child is taken seriously, she responds seriously—by making a responsible inner commitment to personal achievement and growth. Often a firstborn child is conscientious and well organized—a list maker. "These wonderful traits are the perks of being first," explains Norval D. Glenn, Ph.D., professor of sociology at the University of Texas at Austin. "But there are also problems with being first out of the cradle."

Firstborns often suffer from a type of pseudomaturity, explains Leman. "They may act grown-up throughout childhood, because their role models are grown-ups rather than older siblings, only to reject the role of leader in early adulthood." A firstborn is also not the most gracious receiver of criticism, and adults' constant critical comments of his performance may cause the child to become a worried perfectionist. He may fear making mistakes before eyes that he feels are constantly watching him and may grow to hate criticism because it emphasizes the faults that he's trying to overcome.

True to their reputation for excelling, firstborns will rise to the challenge of competition, especially within the family. The arrival of a sibling, for example, may lead a firstborn to wonder, Why is this little crying baby, who can't do anything, getting so much attention? And what happened to all the attention I used to get? Concluding that babyish behavior is the way to go, the youngster may try to reclaim center stage by imitating the baby.

If this doesn't work, she may shift tactics and try to imitate her parents by being helpful in caring for the baby. The child-as-parent role can be overdone, however. The firstborn needs, and deserves, her full share of childhood. Parents can reassure her that she is not being displaced and that she needs to be neither a baby nor a parent to continue to receive love; she can just be herself.

### Raising the first.

Encourage your child's development without demanding perfection. "In particular, the parent of the opposite sex of the firstborn [mother of son, father of daughter] should avoid excessive criticism," says Leman. "Children especially want to please opposite-sex parents. If they conclude that they can't, they may give up." In general, both parents should welcome a firstborn's willingness to achieve, and at the same time should convey the message not only that mistakes are permissible but that everyone makes them.

It's also important to help your child realize for himself that he doesn't have to do everything perfectly. "Teach him to take smaller bites of life and to work on saying no," advises Leman. "And please, encourage his sense of humor. Help him enjoy life."

### The middle child: the diplomat.

Middle children are "born too late to get the privileges and special treatment that firstborns seem to inherit by right," says Leman. And when another child arrives, middle children lose the bonanza that lastborns enjoy—the relaxing of the disciplinary reins, which is sometimes translated as "getting away with murder."

"It's important for all children to feel special in their parents' eyes and to have a quality they feel is valued in the family," explains Jeannie Kidwell, Ph.D., an adjunct professor of psychology at Florida State University and a family therapist in Tallahassee. "In the case of the middle child, it's especially hard to carve out that niche in the family." Neither the achiever nor the baby, the middle child may feel that he has no particular role in the family. Consequently, he may look outside the family to define himself.

"Friends become very important to children in the middle," says Leman. "In outside groups, they find it easier to carve their own identities. They develop friendship skills that firstborns may lack, and they learn to be good team players and club members."

Lacking the benefit of the exceptions parents make for their firstborns and their last-borns, middle children may learn to negotiate, to compromise, to give and take—valuable life skills that will help them succeed. They can become effective managers and leaders because they are good listeners and can cope with varying points of view. By necessity, "middle children get better training for real life than firstborns and babies," says Leman.

Researchers who study birth order say that the middle child is the hardest to describe because she is influenced by so many variables, especially the personalities of her older and younger siblings and the number of years between them. Kidwell finds that middle children suffer the lowest self-esteem if there is a two-year difference between them and their siblings, because they're competing with both the older and the younger child and, in their estimation, they don't measure up to either. If siblings are closer in age (say, a year apart)—and, therefore, more alike—or further apart (say, three years)—and, consequently, quite different—the middle child's self-esteem is stronger. She also finds that middle children have more self-confidence if their siblings are of the opposite sex, because there is less competition. These characteristics hold true throughout childhood, but they're especially noticeable in early childhood, when competition for their parents' attention and affection is at its peak, and in early adolescence, when teenagers are searching for themselves.

## How to raise kids in the middle.

Help your middle child develop self-esteem by recognizing her talents and individuality. You may be less of a cheerleader for your middle child without being aware of it. If your child is developing a competitive sense, help her channel this drive into age-appropriate sports and other competitive activities. If

she displays a talent for listening and mediating, show your appreciation of these skills and encourage your "peacemaker" to speak her mind, to bring her ideas to family discussions, and to share them with others. Make an effort to give your middle child a little extra attention so that she doesn't have to fight for it within the family. If your middle child is two years older and younger than her siblings, be especially sensitive to this child's need to establish her value in your eyes.

Because middle children often feel it necessary to establish themselves through friendships outside the family, help fulfill this need by supporting group activities.

As they try to decide what they want to be when they grow up, "middle children are most likely to become whatever their older siblings are not," says Kidwell. "They bounce off the kids directly above them, deliberately taking on traits and interests that will save them from having to compete with big brother or sister. This is particularly true with an older sibling of the same sex."

If the oldest boy is a good athlete, the second may try hard to get a good report card. As parents, we can understand this natural tendency of a child to go in the opposite direction of an older sibling as a way of carving out a personal identity. And while we support our children's efforts to be what they want to be, we also should refrain from typing them "the jock" and "the brain." Instead, we can let our children know that we think of each of them as a whole, lovable child whose many talents can develop over the years.

## The second-born child.

Because slightly more than one third of American families today have only two children, many parents find themselves thinking in terms of the firstborn and the second-born. The second-born child, however, does share some characteristics with the middle child. Like the middler, the second-born is likely to search for ways to be different from the firstborn child. If the firstborn is neat, the second-born may be messy. The second-born also shares characteristics with the last-born, the "baby."

"A lot depends on the family dynamics, particularly family spacing," says Kidwell. "Two children spaced two years apart may develop a par-

ticularly intense rivalry, feeling they can't play the same role in the family." When there are more years between the children, the second not only may look up to his big brother or sister but may fruitlessly spend a good portion of his childhood trying to catch up to the older sibling.

## How to raise a second child.

Let your second child choose his own role—whether it's the same as or different from that of the older sibling. Be flexible in your expectations of your kids and whatever roles they select. If one chooses to be involved in sports or drawing while the other spends every free moment in the school library, accept it, but also be aware of, and support, the activities they enjoy together (say, listening to music, having you read to them).

Make sure that each child gets one-on-one time with you. When you're with both children, find ways to treat them equally, yet as individuals, too.

## The last-born child: the baby.

The baby of the family is often given an extra dose of affection and attention, as well as a dispensation from rules. Seasoned parents know how fast childhood goes by, so they often justify their permissiveness by telling themselves, He's our last, so let's enjoy him as long as we can.

The positive consequences of this more permissive upbringing are that many last-borns are fun-loving, affectionate, and persuasive. They often grow up to become successful salespeople, counselors, and teachers.

On the negative side, the endless fawning over and praise of these youngsters—primarily because of their place in the family—may leave them feeling that their families do not take them seriously. "And," says Leman, "there's another difficult aspect to the charming last-born's life. She grows up being coddled one minute as a darling little baby, but the next minute she's compared unfavorably with an older sibling. She can't clear the table without spilling something. She can't clean up her room by herself. She can't walk as fast as everyone else through the amusement park. As a result of such conflicting experiences, last-borns can be extremely self-confident in some ways and insecure in others."

Having learned that, as the baby of the family, they cannot *insist* on anything, some last-borns have learned to beg and cajole very effectively—sometimes through smiles, sometimes through tears. The effect is the same: They get their way.

## Bringing up baby.

Since he is the youngest, the last-born may be introduced by his parents as "our baby" even when he is an adult. Let your child grow up when it's time to grow up. Teach him to accept age-appropriate responsibilities. Praise him for carrying out reasonable chores. Avoid doing his chores yourself simply because it's easier on you. Don't let him get away with murder.

Though your baby is adorable, beware of setting him up to perform whenever anyone visits. Display your love for him at times when he is not being adorable, when he's not the center of attention. If you worry that you don't pay enough attention to your child or that it fluctuates, make an effort to give attention to your last-born consistently. This way your baby will learn that he doesn't have to be charming or a cutup to catch your eye, that he can count on it "for free."

## Appreciating kids for themselves.

Birth order—along with gender, the child's temperament, and parental influence—is certainly a contributing factor in a youngster's personality, but it's important to focus on your child as a unique individual. By making judgments primarily on the basis of "where the chips fall," parents may lose the opportunity to appreciate their children for who they really are and what each child has to offer. Regardless of whether they were born first, last, or somewhere in between, they're special.

# How Schools Perpetuate Illiteracy

*To break the cycle of illiteracy—how "the poor get poorer"—schools must help parents understand how to help their children at home.*

La Vergne Rosow

**La Vergne Rosow** is a literacy volunteer, a community college literacy and ESL instructor, and a literacy consultant. Her address is P.O. Box 85, Huntington Beach, CA 92648.

"What's this word?" 9-year-old Mitzi asked her mother.

"What word?"

"This one," she said as she crashed her finger down on the first of 10 words she had to do for homework.

"Uh, well, you know you're supposed to sound it out. Now sound it out."

"I did! *Do or. Do or. Do or!*" She'd learned her lessons well. "D-o" spells *do* and "o-r" spells *or*. Both child and mother knew how to sound out a word they couldn't read, and Mitzi was skillful at finding the little words in the big words, too. "How do I make a sentence with 'do or'?" she asked as she turned over the packet of papers.

"Um, well, I can think of it, but when I try to tell you it, it don't come out right. Just do the best you can. I'm not supposed to tell you *everything*," the young mother said, trying to maintain some semblance of dignity before her child.[1]

The little girl turned the packet over again to try the next word. She was supposed to write a sentence with each of the 10 words on the mimeographed list. By Friday, having done each of 4 activities with the words, she was expected to be able to spell all 10 words on a test. This was only day 2 of a 4-day homework assignment. (Later Mitzi's mom explained that just figuring out what the words on the list were was only part of the problem. Then they had to construct sentences that had only words they could already spell. The proposed sentences always grew shorter and shorter as the struggle progressed.) Ten minutes had passed, and Mitzi still hadn't written the first sentence.

Suddenly she said, "Is it *door?*" and then turned the packet over to start writing.

"Um, no, I don't think so. I think that's spelled another way," her mother answered thoughtfully.

"Well, then, how do you spell *door?*"

"I think it's dore, you know, *dore.*"

## A True Life Drama

The little girl seemed to be trying to take in the logic of her mother's phonetic performance. I leaned forward, hoping to be invited into the dialogue, but heard instead the echo of a literacy and language lecture by Steve Krashen on how the rich get richer. Those who are rich in literacy fortify their children with good stories and beautiful books long before they enter school; the poor readers don't even understand that process and so perpetuate illiteracy from generation to generation.[2] Now, having no invitation to intervene, I was forced to witness this true life drama of what Krashen calls how "the poor get poorer."

Having already repeated the 1st grade, Mitzi was facing the dreaded prospect of failing the 2nd, due to poor performance in language arts. Her mother was an adult nonreader. "I can read the words," she had explained, "but when it comes to explaining it, it's just like a wall goes up, and I can't say what I mean." By a wall going up, I'd immediately figured she was talking about stress, the *Affective Filter*[3] that stops learning and performance. But Mitzi's mom meant instead that she couldn't comprehend text. I was there to help her learn to read when Mitzi had come home from school. Not knowing whether the child knew why I was visiting her mom, and having gotten no introduction, I was not free to move in on the mother/daughter ritual that served only to teach Mitzi that schoolwork is tough and she is never able to do it well.

Krashen had lectured about the ease with which students accustomed to print-rich environments breeze through schoolwork on words they had already learned through pleasure reading. "Those who are readers typically know what most of the words mean already. They have seen them before, in Judy Blume's novels or in Dungeons and

# When children of the literate elite need help, their parents can fill in the blanks the school has missed. When children of the print poor need help, they have nowhere to turn.

Dragons. . . .''[4] Meanwhile, children from nonprint homes and classrooms are left to flesh out the loser's end of the bell-shaped curve. When children of the literate elite need help, their parents can fill in the blanks the school has missed. When children of the print poor need help, they have nowhere to turn. The girl who already knows 9 of the 10 assigned spelling words from pleasure reading will make a 100 percent if she studies the 1 unknown word and 90 percent if she does nothing. The girl who can't read will be faced with 10 new words, an almost overwhelming task of memorization. If she really struggles, she'll earn a C-. In school, that is how the rich get richer and the poor get poorer. They'll imagine that if they had just studied a little harder or worked a little longer they would have done better. "And like the victims of child abuse, they blame themselves."[5] I'd heard the lecture . . . more than once. School is a test . . . to see who already knows the most and to see whose parents can do the best job. Now I was witnessing the demonstration.

## From One Generation to the Next

After 30 or 45 minutes of guesswork, Mitzi ran out to play, knowing that her faithful mother would be waiting to help her with another hour and a half of homework when she came in.[6] She couldn't know that the production of sentences is a test, a call for *output* that shows what the reader already knows; output is simply anything the learner can say or write. Sentence production

was not *input* designed to give the new or nonreader information.[7] Based on what is understandable and relevant to the learner, input becomes acquired without learner effort. Nor could Mitzi's mom know that this assignment was difficult because it employed a bottom-up strategy. It required that the learner remember all sorts of meaningless little pieces of the language, like "do," and put them into bigger pieces: sentences. She had been told that if she did this enough, she would know how to spell, and that would then help her

## Teachers Can Foster Family Literacy

Illiteracy does run in families, but we can end it in our classrooms. And, with funds for extra supplies, books, released time, and help from our schools, K-12 teachers can extend a hand to the parents of the "Mitzis" in our classrooms. We can:

• Make our classrooms examples of "print-rich environments" by providing plenty of books, magazines, posters, and notes.
• Invite parents to story times or other literacy events and help them to enjoy these occasions with their children. Help parents to understand that good questions are designed to stimulate thought, not extract correctness.
• Send books home that we have read to the children. Tell parents that talking about books will help their children learn to appreciate literature.
• Communicate with parents in clear language; find speakers of their languages when they are not proficient in English.
• Tell parents about adult literacy services such as Adult Basic Education and Literacy Volunteer programs. Encourage them to seek help, assuring them that it is never too late to learn to enjoy reading; but forewarn people of possible disappointments like the numbers of months on waiting lists, so that initial problems don't seem like personal affronts.
• Tell parents about local library story hours and services, and invite the librarian to meet them.
• Teach parents how to identify good book features such as: predictable text, Caldecott and Newberry Medalists, their own children's recognition and delight over books made familiar at school. Perhaps a very simple, large-type checklist can help.
• Teach parents not to fall for gro-

cery and drug store workbooks and other skill-level materials. Then point out where they can buy inexpensive books in the neighborhood, such as used book stores, flea markets, library sales, school purchase bargains (Scholastic Books), and chain stores.
• Visit children and parents in their homes to gain insights into their interests. In the process, you may find resources for the entire classroom, such as a parent who can sing folksongs.

For *homework*, teachers should assign enrichment tasks—not activities that ask students to finish incomplete classroom work, use materials that are not available, or obtain teaching at home when none may be available. Instead, the school-related homework should foster love of learning and build a bridge between classroom activities and life at home. For example, teachers can:
• Encourage children to read nursery rhymes or songbooks already made familiar at school.
• Suggest family projects such as handprint collections or pressed flowers, which will be used for school writing; in turn, the writing projects will then be returned to the home as reading materials.
• Give directions for making finger- and hand-puppets that match poems learned at school, and invite students to roleplay or dramatize stories from home for their classmates at school.

Making school/home connections with the parents of the Mitzis in your classrooms is a tough task—but a very good investment. Breaking the cycle of illiteracy continues to pay off generation after generation. □

—La Vergne Rosow

reading; in reality, only those students who are already readers can back into this kind of task successfully. She couldn't know that no struggle would have been involved in pulling a part (a word) out of a whole, such as a real story.

For Mitzi and her mom, there was never any storytelling or picture book enjoyment. But because Mitzi's mother was bent on not having her child do poorly in school the way she herself had, night after night, they labored over writing sentences for sounds like "door."

Finally, Mitzi had hit the word *floor,* and when she said it, her mother realized there was a pattern connection. "Yes, now, if that one's *floor,* what's this one?" she asked pointing back to word number one.

"But you said . . . " Mitzi, a very bright child, had already learned in one lesson the spelling "d-o-r-e."

I wondered what if, instead of *floor,* the familiar word had been *look* or *poor* or *boot.* What other reasonable and wrong connection might have been triggered? How many little transfers of poverty occur in the name of homework each night across this land as illiteracy passes from one generation to the next?

## Keeping Secrets from the Have-Nots

Who is accountable when all the mothers of all the Mitzis just don't measure up? Without knowing the futility of their efforts and the waste of their scarce funds, how many take the cue from this kind of school assignment and buy grocery store workbooks to occupy what would be pleasure book times for the literate elite?

Why aren't mother and child seeing beautiful pictures in books brought home from school and sharing favorite stories that Mitzi has heard again and again in class instead of impoverished little mimeographs with lists of meaningless words? Who profits when the values of the literate haves are kept secret from the illiterate have-nots? Surely we know too much of the reading process to pretend this disparity is created in ignorance. The assignment to sound out "do or" and to produce a sentence from it robs Mitzi of real reading time, but Mitzi doesn't know that. And Mitzi's mother doesn't know that. Can this kind of "literacy lesson" pass as a naive accident in our bountiful domain where consistently "the poor get poorer"?

[1] A 1988 survey of adult nonreaders showed that the biggest reason adults seek literacy help is self-esteem. L. Rosow, (November 1988), "Adult Illiterates Offer Unexpected Cues into the Reading Process," *Journal of Reading*: 120-124.
[2] S. D. Krashen, (1988), USC lecture notes (unpublished).
[3] Krashen describes the *Affective Filter,* the metaphor for the stress barrier that prevents new information from coming into the brain and appropriate known information from being accessed. S. D. Krashen, (1985), *Inquiries and Insights: Second Language Teaching, Immersion and Bilingual Education, Literacy,* (Hayward, Calif.: Alemany Press, a division of Janus Book Publishers, Inc.), pp. 10-11.
[4] Ibid, p. 108.
[5] Ibid.
[6] Not every nonreading mother is so faithful. The mother of another 9-year-old child, Arthur, had a thousand important things to keep her from having to face working with her child on school assignments. L. Rosow, (November 1989), "Arthur: A Tale of Disempowerment," *Phi Delta Kappan* 71, 3: 194-199.
[7] For a comprehensive discussion of input vs. output, see S. D. Krashen, (1989), "We Acquire Vocabulary and Spelling by Reading: Additional Evidence for the Input Hypothesis," *Modern Language Journal* 73, IV: 440-464.

*Author's note:* I am pleased to report that through subsequent tutoring, Mitzi's mother has just finished reading the first book of her life.

I would like to thank Professors David Eskey and William Rideout, Jr., for help with the Mitzi case.

*How Teachers Can Help Ease the Pain*

# Children of Divorce

## Candy Carlile

*Candy Carlile is Assistant Professor of Education, University of Mary Hardin-Baylor, Belton, Texas.*

The structure of the American family is rapidly changing. In the 1960s 60 percent of American families could be described as traditional, with two parents, one at home, and two or three children. Only about 7 percent of U.S. families are now considered to be "traditional" (Elkind, 1986). Today we can expect 50 percent of all first marriages to end in divorce (Glick, 1984; Weitzman, 1985), with an even higher rate of divorce for re-marriages (Berns, 1985). By the year 2000, it is expected that 60 percent of all U.S. children will spend some part of their lives in single-parent homes (Jellinek & Klavan, 1988).

Literally millions of children in classrooms across America are desperately trying to adjust to the personal tragedy of divorce. This process can be made easier for these children when sensitive, caring teachers work to create a safe, nurturing classroom environment that promotes the recovery and healing necessary for a child's well-being.

## The Pain of Divorce

Even in the best of situations, divorce is a painful process for every-one. Although children of all ages are affected, perhaps the most vulnerable are those at the elementary school level. Ironically, when these children need parental love, assurance and support the most, their parents are least able emotionally to provide it. Unfortunately, the turmoil often does not stop after the divorce is final. Parental hostility and bitterness may escalate through the years and continue to cause needless pain and suffering that could result in psychological damage to the child.

A 10-year study of children of divorce conducted by Wallerstein and Kelly (1980) cited a number of symptoms that children in such cases might experience. Of these behaviors, the following might be observed in the elementary school classroom: anxiety, depression, regression, asthma, allergies, tantrums, daydreaming, overaggressive behavior, withdrawal from relationships, poor school performance, frequent crying or absence of emotion, and difficulty in communicating feelings. If any of these symptoms persist, professional counseling should be sought immediately for the child.

Children are remarkably resilient, however. Although they experience a great deal of pain and feelings of loss, most can and will recover from the trauma of divorce (Bienenfeld, 1987). With the help of an understanding teacher, the classroom can become the brightest spot in a child's life during this difficult time.

## Things To Know About Divorce

Although children react differently to divorce depending upon age, maturity and individual situations, teachers need to be aware of some generalities to fully understand the plight of their students.

■ Children of divorce, as well as parents, go through a classic mourning process after divorce, much like after a death in the family. They experience disbelief, then anxiety, anger, sadness, depression and eventually, if given reassurance, acceptance of the divorce (Bienenfeld, 1987).

■ 80 to 90 percent of children recover from the initial shock of divorce in about a year (Jellinek & Klavan, 1988).

■ Boys react more intensely than girls to the loss of their fathers from the home. They are sometimes angry with their mothers for either causing the divorce or driving their fathers away (Dodson, 1987). From elementary school right through high school, boys from single-parent homes were more often classified as "low achievers" than children from intact families (NAESP & Charles F. Kettering Foundation, 1980).

From *Childhood Education*, Summer 1991, pp. 232-234. Reprinted by permission of Candy Carlile and the Association for Childhood Education International, 11141 Georgia Avenue, Suite 200, Wheaton, MD. Copyright © 1991 by the Association.

■ A common reaction of children of divorce who have been rushed into adult roles and responsibilities is to seek early escape from their childhoods. In such cases, these feelings can result in girls becoming sexually precocious and contemptuous of the parent who has been overdependent on them (Hetherington, 1981).

■ 95 percent of divorced parents with custody are mothers (Dodson, 1987). On an average, divorced women and their minor children experience a 73 percent decline in their standard of living in the first year after divorce (Weitzman, 1985). This may result in children having to move into less expensive dwellings and perhaps assume new or increased latchkey responsibilities as mothers struggle to make ends meet financially.

■ Children of divorce are more apt to be late to school or late more often and to miss school altogether. They are also more likely than their counterparts from intact families to spontaneously skip school (NAESP & Charles F. Kettering Foundation, 1980).

■ Teachers have discovered that Mondays and Fridays are especially difficult days for children of divorce (Francke, 1983). Leaving one parent at the end of the week and the other on Sunday can often be too much of an emotional overload for a young child. Anxiety, sadness and tears in the classroom on those days may be a result of the added stress.

## A Place To Heal

If children are to recover from the trauma of divorce, they must have a buffer zone between them and parental conflict. Bienenfeld (1987) encourages parents to establish such a neutral zone by refraining from fighting and arguing when their children are present. Unfortunately, this doesn't always happen, and the classroom provides the only "conflict-free" haven for these children. With a little extra effort and planning, we can make

our elementary school classrooms much more than simply havens. We can make them places where children can begin to heal and become whole again.

## What Teachers Can Do To Help

■ *Know your children.* Children of divorce are usually not eager to talk about their family problems for fear of being perceived as different. It is a teacher's responsibility to identify children of divorce at the beginning of each school year, either through school records or information derived from other teachers. It's also helpful to know when the parents separated to determine approximately where the child is in terms of the healing process. Confer with parents of all students as often as possible to remain aware of other family crises that may occur during the school year.

■ *Talk about feelings.* In a survey of approximately 100 children of divorce, preschool through teen, two emotions were discovered to be predominant in interviews with the children: anger and sadness (Francke, 1983). Guilt, grief, loss, helplessness, loneliness, rejection and anxiety are also common emotions experienced by children before, during and after divorce. Children need to know that it's okay to have these feelings and

that they are not alone. If they hesitate to verbalize their feelings, they should be given the opportunity to express themselves in other ways. The use of puppets and dolls (Francke, 1983), unstructured drawings (Bienenfeld, 1987), role-playing and creative writing are a few of the strategies found to be successful in the classroom.

■ *Bibliotherapy.* Using fictional books to help children through difficult times in their lives is certainly not a new strategy for elementary school teachers. Fortunately, a number of noteworthy juvenile books deal with the topic of divorce. Some are for independent reading by children, but I have found the most effective use of these books is to read them aloud to students and then discuss them together. This way the teacher is able to reach everyone—those who are dealing with divorce on a personal level and the other children who can always benefit from a lesson in understanding and kindness. (See Figure 1 for titles.)

■ *Make children aware they are not alone.* Through instructional activities, teach children about the many different types of family structures in today's society. Have children make individual booklets that tell about their families. Construct a class bulletin board using photos of family members. As a

---

**Figure 1. Children's Books and Other Sources**

Bienenfeld, F. (1980). *My mom and dad are getting a divorce.* St. Paul: EMC Corporation.
Blue, R. (1972). *A month of Sundays.* New York: Franklin Watts.
Brown, L. K., & Brown, M. (1986). *Dinosaur's divorce.* New York: Atlantic Monthly.
Cain, B., & Benedek, E. (1976). *What would you do? A child's book about divorce.* Indianapolis: The Saturday Evening Post Co.
Goff, B. (1969). *Where is daddy? The story of a divorce.* Boston: Beacon.
Kindred, W. (1973). *Lucky Wilma.* New York: Dial.
Lexau, J. (1971). *Me day.* New York: Dial.
Perry, P., & Lynch, M. (1978). *Mommy and daddy are divorced.* New York: Dial.
Pursell, M. S. (1977). *A look at divorce.* Minneapolis: Lerner.
Sitea, L. (1974). Zachary's divorce. In M. Thomas & C. Hart (Eds.), *Free To Be You and Me* (pp. 124-7). New York: McGraw-Hill.
Stanek, M. (1972). *I won't go without a father.* Chicago: Albert Whitman.
Zolotow, C. (1971). *A father like that.* New York: Harper & Row.

cooperative learning activity, have children cut pictures from magazines illustrating different types of family structures. These pictures can be placed in a classroom story-starter file or glued to a piece of posterboard to make a collage.

■ *Modify your language.* Be sure home correspondence, assignments, classroom assignments and school events allow for the variety of family structures represented within your classroom. A child may want to bring a grandparent to Open House or create a Mother's Day card for an aunt, a stepmother or the teacher down the hall. While divorce is no longer considered a social stigma, a child who attends Parents' Night with someone other than a parent can needlessly experience a great deal of personal embarrassment due to unthinking school personnel and children's insensitivity.

■ *Be tolerant of behavior changes.* The majority of children trying to cope with divorce experience a change in behavior. An increase in anxiety, restlessness, decreased concentration and daydreaming may be observed. The change may be immediate or gradual—with children responding to their own internal timetables (Wallerstein & Kelly, 1980). Lonely children may arrive at school early and stay late to receive as much time and attention from the teacher as possible (Francke, 1983).

Teachers must be patient with these children and deal with each case individually. When a child has had an especially bad day, extra time may need to be given for work that was not completed, or perhaps the child might be granted a "time out" from the classroom. Sometimes, a few classroom rules may need bending in order for children to regain some control of their emotions and their lives.

■ *Keep communication open with parents.* Divorce tends to complicate communication between teachers and parents. Simply scheduling parent-teacher conferences can become a major ordeal. Both parents may demand separate conferences, or neither parent may be able to come for the time you have scheduled. For the child's sake, it's important to make the extra effort necessary to keep parents informed of what's happening at school and to stay informed yourself. If necessary, make adjustments in conference times, or make evening telephone calls when parents are home from work.

Also keep in mind that the child may be having to adjust to two households now; books, homework assignments and notes about school progress or upcoming events may be left one place when they are needed at another. An additional matter to consider is that the child's transportation to and from school may also change with parental separation. With the increase in kidnappings by noncustodial parents, it is helpful for school personnel to be informed of which parent has been awarded legal custody of the child. Then, at least, it is possible for the custodial parent to be notified in case someone else arrives to pick the child up during school hours.

## The Classroom and Beyond
The trend toward divorce in America is definitely not on the decline. Female-headed families are increasing 10 times as quickly as two-parent families. As a result, the number of emotionally troubled children in classrooms continues to grow with each new semester. In many cases, teachers are providing the only safety net for these children (Francke, 1983). Schools can no longer ignore the problem and must begin to support teachers by providing training that enables them to better understand and deal with children of divorce. In addition, budgets must be stretched to ensure that guidance counselors are in place at the elementary school level. Unless more progress is made toward reaching out to these children, some predict that as many as three out of four children of divorce will themselves get divorced. Can we afford having this prediction become a reality?

### References
Berns, R. M. (1985). *Child, family, community.* New York: Holt, Rinehart & Winston.

Bienenfeld, F. (1987). *Helping your child succeed after divorce.* Claremont, CA: Hunter House.

Dodson, F. (1987). *How to single parent.* New York: Harper & Row.

Elkind, D. (1986). Helping parents make healthy educational choices for their children. *Educational Leadership, 44*(3), 36-38.

Francke, L. B. (1983). *Growing up divorced.* New York: Linden Press/Simon & Schuster.

Glick, P. C. (1984). Marriage, divorce and living arrangements: Prospective changes. *Journal of Family Issues, 5,* 7-26.

Hetherington, E. M. (1981). Children and divorce. In R. W. Henderson (Ed.), *Parent-child interaction: Theory, research and prospects* (p. 52). New York: Academic Press.

Jellinek, M., & Klavan, E. (1988, September). The single parent. *Good Housekeeping,* p. 126.

National Association of Elementary School Principals & Charles F. Kettering Foundation. (1980). One-parent families and their children: The schools' most significant minority. *Principal, 60,* 31-37.

Wallerstein, J. S., & Kelly, J. B. (1980). *Surviving the breakup.* New York: Basic Books.

Weitzman, L. J. (1985). *The divorce revolution.* New York: The Free Press.

# Single-Parent Families: How Bad for the Children?

K. ALISON CLARKE-STEWART

*Alison Clarke-Stewart is a professor in the Program in Social Ecology at the University of California, Irvine. She has written extensively about the various environments that influence children's development, including the family and day care. Currently she is doing research on how divorce and child custody affect children. Her books include:* Daycare *and* Child Development in the Family.

**Researchers know many factors that make divorce harder for children to endure—and the school can't do much about them. But teachers can help keep school from being one more problem.**

Six-year-old Nathaniel makes his own lunch before he goes to school. Nine-year-old Katherine comes home to an empty house and spends the afternoon watching television. Twelve-year-old Jason does the shopping, babysits for his younger sister, and sighs a lot. There's no question, children today do not live the protected, dependent existence that most of their parents—and teachers—did as youngsters. Responsibilities are thrust upon children at earlier and earlier ages. Expectations for their independence and achievement are high. Many of them experience daily stress.

One contributing factor in the complex web of contemporary economics and life-styles is the increased frequency with which children are growing up in single-parent families. A high proportion of these families are the result of divorce, and it is specifically on the distinctive situation of such families that this paper will focus.

Today, in the United States, one schoolchild in three has parents who are divorced. Thirty percent of these children live in stepfamilies. The other 70 percent live with their mothers or fathers alone.

What are the consequences of their parents' divorcing for children's lives, development, and achievement? Are these children "at risk"? If so, how much, and for how long? Should unhappy parents have stayed together "for the sake of the children"? Behavior problems observed in children from "broken homes" are often attributed to the parents' divorce, but is this always an accurate assessment? Are

From *NEA Today*, January 1989, pp. 60-64. Reprinted by permission of the National Educational Association of the United States.

there ways that schools and teachers can help children with problems rooted in their parents' divorce?

As divorce has become more and more common in this society, researchers have asked these questions, and the answers they have come up with are both worrying and encouraging. Worrying, because their observations show that children do indeed suffer, and suffer severely, when their parents get divorced. Encouraging, because they also show that negative effects on children's psychological well-being are not inevitably long-lasting. Children can be helped through the painful transition of their parents' divorce to a healthy, happy, and well-adjusted life.

## How Divorce Hurts

The effects of divorce begin long before the divorce itself, for both parents and children. In one study, observations of children as long as 11 years before their parents separated showed the effects of predivorce family stress. Boys in families in which the parents subsequently divorced were more impulsive and aggressive than boys in nondivorcing families. For parents, the effects begin to show in the years before the separation, through such symptoms as headaches, fatigue, weight loss, depression, anxiety, and mood swings—and these symptoms intensify after the separation. On a scale of stressful life events, separating from a spouse is second in intensity only to the death of a spouse. Over 40 percent of the adults going through a divorce report suffering from at least five physical or psychological symptoms; one-fifth need psychiatric help or hospitalization.

For children, too, the initial reaction to their parents' separation is traumatic. Children whose parents get divorced are initially distraught, shocked, afraid for their own futures. It doesn't make it any easier that one in three of their friends may be in the same boat. Losing *their* mother or *their* father is devastating. Their world turns upside down. Divorce is most devasting for "innocent victims"—those who have no control over its initiation—and children never initiate divorces.

In one study, interviews with children whose parents were getting divorced showed that none of them were happy about their parents' divorce, even if the parents were often in violent conflict with each other. More than three-quarters of the children opposed the divorce strongly, and even five years later one-third were still disapproving, dissatisfied, and intensely unhappy. The nuclear family is all the child knows, so children inevitably experience a strong feeling of loss—of the family unit, of security, and of their fairy-tale fantasy of "happily ever after."

After the divorce, the losses continue. For some things in life—and par-

---

**Not one child was happy about a family divorce, even if the parents were often in violent conflict with each other.**

---

ents may be among them—two is always better than one. One parent can be in only one place at a time, and for parents going through a divorce, that place is most often work, therapy, or the lawyer's office. One parent can have only one point of view, and for divorcing parents that point of view is most often their own. One parent can model only one gender role, give only so many hugs, offer so much discipline, and earn so much money.

Parents going through a divorce and the period following it are overwhelmed, overworked, and disorganized. There is not enough time for work or for themselves. They are absorbed in their own problems of survival, in their involvement in work (for many women, for the first time), in dating, in self-improvement, and in the search for support.

The children are often neglected. In the first couple of years after the divorce, children have less regular bedtimes and mealtimes, eat together as a family less, hear fewer bedtime stories, and are more often late for school. Discipline is less consistent, positive, and affectionate. And perhaps most salient of all, the aftermath of divorce brings economic disaster for most mothers and children.

Recent studies in a number of states have shown that after a divorce women suffer a drastic drop in income and

standard of living—in California, for example, a drop of 73 percent. Men's standard of living improves—42 percent in the states included in this study. Most women are not prepared to support themselves financially, even if they worked before the divorce. They commonly receive inequitable divorce settlements, no lifetime alimony, and a limited amount of spousal and child support (often not paid). They have few job prospects, no job histories, limited earning potential, and no careers. Because 90 percent of children in divorced families live with their mothers, this economic disaster directly affects the children. No-fault divorce has created a new impoverished class. More than half of poor families are made up of single mothers with children—and a sizable proportion of these mothers are divorced.

But it's not just the poverty that's hard to live with. It's the *drop* in income—and the more affluent the family, the harder that is to handle. Giving up Junior League friends to live on Hamburger Helper and food stamps is not only economically stressful, it's demoralizing as well.

Small wonder that children from divorced families are more likely than others to become juvenile delinquents, psychiatric patients, suicide victims. More than half have trouble in school—the result of depression, anxiety, guilt, loneliness, low self-esteem, low achievement, and bad behavior.

## Getting over Divorce

The good news is that these effects are not inevitable and they don't have to be long-lasting. Divorce is a painful, negative experience for everyone involved. But people—children especially—are resilient, and time heals. The first year after the divorce is the worst emotionally, and it gets worse before it gets better. But by two or three years after the divorce, in most families, routines are back to normal, physical symptoms have disappeared, the intense psychological stress is over, and adults and children have improved self-esteem and are functioning competently.

The process of adjusting to divorce and subsequent life in a single-parent family is smoother and easier for some adults and children than for others. Some individuals bounce back within a year or two. Others never really get over the experience. Although children whose parents get divorced are "at risk" for psychological and behavioral problems, these problems are not *inevitable*. Researchers currently are probing into the conditions and personal qualities that determine whether a child makes a quick and complete recovery from divorce and a positive adjustment to life in a single-parent family. They have found a number of factors that seem to be critical.

*Age.* One important determinant of children's reactions to their parents' divorce is age. The younger a child is, the better the prognosis for a complete adjustment. Preschool children don't know what "divorce" is. They don't understand what's going on, and they react to their parents' separation with bewilderment, fear, and regression. But in the long run, they are the most likely to be emotionally unscathed.

Very young children have spent less time in a conflicted family. Their familiarity with and attachment to the family unit is less. And the parents themselves are younger, which makes their recovery easier.

Children who are 6 to 8 years old when their parents divorce understand what is going on better than younger children, but they hurt more. They yearn for the lost parent, and they feel rejected, torn in two, angry at the custodial parent. They don't have a well-developed sense of time, nor do they understand the nature of blood ties. So when they are with one parent they miss the other. They are afraid that while they're apart, the missing parent will find another son or daughter and forget them.

Over the long run, a bare majority of these children adjust fairly well. In a study of 60 divorced families in California by Judith Wallerstein, for example, 10 years after the divorce, 40 percent of the children who had been in this age range at the time of divorce were still functioning poorly.

Children who are 9 to 12 years old when their parents divorce are more upset than younger children. Their parents tell them more about the reasons for the divorce. They often align with one parent (usually the custodial parent) against the other. They are the most likely of all to suffer psychosomatic symptoms of stress and sup-

pressed anger and to have problems in achievement and conduct at school.

---

# One parent can model only one gender role, give only so many hugs, offer so much discipline, and earn so much money.

---

An increase in household responsibilities and the need to make money often thrust these children into a precocious independence that may include premature sexual awareness or sexual activity.

Similarly, young adolescents, 13 to 16 years old, may be pushed too fast into independence by their parents' divorce. At the best of times, early adolescence is a vulnerable period of shaky self-esteem and conflicts over autonomy. A divorce may precipitate an adolescent's dropping out of school, getting pregnant, or getting into trouble with the law. Young adolescents react to their parents' divorce with unrealistic anguish, anxiety, and outrage: How could you do this to me? Along with the children who are 9 to 12 at the time of the divorce, they have the bleakest long-term outlook. In Wallerstein's study, slightly over half the children in this age range were doing poorly 10 years later.

*Sex.* For a variety of reasons, divorce is harder on boys than on girls, and boys are more likely to have problems. Boys are more vulnerable in general, and boys—who, like girls, are usually in a mother's custody—are most likely to lose the parent who is their gender-role model and the stronger authority.

*Family competence and confidence.* Adults who are more intelligent, assertive, self-assured, well-educated, creative, imaginative, mature, emotionally stable, tolerant of frustration, good at coping, willing to take risks, and socially bold are better able than most to deal with divorce and single parenthood, and so are their children.

Similarly, children with strong personal qualities tend to handle the divorce situation more easily. Ironically, however, the children who are most

likely to need such strong personal qualities, because their parents are getting divorced, are least likely to possess them, because they are more likely to have grown up in an unharmonious family environment.

*Economic situation.* Perhaps the single best predictor of the long-term consequences of divorce is the family's financial situation. The drastic drop in income and economic insecurity that accompany many divorces present severe challenges for both parents and children. Stories of single-parent families struggling for survival—living on cold cereal for dinner and trying to keep up the mortgage payments or moving from opulent abodes to tiny apartments in impoverished neighborhoods—are common. These changes inevitably lead to depression and resentment. For children, the economic drop packs a triple whammy: they lose material objects and opportunities, they lose status with their peers, and they are victims of their mothers' distraction and depression. Economic factors have a powerful effect on parents' and children's adjustment to divorce.

*Parents' caring and availability.* Children's relationships with both their parents after the divorce are very important for a healthy adjustment. These relationships, researchers have found, depend in large part on the child's continuing contact with both parents and on the ability of both parents to provide adequate supervision and consistent, authoritative discipline balanced by ample affection.

Because good relations with both parents have been found to be important for children, many states now award joint or shared custody of children to divorcing parents. Such arrangements sound ideal. The children do not "lose" a parent. They receive a more balanced exposure to two adults. Both parents continue to contribute fully to childrearing. And there is a greater likelihood that the expenses of child support will be shared. For the parents, there is regular and reliable relief from child care as well as the opportunity to make important decisions about the child and to offer daily, not Disneyland, care.

Little is known, however, about whether children really do better in joint custodial arrangements. Existing research is based on small, self-selected samples, and the results of different studies are not entirely consistent. There do seem to be some benefits of joint custody in terms of stress, satisfaction, self-esteem, and symptoms—if joint custody was the choice of the parents rather than of the courts. There is also some evidence that parents with joint custody are less likely than parents with sole custody to return for relitigation of the custody arrangement—again, if they themselves originally chose joint custody.

Court-ordered joint custody, however, may not have any of these benefits. Recent evidence, again collected by Judith Wallerstein, suggests that two years after the divorce, children in court-ordered joint custody arrangements are not doing as well as children in families where the court ordered sole custody. A possible reason is that in the families with court-ordered joint custody, the parents retained a rigid (court-ordered) 50-50 custody split, while only half the couples who had chosen joint custody were still following a 50-50 split. The others had slipped into the more conventional weekday/weekend division of time.

Whatever the legal arrangement, what is most important from the children's perspective is the *quality* of their relationship with both parents. If either parent disappears from the family, if either parent is rejecting, the child will suffer. To promote their children's satisfactory adjustment, parents must look out for the children's needs as well as their own, and not become overly self-absorbed—a challenge when they, too, are hurting.

*Parents' current relationship.* Children also suffer more if their parents are hostile toward each other. Some divorce researchers have gone so far as to suggest that the reason children of divorced parents have problems is not that they are separated from one of their parents but that their parents continue to fight overtly—sometimes violently—in front of them. In numerous studies, parental conflict or cooperation before and after the divorce has been found to predict both parents' and children's psychological well-being. It is most damaging to children when parents go on fighting and neglect the child or use the child as a pawn in their continued battling—

for example, through custody relitigation or child-snatching.

*Stability of circumstances.* Another factor that makes adjusting to a divorce difficult for children is the number of changes that inevitably accompany divorce. Moving to a new town and leaving old associations behind immediately upon separation may be the best thing for the parent, but it is not usually best for the child. The more changes children experience—moving to a new neighborhood, starting a new school, having mother start a job, going through repeated separations and reconciliations, living with changes in the custody arrangement—

---

## What is most important from the child's perspective is the *quality* of his or her relationships with both parents.

---

the harder it is to adjust. When parents remarry and the child becomes part of a stepfamily—which happens 1,300 times every day in this country—the change may, again, be good for the parent's mental health but not necessarily for the child's, since it adds new relationships, new conflicts, new rivalries, new uncertainties, and new complexities.

Despite the problems of separation and transition to a new family form, in certain limited ways children can benefit from change. Children who move to a new class or a new school a year or two after the divorce, for example, have had a chance to adjust to living in a divorced family. The change gives them the opportunity to shed any bad reputation they may have made for themselves during the time of emotional crisis and go on to more positive relationships and achievements.

*Access to outside help.* Finally, the parents and children who adjust best to divorce are those who get help. Divorce is a trauma it's hard to go through alone, and adults and children alike benefit from the opportunity to talk about their experiences to sympathetic and supportive listeners. These listeners may be family members,

friends, teachers, counselors, therapists, or other people who are going through divorce. Social support, from either a network of emotionally supportive and accepting friends or participation in social or professional groups, has been found to buffer stress. What's important is that divorcing parents and children be assured that they are worthy, that they are loved, and that things will—eventually—get better. If they can be given advice about how to speed the process of things getting better, or if they are provided with tangible services, from laundry to loans, this also is helpful.

## What Can Teachers Do?

In any year, in any class, the odds are high that there will be some children who are going through some phase of a parental divorce or remarriage. Teachers may be puzzled, annoyed, or completely frustrated by the effects of these events on the children's behavior in school. What can they do to assist these children and allay their own frustrations?

For one thing, teachers should try to be well-informed about what to expect from children under these circumstances. They should know that children, especially boys, are likely to act up and act out, to be distracted and withdrawn, to let their schoolwork slide, for as long as two years after their parents separate. During this time, these children, and their parents, need support and sympathy, not judgmental evaluations and criticism.

Teachers can attend workshops, read books, talk to their colleagues about the problems divorce creates and about possible solutions to those problems. Many schools now offer group programs for children whose parents are divorced, and there is growing evidence that these programs are helpful in children's adjustment.

Children whose parents divorce go through a slow and painful process of coming to understand and cope with the divorce and their new lifestyle and often reduced circumstances. This process can be guided—and children's adjustment can be eased—but time and support are necessary.

Children need to acknowledge the reality of their parents' separation, disengage from the parents' conflict, resolve their own feelings of loss and anger, accept the permanence of the divorce, and achieve realistic hopes and dreams for themselves. All this takes time. Classroom teachers can give children whose parents have just split up a break for some period of adjustment and transition, reducing their stress with lighter assignments and extra attention. Being patient and sympathetic is likely to pay off in the end.

Another way teachers can alleviate the problems created by divorce is by raising the consciousness of their other students about what divorce means and about what children whose parents are divorcing might be experiencing. Later on, teachers can help children whose parents are divorced by offering them a fresh start after they have made the initial adjustment to the divorce. In new classes or workgroups, their fellow students won't be biased by any bizarre or disruptive behavior they may have shown in the immediate aftermath of the divorce.

Looking more toward the future, teachers should do as much as they can to prepare their students for adult life in the twenty-first century. Two points are particularly important here. Students need preparation for the difficulties and challenges of marriage and family life, so that they won't take lightly the decisions they'll be making about when and whom to marry and when to have children. Girls need preparation to pursue lucrative careers and to be self-supporting. This is no longer a feminist issue alone. It is an issue of economic survival.

Divorce is a social phenomenon that affects us all. It is up to all of us, then, to help children and their parents cope with it as well as they can.

## For Further Reading

*Divorce.* Sharon J. Rice and Patrick C. McKenry. Sage Publications, 1988. A systematic summary of recent research on the sociological and psychological processes involved in divorce.

*Growing Up Divorced.* Linda Bird Franke. Linden Press/Simon & Schuster, 1983. This is one of the many books available for parents—to inform, to educate, and to assist in their challenging task of rearing children after divorce. It provides an excellent review of the research demonstrating how divorce presents a series of crises for children, depending on their age and sex.

*Interventions for Children of Divorce: Custody, Access, and Psychotherapy.* Walter F. Hodges. Wiley, 1986. For those who are interested in the kinds of therapy and support programs currently available for children of divorce, this book offers an introduction. It also gives a thorough review of research showing the effects of divorce on adults and children.

*Mothers and Divorce: Legal, Economic, and Social Dilemmas.* Terry Arendell. University of California Press, 1986. *The Divorce Revolution.* Lenore Weitzman. Free Press, 1985. The sociologist authors of these books explore the dire economic and social consequences of divorce for modern middle-class single mothers. Both call for drastic reforms to make divorce legislation more equitable for men and women and to provide adequate support for child rearing.

"Single Parent Families: A Bookshelf: 1978-1985." Benjamin Schlesinger. *Family Relations,* vol. 35, pp. 199-204, 1986. This article lists 80 books and special issues of journals on single parents that appeared between 1978 and 1985. A hint of the vast literature available on this subject, this annotated list suggests where to start reading.

"Single Parenting: A Filmography." Lee Kimmons and Judith A. Gaston. *Family Relations,* vol. 35, pp. 205-211, 1986. This annotated listing of films provides teachers with a description of a broad range of available films, filmstrips, and videotapes that deal with the single-parent experience. All would be useful for classes, support groups, or workshops.

# Where Are the Parents?

## John McCormick

By the 25th spring of her increasing discontent, Marijke Raju was ready to retaliate. She was fed up with indulgent parents who let third graders play baseball or hit the mall rather than finish their homework. And she'd had her fill of nonacademic interruptions—bus-boarding drills today, an assembly to unveil the school's chocolate-sales drive tomorrow—that clutter her third graders' schedule in the middle-class Chicago suburb of Northlake, Ill. "You're the parent, the nurse, the policeman, the social worker and, very last, you are the teacher," she says. To make matters still worse, those children who don't encounter rigor at home resent the discipline Raju imposes at school. So, last May, when someone slashed her tire in the parking lot, Raju decided *someone* should pay—and that someone should be a parent.

As it played out, an administrator reimbursed Raju before she could reach the school's parents' auxiliary. But the incident—and the target of Raju's ire—reflects a new reality. In faculty rooms across America, hypercriticism of the nation's educators is beginning to meet its match. Teachers are losing patience with demanding but unsupportive parents who blame everyone but themselves for Johnny's tepid performance. Judging by what they do rather than the lip service the offer, many of today's parents plainly put their own needs, and especially their careers, ahead of their children. While some of that is understandable, particularly in households where merely keeping food on the table is a dicey proposition, the unpleasant consequence is a void schools cannot fill. Equally frustrating are the worthy but increasing intrusions—lessons in everything from AIDS awareness to self-esteem to handgun safety—that a too busy society now expects its

schools to impart. "We've asked schools to do too much," laments Brown University education expert Theodore Sizer. "Teachers aren't parents."

To the schools we consign our most prized possessions: our children and our tax dollars. But many of the nation's 45 million schoolchildren are woefully unprepared for each day's work. Some days it seems that fewer kids come to school hungry because their parents are poor than come tired because parents let them watch television too late. Teachers' efforts to boost achievement must navigate a flood tide of societal changes—high numbers of broken homes and working parents, to name two—that reduce the amount of influence kids get from authority figures at home. "What we used to call 'teaching' is now morning-to-night service to families," says Louise Sundin, president of the Minnesota Federation of Teachers. "Some days it looks like nobody else is helping."

The parents most driven professionally can be the least helpful at school. Many behave as though the school exists for their child alone; a particularly annoying subspecies of the self-absorbed pulls kids out of class for family vacations *and* asks teachers to prepare a week's lessons, presumably to be administered by the ski patrol. Connecticut educator Peter Buttenheim reserves the term "designer parents" for a growing, affluent cadre obsessed by the end product of education rather than the process. Designers typically suspect that *their* children's needs aren't being met, and treat even bright and enthusiastic teachers much as they would an unproven auto mechanic.

"Affluenza," as it is known in the trade, takes many forms. Veteran teachers, faced with a generation of passive learners weaned on television, say too many parents have lost their good

sense or their spine. New Haven teacher Wendy Wells says her well-heeled and media-savvy students display plenty of surface sophistication, but lack critical powers of observation and the desire to study things in depth. "We don't teach as much because kids don't come with the same work ethic," she says. "Homework isn't done because the family went to the 'Ice Capades'."

Changes in family life has distanced parents from schools. Parents' lives are so hectic that schools often can't find them when problems arise; one mother informed a suburban Chicago school that she didn't give her unlisted telephone number to *anyone*. With so many parents working, one third of all elementary students return to empty homes. Home life is so closely tied to school performance that 70 percent of elementary principals now keep formal records of each child's family structure. (Fully 97 percent of the National Association of Elementary School Principals think children from single-parent homes pay a price academically.)

For many teachers, the dysfunctional family is more than an abstract term. Some kids reach kindergarten without having been read to or even talked to, and can interact with other children only by hitting them. Schools nationwide try to educate students who disappear for weeks without explanation; of the 26 seventh graders in one Los Angeles music-appreciation class, only four showed up regularly last year. And in drug-education classes, teachers often wonder who's teaching whom. "They say, 'I went to my uncle's house and they were measuring drugs on the scales'," says Helene Sapadin of New Haven, Conn. "Here we are saying that drugs are bad, and we're talking about their *families*."

When parents can't or won't convey

---

## WARD CLEAVER, PHONE HOME

**Parents are pressed for time**
73% of mothers with school-age children work outside the home. Nearly one fourth of all children under age 18 live with a single parent, and only 7% of school-age children live in a two-parent household where there is only one wage earner.

**So schools teach the new facts of life**
According to one survey, almost all elementary schools (95%) teach drug education, and more than half start teaching it in kindergarten. Most (72%) teach sex education.

SOURCES: BUREAU OF LABOR STATISTICS; NATIONAL ASSOCIATION OF ELEMENTARY SCHOOL PRINCIPALS

---

crucial information to their children, legislatures and school boards rush to the rescue. Allan Vann, author of a book on bloated school curricula, likens the process to pouring water into an already filled glass. "Named *one* subject that's been *dropped* from elementary schools in the 1980s," grumped a recent newsletter from the principals' association. "Now, think about the subjects that have been *added:* AIDS, sex- and drug-abuse education, hygiene, family-life training, nutrition and fitness, environmental education, conflict resolution . . ." The list will never be inclusive. "Who's against bike safety?" asks Bruce Berndt, president of the Chicago Principals' Association. "But how much time should we spend on something like that?"

The most common argument for the swollen nonacademic curriculum is that if schools don't impart these often crucial lessons, no one else will. Consider the burden of teachers at Miami Beach Senior High School, who must acculturate a student body of 2,100 students of 67 nationalities. Principal Daniel Tosado says there is no other institution to help

poor immigrant students and their families. But some educators say that misses the larger point. If south Florida mobilized church groups, nationality associations or elderly volunteers to help families with language training and social-service referrals, couldn't Tosado's staff devote more time to the classwork students will need if they're to achieve their dreams of a better life?

If teachers feel overwhelmed, many parents feel unwelcome. For too long some schools made parents feel like intruders. "We restricted conferences to certain days and we didn't welcome parents into classes," says Bob Chase, vice president of the National Education Association. "The barriers were unspoken but they suggested that we were the professionals." Moreover, the popularity of teacher-bashing during the 1970s and early 1980s made teachers nationwide feel defensive; undoubtedly many deflected their discomfort back at parents. Chase now thinks such barriers are falling. "Teachers are reaching out," he says. "We need the community's help."

Too often, though, both parents are teachers recite the timeworn mantra—"Parents and schools must work together"—and then blunder along separately. If any group should be capable of closing the gap it's the Parent Teacher Association. And PTA national president Ann Lynch is trying to set an agenda for a different demographic age. One example: chapters are urged to divide the old monthly meetings into morning, evening and weekend sessions so every working parent can participate. "We're hoping schools that say, 'We want parental involvement' will back that up with outreach programs," she says. "Too many parents don't have relationships with schools until there's a problem."

Terrel Bell, a former U.S. Education secretary, suggests a more formal approach: he would have every state require annual, written agreements between parents and schools as a precondition for enrollment. Among other things, parents would warrant that each child will get a good night's sleep, arrive at school on time and have a place at home to study. "This would impress on many parents their obligation," says Bell. "You get the service free but you

*Fathers and mothers blame everyone but themselves for Johnny's tepid academic performance*

---

have to make the commitment." In experiments around the nation, the San Francisco-based Quality Education Project has found that merely asking parents to sign pledges similar to Bell's proposed contract makes them feel far more accountable for their children's schoolwork. Indianapolis educators use a different approach: they search out parents at major employers for lunchtime workshops on such topics as helping a child learn to read. Minneapolis offers Success by 6, an amalgam of business, labor, government, health and education initiatives to help parents nurture the skills their kids will need to flourish in the early grades.

Many educators say there is no tactful way to impress on parents how much impact their priorities have on their children—and how important it is that they get involved at school. When academic or behavior problems arise, teachers routinely rearrange their professional lives to schedule special meetings at times convenient for parents. Not enough parents, they say, ever offer to do the same.

In the end, we've decided as a culture that education is too important to be left just to the educators, and that parenting is too important to be left solely to the parents. Those axioms, as a practical matter, lead to shared power and shared responsibilities. They can be a prescription for resentment and neglect—or an opportunity to raise a child successfully. For the moment, teachers would prefer to emphasize the latter. Heed us, they're crying. Help us. Help us help your children.

*With Karen Spinger in Chicago, Patrick Rogers in New York, Leslie Barnes in San Francisco and Peter Katel in Miami*

# Appropriate Educational Practices

- Preschool and School-Age Programs (Articles 18–24)
- Assessment (Articles 25–27)
- Special Needs (Articles 28–30)

Instruction versus guidance, systematic versus emergent, teacher-chosen versus child-initiated. These are some of the ideas around developmentally based education that are currently debated by caregivers, teachers, parents, and school boards. The principles and philosophies behind these discussions are complex. Those involved in the discussions are firm in their views.

Some hold that young children must be prepared for the twenty-first century, which is arriving soon as the postindustrial information technology-based era. They sense the urgency of transformed skills and abilities that will be necessary to function effectively in society. To be next century's adults, today's children require an infusion of powerful instruction and many believe early childhood is the time to begin. Those on this side of the debate believe direct instruction, based on visionary goals, and use of academic tools (such as workbooks, basal readers, sequenced tasks, and paper/pencil) are appropriate practice to prepare young children for entry to the next century. Achievement is verified by testing, an important measurement to advocates of national standards.

The other side of the debate, while affirming the necessity of preparation, emphasizes young children's learning in the immediate present rather than the future. To them, the path to effective adult skills and abilities is developmental. Young children learn through exploration of physical objects and their instruction is embedded in the activity itself. The urgency they sense is for children to engage the world and construct their own knowledge. Appropriate practice, to developmentalists, is child-initiated activity, based on emergent goals, using objects of the physical world as tools of learning.

The strength of today's debate over appropriate practice in early childhood indicates another swing of the educational philosophy pendulum. The pendulum has always swung, and this time it involves an early childhood community that is more sure of its knowledge and more mature in its practices. It is also a community more divided over its philosophy than on earlier swings.

As knowledge and practice expand, a seeming paradox may be occurring that causes a rupture in philosophy. When any professional community grows, it divides its tasks. The early childhood education community is no exception: one group studies children, another designs curriculum, still another teaches. Knowledge of children is built by some, while practice with children is perfected by others. If the two work behind closed doors, they may achieve differing goals, while still using each other's language. Early childhood philosophy is further influenced by opinions from other fields when state or national conditions shift attention to education.

This process is similar to a cottage business that grows into an industry. Concepts once designed and executed locally are now designed in one department to be engineered elsewhere. The product will probably not emerge as it was originally intended. The early childhood profession is currently in danger of the same growth problem. Curricular concepts are being predesigned for children to engineer with little variability. Practices with children become less dependent on the individuals in the groups and more dependent on commercial sourcebooks. The trade-off is a homogenized program, developmental only by the label.

Some early childhood educators may be losing their original intention. The current debates indicate this is true. The reason for a sense of loss is that attention is shifting from the children, whose development they mean to ensure, to the products of education. The search for "how to's" can lead to the assumption that the instant curriculum can truly be developmentally appropriate, or that a prepackaged, sterile environment will automatically result in quality. The press to prove child achievement should be recognized as a short-term educational product.

Authentic appropriate practice, based on children's development, has no short cuts and cannot be trivialized. By detailing specifics of routines and procedures and materials and resources suitable for young children, however, the early childhood profession strengthens its identity. It is a helpful exercise to ensure the match of practice with childhood. Putting thought and planning and process behind the words involves using knowledge of child development to inform caregiving decisions and curricular choices. This is also an exercise in teacher autonomy; to own and value the work of the profession.

The current debate on developmentally appropriate practice is a healthy one, calling for knowledge to remain based on young children and practice to resist standardization. How the early childhood community's perception of appropriate practice will evolve by the twenty-first century remains an open question.

### Looking Ahead: Challenge Questions

Based on your philosophy of education, what is the optimal level of structure appropriate in preschool? In kindergarten? In primary grades? How would specific program components reflect optimal structure?

Should young children be retained in kindergarten? If so, for what reasons? How does grade retention relate to developmentally appropriate practice?

What role does television play in children's learning today? What should television provide for children in the future?

What are the most important components of a developmentally appropriate after-school program for the primary grades?

What is a teacher's role in early intervention for young children with special needs?

How can the physical environment be arranged to encourage children's use of language?

# Guidelines for Appropriate Curriculum Content and Assessment in Programs Serving Children Ages 3 Through 8

### A POSITION STATEMENT OF THE
## National Association for the Education of Young Children
### AND THE
## National Association of Early Childhood Specialists in State Departments of Education

### Adopted November 1990

## *Background information*

The National Association for the Education of Young Children (NAEYC) and the National Association of Early Childhood Specialists in State Departments of Education (NAECS/SDE) jointly developed these guidelines to inform decisions about curriculum content and assessment in programs serving children 3 through 8 years of age. The purpose of this document is to guide teachers and supervisors to: (1) make informed decisions about appropriate curriculum content and assessment, (2) evaluate existing curriculum and assessment practices, and

(3) advocate for more appropriate approaches. This document is designed to assist teachers and administrators with only one part of their complex jobs—their important roles as curriculum decision makers and evaluators.

Curriculum decisions not only involve questions about **how** children learn, but also **what** learning is appropriate and **when** it is best learned (Katz, 1989). In addition, the way learning is assessed directly influences what is taught and when it is expected to be learned. Therefore, these guidelines address both curriculum and assessment. The early childhood profession believes that curriculum and assess-

ment should be planned based on the best knowledge of theory and research about how children develop and learn, with attention given to individual children's needs and interests in relation to program goals.

**Curriculum** is an organized framework that delineates the content children are to learn, the processes through which children achieve the identified curricular goals, what teachers do to help children achieve these goals, and the context in which teaching and learning occur. The early childhood profession defines curriculum in its broadest sense, encompassing prevailing theories, approaches, and models. **Assessment** is the process of observing, recording and otherwise documenting the work children do and how they do it, as a basis for a variety of educational decisions that affect the child, including planning for groups and individual children, and communicating with parents. Assessment encompasses the many forms of evaluation available to educational decision makers. Assessment in the service of curriculum and learning requires teachers to observe

---

*It is important to explain how the scope of these guidelines, for 3- through 8-year-olds, was determined. NAEYC defines "early childhood" as birth through age 8. We have not changed our position that education begins at birth. However, curriculum and assessment for infants and toddlers looks different from what is described here. In fact, many infant specialists object to the use of the word "curriculum" with infants. Because this document is a joint position statement of NAEYC and NAECS/ SDE and we assume one of its primary audiences will be public school personnel, we originally conceived the document to address the age range of 4- through 8-year-olds to be compatible with the early childhood unit concept recommended by the National Association of State Boards of Education (1988). We chose to expand the scope to address 3-year-olds in anticipation of future trends toward increased educational services for this age group in public schools, Head Start, and child care programs.*

---

and analyze regularly what the children are doing in light of the content goals and the learning processes. . . .

## Guidelines for curriculum content and assessment for 3- through 8-year-olds

The National Association for the Education of Young Children (NAEYC) and the National Association of Early Childhood Specialists in State Departments of Education (NAECS/SDE) jointly developed the following guidelines to inform decisions about what constitutes appropriate curriculum content and assessment procedures in programs serving children ages 3 through 8. Decisions about curriculum and assessment are among the most important decisions that educators make. Curriculum and assessment decisions usually reflect a compromise of sorts among the many parties who have an interest in what is taught and learned in schools: parents, community leaders, subject-matter experts, as well as professional educators. NAEYC and NAECS/SDE believe that early childhood educators bear a responsibility to ensure that such decisions are based on current knowledge about child development and learning as well as knowledge of individual children.

The purpose of these guidelines is to ensure that the knowledge base of early childhood education is applied when decisions are made about curriculum and assessment for young children, 3 through 8 years. Curriculum and assessment decisions must be based on knowledge of what is age-appropriate as well as what is individually appropriate, if we truly want all children to learn and succeed in school and in life. Similarly, curriculum content and assessment procedures in a free society such as ours should reflect the ideals of a participatory democracy such as personal autonomy, decision making, equality, and social justice. Schools should not only teach about democratic values but should provide opportunities for children "to live democratically in the microcosm of the classroom" (Kessler, in press).

Curriculum content (what children are to learn), learning processes (how children learn), instructional strategies (how to teach), environment (the learning context), and assessment

strategies (how to know that learning has occurred and what curriculum adjustments are needed) are all interrelated and constitute the educational program. A complete discussion of these topics is beyond the scope of this document. For more information on NAEYC's positions on appropriate instructional strategies and learning processes, see *Developmentally Appropriate Practice in Early Childhood Programs Serving Children From Birth Through Age 8* (1987), edited by S. Bredekamp.

## Guidelines for curriculum content

The guidelines in this document apply to educational programs for **all** children ages 3 through 8. Recently, many specialized programs, such as those for children identified as at-risk, gifted, developmentally delayed, learning disabled, physically or emotionally disabled, have been developed primarily because traditional curriculum and classroom practice have not been responsive to a wide range of individual differences. Developmentally appropriate curriculum and practices, such as those described in this document, are more likely to accommodate to a broader range of individual differences. When a child requires specialized services that go beyond what can be provided within regular classroom experiences, then those services should be provided in programs that also meet these guidelines.

**Guidelines are standards or principles by which to make a judgment or determine a course of action.** The following statements are guidelines to use in making decisions about developing and/or selecting curriculum content for young children (what children are expected to know and be able to do). Guidelines are followed by elaborating paragraphs. To judge curriculum appropriate and acceptable, positive evidence should exist that **all** guidelines are met. Curriculum should be evaluated at the level of implementation, as well as at previous points in time when curriculum decisions are made. For instance, a curriculum decision made at a district or agency level may appear to conform to the guidelines, but when implemented at the classroom level, it may not. Likewise, if

curriculum appears to be weak in meeting one or more guidelines, it may be possible to compensate for the weakness during implementation by teachers in classrooms.

**1.** **The curriculum has an articulated description of its theoretical base that is consistent with prevailing professional opinion and research on how children learn.**

Curriculum should be grounded in the most current knowledge of child development and learning. The prevailing world view reflects a developmental, interactive, constructivist approach to learning that is not limited to the almost exclusively behaviorist approach that permeated curriculum and assessment in this country for the past several decades.

**2.** **Curriculum content is designed to achieve long-range goals for children in all domains—social, emotional, cognitive, and physical—and to prepare children to function as fully contributing members of a democratic society.**

Curriculum should address the development and learning of the whole child. This means that curriculum in primary grade schools must attend to social, emotional, and physical goals as well as cognitive goals. Likewise, programs for 3- and 4-year-olds need to address cognition as well as social, emotional, and physical development. In addition, curriculum content and processes should reflect democratic ideals of community involvement, liberty, freedom of choice, equality, fairness, and justice.

**3.** **Curriculum addresses the development of knowledge and understanding, processes and skills, dispositions and attitudes.**

The acquisition of knowledge and the mastery of skills is accomplished so as to ensure that children will be disposed to apply the knowledge or skill and so that children associate positive feelings with the learning (Katz, 1989). For example, if reading instruction is limited to drill and practice on phonics and word attack skills, children may choose to not read because they find no pleasure or satisfaction in reading or do not understand what they decode. On the other hand, if children are motivated to get meaning from reading, they are more likely to respond to instruction in use of phonetic cues.

## 4. Curriculum addresses a broad range of content that is relevant, engaging, and meaningful to children.

The human mind is a pattern detector; the child naturally attempts to make meaning out of every experience. As a result, what is meaningful is always more easily learned, understood, and remembered. Effective curriculum develops knowledge and skills in a meaningful context, not in isolation. For example, children learn numerals and number concepts by counting real objects, not by filling in workbook pages. Children learn letters and their sounds from using them in their name, signs, or stories that are meaningful to them, rather than by tracing them on a page or reciting the alphabet repeatedly. The younger the child, the more important it is to provide curriculum content that is close to the child's experience and therefore more likely to be meaningful.

## 5. Curriculum goals are realistic and attainable for most children in the designated age range for which they were designed.

Curriculum planning should adjust for normative differences in children's development and learning. Children should not be expected to comprehend abstract/symbolic concepts or master skills or content that can be acquired much more easily later on. To some extent, this guideline addresses the issue of efficiency in teaching and learning. For instance, first, second, and third grade teachers all report that children cannot comprehend place value; they spend hours trying to teach this abstract concept and children either become frustrated or resort to memorizing meaningless tricks. This is an example of an unrealistic objective that could be attained much more easily later on.

Curriculum decisions about when children are expected to acquire knowledge and skills are based on age-group, individual, and cultural expectations. Curriculum expectations of young children are flexible and dynamic, rather than deterministic and lock-step, since there is no universal sequence of skills development. The curriculum allows for children to work at different levels on different activities and does not require all the children to do the same thing at the same time. Decisions about when knowledge and skills are introduced and/or expected to be accomplished are based on knowledge of the prior experiences of individual children in a group, knowledge of prerequisite intellectual structures, and knowledge about typical patterns of development and learning.

## 6. Curriculum content reflects and is generated by the needs and interests of individual children within the group. Curriculum incorporates a wide variety of learning experiences, materials and equipment, and instructional strategies, to accommodate a broad range of children's individual differences in prior experience, maturation rates, styles of learning, needs, and interests.

Curriculum planning should anticipate the interests that are typical of children of different ages and also emerge from the interests that children demonstrate. Interest can also be generated by exposing children to events, materials and people that children would not experience otherwise. Educators must choose which of children's interests to support and which to ignore. In addition, educators have a responsibility to nurture certain interests, particularly those that are tied to cultural values such as the value of children's autonomy and creative experience.

## 7. Curriculum respects and supports individual, cultural, and linguistic diversity. Curriculum supports and encourages positive relationships with children's families.

The curriculum embraces the reality of multiculturalism in American society by providing a balance between learning the common core of dominant cultural knowledge (for example, the English language, democratic values) and knowledge of minority cultures. Curriculum accommodates children who have limited English proficiency. All the cultures and primary languages of the children are respectfully reflected in the curriculum.

## 8. Curriculum builds upon what children already know and are able to do (activating prior knowledge) to consolidate their learning and to foster their acquisition of new concepts and skills.

For example, there is no body of knowledge possessed by all children of the same age, just as there is no universal sequence of learning. Because children bring meaning to learning experiences based on their past experiences and individual development, different children acquire different learnings from the same experience. As a result, curriculum for young children should not be based on a rigid scope and sequence but should help children connect new learning to what they already know and are able to do.

## 9. The curriculum provides conceptual frameworks for children so that their mental constructions based on prior knowledge and experience become more complex over time.

Conceptual organizers such as themes, units, or projects give children something meaningful and substantive to engage their minds. It is difficult for children to make sense of abstract concepts such as colors, mathematical symbols, or letter sounds when they are presented at random or devoid of any meaningful context.

## 10. Curriculum allows for focus on a particular topic or content, while allowing for integration across traditional subject-matter divisions by planning around themes and/or learning experiences that provide opportunities for rich conceptual development.

Children's learning is not compartmentalized or divided into artificial subject matter distinctions. The purpose of integrating curriculum is to reflect the natural way children learn and also to help children make connections between what they learn at home and in the program, between what they learn in school and the real world, and between different disciplines or subject matter areas (British Columbia Ministry of Education, 1990). The curriculum provides for long blocks of time to bring naturally related subjects together and does not require minimal time allotments for instruction in discrete subject matter. For example, children read and write about a science experiment they have done or measure and estimate the number of blocks they will need to build a store.

**11.** The curriculum content has intellectual integrity; content meets the recognized standards of the relevant subject-matter disciplines.

Regardless of the age of the child, educators have a responsibility to respect the knowledge base of the appropriate disciplines when formulating curriculum. In an attempt to simplify content, curriculum developers sometimes present inaccurate, misleading, or potentially confusing information. If the specific content is related to a particular discipline, then it should be as accurate as possible (although children's constructions of knowledge will not mirror adult conceptions.) For example, science curriculum should be factual and not promote magical thinking in children; likewise, children should be exposed to literature, poetry, and works of art and music of recognized quality.

**12.** The content of the curriculum is worth knowing; curriculum respects children's intelligence and does not waste their time.

Content should be included in curriculum for specific age groups because it is important for children to learn to function capably in their world. Content goals should include what children can learn efficiently and effectively at this time. Children and teachers should not have to waste time trying to address content that is meaningless, or could be learned much more easily when the child is older.

**13.** Curriculum engages children actively, not passively, in the learning process. Children have opportunities to make meaningful choices.

The curriculum provides for children's direct experience before moving to more abstract levels of understanding. The curriculum or learning experience builds on children's prior learning and previous knowledge, thus sensory experience is not prerequisite in every situation but vital when introducing new concepts or information. Encouraging and permitting children to make real choices fosters interest and engagement. For instance, children should have opportunities to express their own ideas in writing and to read books of their choosing as well as those that the entire group will address.

**14.** Curriculum values children's constructive errors and does not prematurely limit exploration and experimentation for the sake of ensuring "right" answers.

Overemphasis on standardized test scores and the acquisition of basic skills has made teachers and parents uncomfortable with the natural process of the child's construction of knowledge. The fact is that teachers can learn a great deal about children's thinking and reasoning and level of cognitive development by attending to their "wrong" answers.

**15.** Curriculum emphasizes the development of children's thinking, reasoning, decision-making, and problem-solving abilities.

Curriculum emphasizes both content and process, what children need to know and be able to do. Curriculum content gives meaning to process, rather than focusing on isolated facts. Skills are taught in the context of activities that are meaningful to the child, rather than teaching skills in isolation (Lloyd-Jones & Lunsford, 1989).

**16.** Curriculum emphasizes the value of social interaction to learning in all domains and provides opportunities to learn from peers.

Social interaction with peers and adults is essential for children to develop real understanding. Social interaction also provides opportunities for children to learn cooperation and other kinds of positive social behavior. Multi-age grouping is one strategy to promote social interaction among individual children and their more capable peers, an effective way of enhancing language competence and generally assisting children's progress to the next level of development and understanding.

**17.** Curriculum is supportive of children's physiological needs for activity, sensory stimulation, fresh air, rest, hygiene, and nourishment/ elimination.

Curriculum should respect and meet children's physical needs while also promoting children's independent functioning and ability to meet their own needs. Children should not be required to sit still for long periods without a break. Under no circumstances should children who need regular opportunities to move their bodies be kept indoors to complete tasks or deprived of food as punishment.

**18.** Curriculum protects children's psychological safety, that is, children feel happy, relaxed, and comfortable rather than disengaged, frightened, worried, or stressed.

Decisions about curriculum should respect children's psychological safety. For instance, the content itself should not generate fear or confusion, nor should the premature expectation of mastery of skills generate stress.

**19.** The curriculum strengthens children's sense of competence and enjoyment of learning by providing experiences for children to succeed from their point of view.

Sometimes teachers seem to use as their primary criterion for selecting curriculum, "But the children just love it!" Enjoying the curriculum is an important but insufficient criterion for curriculum selection. Worthwhile curriculum does not have to entertain children. Instead, children's enjoyment can derive from positive feelings about self and meaningful learning, as they realize their own progress and growing competence.

**20.** The curriculum is flexible so teachers can adapt to individual children or groups.

The curriculum suggests alternatives as well as assumes that teachers will use their own professional judgment.

## Suggestions for using the curriculum guidelines

Developing curriculum or deciding whether a particular curriculum is appropriate for a specific group of children is a complex task that requires consideration of many variables. To facilitate the task of using the Curriculum Guidelines, we have phrased each of the guidelines as a question. We suggest that a curriculum committee, composed of six to eight teachers, review a proposed curriculum by subjecting it to these questions. An approved curriculum would be one for which a group of early childhood professionals could consensually agree in the affirmative to each of the following questions:

**1.** Does it promote interactive learning and encourage the child's construction of knowledge?

**2.** Does it help achieve social, emotional, physical, and cognitive goals?

**3.** Does it encourage development of positive feelings and dispositions toward learning while leading to acquisition of knowledge and skills?

**4.** Is it meaningful for these children? Is it relevant to the children's lives? Can it be made more relevant by relating it to a personal experience children have had or can they easily gain direct experience with it?

**5.** Are the expectations realistic and attainable at this time or could the children more easily and efficiently acquire the knowledge or skills later on?

**6.** Is it of interest to children and to the teacher?

**7.** Is it sensitive to and respectful of cultural and linguistic diversity? Does it expect, allow, and appreciate individual differences? Does it promote positive relationships with families?

**8.** Does it build on and elaborate children's current knowledge and abilities?

**9.** Does it lead to conceptual understanding by helping children construct their own understanding in meaningful contexts?

**10.** Does it facilitate integration of content across traditional subject matter areas?

**11.** Is the information presented accurate and credible according to the recognized standards of the relevant discipline?

**12.** Is this content worth knowing? Can it be learned by these children efficiently and effectively now?

**13.** Does it encourage active learning and allow children to make meaningful choices?

**14.** Does it foster children's exploration and inquiry, rather than focusing on "right" answers or "right" ways to complete a task?

**15.** Does it promote the development of higher order abilities such as thinking, reasoning, problem solving, and decision making?

**16.** Does it promote and encourage social interaction among children and adults?

**17.** Does it respect children's physiological needs for activity, sensory stimulation, fresh air, rest, and nourishment/elimination?

**18.** Does it promote feelings of psychological safety, security, and belonging?

**19.** Does it provide experiences that promote feelings of success, competence, and enjoyment of learning?

**20.** Does it permit flexibility for children and teachers?

## Guidelines for appropriate assessment

Assessment is the process of observing, recording and otherwise documenting the work children do and how they do it, as a basis for a variety of educational decisions that affect the child. Assessment is integral to curriculum and instruction. In early childhood programs, assessment serves several different purposes: (1) to plan instruction for individuals and groups and for communicating with parents, (2) to identify children who may be in need of specialized services or intervention, and (3) to evaluate how well the program is meeting its goals.

The following guidelines first address the primary use of assessment: for planning instruction and communicating with parents. Guidelines for screening and program evaluation follow. (For additional information on the topic of assessment, see also NAEYC's Position Statement on Standardized Testing of Young Children (NAEYC, 1988) and Unacceptable Trends in Kindergarten Entry and Placement (NAECS/SDE, 1987), and Kamii (1990).)

**Guidelines for planning instruction and communicating with parents.** Assessment of children's development and learning is absolutely necessary if teachers are to provide curriculum and instruction that is both age-appropriate and individually appropriate. An initial assessment is necessary for teachers to get to know children and to adjust the planned curriculum. The appropriate use of initial assessment is to find out what children already know and are able to do and to use this information to adjust the curriculum to the individual children. Too often, initial assessment takes the form of "readiness testing" with young children or "achievement testing" with older children, the results of which are used to exclude children from the program, track them by ability, or otherwise label them. How the initial assessment is conducted

will determine the accuracy and usefulness of the findings. To provide an accurate picture of children's capabilities, teachers must observe children over time; information obtained on one brief encounter may be incomplete or distorted. Likewise, initial assessment information must be used to adjust curriculum and instruction. If assessment data are ignored and no adjustments are made, then the data should not be collected. Moreover, assessment data should be used to bring about benefits for children such as more individualized instruction; it should not be used to recommend that children stay out of a program, be retained in grade, or be assigned to a segregated group based on ability or developmental maturity.

The following principles should guide assessment procedures for children ages 3 through 8:

**1.** Curriculum and assessment are integrated throughout the program; assessment is congruent with and relevant to the goals, objectives, and content of the program.

**2.** Assessment results in benefits to the child such as needed adjustments in the curriculum or more individualized instruction and improvements in the program.

**3.** Children's development and learning in all the domains—physical, social, emotional, and cognitive—and their dispositions and feelings are informally and routinely assessed by teachers' observing children's activities and interactions, listening to them as they talk, and using children's constructive errors to understand their learning.

**4.** Assessment provides teachers with useful information to successfully fulfill their responsibilities: to support children's learning and development, to plan for individuals and groups, and to communicate with parents.

**5.** Assessment involves regular and periodic observation of the child in a wide variety of circumstances that are representative of the child's behavior in the program over time.

**6.** Assessment relies primarily on procedures that reflect the ongoing life of the classroom and typical activities of the children. Assessment avoids approaches that place children in artificial situations, impede the usual learning and developmental experiences in the classroom, or divert chil-

5. The younger the child, the more critical it is that the screening activities involve the manipulation of toys and materials rather than pictures and paper/pencil tasks.

6. If the results of the screening indicate that a child has not performed within an average developmental range, the child is seen individually by an experienced diagnostician who is also an expert in child development.

7. If a comprehensive diagnostic process is recommended after screening, key conditions warranting the implementation of this process should be delineated and documented for the parents in writing in non-technical language they can understand. Throughout the assessment process, parents must be informed in writing about diagnostic resources, parent rights and reasons for referral, as well as rights of refusal.

**Guidelines for program evaluation and accountability.** Whenever children are served in a program, it is essential that the program be evaluated regularly to ensure that it is meeting its goals and that children and families are benefitting from participation. In recent years, standardized test scores have become the primary vehicle for demonstrating that schools and teachers are accountable. Too often, this practice has led to blaming children who are ill-served by the program or punishing districts that do not measure up to expectations without examining all components of the program. Overreliance on standardized achievement test scores as the only indicator of program effectiveness has had a detrimental effect on curriculum. Therefore, any effort to reform curriculum must be matched by testing reform. Data obtained through program evaluation should be used to identify areas in need of staff development or other support.

The following guidelines are designed to guide program evaluation efforts:

1. In constructing assessment procedures related to evaluating programs or determining program accountability, no other stated principles of curriculum or assessment are violated.

2. Performance data of children collected by teachers to plan instruction are summarized and quantified by teachers and administrators to use in evaluating how well the program is meeting its goals for children and families.

3. The program uses multiple indicators of progress in all developmental domains to evaluate the effect of the program on children's development and learning. Group-administered, standardized, multiple-choice achievement tests are prohibited before third grade, preferably fourth. (See Kamii, Ed., 1990.)

4. All components of the program are evaluated to judge program effectiveness within the overall context of opportunities provided for children and families, including staff development and evaluation, parent satisfaction and feelings about how well the program serves their children and their opportunities for involvement, administration, physical environment, and health and safety. Results of outside, independent evaluation such as that obtained from program accreditation is useful in program evaluation.

5. Programs which are mandated to use a standardized test of children's progress for program evaluation or accountability purposes employ a sampling method whenever feasible. This approach eliminates the need to subject all children to a testing procedure which can consume large blocks of time, cause undue stress, and produce results which are used for unwarranted decisions about individual children.

## Applying the assessment guidelines

As with curriculum decisions, assessment decisions should reflect the consensual opinion of early childhood professionals as well as assessment experts. To facilitate this process, we have phrased the foregoing guidelines as questions. Evaluation of current or proposed assessment procedures and/or instruments should result in affirmative responses to **all** of these questions.

### Questions to ask in evaluating a program's assessment procedures

1. Is the assessment procedure based on the goals and objectives of the specific curriculum used in the program?

2. Are the results of assessment used to benefit children, i.e., to plan for individual children, improve instruction, identify children's interests and needs, and individualize instruction, rather than label, track, or fail children?

3. Does the assessment procedure address all domains of learning and development—social, emotional, physical, and cognitive—as well as children's feelings and dispositions toward learning?

4. Does assessment provide useful information to teachers to help them do a better job?

5. Does the assessment procedure rely on teachers' regular and periodic observations and record-keeping of children's everyday activities and performance so that results reflect children's behavior over time?

6. Does the assessment procedure occur as part of the ongoing life of the classroom rather than in an artificial, contrived context?

7. Is the assessment procedure performance-based, rather than only testing skills in isolation?

8. Does the assessment rely on multiple sources of information about children such as collections of their work, results of teacher interviews and dialogues, as well as observations?

9. Does the assessment procedure reflect individual, cultural, and linguistic diversity? Is it free of cultural, language, and gender biases?

10. Do children appear comfortable and relaxed during assessment rather than tense or anxious?

11. Does the assessment procedure support parents' confidence in their children and their ability as parents rather than threaten or undermine parents' confidence?

12. Does the assessment examine children's strengths and capabilities rather than just their weaknesses or what they do not know?

13. Is the teacher the primary assessor and are teachers adequately trained for this role?

14. Does the assessment procedure involve collaboration among teachers, children, administrators, and parents? Is information from parents used in planning instruction and evaluating children's learning? Are parents informed about assessment information?

15. Do children have an opportunity to reflect on and evaluate their own learning?

**16.** Are children assessed in supportive contexts to determine what they are capable of doing with assistance as well as what they can do independently?

**17.** Is there a systematic procedure for collecting assessment data that facilitates its use in planning instruction and communicating with parents?

**18.** Is there a regular procedure for communicating the results of assessment to parents in meaningful language, rather than letter or number grades, that reports children's individual progress?

## Questions to ask in evaluating screening/diagnostic procedures

**1.** Are screening test results used only as a first step in a systematic diagnostic procedure for identifying children with special needs? Are screening test results **never** used to deny children entrance to a program or as the sole criterion for assignment to a special program?

**2.** Are the screening tests used reliable and valid for the purpose for which they are used? Are the technical adequacies of standardized measures carefully evaluated by knowledgeable professionals?

**3.** Are parents informed in advance when children are screened? Is the purpose and procedure carefully explained to parents and are parents permitted to stay with their child if desired?

**4.** Is the screener knowledgeable about young children and able to relate to them in a positive manner?

**5.** Does the screening procedure involve concrete hands-on activities rather than paper-and-pencil tasks?

**6.** Does the screening procedure lead to systematic diagnosis of potential handicapping conditions or health problems for the children for which this is warranted?

**7.** Are parents informed of the procedures and their rights throughout the screening/diagnosis procedure?

## Questions to ask in evaluating program evaluation procedures

**1.** Is the program evaluation procedure

---

# Model of Learning and Teaching

| What Children Do | What Teachers Do |
|---|---|
| **Awareness** | |
| Experience | Create the environment |
| Acquire an interest | Provide opportunities by introducing |
| Recognize broad parameters | new objects, events, people |
| Attend | Invite interest by posing problem or |
| Perceive | question |
| | Respond to child's interest or shared |
| | experience |
| | Show interest, enthusiasm |
| **Exploration** | |
| Observe | Facilitate |
| Explore materials | Support and enhance exploration |
| Collect information | Provide opportunities for active |
| Discover | exploration |
| Create | Extend play |
| Figure out components | Describe child's activity |
| Construct own understanding | Ask open-ended questions, "What |
| Apply own rules | else could you do?" |
| Create personal meaning | Respect child's thinking and rule |
| | systems |
| | Allow for constructive error |
| **Inquiry** | |
| Examine | Help children refine understanding |
| Investigate | Guide children, focus attention |
| Propose explanations | Ask more focused questions, "What |
| Focus | else works like this? What |
| Compare own thinking | happens if?" |
| with that of others | Provide information when requested, |
| Generalize | "How do you spell?" |
| Relate to prior learning | Help children make connections |
| Adjust to conventional rule | |
| systems | |
| **Utilization** | |
| Use the learning in many | Create vehicles for application in real |
| ways; learning becomes | world |
| functional | Help children apply to new situations |
| Represent learning in various | Provide meaningful situations to use |
| ways | learning |
| Apply to new situations | |
| Formulate new hypotheses | |
| and repeat cycle | |

---

congruent with all other stated principles of curriculum and assessment?

**2.** Does the program evaluation summarize and quantify the results of performance-based assessments of children's progress conducted by classroom teachers?

**3.** Does the program evaluation incorporate many indicators of children's progress, rather than standardized, group-administered achievement test scores?

**4.** Does the program evaluation address all components of the delivery of the program instead of being limited to measuring outcomes for children?

**5.** Is sampling used in situations where the administration of a standardized achievement test is mandated?

# References

American Association for the Advancement of Science. (1989). *Science for all Americans: A project 2061 report on literacy goals in science, mathematics, and technology.* Washington, DC: Author.

Association for Supervision and Curriculum and Development. (1989). *Toward the thinking curriculum: Current cognitive research.* Alexandria, VA: Author.

Bennett, W. J. (1988). *First lessons.* Washington, DC: U.S. Department of Education.

Biber, B. (1984). *Early education and psychological development.* New Haven, CT: Yale University Press.

Bredekamp, S. (Ed.). (1987). *Developmentally appropriate practice in early childhood programs serving children from birth through age 8.* (ex. ed.). Washington, DC: NAEYC.

British Columbia Ministry of Education. (1990). *Primary Program Resource Document.* Victoria, British Columbia: Author.

Chittenden, E., & Courtney, R. (1989). Assessment of young children's reading: Documentation as an alternative to testing. In D. Strickland (Ed.), *Emerging literacy: Young children learn to read and write.* Newark, DE: International Reading Association.

Connecticut Department of Education. (1988). *Guide to program development for kindergarten.* Hartford, CT: Author.

DeVries, R., & Kohlberg, L. (1989). *Constructivist early education: Overview and comparison with other programs.* Washington, DC: NAEYC.

Eisner, E. (1990). Who decides what schools teach? *Phi Delta Kappan, 71*(7), 523–526.

Eisner, W. E., & Vallance, E. (Eds.). (1974). *Conflicting conceptions of curriculum.* Berkeley: McCutchan.

Elkind, D. (1976). *Child development and education.* New York: Oxford University Press.

Elkind, D. (1987). *Miseducation: Preschoolers at risk.* New York: Knopf.

Engel, B. (1990). An approach to evaluation in reading and writing. In C. Kamii (Ed.), *Achievement testing in early childhood education: Games grown-ups play.* Washington, DC: NAEYC.

Erikson, E. (1963). *Childhood and society.* New York: Norton.

FairTest (National Center for Fair and Open Testing). (1990). *Fallout from the testing explosion: How 100 million standardized exams undermine equity and excellence in America's public schools (3rd edition).* Cambridge, MA: FairTest.

Ferreiro, E., & Teberosky, A. (1982). *Literacy before schooling.* Portsmouth, NH: Heinemann.

Garbarino, J. (1989). Early intervention in cognitive development as a strategy for reducing poverty. In G. Miller (Ed.), *Giving children a chance: The case for more effective national policies.* (pp. 23–26). Washington, DC: National Policy Press.

Goodman, K., Goodman, Y., & Hood, W. (1989). *The whole language evaluation book.* Portsmouth, NH: Heinemann.

Hirsch, E. (1987). *Cultural literacy: What every American needs to know.* Boston: Houghton Mifflin.

Illinois Association for Supervision and Curriculum Development. (1989). *Early childhood screening.* Normal, IL: Author.

International Reading Association. (1989). *Literacy development and prefirst grade.* Newark, DE: Author.

Jones, E. (1989). *Emergent curriculum: Planning and letting go.* Unpublished paper. Pasadena, CA: Pacific Oaks College.

Kamii, C. (1982). *Number in preschool and kindergarten: Educational implications of Piaget's Theory.* Washington, DC: NAEYC.

Kamii, C. (Ed.). (1990). *Achievement testing in early childhood education: The games grown-ups play.* Washington, DC: NAEYC.

Kamii, C., & DeVries, R. (1980). *Group games in early childhood education.* Washington, DC: NAEYC.

Katz, L. G. (July, 1989). *Pedagogical issues in early childhood education.* Unpublished document.

Katz, L. G., & Chard, S. (1989). *Engaging children's minds: The project approach.* Norwood, New Jersey: Ablex.

Kessler, S. (in press). Reconceptualizing early childhood education. *Early Childhood Research Quarterly.*

Kleibard, H. (1986). *The struggle for the American curriculum.* Boston: Routledge & Kegan Paul.

Lloyd-Jones, R., & Lunsford, A. A. (Eds.). (1988). *The English Coalition Conference: Democracy through language.* Urbana, IL: National Council of Teachers of English.

Maryland State Department of Education. (1989). *Standards for implementing quality prekindergarten education.* Baltimore, MD: Maryland State Department of Education, Division of Instruction, Language, and Supplementary Programs. (ERIC Document Reproduction Service No. ED 238 525.)

Meisels, S. J. (1985). *Developmental screening in early childhood: A guide.* (rev. ed.). Washington, DC: NAEYC.

Missouri Department of Elementary and Secondary Education. (May, 1989). *Project contruct: Curriculum and assessment specifications.* St. Louis, MO: Author.

National Association for the Education of Young Children. (1988). Position statement on standardized testing of young children 3 through 8 years of age. *Young Children, 43*(3), 42–47.

National Association of Early Childhood Specialists in State Departments of Education. (1987). *Unacceptable trends in kindergarten entry and placement.* Unpublished paper.

National Association of Elementary School Principals. (1990). *Early childhood education and the elementary school principal.* Alexandria, VA: Author.

National Association of State Boards of Education. (1988). *Right from the start: The report of the NASBE task force on early childhood education.* Alexandria, VA: Author.

National Commission on Social Studies in the Schools. (1989). *Charting a course: Social studies for the 21st century.* Washington, DC: Author.

National Commission on Testing and Public Policy. (1990). *From gatekeeper to gateway: Transforming testing in America.* Chestnut Hill, MA: Author.

National Council of Teachers of Mathematics. (1989). *Curriculum and evaluation standards for school mathematics.* Reston, VA: Author.

Rosegrant, T. (1989). The developmental characteristics of three-and-a-half- to five-and-a-half-year-olds and implications for learning. Unpublished paper.

Rothman, R. (May, 1989). What to teach: Reform turns finally to the essential question. *Education Week. 1*(8), 10–11.

Shepard, L. A., & Smith, M. L. (1988). Escalating academic demand in kindergarten: Some nonsolutions. *Elementary School Journal, 89*(2), 135–146.

Smith-Burke, M. T. (1985). Reading and talking: Learning through interaction. In Jaggar, A., & Smith-Burke, M. T. (Eds.). *Observing the language learner.* Newark, DE: International Reading Association.

Spodek, B. (1977). What constitutes worthwhile educational experiences for young children. In B. Spodek (Ed.). *Teaching practices: Reexamining assumptions* (pp. 1–20). Washington, DC: NAEYC.

Spodek, B. (1985). Goals and purposes of educational programs for 4- and 5-year-old children. Final report of the Commission on Appropriate Education. Unpublished document.

Spodek, B. (1988). Conceptualizing today's kindergarten curriculum. *The Elementary School Journal, 89*(2), 203–212.

Spodek, B. (in press). What should we teach kindergarten children? *Educational Leadership.*

Strauss, S. (1987). Educational-developmental psychology and school learning. In L. Liben (Ed.). *Development and learning: Conflict or congruence?* Hillsdale, NJ: Erlbaum.

Teale, W. H. (1988). Developmentally appropriate assessment of reading and writing in the early childhood classroom. *The Elementary School Journal, 89*(2), 173–184.

Teale, W., & Sulzby, E. (Eds.). (1986). *Emergent literacy: Writing and reading.* Norwood, NJ: Ablex.

Vygotsky, L. S. (1978). *Mind in society: The development of psychological processes.* Cambridge, MA: Harvard University Press.

Vygotsky, L. S. (1981). The genesis of higher mental functions. In J. V. Wertsch (Ed.). *The concept of activity in Soviet psychology.* Armonk, NY: M. E. Sharpe.

# Synthesis of Research on Grade Retention

*Although grade retention is widely practiced, it does not help children to "catch up." Retained children may appear to do better in the short term, but they are at much greater risk for future failure then their equally achieving, non-retained peers.*

LORRIE A. SHEPARD
AND MARY LEE SMITH

**Lorrie A. Shepard** is Professor of Research and Evaluation Methodology, University of Colorado School of Education, Campus Box 249, Boulder, CO 80309. **Mary Lee Smith** is Professor of Educational Psychology, Arizona State University College of Education, Tempe, AZ 85287. They are the authors of the 1989 book, *Flunking Grades: Research and Policies on Retention*, published by the Falmer Press in London.

Retaining students in grade is often used as a means to raise educatonal standards. The assumption is that by catching up on prerequisite skills, students should be less at risk for failure when they go on to the next grade. Strict enforcement of promotion standards at every grade is expected both to ensure the competence of high school graduates and lower the dropout rate because learning deficiencies would never be allowed to accumulate. Despite the popular belief that repeating a grade is an effective remedy for students who have failed to master basic skills, however, the large body of research on grade retention is almost uniformly negative.

## Research Evidence

The purpose of this article is to summarize research-based conclusions regarding the effects of grade retention. We then address the discrepancy between research and practice and consider alternatives to retention.

*How many students repeat a grade in school?* Although no national statistics have been collected on grade retention, we recently (1989a) analyzed data from 13 states and the District of Columbia. Our estimate is that 5 to 7 percent of public school children (about 2 children in every classroom of 30) are retained in the U.S. annually. However, annual statistics are not the whole story. A 6 percent annual rate year after year produces a cumulative rate of nonpromotion greater than 50 percent. Even allowing for students who repeat more than one grade, we estimate that by 9th grade approximately half of all students in the U.S. have flunked at least one grade (or are no longer in school). This means that, contrary to public perceptions, current grade failure rates are as high as they were in the 19th century, before the days of social promotion.

*Does repeating a grade improve student achievement?* In a recent meta-analysis of research, Holmes (1989) located 63 controlled studies where retained students were followed up and compared to equally poor-achieving students who went directly on to the next grade. Fifty-four studies showed overall negative effects from retention, even on measures of academic achievement. This means that when retained children went on to the next grade they actually performed more poorly on average than if they had gone on without repeating. Suppose, for example, that retained and control groups both started out at the 10th percentile on standardized achievement tests at the end of 1st grade. The retained group was made to repeat 1st grade while the control group was promoted to 2nd grade. Two years later when the retained children completed 2nd grade, they might be (on average) at the 20th percentile. However, the control children, who started out equally deficient, would finish 2nd grade achieving ahead of their retained counterparts by 0.31 standard deviation units, or at roughly the 30th percentile on average.

When Holmes selected only the 25

Lorrie A. Shepard and Mary Lee Smith, "Synthesis of Research on Grade Retention," *Educational Leadership*, Vol. 47, No. 8, May 1990, pp. 84-88. Reprinted with permission of the Association for Supervision and Curriculum Development.

studies with the greatest degree of statistical control, the negative effect of retention was again confirmed. In the 9 positive studies (out of 63), the apparent benefit of retention tended to diminish over time so that differences in performance between retained and control children disappeared in later grades.

*Does nonpromotion prevent school dropouts?* In a typical end-of-year news story, *USA Today* (Johnson 1988) reported that one-quarter of the 1st graders in a Mississippi community would be held back because they "can't read at a 1st-grade level." Consistent with the view that retention will repair deficient skills and improve students' life chances, the principal explained her decision: "In years past, those students would have been promoted to 2nd grade. Then they might have dropped out in five, six, or seven years."

Researchers of the dropout phenomenon have consistently found a significant relationship between grade retention and dropping out—in the opposite direction, however, from the one imagined by the Mississippi principal. Dropouts are five times more likely to have repeated a grade than are high school graduates. Students who repeat two grades have a probability of dropping out of nearly 100 percent (Association of California Urban School Districts 1985). In the past, these findings were ignored because poor achievement could be the explanation for both grade retention and dropping out. More recently, Grissom and Shepard (1989) conducted three large-scale studies, involving from 20,000 to 80,000 students each. They examined the retention-dropout relation after controlling for achievement and found that with equally poor achievement (and controlling for other background characteristics associated with dropping out), students who repeated a year were 20 to 30 percent more likely to drop out of school. For example, in Austin, Texas, African-American males with below average achievement have a 45 percent chance of dropping out of school; but African-American males with identical achievement scores who have repeated a year of school have a 75 percent chance of leaving school before graduation. A substantially increased risk for dropping out after

**FLUNKING GRADES · RESEARCH AND POLICIES ON RETENTION**

EDITED BY LORRIE A SHEPARD AND MARY LEE SMITH

The Falmer Press
Education Policy Perspectives Series

repeating a grade was found even in a large affluent suburban school district with only a 4 percent dropout rate.

*What are the emotional effects of retention?* In a much-quoted study of childhood stressors by Yamamoto (1980), children rated the prospect of repeating a grade as more stressful than "wetting in class" or being caught stealing. Going blind or losing a parent were the only two life events that children said would be more stressful than being retained. The negative connotations of being held back pervade the American school culture. When Byrnes (1989) interviewed children and used euphemisms to refer to spending two years in the same grade, even 1st graders said, "Oh, you mean flunking." Eighty-seven percent of the children interviewed said that being retained made them feel "sad," "bad," "upset," or "embarrassed." Only 6 percent of retained children gave positive answers about how retention made them feel, like, "you learn more," or "it lets you catch up." Interview transcripts from both high-achieving students and retained students revealed a widely shared perception that retention is a necessary punishment for being bad in class or failing to learn.

Holmes' (1989) synthesis of controlled studies included nearly 50 studies with some social or emotional outcome measures. On average, Holmes found that retained students do more poorly than matched controls on follow-up measures of social adjustment, attitudes toward school, behavioral outcomes, and attendance.

The above research findings indicate, then, that contrary to popular belief,

repeating a grade actually worsens achievement levels in subsequent years. The evidence contradicts commonsense reasoning that retention will reduce school dropout rates; it seems more likely that school policies meant to increase the number of grade retentions will exacerbate dropout rates. The negative social-emotional consequences of repeating represents the only area where conventional wisdom is consistent with research findings: kids have always hated being retained, and the studies bear that out.

## Reconciling Research and Practice

Policies of grade retention persist in the face of negative evidence because teachers and parents cannot conduct controlled experiments. Without controlled comparisons, retention looks as if it works, especially if you believe that it does. Consider how the performance of individual retained and control children is interpreted by teachers. A control child does very poorly academically, is considered for retention, but is socially promoted. Consistent with the 30th percentile figure quoted from the Holmes (1989) study above, the control child ends up in the bottom half of the class, still struggling. Teachers then say, "If only we had retained him, his performance would have improved." Meanwhile, a comparable child does repeat, shows improvement during the repeat year on some skills, but in the next grade does even more poorly than the control child. Believing that retention helps, however, and without being able to see the controlled comparison, teachers accept any improvement during the repeat year itself as proof that retention works; and about poor performance in the next grade they say, "He would have done even more poorly without the extra year," or "At least we tried."

Schools are also under considerable political pressure to maintain acceptably high levels of grade retention as proof of high standards. Public belief in the efficacy of retention creates a powerful mandate: Flunk poor-achieving students for their own good as well as society's good. Without a simple way to explain to the public that at-risk students are more likely to learn and stay in school if not retained, schools may sacrifice the best interests of individual children to appease popular demands.

What alternatives are there to retention? There are numerous ways to provide extra instructional help focussed on a student's specific learning needs within the context of normal-grade promotion. Remedial help, before- and after-school programs, summer school, instructional aides to work with target children in the regular classroom, and no-cost peer tutoring are all more effective than retention. Unlike retention, each of these solutions has a research base showing positive achievement gains for participating children over controls. Cross-age peer tutoring, for example, where an average 5th grade student might tutor a 2nd grader who is behind in math, shows learning gains for both the target students and the tutors (Hartley 1977).

One of the fears about social promotion is that teachers will pass on deficient students endlessly as if no one had noticed their problem. Rather than ban retention but do nothing else, creative groups of teachers in a few schools have developed staffing teams (of regular teachers) to work out plans with the next-grade receiving teachers about how to address the learning difficulties for students who otherwise would have been retention candidates. Similarly, some schools "place" poorly performing students in the next grade with a formally agreed upon Individualized Educational Plan (IEP), akin to the special education model of intervention. The decision to allow a deficient student to advance to the next grade with a plan for special help is analogous to prevalent school policies for gifted students. Instead of double promoting academically gifted students, schools keep them in their normal grade and provide them with enriched instruction. There are two reasons enrichment is preferred over skipping grades. First, normal grade placement is better socially for academically able students. Second, these able children are not equally advanced in every subject, and the amount they are ahead does not come in convenient nine-month units. Parallel arguments can be used to explain why retention does not improve achievement but promotion plus remediation does. Finally, there is reason to believe that struggling students need a more inspired and engaging curriculum, one that involves them in solving meaningful problems, rather than repetitive, by-rote drills on basic skills. Outmoded learning theories (e.g., Thorndike's [1972] S-R bonds and behaviorism's programmed instruction [Mager 1962]) require children to master component skills before they are allowed to go on to comprehension and problem solving; this theory consigns slow learners to school work that is not only boring but devoid of any connection to the kinds of problems they encounter in the real world.

The second wave of educational reform, exemplified by curricular changes in California and the new standards of the National Council of Teachers of Mathematics, is based on more current learning theory from cognitive and constructivist psychology (Resnick 1987, Wertsch 1985), which holds that skills cannot be learned effectively nor applied to new problems unless the skills are learned in context. For example, students who are given lots and lots of problems to solve about how much tile to buy to floor a room with irregular dimensions and how much paint to buy are more likely to be better at both multiplication facts and problem solving than students who must memorize all

---

### Highlights of Research on Grade Retention

A synthesis of the research on grade retention shows that:

• Grade failure rates are as high as they were in the 19th century, before the days of social promotion: Although annual statistics show only about a 6 percent annual rate for retention, year after year that produces a cumulative rate of nonpromotion greater than 50 percent. By 9th grade approximately half of all students in the U.S. have flunked at least one grade (or are no longer in school).

• Retained children actually perform more poorly on average when they go on to the next grade then if they had been promoted without repeating a grade.

• Dropouts are five times more likely to have repeated a grade than are high school graduates. Students who repeat two grades have a probability of dropping out of nearly 100 percent.

• Children in Yamamoto's (1980) study of childhood stressors rated the prospect of repeating a grade as more stressful than "wetting in class" or being caught stealing. The only two life events they felt would be more stressful than being retained were going blind or losing a parent. Both high-achieving and retained students interviewed by Byrnes (1989) viewed retention as a necessary punishment for being bad in class or failing to learn.

• There are many alternatives to retention that are more effective in helping low achievers. These include remedial help, before- and after-school programs, summer school, instructional aides to work with target children in the regular classroom, and no-cost peer tutoring. Groups of teachers in some schools have developed staffing teams to work out plans with the next-grade receiving teachers about how to address the learning difficulties for students who otherwise would have been retention candidates. Some schools "place" poor performing students in the next grade with a formally agreed upon Individualized Educational Plan (IEP), akin to the special education model of intervention.

• The annual cost to school districts of retaining 2.4 million students per year is nearly $10 billion. Summer school costs only approximately $1,300 per student compared to $4,051 for a repeated grade. At a wage of $6 an hour for an aide, it would take the savings from only 1.6 retained students to have an extra adult in every classroom full time to give extra attention to low achieving students.

---

**Remedial help, before- and after-school programs, summer school, instructional aides to work with target children in the regular classroom, and no-cost peer tutoring are all more effective than retention.**

# Children rated the prospect of repeating a grade as more stressful than "wetting in class" or being caught stealing.

retained to more effective instructional programs.

## The Futility of Flunking

Researchers have not been able to tell why retention doesn't work as intended. Some speculate that the negative emotional effects of repeating harm subsequent learning. Others suggest that going through the same material again is a crude and ineffective way to individualize instruction since a child may be more than one year behind in some subjects and only a few months behind in others. Because retention itself is considered to be the treatment, there is usually no additional effort to correct the poor quality of teaching and learning that occurred the first time through. In other words, the child may have failed to achieve grade-level standards because the programs or teachers he had were ineffective. Merely repeating the same curriculum or instruction is not likely to fix the problem. If extra money exists to support remediation along with retention, then educators

their multiplication tables before confronting even one such problem.

How much does retention cost? Can the dollars saved by not retaining students be reallocated to more effective alternatives? Based on an annual retention rate of 6 percent and a per pupil cost of $4,051 (U.S. Department of Education, Center for Education Statistics), we estimated that U.S. school districts spend nearly $10 billion a year to pay for the extra year of schooling necessitated by retaining 2.4 million students (see study cited in author's note at end of article).

Ten billion dollars would go a long way to pay for remedial programs, summer school, classroom aides, or reduced class size to help at-risk students learn. For example, summer school costs only approximately $1,300 per student compared to $4,051 for a repeated grade. Even special education help for a learning disabled child costs on average only $1,600 (half of which is spent on testing and staffing instead of instruction). At a wage of $6 an hour for an aide, it would take the savings from only 1.6 retained students to have an extra adult in every classroom full time.

Ironically, however, retention does not appear as a line item in any educational budget. No jurisdiction appears to bear the cost of the extra year. Because most students do not stay in the same district for 13 years of school, it does not matter to local districts that some students take 14 years. If a student stays in a district only 4 years, then the cost of grades 1–2–3–4 is the same as grades 1–2–3–3. Even states are not aware that they are paying for an extra year. Because the real cost of retention is never explicitly acknowledged, local educators find it difficult to redirect savings from students not

## No Benefits from Kindergarten Retention

The decade of the 1980s saw a dramatic rise in the number of children asked to repeat kindergarten. In districts with special programs for "unready" kindergartners, as many as 50 percent were held back (California Department of Education 1988). An extra year before 1st grade is now offered in a variety of different forms: transition classrooms before 1st grade, developmental kindergarten before kindergarten, and straight repeating of kindergarten. According to its advocates, kindergarten retention, because it is intended to prevent school failure caused by immaturity, is different from retention in later grades.

Controlled studies do not support the benefits claimed for extra-year programs, however, and negative side effects occur just as they do for retention in later grades. In a review of 16 controlled studies on the effects of extra-year programs, the predominant finding is one of no difference (Shepard 1989). For example, when researchers followed extra-year children to the end of 1st grade or as far as 5th grade and compared their performance to unready children whose parents refused the extra year, the extra-year children performed no better academically despite being a year older for their grade. The conclusion of "no benefit" holds true even for studies where children were selected on the basis of immaturity rather than for academic risk, and even where a special transition curriculum was offered rather than repeating regular kindergarten.

Although the majority of teachers believe that retention in kindergarten does not carry a social stigma "if handled properly," extra-year children are more likely to have lower self-concepts and poorer attitudes toward school compared to controls (Shepard 1989). Parent interviews reveal both short-term and long-term distress associated with the retention decision such as teasing by peers, tears because friends are going on, and references years later like, "If I had only been able . . . , I would be in 3rd grade now." (Shepard and Smith 1989b).

Various analysts have suggested that kindergarten retention is an educational fad, gaining popularity because of the apparent need to remove unready children from increasingly narrow academic demands in kindergarten and 1st grade. Long periods of seat work, worksheets, and "staying in the lines" are required of children, inconsistent with the normal development of 5- and 6-year-olds. Ironically, retention and holding children out of school, intended to protect them from inappropriate expectations, actually contribute to the escalation of demands, thereby placing more and more children at risk. As kindergartens become populated with 6-year-olds who have had 3 years of preschool, teachers find it difficult to teach to the normal 5-year-olds in the class. The problem can only be solved with more developmentally appropriate curriculum in the early grades and reform of harmful instructional practices, something that many national associations have called for, including the National Association for the Education of Young Children, the National Association of State Boards of Education, the Association for Childhood Education International, the Association for Supervision and Curriculum Development, the International Reading Association, the National Association of Elementary School Principals, and the National Council of Teachers of English. Until this problem of kindergarten retention is addressed on a national scale, educators must deal with its consequences—which will negatively affect the quality of education at every level of schooling.

—Lorrie A. Shepard and Mary Lee Smith

should ask why students can't receive the extra help in the context of their normal grade placement.

The public and many educators find it difficult to give up on retention. To do so seems to mean accepting or condoning shamefully deficient skills for many high school graduates. It is easier for the public to credit research findings that retention harms self-esteem and increases the likelihood of dropping out than to believe the most critical finding—that retention worsens rather than improves the level of student achievement in years following the repeat year. Only with this fact firmly in mind, verified in over 50 controlled studies, does it make sense to subscribe to remediation and other within-grade instructional efforts which have modest but positive evidence of success. Perhaps the futility of flunking students to make them learn would be more obvious if it were recognized that statistically, social promotion has been dead for at least 10 years (i.e., cumulative retention rates are very high). Today's graduates and dropouts are emerging from a system that has imposed fierce non-promotion rates, flunking between 30 and 50 percent of all entering students at least once in their school careers. Strict promotion standards have been enforced for a decade and, as would have been predictable from the retention research findings on achievement, have not appreciably improved the performance of current graduates. Ultimately, hopes for more dramatic improvements in student learning (than can be expected from promotion plus remediation) will only come from thoroughgoing school changes —more support and opportunities for teachers to work together in addressing the problems of hard-to-teach children (Martin 1988), and curricular reforms designed to engage all children

## U.S. school districts spend nearly $10 billion a year to pay for the extra year of schooling necessitated by retaining 2.4 million students.

in meaningful learning tasks that provide both the context and the purpose for acquiring basic skills (Resnick 1987).

*References*

Association of California Urban School Districts (ACUSD). (1985). *Dropouts from California's Urban School Districts: Who Are They? How Do We Count Them? How Can We Hold Them (or at Least Educate Them)?* Los Angeles: ACUSD.

Byrnes, D. A. (1989). "Attitudes of Students, Parents, and Educators Toward Repeating a Grade." In *Flunking Grades: Research and Policies on Retention*, edited by L.A. Shepard and M.L. Smith. London: The Falmer Press.

California Department of Education. (1988). *Here They Come: Ready or Not! Report of the School Readiness Task Force.* Sacramento: CDE.

Grissom, J.B., and Shepard, L.A. (1989). "Repeating and Dropping Out of School." In *Flunking Grades: Research and Policies on Retention*, edited by L.A. Shepard and M.L. Smith. London: The Falmer Press.

Hartley, S.S. (1977). "Meta-Analysis of the Effects of Individually Paced Instruction in Mathematics." Unpublished doctoral dissertation, University of Colorado at Boulder.

Holmes, C.T. (1989). "Grade-Level Retention Effects: A Meta-Analysis of Research Studies." In *Flunking Grades: Research and Policies on Retention*, edited by L.A. Shepard and M.L. Smith. London: The Falmer Press.

Johnson, H. (April 15–17, 1988). "Reforms Stem a 'Rising Tide' of Mediocrity," *USA Today*: 1–2.

Mager, R.F. (1962). *Preparing Instructional Objectives.* Fearon Publishers.

Martin, A. (1988). "Screening, Early Intervention, and Remediation: Obscuring Children's Potential." *Harvard Educational Review* 58: 488–501.

Resnick, L.B. (1987). *Education and Learning to Think.* Washington, D.C.: National Academy Press.

Shepard, L.A. (1989). "A Review of Research on Kindergarten Retention." In *Flunking Grades: Research and Policies on Retention*, edited by L.A. Shepard and M.L. Smith. London: The Falmer Press.

Shepard, L.A., and M.L. Smith, eds. (1989a). *Flunking Grades: Research and Policies on Retention.* London: The Falmer Press.

Shepard, L.A., and M.L. Smith. (1989b). "Academic and Emotional Effects of Kindergarten Retention in One School District." In *Flunking Grades: Research and Policies on Retention*, edited by L.A. Shepard and M.L. Smith. London: The Falmer Press.

Thorndike, E.L. (1922). *The Psychology of Arithmetic.* New York: Macmillan.

Wertsch, J.V., ed. (1985). *Culture, Communications, and Cognition: Vygotskian Perspectives*, 1985 vol. New York: Cambridge University Press.

Yamamoto, K. (1980). "Children Under Stress: The Causes and Cures." *Family Weekly, Ogden Standard Examiner*: 6–8.

*Authors' note:* Portions of this article were developed for the Center for Policy Research in Education Policy Briefs. (1990, January). "Repeating Grades in School: Current Practice and Research Evidence." New Jersey: Rutgers, The State University of New Jersey.

# Understanding Bilingual/Bicultural Young Children

## Lourdes Diaz Soto

*Dr. Lourdes Diaz Soto is Assistant Professor of Early Childhood Education at The Pennsylvania State University. A former preschool teacher, she studies the learning environments of culturally and linguistically diverse young children.*

Early childhood educators have long created exciting and enriching environments for young children but may find an additional challenge when attempting to meet the needs of bilingual/bicultural learners. Teachers currently working with young linguistically and culturally diverse children have asked questions such as: "I feel confident with the art, music and movement activities I have implemented, but how can I best address the needs of speakers of other languages? Are there specific educational strategies that I should incorporate to enhance second language learning? What practical applications can I gain from the research evidence examining second language learning and successful instructional approaches in bilingual early childhood education?"

This review examines:

● demographic and educational trends pointing to the growing numbers of

**More and more bilingual/bicultural children are appearing in early childhood classrooms across the country.**

bilingual/bicultural young children in America today

● misconceptions about young children learning a second language

● successful educational approaches in early childhood bilingual education

● practical applications of existing research which can be readily implemented by early childhood educators.

### Demographic and educational trends

Although the reliability of statistics over the past nine years describing the size and characteristics of the non-English language background (NELB) population has been questioned (Wong Fillmore, in press), it is clear from existing data and projections that language minority students comprise an increasing proportion of our youngest learners. The number of NELB children

aged birth to 4 years old rose steadily from 1.8 million (1976) to a projected 2.6 million in 1990, while the number of children aged 5 to 14 are projected to rise from 3.6 million to 5.1 million in the year 2000 (Oxford, 1984). Additional evidence points to "minority" enrollments, which include culturally diverse learners, ranging from 70 percent to 96 percent in the nation's 15 largest school districts (Hodgkinson, 1985).

Immigrant children from diverse, developing nations such as Haiti, Vietnam, Cambodia, El Salvador, Guatemala, Honduras, and Laos are entering classrooms which are usually unprepared to receive them. La Fontaine (1987) estimates that two-thirds of school-age, language-minority children may not be receiving the language assistance needed to succeed in school. This situation is bound to intensify with the projected increases in total school-age population of language-minority students, ranging from 35 percent to 40 percent by the year 2000 (Oxford, 1984). Existing demographic data provides evidence that meeting the educational needs of bilingual/bicultural young children is an important mandate for our schools.

The field of Bilingual Early Childhood Education has evolved from two educational domains, contributing to differing philosophies and practices. The elementary domain has, with some exceptions, largely emphasized formal language learning instruction; while the early childhood domain has emphasized a variety of approaches including natural language acquisition. Based upon existing bilingual research and what we know about how young children develop, a supportive, natural, language-rich environment, affording acceptance and meaningful interactions, appears optimal.

Early childhood educators are faced with a recurrent challenge, however, when programs earmarked for speakers of other languages are continually viewed as compensatory, or incorporate deficit philosophies. The practice of many instructional programs has been to develop English proficiency at the expense of the native language. The latter approach is called "subtractive" (Lambert, 1975) because the language learning process substitutes one language for another. This form of "bilingual education" may be a misnomer, since it continues to foster monolingualism (Snow & Hakuta, 1987).

Language learning and cultural enhancement need to be viewed as a resource, and not as a deficiency. Garcia (1986) has suggested that early childhood bilingualism includes the following characteristics:
• the child is able to comprehend and produce linguistic aspects of two languages
• the child is exposed naturally to two systems of language as used in the form of social interaction during early childhood
• both languages are developed at the same time.

Garcia (1983) notes that definitions of early childhood bilingualism must consider linguistic diversity, as well as social and cognitive parameters. Teachers of young children need a broad educational framework because a child's social, mental, and emotional worlds are an integral part of language learning.

Simplistic categorizations of bilingual children are not appropriate, since a variety of dimensions and possibilities exist for individual learners. Both experienced and novice bilingual/bicultural educators have noted differing educational terminology, reflecting the political mood of the nation. The table on page 32 illustrates the variety of terms in use. For example, the term "limited English proficient" (LEP) often cited in the literature points to a child's limitation rather than strength. The definitions proposed by Snow (1987) provide both clarity and recency, and are presented in the table in an attempt to show the range of concepts related to second language education. Casanova (1990) introduced the term "speakers of other languages" (SOL), helping to portray a positive attribute. The addition of the term "speakers of other languages" seems especially useful because there is ample documentation of the existence of both bilingual and multilingual young children in our schools.

Educators need to think in terms of "additive" (Lambert, 1975) bilingualism by incorporating practices which will enhance, enrich, and optimize educational opportunities for second language learners. Minimum standards and compensatory approaches are likely to sustain the existing educational difficulties faced by second language learners, speakers of other languages (SOL), and monolingual (EO) learners currently being deprived of a second language.

## Misconceptions about young learners

A variety of misconceptions about second language acquisition and young learners exists (McLaughlin, 1984). **One misconception is that young children acquire language more easily than adults.** This idea was borne of the assumption that children are biologically programmed to acquire languages.

Although we know that early, simultaneous bilingualism will not harm young children's language development, and that they are capable of acquiring a second language without explicit instructions, it is a myth to think that children find the process "painless" (Hakuta, 1986).

Experimental research comparing young children and adults in second language learning has consistently indicated poorer performance by young children, except in pronunciation. Factors leading to the impression that young children acquire languages more easily are that children have fewer inhibitions, and greater frequency of social interactions (McLaughlin, 1984).

**A second, related misconception states that the younger the child, the more quickly a second language is acquired.** There is no evidence of a critical period for second language learning with the possible exception of accent (Hakuta, 1986). Studies reported by Krashen, Long, and Scarcella (1979), which examine rate of second language acquisition, favor adults. In addition,

### Table. Explanation of Terms Used in Second Language Education

| | |
|---|---|
| **Linguistic minority student** | *speaks the language of a minority group, e.g., Vietnamese* |
| **Linguistic majority student** | *speaks language of the majority group, i.e., English in the U.S.* |
| **Limited English proficient** | *any language background (LEP) student who has limited speaking skills in English as a second language* |
| **Non-English proficient (NEP)** | *has no previous experience learning English; speaks only the home language* |
| **English Only (EO)** | *is monolingual English speaker* |
| **Fluent English proficient** | *speaks both English and another language at home. This student speaks English fluently, e.g., ethnically diverse student born in the U.S., who speaks a second language at home.* |

(Adapted from Snow, 1987)

adolescent learners acquire a second language faster than younger learners. Young children who receive natural exposure to a second language, however, are likely to eventually achieve higher levels of second language proficiency than adults.

It may be that "threshold levels" (Cummins, 1977; Skutnabb-Kangas, 1977) of native language proficiency are needed by young language minority learners in order to reap the benefits of

# It is not true that young children learn a new language more quickly and easily than adults.

becoming bilingual. Young children, as a rule, will eventually catch up to, and surpass, most adults, but we need to provide them with a necessary gift of time.

**A third misconception is that there is a single path to acquiring a second language in childhood.** Wong Fillmore's (1976, 1985, 1986) research emphasizes the complex relationship among individual differences in young second language learners. Wong Fillmore (1985) suggests that three interconnected processes, including the social, linguistic, and cognitive domains, are responsible for variability in language learning. Learner characteristics contribute substantially to differential second language learning in children, but the relationship between learner characteristics and outcomes is not simple. No one characteristic can determine language learning (e.g., gregariousness) because variables such as situations, input, and interactions are also important (Wong Fillmore, 1986).

The research viewing individual differences points to the fact that young learners' second language acquisition abilities vary a great deal and are dependent upon social situations. Teachers of young children need to be cognizant of these variabilities by becoming keen observers of existing knowledge and abilities (Genishi, 1989). The assessment of language is a complex en-

deavor, and informal observations and teacher documentation can be extremely valuable tools. Readers are referred to Genishi and Dyson (1984) for a practical and sensitive review of how to assess progress in second language acquisition.

The second language learning process cannot be isolated from the young child's cultural learning. Ethnographic studies examining linguistically and culturally diverse children have found that classroom patterns also need to be culturally responsive, since differing approaches may work well with diverse children. For instance, Phillips (1972) found that Native American children were more willing to participate in group speaking activities than non-Native American children. Also, Au and Jordan (1981) found that reading and test scores improved when teachers incorporated narrative speech patterns such as talk story and overlapping speech into classroom routines with native Hawaiian children. Young children need to develop a positive and confident sense of biculturalism.

A great deal of trial and error takes place when a young child acquires a second language (McLaughlin, 1984). Learning to walk may serve as an example of another skill where exploration and experimentation are necessary. Young children progress at their own rate and persist until the skill is mastered. An accepting attitude is necessary during the trial and error phases of language acquisition. Rigid instructional practices emphasizing grammar construction are not appropriate because they can confuse and interfere with the natural developmental progression of second language acquisition (Felix, 1978, Lightbrown, 1977). The developmentally appropriate instructional practices advocated by NAEYC (Bredekamp, 1987) apply to second language learners as well. Young bilingual/bicultural children experience the same developmental progressions, with additional challenges involving second language/cultural learning.

## Successful instructional approaches

In the United States, bilingual education is typically defined as an educational program for language minority students, in which instruction is provided in the child's primary language

while the child acquires sufficient English skills to function academically. As noted earlier, an *additive* approach focuses on enrichment by the addition of a second language while supporting the native language, and a *subtractive* approach teaches a second language as a replacement, often at the expense of the native language. Programs that offer no aid to students learning a second language are referred to as "sink or swim" or "submersion" efforts (Snow, 1987). While it is beyond the scope of this paper to examine the pervasive "English Only" attitudes in our nation today, it should be noted that bilingual instruction is controversial, and that the sociopolitical climate has often prompted the needs of young bilingual/bicultural children to be overlooked. It is also often the case that programs purporting to include bilingual approaches, in truth, emphasize English only, and a "sink or swim" approach.

Nevertheless, three bilingual education approaches are prevalent for preschoolers and early elementary school students (Ovando & Collier, 1985). The **transitional** approach is widespread and emphasizes the rapid development of English language skills, so the student can participate in the mainstreamed setting as soon as possible. Native language instruction is used initially but the major focus is generally to quickly transfer the learner to the mainstreamed setting. We need to look carefully at these programs in light of Cummins' (1979, 1984, 1985) research, emphasizing the need for learners to obtain optimal levels of native language proficiency.

The **maintenance/developmental** approach emphasizes the development of language skills in the home language, with an additional goal of English mastery. This strategy enhances the child's native language and allows learners to gain concepts in the native language while introducing English as a Second Language (ESL). Children are usually served by additional "pull out" English as a Second Language (ESL) instruction from teachers trained in ESL methods.

The **two-way** bilingual approach serves both the language majority and the language minority, expecting both groups of learners to become bilingual, and to experience academic success. An advantage of the two-way bilingual approach is that children are afforded an opportunity to participate in culturally and linguistically diverse intergroup relations. Recent research points to long-term attitudinal effects from this newly emerging bilingual approach (Collier, 1989).

The role of Head Start in Bilingual Early Childhood Education needs to be acknowledged in light of exemplary service for over 25 years (U.S. Department of Health and Human Services, 1990). Soledad Arenas (1980) describes a bilingual early childhood Head Start effort initiated by Administration for Children, Youth and Families (ACYF). Four contracts were awarded throughout the nation, including: Un Marco Abierto at the High/Scope Center in Ypsilanti, Michigan; Nuevas Fronteras de Aprendizaje at the University of California; Alerta at Columbia University; and Amanecer in San Antonio, Texas. Each program differed considerably, but was based upon an additive philosophy, and serviced Spanish-speaking Head Start children. The evaluation conducted by Juarez and Associates (1980), viewing the impact of the programs over a three-and-a-half year period, found the bilingual preschool curricula to be effective for both Spanish and English preferring young children. In addition, the evaluation concluded that parent and teacher attitudes were favorable, that models can be implemented in differing geographical locations, and that dual language strategies were most related to positive child outcomes.

An important and thorough review of bilingual education research involving 23 different programs found that preschool, elementary, and middle school children who were enrolled in the bilingual programs reviewed, outperformed children on a variety of standardized measures in nonbilingual programs, regardless of the language used for testing (Willig, 1985). Also, research examining bilingualism and cognitive competence favors the attainment of higher levels of bilingual proficiency (Barrik & Swain, 1974; Cummins & Gulutson, 1974; Cummins & Mulcahy, 1976; Duncan & De Avila, 1979; Lessler & Quinn, 1982; Peal & Lambert, 1962; Skutnabb-Kangas, 1977; Hakuta, 1986). Advanced bilingualism has been found to be associated with cognitive flexibility and divergent thinking (Hakuta, 1986). These are powerful findings in an era when the usefulness of bilingual approaches continues to be questioned.

It has been suggested that successful programs progress from native language instruction to initial second language learning, to a stage of enrichment and eventually a return to the native language instruction via the incorporation of literature and social studies, in order to incorporate a healthy sense of biculturalism (Krashen & Biber, 1988). The three components of successful programs serving limited English proficient children reviewed by Krashen and Biber include:

● high-quality subject matter instruction in the native language without concurrent translation

● development of literacy in the native language

● comprehensible input in English

The Carpinteria Preschool Program (Keatinge, 1984; Krashen & Biber, 1988) is particularly interesting because of the emphasis on native language instruction. The children in this program received instruction in Spanish, yet outperformed comparison learners on a test of conversational English (Bilingual Syntax Measure), and exceeded published norms on tests of school readiness (School Readiness Inventory), and academic achievement (California Achievement Test). This particular program supports Cummins' (1984) contention that learners need to obtain a "threshold level" or optimal level of native language proficiency. It appears that native language instruction actually gave students an advantage in their acquisition of a second language.

What can we conclude from this discussion? In an attempt to summarize selected research findings regarding second language acquisition and successful approaches to bilingual education, a list of practical classroom applications is proposed.

## Practical applications for teachers of young children

As a caretaker in a decision-making capacity, the early childhood educator plays a critical role in the lives of linguistically and culturally diverse young children. The early childhood setting becomes a home away from home, the first contact with non-family members, the first contact with culturally different people, and the first experience with non-native speakers. A teacher's attitude and knowledge base is crucial in setting the educational goals of acceptance and appreciation of diversity (Ramsey, 1987). The possibilities are endless for teachers of young children who, as role models, are in a unique position to establish the tone, or "classroom climate," through decision making, collaboration, interactions, and activities.

Teachers of young children are currently implementing a variety of educationally sound strategies. In addition, based upon the recent research, and what we know about young children, we can:

1. Accept individual differences with regard to language-learning time frames. It's a myth to think that young children can learn a language quickly and easily. Avoid pressures to "rush" and "push out" children to join the mainstream classrooms. Young children need time to acquire, explore, and experience second language learning.

2. Accept children's attempts to communicate, because trial and error are a part of the second language learning process. Negotiating meaning, and collaboration in conversations, is important. Children should be given opportunities to practice both native and newly established language skills. Adults should not dominate the conversations; rather, children should be listened to. Plan and incorporate opportunities for conversation such as dramatic play, storytime, puppetry, peer interactions, social experiences, field trips, cooking and other enriching activities.

3. Maintain an additive philosophy by recognizing that children need to acquire new language skills instead of replacing existing linguistic skills. Afford young children an opportunity to retain their native language and culture. Allow young learners ample social opportunities.

4. Provide a stimulating, active, diverse linguistic environment with many opportunities for language use in meaningful social interactions. Avoid rigid or didactic grammatical approaches with young children. Children enjoy informal play experiences, dramatizations, puppetry, telephone conversations, participation in children's literature, and social interactions with peers.

5. Incorporate culturally responsive experiences for all children. Valuing each child's home culture and incorporating meaningful/active participation will enhance interpersonal skills, and contribute to academic and social success.

6. Use informal observations to guide the planning of activities, interactions, and conversations for speakers of other languages.

**7.** Provide an **accepting** classroom climate that values culturally and linguistically diverse young children. We know that young children are part of today's natural resources, capable of contributing to tomorrow's multi-cultural/multilingual society.

## References

Arenas, S. (1980, May/June). Innovations in bilingual/multicultural curriculum development. *Children Today*. Washington, DC: U.S. Government Printing Office No. 80–31161.

Au, K., & Jordan, C. (1981). Teaching reading to Hawaiian children: Finding a culturally appropriate solution. In H. T. Trueba & G. P. Guthrie (Eds.), *Culture and the bilingual classroom: Studies in classroom ethnography*. Cambridge, MA: Newbury House.

Baker, C. (1988). *Key issues in bilingualism and bilingual education*. Clevedon, Avon, England: Multilingual Matters, Ltd.

Barrik, H., & Swain M. (1974). English-French bilingual education in the early grades: The Elgin study. *Modern Language Journal, 58*, 392–403.

Bredekamp, S. (1987). (Ed.). *Developmentally appropriate practice in early childhood programs serving children from birth through age 8*. Washington, DC: NAEYC.

Casanova, U. (1990). *Shifts in bilingual education policy and the knowledge base*. Tuscon, AZ: Research Symposia of the National Association of Bilingual Educators.

Dulay, H., & Burt, M. (1974). Natural sequences in child second language acquisition. *Language Learning, 24*, 37–53.

Duncan, S. E., & DeAvila, E. (1979). Bilingualism and cognition: Some recent findings. *NABE Journal, 4*, 15–50.

Escobedo, T. (1983). *Early childhood bilingual education. A Hispanic perspective*. New York: Teachers College Press, Columbia University.

Felix, S. W. (1978). Some differences between first and second language acquisition. In C. Waterson & C. Snow (Eds.), *The development of communication*. New York: Wiley.

Garcia, E. (1983). *Early childhood bilingualism*. Albuquerque: University of New Mexico.

Garcia, E. (1986). Bilingual development and the education of bilingual children during early childhood. *American Journal of Education, 11*, 96–121.

Collier, V. (1989). Academic achievement, attitudes, and occupation among graduates of two-way bilingual classes. Paper presented at the American Educational Research Association, San Francisco, California.

Contreras, R. (1988). *Bilingual education*. Bloomington, IN: Phi Delta Kappa.

Cook, V. J. (1973). The comparison of language development in native children and foreign adults. *International Review of Applied Linguistics in Language Teaching, 11*, 13–29.

Cummins, J. (1977). Cognitive factors associated with intermediate levels of bilingual skills. *Modern Language Journal, 61*, 3–12.

Cummins, J. (1979). Linguistic interdependence and the educational development of bilingual children. *Review of Educational Research, 49*(2), 222–251.

Cummins, J. (1984). *Bilingualism and special education: Issues in assessment and pedagogy*. Clevedon, Avon, England: Multilingual Matters, Ltd.

Cummins, J. (1985). The construct of language proficiency in bilingual education. In James Alatis & John Staczek (Eds.), *Perspectives on bilingualism and bilingual education* (pp. 209–231). Washington, DC: Georgetown University.

Cummins, J., & Gulutson, M. (1974). Some effects of bilingualism on cognitive functioning. In S. Carey (Ed.), *Bilingualism, biculturalism and education*. Edmonton: University of Alberta.

Cummins, J., & Mulcahy, R. (1978). Orientation to language in Ukrainian-English bilingual children. *Child Development, 49*, 1239–1242.

Genishi, C. (1984). *Language assessment in the early years*. Norwood, NJ: Ablex.

Genishi, C. (1989). Observing the second language learner: An example of teachers' learning. *Language Arts, 66*(5), 509–515.

Hakuta, K. (1986). *Mirror of language. The debate of bilingualism*. New York: Basic.

Hodgkinson, H. (1985). *All one system: Demographics of education, kindergarten through graduate school*. Washington, DC: Institute for Educational Leadership, Inc.

Juarez & Associates (1980). Final report of an evaluation of the Head Start bilingual/bicultural curriculum models. Washington, DC: U.S. Department of Health and Human Services. No. 105–77–1048.

Keatinge, R. H. (1984). An assessment of the pinteria preschool Spanish immersion program. *Teacher Education Quarterly, 11*, 80–94.

Kessler, C., & Quinn, M. (1982). Cognitive development on bilingual environments. In B. Hartford, A. Valdman, & C. Foster (Eds.), *Issues in international bilingual education*. New York: Plenum.

Krashen, S., & Biber, D. (1988). *On course: Bilingual education's success in California*. Sacramento: California Association for Bilingual Education.

La Fontaine, H. (1987). *At-risk children and youth—The extra educational challenges of limited English-proficient students*. Washington, DC: Summer Institute of the Council of Chief State School Officers.

Lightbron, P. (1977). French second language learners: What they're talking about. *Language Learning, 27*, 371–381.

McLaughlin, B. (1984). *Second-language acquisition on childhood: Volume 1: Preschool children*. Hillsdale, NJ: Erlbaum.

Ovando, C., & Collier, V. (1985). *Bilingual and ESL classrooms*. New York: McGraw-Hill.

Oxford, C., et al. (1984). Demographic projections of non-English background and limited English-proficient persons in the United States in the year 2000. Rosslyn, VA: InterAmerica Research Associates.

Peal, E., & Lambert, W. (1962). The revelations of bilingualism to intelligence. *Psychological Monographs, 76*(27), 1–23.

Phillips, S. (1972). Participation structures and communicative competence: Warm Springs children in community and classroom. In C. Cazden, V. John, & D. Hymes, (Eds.), *Functions of language in the classroom*. New York: Teachers College, Columbia University.

Ramsey, P. (1987). *Teaching and learning in a diverse world*. New York: Teachers College Press, Columbia University.

Skutnabb-Kangas, T. (1977). *Bilingualism or not: The education of minorities*. Clevedon, Avon, England: Multilingual Matters, Ltd.

Sleeter, C., & Grant, C. (1987). An analysis of multicultural education in the United States. *Harvard Educational Review, 57*(4), 421–444.

Snow, M. (1987). *Common terms in second language education: Center for Language Education and Research*. Los Angeles: University of California.

Snow, C., & Hakuta, K. (1987). *The costs of monolingualism*. Unpublished monograph, Cambridge, MA: Harvard University.

Soto, L. D. (in press). Alternate research paradigms in bilingual education research. In R. Padilla and A. Benavides (Eds.), *Critical perspectives on bilingual education research*. Phoenix: Bilingual Review/Press.

Soto, L. D. (in press). Success stories. In C. Grant (Ed.), *Research directions for multicultural education*. Bristol, PA: Falmer Press.

Swain, M. (1987). Bilingual education: Research and its implications. In M. Long and J. Richards (Eds.), *Methodology in TESOL*. Cambridge, MA: Newbury House.

U.S. Department of Health and Human Services. (1990). Head Start: A child development program. Washington, DC: Office of Human Development Services, Administration for Children, Youth and Families.

Willig, A. (1985). A meta-analysis of selected studies on the effectiveness of bilingual education. *Review of Educational Research, 55*(3), 269–317.

Wong Fillmore, L. (1976). *The second time around: Cognitive and social strategies*. Unpublished doctoral dissertation, Stanford University, Stanford, CA.

Wong Fillmore, L. (1985). *Second language learning in children: A proposed model*. Proceedings of a conference on issues in English language development, Arlington, VA. ERIC Document 273149.

Wong Fillmore, L. (in press). Language and cultural issues in early education. In S. Kagan (Ed.), *The care and education of America's young children: Obstacles and opportunities*. The 90th yearbook of the National Society for the Study of Education.

Wong Fillmore, L., & Valadez, C. (1986). **Teaching bilingual learners. In M. Wittrock (Ed.), *Handbook of research on teaching*. New York: Macmillan.

# Structure Time & Space
# To Promote Pursuit of Learning
# in the Primary Grades

## Marianne Gareau
## and Colleen Kennedy

*Marianne Gareau is a first grade teacher at LaPerle Elementary School in Edmonton, Alberta, Canada. She has also worked as an Elementary Consultant with the Alberta Department of Education.*

*Colleen Kennedy, M.Ed., teaches a combined class of first and second grade children at Richard Secord School in Edmonton, Alberta, Canada. Both authors pursue a continuing interest in the study of child development and applications to classroom practice.*

As the bell rang, signaling the beginning of Greenvale School's day, seven-year-old John joined a large group of children who were looking for a place to sit on the stairs that surrounded the open library. When most of the children were seated, Mrs. McNeil, the principal, began reading aloud from a book. After she had finished, several children shared stories they had written and then everyone began moving toward their classrooms. John stayed behind for a few minutes to select new library books. When he arrived at the classroom, a number of children were already engaged in quiet reading activities. John quickly selected an insect book from the science display and nestled down on the rug to read.

At 9:30 the teacher, Mr. Woodland, moved to the story area. John returned his book to the science area and found a place close to Mr. Woodland. As soon as Mr. Woodland finished reading the story, children began leaving the group to collect their writing folders and find a place to write. John preferred to work in the quiet area by the storage cupboard. He opened his folder and reviewed what he had written the day before. A small group of children was talking with Mr. Woodland, and John knew that unless he needed some assistance, he would have a large block of time in which to work on his insect story. Toward the end of the writing session, the teacher came by and John showed him the beginning portion of his story. Mr. Woodland offered a few suggestions. Then it was time for recess.

After recess, John went straight to the planning board. It was learning center time, and he wanted to join the group that was working on a large papier maché dragon in the work area next door.

After lunch, the whole class gathered together for a large-group session. The VIP (a child, identified as the Very Important Person for the day) initiated the afternoon activities by inviting the group to talk about the calendar, while Mr. Woodland wrote on a piece of chart paper at the back of the group. John knew that toward the end of the group session, the class would be invited to read Mr. Woodland's story. He wondered if Mr. Woodland was writing about insects. Later in the afternoon, the children went to gym class and then returned to their classroom to participate in math activities. John and a small group of children worked with Mr. Woodland on two-digit place value, while the rest of the students worked on math activities individually and in small groups.

This vignette gives a glimpse of what we believe to be appropriate educational programming for primary grade children. We base this belief on what we know about young children—their developmental characteristics and the ways in which they learn best—and on our philosophy of education and general goals in primary edu-

## Children's characteristics should dictate the use of space and time in the classroom.

cation programs. These two important aspects provide the impetus for a fuller discussion of the appropriate use of time and space to support children in engaging in meaningful learning experiences. Teachers need to be aware of the developmental characteristics of young children and of the overall goals of the primary program. Therefore, we discuss the use of time and space in primary classrooms, referring to what is known about how young children learn best and relating this to our introductory vignette.

## *Organizing the classroom day*

For a child in the preoperational stage, time is purely subjective: "A long time" may be a minute or an hour, depending on the activity in which the child is engaged. As young children develop, they move from this subjective concept of time to a more objective one. Being able to put events in temporal order and understanding the possibility of time units, for instance, are later developments. In primary programs, the child must learn to use time; it is through managing time that a child can best gain an understanding of it.

We often hear adults speak of children's "short attention spans" when what they are referring to is that young children who are not interested in certain tasks, or who are not motivated, tend to look for something else to do. If we think instead of a child's "task-orientation time," the time a child will pursue an activity that is interesting and meaningful, we have a more productive approach to facilitating children's learning (Nash, 1979). Our challenge as educators is to discover what we can do to increase task-orientation time, since we know that children will learn more with increased concentration on tasks.

### Task-oriented timetables

Research studies reported by Nash (1989) suggest that, in many kindergarten programs, a child's task orientation actually decreases from the beginning to the end of the year. Classroom observations indicated that such reductions were related to interruptions scheduled into the program. Well-intentioned teachers, believing they should accommodate the children's short attention span by planning frequent changes in activity, were in essence contributing to the problem!

Therefore, we need to modify our timetable to place the emphasis on tasks rather than on time. If we continually make decisions for children based on scheduled times rather than on completion of tasks, we discourage growth in attention span. Instead, we should provide children with large blocks of time to engage in meaningful activities and projects, and eliminate routines that interrupt their work. Although children at this age may be easily distracted, they are also capable of periods of intense concentration when engaged in meaningful activities. In the introductory vignette, the schedule is organized according to developmental needs of children in this age group. Learning is accomplished in an integrated fashion, with large blocks of time scheduled for reading, writing, and math activities, and every attempt made to minimize disruptions or interruptions of the children's activities. Children have the opportunity to develop their language skills through naturally occurring interactions with the teacher and with their peers, both on a one-to-one basis and in small groups. Children may also exhibit pensiveness and should be allowed time to ponder and reflect. If John knows that he has a large block of time to work on his insect story, he will feel free to take the time he needs to collect his thoughts, ideas, and information before and as he writes. John also realizes that this is a continuing project that does not have to be finished in one day.

### Whole-group routines and activities

Whole-group activities that are likely to interest most of the children can be placed later in the school day. As the time for these activities approaches, teachers should alert children to the need to bring closure to their tasks. In John's classroom, the "traditional" opening activities have been placed in the middle of the day. Such an approach takes advantage of children's strong interest and motivation in getting immediately involved in individual learning activities at the start of the day. After lunch, children are more ready to come together as a large group.

Because they make time and events visible, planning boards can be very useful. They encourage children to recognize the beginning and end of an activity and to develop insight into planning their activities and managing their time. In our classroom at Greenvale School, children assume responsibility for their own learning by selecting their center time activities at the planning board.

---

**If we continually make decisions for children based on scheduled times rather than on completion of tasks, we discourage growth in attention span. Instead we should provide children with large blocks of time to engage in meaningful activities and projects, and eliminate routines that interrupt the child's work.**

---

## *Figure 1.* Sample timetable

| | |
|---|---|
| 9:00 A.M. | Assembly (three times each week) |
| 9:15 A.M. | Quiet Reading |
| 9:25 A.M. | Shared Reading/Read to Class |
| 9:35 A.M. | Writing (whole group conferencing, quiet writing, shared writing) |
| 10:20 A.M. | Recess |
| 10:35 A.M. | Centers (Integrated Curriculum) |
| 11:30 A.M. | Lunch |
| 12:45 P.M. | Opening Activities (story, calendar, number line, time, weather, feelings chart, message, show-and-tell) |
| 1:20 P.M. | Physical Education/Music |
| 2:20 P.M. | Recess |
| 2:35 P.M. | Math Lesson and Math Centers |
| 3:35 P.M. | Dismissal |

We should also establish routines that are reasonable and make sense to children. As much as possible, these routines should meet the child's (rather than the adult's) needs. For example, taking off coats and hanging them up when coming in makes sense, but sitting quietly and waiting until everyone completes a worksheet does not. When routines are appropriate, there is a "flow" to the school day that children respond to well and find comfortable. In John's classroom, the children do not have to wait for the teacher to tell them what to do next. Because they have developed meaningful routines, they can move from one learning activity to another with minimal direction from the teacher and little disruption to the flow of daily learning activities. Figure 1 shows the timetable followed in John's classroom.

### *Organizing the learning environment for children*

In discussing ways to organize the classroom, Nash (1979) outlines four basic steps:

**1.** Develop a philosophy and general objectives.

**2.** Clarify knowledge of child development and ways of learning.

**3.** Decide on basic learning areas.

**4.** Look at children's behavior and arrange the classroom to reduce distractions.

### General objectives for primary children

The first step consists of developing a philosophy and general objectives. Many well-known experts such as Katz (1987, 1988), Nash (1976), and Bredekamp (1987) have identified the following fundamental goals for a sound educational program for young children:

● learn about and like themselves

● develop positive feelings about learning through experiencing success

● select, plan, and organize their own learning activities for a significant portion of the program day

● engage in meaningful activities with language and literacy

In providing an environment where children can learn about and like themselves, teachers and other adults must first of all demonstrate true affection for the children. Children who know they are cared for will feel safe enough to talk about themselves and get to know themselves well. Since modeling is one of the most powerful tools for learning, children who are treated with respect and trust will tend to develop a positive self-concept and a respectful attitude toward others.

The best way for children to develop positive feelings about learning is through achieving success in their tasks. This requires an environment that presents children with a variety of open-ended learning activities to accommodate their different abilities and interests. For example, children in Greenvale School choose stories according to their reading level and interest. They also work on math activities individually or in small groups rather than as a whole class.

Children are capable of assuming responsibility for their own learning. When a teacher organizes the classroom environment to allow children choices in planning and organizing their activities for a portion of the day, they become even more skilled at directing their own learning. John's obvious sense of control over his writing activities is a good example of this.

Finally, it is important for young children to engage in many meaningful activities with language and literacy. Since reading and writing are basic skills of early schooling, much of the school day should be connected to acquiring and practicing language use. Children should have daily opportunities to interact with others, to read and be read to, and to write selections of their own choosing.

These goals recognize the importance of providing children with meaningful experiences that will prepare them to be lifelong learners. Elementary school teachers can achieve these goals by providing a classroom environment that is compatible with developmental characteristics of young children. Children's innate desire to make sense of the world, to experiment, discover, and create, must be reflected in the classroom organization.

### Matching the program to developmental characteristics

The second step involves clarifying our knowledge of children's development and ways of learning. Children between the ages of four and seven share many characteristics (Norris & Boucher, 1980; Feeney, Christensen, & Moravcik, 1983; Beaty, 1986). For example, they experience growth spurts, which may cause instability, awkwardness, and an increased need for movement. Small muscles and bones are not completely formed or developed; therefore, fine-motor tasks still present a challenge for many children. Most children of this age are naturally farsighted, and activities requiring close work such as printing are very tiring. Children's hearing is not fully developed, and phonics-related activities requiring close attention to

small details may be inappropriate. In organizing the classroom program, teachers should be aware of these physical conditions.

Touch and movement are crucial to young children's learning. Memory is largely associative and needs to be linked to a particular experience or action. This is one reason field trips and projects are particularly powerful learning activities. Thought does not always precede action; although children may carry out plans made in advance, plans may also evolve during an activity (Norris & Boucher, 1980). Teachers should capitalize on this characteristic and give their children activities open-ended enough to involve both planning and spontaneous innovation.

## Learning areas related to children's interests

In the introductory vignette, the teacher applies his knowledge of child development by providing the children with opportunities to learn through activity, in small groups, and on a one-to-one basis. He also recognizes that children learn in different ways and provides a variety of learning areas in the classroom, as well as the opportunity to make choices. The third step in structuring the learning environment is to decide on basic learning areas such as reading-writing, math-science, and fine arts areas. In these areas teachers can develop units of study that capitalize on children's inter-

*Figure 2.* **John's classroom at Greenvale School**

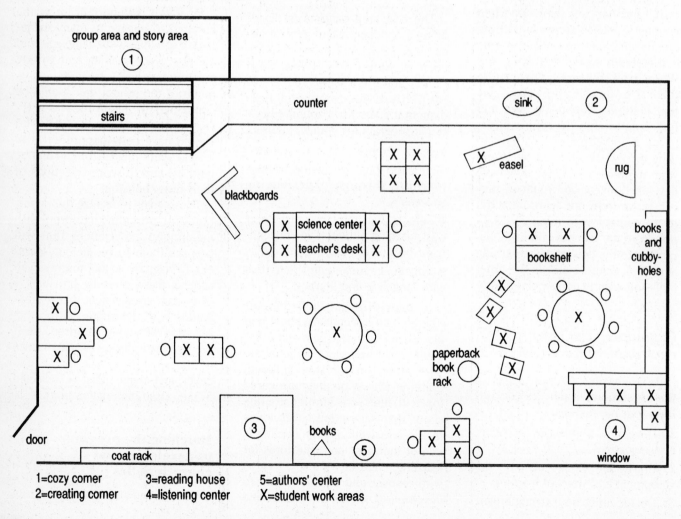

1=cozy corner    3=reading house    5=authors' center
2=creating corner    4=listening center    X=student work areas

dren from their natural learning processes.

**7.** Assessment relies on demonstrated performance, during real, not contrived activities, for example, real reading and writing activities rather than only skills testing (Engel, 1990; Teale, 1988).

**8.** Assessment utilizes an array of tools and a variety of processes including but not limited to collections of representative work by children (artwork, stories they write, tape recordings of their reading), records of systematic observations by teachers, records of conversations and interviews with children, teachers' summaries of children's progress as individuals and as groups (Chittenden & Courtney, 1989; Goodman, Goodman, & Hood, 1989).

**9.** Assessment recognizes individual diversity of learners and allows for differences in styles and rates of learning. Assessment takes into consideration children's ability in English, their stage of language acquisition, and whether they have been given the time and opportunity to develop proficiency in their native language as well as in English.

**10.** Assessment supports children's development and learning; it does **not** threaten children's psychological safety or feelings of self-esteem.

**11.** Assessment supports parents' relationships with their children and does not undermine parents' confidence in their children's or their own ability, nor does it devalue the language and culture of the family.

**12.** Assessment demonstrates children's overall strengths and progress, what children **can** do, not just their wrong answers or what they cannot do or do not know.

**13.** Assessment is an essential component of the teacher's role. Since teachers can make maximal use of assessment results, the teacher is the **primary** assessor.

**14.** Assessment is a collaborative process involving children and teachers, teachers and parents, school and community. Information from parents about each child's experiences at home is used in planning instruction and evaluating children's learning. Information obtained from assessment is shared with parents in language they can understand.

**15.** Assessment encourages children to participate in self-evaluation.

**16.** Assessment addresses what children can do independently and what they can demonstrate with assistance, since the latter shows the direction of their growth.

**17.** Information about each child's growth, development, and learning is systematically collected and recorded at regular intervals. Information such as samples of children's work, descriptions of their performance, and anecdotal records is used for planning instruction and communicating with parents.

**18.** A regular process exists for periodic information sharing between teachers and parents about children's growth and development and performance. The method of reporting to parents does not rely on letter or numerical grades, but rather provides more meaningful, descriptive information in narrative form.

**Guidelines for identifying children with special needs.** Another major purpose of assessing children is to identify children with special needs in order to ensure that they receive appropriate services and/or intervention. The identification process involves at least two steps: screening and diagnosis. Screening is a brief assessment procedure designed to identify children who **may** have a learning problem or handicapping condition that requires more intensive diagnosis based on many sources of information, including that obtained from parents and expert diagnosticians (Meisels, 1985). Formal screening is warranted when parents, teachers, or other professionals suspect that a child may have such a problem. Screening should never be used to identify second language learners as "handicapped," solely on the basis of their limited abilities in English. The word "screening" is sometimes used erroneously to refer to the administration of formal or informal readiness tests by which teachers get to know children so they can begin the process of tailoring the curriculum that they planned for all the children to the individual children in their group. This process is more accurately described as assessment for planning instruction and therefore the guidelines above apply to these situations.

Components of the screening proc-

ess (ILASCD, 1989) typically include a range of activities which allow the screener to observe and record children's physical health, fine/gross motor skills, social interactions, emotional expressions, communication competence, concept development, and adaptive skills. A parent interview obtains the following information, at a minimum: medical history, general health, family health concerns, serious or chronic illness, family composition, parent perception of child's social-emotional and cognitive development.

The following principles (ILASCD, 1989; Maryland Department of Education, 1989) should guide assessment procedures used to identify children's special needs:

**1.** Results of screening tests are **not** used to make decisions about entrance to school or as the single criterion for placement in a special program, but rather are used as part of a thorough process of diagnosis designed to ensure that children receive the individual services they need.

**2.** Any standardized screening or diagnostic test that is administered to a child is valid and reliable in terms of the background characteristics of the child being tested and the test's intended purposes. This is determined by a careful review of the reliability and validity information that is provided in the technical manual that accompanies the test and of independent reviews of tests such as those available in Buros' Mental Measurement Yearbook.

**3.** When a child is formally tested, the procedures conform with all regulations contained in P.L. 94–142. Parents are informed in advance, and information about the test and test results are shared with the child's parents. Any interpretation of test scores describes, in non-technical language, what the test covered, what the scores do and do not mean (common misinterpretations of the test scores) and how the results will be used. Allowances are made for parents to remain with the child during screening, if desired.

**4.** The screener approaches all interactions with children in a positive manner. The screener has knowledge of and prior experience with young children in order to score the measure accurately and support the validity of the results.

# Classroom space should be used to complement children's developmental characteristics: The needs to move, touch, experience variety, and make decisions.

ests. John's interest in insects has been incorporated into the science center, which includes live insects brought in by the children. This in turn leads to a writing activity on this topic. Because children learn in an integrated fashion, attempts should be made to connect the learning areas whenever possible.

## Children's behavior determines room arrangement

In Nash's (1979) fourth step, she proposes that we look at children's behavior to decide how to set up these learning areas. One of our tasks as teachers is to assist children in making sense of their world, or "making connections." One way in which children grow toward logical thinking is by repeatedly experiencing connections between things. In organizing the classroom space, we should at-

tempt to position learning materials close to others with related learning objectives. Children's curiosity will then be a positive feature, since they can add what attracts their attention to their present activity. Finally, space should be arranged to reduce distractions. Grouping can be made according to quiet or noisy activities, clean and messy ones. Figure 2 presents a view of John's classroom at Greenvale School.

## *Use time and space to support development*

If we are to be effective teachers, we must understand developmental characteristics of children and use these as a basis for designing our programs. When we identify children's characteristics as intrinsic to their particular stage of development, we are more likely to

view these characteristics in a positive light. Rather than imposing a structure that is counter to children's natural ways of learning, we will design our timetables and our classroom environments to accommodate and capitalize on these ways of learning. The result of such planning is children who retain their innate motivation and interest in learning.

## References

Beaty, J. J. (1986). *Observing development of the young child.* Columbus, OH: Merrill.

Bredekamp, S. (Ed.). (1987). *Developmentally appropriate practice in early childhood programs serving children from birth through age 8.* (exp. ed.). Washington, DC: NAEYC.

Feeney, S., Christensen, D., & Moravcik, E. (1983). *Who am I in the lives of children? An introduction to teaching young children.* (2nd ed.). Columbus, OH: Merrill.

Katz, L. (1987). What should young children be doing? *The Wingspread Journal, 9*(2), 1–3.

Katz, L. (1988). Engaging children's minds: The implications of research for early childhood education. In C. Warger (Ed.), *A resource guide to public school early childhood programs* (pp. 35–52). Alexandria, VA: Association for Supervision and Curriculum Development.

Nash, C. (1976). *The learning environment.* Toronto: Methuen.

Nash, C. (1979). *A principal's or administrator's guide to kindergarten.* Toronto: Ontario Institute for Studies in Education.

Norris, D., & Boucher, J. (Eds.). (1980). *Observing children through their formative years.* Toronto: Toronto Board of Education.

# Why Not Academic Preschool?   (Part 1)*

## Ideas That Work With Young Children

### Polly Greenberg

*Polly Greenberg has been an early child-hood educator for many decades. On a continuum of one-to-ten, ten being a per-fectly developmentally appropriate teacher, colleagues (playfully) rate Polly 8-1/2.*

**?** I am a preschool director. I have looked into NAEYC's accreditation system to see whether I want to discuss getting into it with our board and staff. I see the obvious advantages—it would look good to parents and prospective parents, be a morale booster to staff, and be a vehicle for improving our program. Of course we seek educational excellence. We want to be the best.

This is where I balk at accreditation. *We* believe that 3- and 4-year-olds can *learn*, and *expect* them too. Our parents are educated and would never put up with an inferior program where children just play. Yet reading NAEYC's materials, and other current publications, I sense that it is the *academic* approach that may be "inferior." We also believe in strong discipline. Life requires it. Truth to tell, I do feel in a quandary. Can you clarify this?

**O**n the most important point you raise, all leaders of early childhood education (whether expert practitioners, or teacher educators,

*Future editions of *Young Children* will address other major goals, which program serves them best, and the repercussions of these programs in later life.

or specialists like researchers or theoreticians, or teachers who specialize in the needs of children with unusual disabilities or in areas such as language, literacy, one or two of the arts) would agree: **We all believe that 3- and 4-year-olds can learn; we all expect them to learn.** We all agree that self-esteem is an *essential* for optimal development to take place; and we all are quick to state that **a big part of a child's self-esteem comes from feeling competent—from becoming increasingly competent in "things that count in the child's world."** (This is why children from corners of our culture where adults believe—because their lives have taught them so—that children should learn to protect themselves physically feel *good*, not *bad*, if they're daring fighters. In *their* world, being a good fighter is a "thing that counts.") Like you, we also believe strongly in discipline—**self**-discipline.

### Two major sharply contrasting approaches to early childhood education

There are two major, sharply contrasting approaches to these shared goals, two sharply contrasting philosophies (models) of education for 3-, 4-, and 5-year-olds—and many carefully conceptualized (or carelessly occur-ring) variations at all points along a continuum within both of these very broad categories. Seldom do we see *excellent* examples of *either* philosophy. The majority of excellent programs mix aspects of each model. Because understanding the differences between the models is so important, this article will be in two parts, in order to explore the subject.

### The first early childhood education philosophy is exemplified in traditional American nursery/kindergarten/first grade education (1920/present)

The child is believed to be an active learner who learns best when she

- moves at will, becomes involved in something, usually with other children (purposefulness and creative thinking are encouraged)
- makes *major* choices—chooses among a variety of worthwhile "live" activities ("live" meaning that the child is not choosing only among worksheets)
- initiates and "does" within a richly prepared indoor and outdoor environment (initiative is encouraged)
- discovers, dismantles, reassembles
- discusses with friends and grown-ups
- grapples with challenges (some of which she inadvertently stumbles into,

From *Young Children*, Vol. 45, No. 2, January 1990, pp. 70-80. Copyright © 1990 by Polly Greenberg, NAEYC, 1834 Connecticut Avenue, N.W., Washington, DC 20009.

and some of which she consciously sets out to conquer)

• constructs understandings, each at her own rate of intellectual development
• plans and collaborates with friends and adults
• solves problems she runs into (not problems that are concocted out of context and set before her in bite-sized portions of "a problem-solving curriculum")
• *creates* concepts and *recreates* or elaborates upon them as she learns something new that seems true but doesn't mesh with what she thought she knew
• works with an interesting, intuitive, endorsing adult who mingles with children as they play and work, and in informal interest groups, skill groups, and social groups—all of them often minigroups
• evaluates her own work and behavior with peer and adult participation
• feels rewarded by the satisfaction of a job well done (intrinsic reward)
• experiences spontaneous encounters with learning as her mind meets interesting or puzzling things that capture her attention and intrigue her, **which always include things related to what adults and older children do, hence generally include pretending to read books by 2 or 3 years of age; writing letters and numerals while playing and drawing somewhere between ages 3 and 7 (typically beginning by 4 or 5 years old); and guess-spelling, asking how to spell words, and real reading at 5, 6, or 7, if not sooner.**

All of this is believed to be best learned through enriched free play and teacher-designed, teacher-guided projects usually planned so they expand upon what the child has freely elected to do. Sophisticated guidance and enrichment intended to ensure that opportunities to develop creativity, imagination, generous amounts of math, science concepts, social studies concepts, language, and literacy, as well as opportunities to learn in all the arts, grow out of or are interplanted in a **naturalized** manner throughout what the child has become absorbed in. Teachers, parents, the community; and supervisors, consultants, and teacher educators connected in one way or another with the program determine what should be included in the curriculum, but it isn't believed that

there is a fixed body of knowledge that children should "master."

Teachers assess children's progress by

• *observing* them;
• *recording and keeping* anecdotal notes about anything of particular interest or very typical emotionally, socially, physically, intellectually, academically, aesthetically, or otherwise;
• *identifying* special needs in any of these areas, and following up or referring as needed;
• *collecting and keeping* samples and photos of their activities; and
• *sharing* extensively in the information- and opinion-gathering process with the child's parent(s) and other staff. (This is how those of us who were trained as nursery educators before the advent of the achievement testing craze that started sweeping into our schools in the '60s were taught to assess young children's progress. Mercifully, "test mania" and related atrocities—such as omitting, deleting, or putting in parentheses children who, for whatever reason, are not in that magical and mythical place called Average—are beginning to be attacked from all sides. See, for example, Kamii, 1990.)

This philosophy of education assumes that what children learn casually and naturally as they live their lives and play their days away is valuable learning, nature's way of educating children, God's way, if you will; and that though it can be improved upon by the careful craftswomen that expert early childhood practitioners are, adults should not *deprive* children of natural learning by making them sit down and be taught at. This philosophy believes not *only* in preparing the environment for excellent play, but *also* that for the child to have **optimal** learning opportunities, adults

(parents or teachers) need to **enrich** the play, **plan** projects, and **teach** children many things somewhat in the same way that one **naturalizes** plants. You carefully arrange your purposeful additions to the landscape here and there and all around in the midst of what's happening there naturally so that to a person stumbling into it, all seems relaxed and natural. We **naturalize** "subjects" and "skills" and the conventional knowledge that we expect children to learn, throughout the children's learning environments (home, school, community).

This naturalizing means that "subjects" are integrated, but more than this: It means that children learn "subject" area "skills" and "subskills" and facts in meaningful contexts, sometimes in thematic, teacher guided projects— **as a need for these skills crops up in activities a child has eagerly elected to involve himself in.** For a long time, there have been as wide a variety of OK ways to do this as there have been first-rate teachers. There have also, for a long time, been published curricula featuring this philosophy. Emphasis is equally on all aspects of each child's development: **Intellectual learning is fostered,** but is not given priority over physical, social, and emotional learning. Various theoretical frameworks are adhered to, but not given priority over children's individual needs. Academics may be informally included in the array of learnings occurring, **but learning is never narrowed to "mere" academics.** You say you believe that children are capable of learning and should learn when 3, 4, and 5 years of age. Developmentally appropriate program people believe this strongly, but resist the idea of *limiting* learning to academics only.

Children have opportunities at school (as they do at home in moderately liter-

> **As they learn a vast amount in all areas through their play and projects, children develop positive self-esteem with regard to their competence in using language and math adeptly, and in thinking in a scientific, self-disciplined, problem-solving mode.**

ate families) to learn letters and sounds and a great deal more that goes into easy early reading, but they learn most of it one child at a time during sociable playing, drawing, and talking times with friends. Children learn

● as they experiment and discover, or
● as a need for the new knowledge comes up **for an individual** in his play and projects, or
● as children's observant teachers purposefully expand upon what a child (or small group) is doing to include literacy experiences, or
● when adults are reading stories to children and conversing about them, or
● when an adult is engaged in an activity and children are invited to join in if they wish.

In the 1940s, '50s, and '60s, when it was the predominant approach to learning in nursery schools, and especially in public kindergartens and first grades, this was called *the language experience approach*; now we know it as *the whole language approach* or *emerging literacy*. There are small differences between language experience and whole language, but from the expert classroom teacher's perspective, they're insignificant.

(It must be admitted that within this broad category of educators who believe in learning through play and projects is a contingent that finds the alphabet anathema and shies away from the sounds of letters as if they would infect children with a fearful anti-education virus. But although some theoreticians "freak at the thought," as one literacy specialist phrased it, many ordinary, very child-development-oriented classroom teachers, and probably *most* parents, certainly most middle-class parents, include exposure to letters and sounds, and friendly explanations, in with everything else they expose 2-, 3-, 4-, and 5-year-old children to at school or at home. Therefore, without "instruction," many children learn about them. As the pendulum now swings away from academic preschool, we are likely to see a return of the 1950s extremists, who shuddered at the thought of phonics—*even if offered in a playful, natural manner*—before children reached first grade.)

The same is true of math. Children have opportunities to figure out numerical relationships as they play and work with objects and people, to count, to make graphs, to classify things, to weigh things, to learn liquid and linear measurement, more and less, bigger and smaller, adding on and taking away, how to recognize numerals—**but all as it comes up in their play and projects,** or as their teachers **extend these play and project activities to include such experiences.** In math learning, understanding (mastering) the basics (the principles involved) should precede memorizing the details (skills and facts).

➜ For children to learn optimally this way, teachers must be given

● **training in**
— child development, including, some of us believe, the depth, interpersonal, and humanistic psychologies,
— observing individual children, including the art and science of taking pertinent notes,
— working informally as equal people with all parents,
— working with specialists as needed in assessing and assisting children and families with special needs,
— recognizing moments when one can connect with a child to develop trust and friendship, from which learning grows (a sophisticated skill),
— creating a complex, stimulating, ever-fresh yet predictable and manageable learning environment including a variety of interlinked learning centers,
— recognizing moments when a child or group of children could learn something new—a new idea, an approach to solving a problem, a new fact, a new skill,
— interjecting thought-provoking comments and queries without interrupting or interfering (a skill that many expert teachers believe intuitive teachers do better than non-intuitive teachers, no matter how well trained),
— helping children with the intricacies and nuances of having and being friends,
— helping children discipline **themselves** (develop inner controls); and
— helping each child feel good about himself or herself throughout all this.
● **authority to use their**
— intuition,
— judgment,
— knowledge,
— materials, and
— resources

in making the moment into a learning encounter—possibly one that can be expanded into a week-long or six-week-long project with depth, dimensions, aspects, and angles "covering" in a web-like way learning in many "subject" areas, totaling educational excellence. (In all honesty, we need to note that a great number of teacher education programs purporting to believe in this general approach to early education do *not* give students a thorough grounding in these things, nor do many work places give teachers the freedoms and support necessary for them to fully use their sensitivities and skills.)

---

# Nature has made the human mind so it seeks stimuli to pique it, thus rapidly expanding thinking processes and knowledge.

---

Said a very good teacher of 3s (who has taught in academic preschools, and now does staff development work in developmentally appropriate programs) when she read this list:

A really good teacher using *any* philosophy should be trained in all this. The problem is, if the principal or director is big on the academic approach to preschool, you never get time to use all this. Your teaching isn't evaluated on these kinds of things. You are evaluated on how orderly and quiet the children are, how well you write up and present each step of your lesson plan, and the children's standardized test scores. It's appreciated if you do all this other too, but it isn't relevant in evaluating you, so you don't spend time doing it and becoming better at it all. You need all this training *and* a chance to perfect your ability to do it in a real, live, three-ring circus classroom, *and* to be evaluated (valued) for these skills. Besides, an academic preschool conditions *parents* to value the wrong approach, too, so your parents are *against* your good teaching, instead of supportive of it.

This general category—currently called **developmentally appropriate practice**—includes approaches, theories, and emphases associated with people such as John Dewey, Patty Hill,

Arnold Gesell, Lucy Sprague Mitchell, Harriet Johnson, Carolyn Pratt, Barbara Biber, Margaret Naumburg, Cornelia Goldsmith, Erik Erikson, Jean Piaget, David Weikart, and David Elkind.

Disparate, far from monolithic, ranging from the original Progressive Educators to the contemporary Piagetian constructivists, this group nonetheless has been characterized by general consensus. This consensus is most recently displayed by the publication of *Developmentally Appropriate Practice* (Bredekamp, 1987) by NAEYC. As one contemporary educator described the process behind that document:

We thrash out all our viewpoints and convictions and produce a broad set of statements we can *all* accept, even though we also cherish our differences.

**This general approach is advocated by NAEYC** now, and has been—with varying emphases over the years—consistently ever since it originated in 1926 as the National Association for Nursery Education. The approach is currently called "developmentally appropriate" early childhood education (with or without the literal numerals or alphabet letters, depending upon which subgroup you're listening to). It's the approach to young children's development and learning taught throughout much of this century by Columbia Teachers College, Bank Street College of Education, Vassar College, Wheelock, Peabody, Sarah Lawrence, the University of Maryland, the Merrill-Palmer Institute, newer programs such as Pacific Oaks and Erikson Institute, and other institutions *specializing* in education for children younger than 6. Mid-century British Infant Schools have used this general approach. Traditional nursery/kindergarten education was developed in tandem with the child study and psychoanalytic psychology movements, and it has absorbed a lot of basics from both. (Since the '60s, it has taken on some basics from other psychologies, too.)

**Currently, this "developmentally appropriate" philosophy is being strongly promoted by all national education associations** that have published position statements on early childhood education. Among them are the National Association of Elementary School Principals, the Association for Supervision and Curriculum Development, and the National Association of

State Boards of Education; **so if you choose to move your school in this direction, you're in good company.** The reason all those leaders are forcefully advocating this kind of educational experience for 3-, 4-, and 5-year-olds—and even for 6- and 7-year-olds—is that a wealth of recent research confirms and corroborates what most expert practitioners have been explaining, writing, and teaching for 100 years: **This is the most effective way to educate young children. It works best in the long run, and with any luck, life *is* longer than 5 or 6 years, so there's no need for 5-year-olds to know everything they will need to know throughout their school and later years.**

## The second early childhood education philosophy is represented by the recently introduced (1960s), basically academic preschool/ kindergarten/first grade

The child is believed to learn best when he

- sits still, pays attention to the teacher who is "instructing," or does assigned, often paper-and-pencil, seatwork (receptivity is praised)
- makes *minor* choices—which color paper he wants for making a patterned craft item (it's expected that he *will* make the craft item; not to do so usually isn't an option)
- obeys and follows directions in the classroom (compliance is rewarded with compliments)
- initiates and "does" only during a brief free play period, at recess, and on his own time at home in a home environment (that *may* be loaded with learning opportunities, and *may* offer an adult to assist the child in interpreting and expanding the learning his mind comes upon; or *may* be an environment in which learning opportunities are starkly limited and in which an adult is not available to promote spontaneous learning)
- discovers, but on a narrowly restricted scale—discovers the right answer from among several possible answers on a workbook page
- discusses, but in a formal, teacher-led, tightly topic-related format; children have little chance to learn through informal conversation with one another while in the classroom
- experiences few intellectual chal-

lenges to grapple with and construct understandings from—his own rate of intellectual development may or may not be recognized, but is seldom honored and responded to in the curriculum that confronts him

- goes along with plans his teacher has made—teachers and children do very little planning *together;* children are expected to tolerate their circumstances good-naturedly
- solves only prefabricated, packaged problems out of a purchased curriculum, if (officially) any; even social problems are usually "solved" for him because the teacher, focused as she is on the academic curriculum she must "cover," doesn't have time to help the child see and test behavioral alternatives, so she tells him the rule and possibly puts him in "the time-out chair to think about it"; very little assertiveness and stridency is "allowed"
- memorizes facts (may create some concepts), waits to be told whether he has gotten them "right" or "wrong," tries again (often guessing, because if that answer was wrong, maybe this answer will be right), doesn't develop *evidence* that he's right or wrong
- works with an almost-always-right adult who approves of him when he's right and disapproves when he is wrong, usually in "instructional" settings, rarely in small interest or social groupings
- awaits, passively, adult evaluation and praise (extrinsic reward) rather than judging for himself whether or not his work is good and his behavior helpful
- experiences reprimands and restraining procedures when he spontaneously encounters something that captures his attention and intrigues him but does not happen to be on the worksheets he has been assigned or in the lesson he's supposed to be attending to

After reading this description of the academic "preschool," an excellent teacher of 3s said:

I used to teach this way. I strolled around my classroom distributing sheets of paper and bundles of brisk directives. I taught like this because that's how my teachers taught *me* all through school. I didn't go to preschool, so I knew no other way.

I went through a teacher education program, but even though what I wanted was kindergarten, or even younger, what I learned was mostly all meant for upper elementary teachers, with some special stuff and caveats tacked on for kindergarten teachers. (I didn't know at the time that there was a special field, at *that* time known as "nursery education," or I would've looked for a school specializing in it, instead of dabbling in it as my elementary-oriented college did.) This was the heyday of cognitive, cognitive, cognitive, too, so they didn't emphasize all the rest of the child. I was flimflammed into skill-by-skill teaching.

When I started work, it was in a preschool I later learned would be called an academic preschool, but until all the debate began in the mid-1980s, I thought it was the way *all* preschools were. It was a top-of-the-line private school. So all the wrong ideas and strategies I had learned were reinforced. I spent my days chiding children. If my aide and I had a child who refused to "perform," we pursued him like furies. I remember the frightened little faces of those who never did well. If tears troubled their eyes, I felt I was reaching them, motivating them. I look back now and feel it was an affront to childhood, just pure intimidation and pretension (which cynics say is the aim of most human behavior anyway). I worry now, praying I didn't char any little hearts with my predictions about how they would never amount to anything if they didn't work harder. They were only 3 years old!

**I didn't realize the extent to which young children are motivated to be like grown-ups and older children, which, in a literate society, includes using the 3Rs.** I didn't trust children to evolve a "mastery" in their own way, each in his own time, if given encouragement and assistance.

In this broad category and philosophy of education, which could be described as a **behavior modification** approach, the schedule includes play periods, but they're brief and are seen as a break for "rest and recreation." Projects and some of the arts are scheduled, but are offered as "enrichment": play and projects are important but peripheral activities, not the core curriculum. The core curriculum is a tightly structured sequence of splinter skills, presented to the child through a strictly structured sequence of instructional steps. These educators believe that all of this is best learned through short periods of separated subject instruction, intended to give the child the necessities for *later* learning *earlier*. This minimizes the importance of the child's *present* age and stage, causing a commentator to remark:

If there were no need for a certain set of years, nature, which is ultra-efficient, would telescope childhood and jump from one to six without all the years in between. They are all there for a *reason*.

It's believed that there is a fixed body of knowledge that 4-year-olds need to

master. Adults either

● don't realize how much more easily children learn abstract academic subskills *later*, say at 6 or 7, or
● believe that learning must be unpleasant to be effective, or
● are unaware that *the same abstract academic* subskills can be taught as the need arises in contexts meaningful to this age group.

Here, the former academic preschool teacher exclaimed:

That's it! That's exactly it! The fact that children need to learn these things doesn't translate to mean they need to learn them *now*, when they're just 3 and 4 years old. It *is* true that I used to think learning was a sort of grim business. I used to envision children huddled around their squadrons of clumped-together school desks, slumped over their work; that was "learning." How funny it seems now! I used to think I was doing a good job when I saw all my docile little children chastened and conforming. Now I look for *joy—love* of learning.

Children's progress is assessed with tests, so there's heavy emphasis on mastery. The degree of children's measurable "performance" in academic tasks is what's valued. Children are positively "reinforced" (given stars, smiles, etc.) for absorbing, at least for the moment, as much memorized information in the form of abstract symbols (letters, shapes) as they reasonably can. Adults control most of the use of space, time, and materials in all early childhood programs in that they arrange and manage all of it, set behavioral standards, and so on. But in the academic preschool there is little if any emphasis on children using most of the space most of the time *in their way*.

This broad category of programs and philosophies features

● direct instruction;
● teacher as minute-by-minute schedule planner;
● emphasis on
—the subskills involved in reading and math,
—symbols representing things (letters, numerals) instead of on examining and exploring the things themselves, and
—conventional knowledge such as days of the week, colors, courtesies, and so on;
● curriculum **prepared outside the classroom—purchased by the pro-**

gram and **"covered" by the "teacher"** (in contrast to curriculum created by the teacher, or purchased curricular materials that provide a sound philosophy, a framework to preclude a piecemeal, mishmash bunch of activities, and many time-saving specifics, but also encourage and enhance teacher creativity and familiarity with the local community);
● "child as the recipient of lessons";
● "sooner is better";
● "learning through a limitless supply of paper-and-pencil worksheets";
● emphasis on mastery and testing;
● "operant conditioning";
● "rewards" as "reinforcement" for "right answers"; and
● authoritarian management.

Here, a child care center head teacher murmurs:

Authoritarian management . . . Before I took a graduate school course in early childhood classroom management, I believed in very strong and stern discipline. But my children had very little **self**-discipline. The minute I'd step away, it would all fall apart. Now I lay it on *less*, so the children have developed *more*, more inner controls. Of course I help them with a great deal of guidance.

This loose group of programs descends from Pavlovian and Skinnerian theory. When these programs were first developed in the 1960s, several of the names we heard most were Carl Bereiter and Seigfried Englemann (later a program that grew out of Bereiter and Englemann's work, DISTAR, was published), and Susan Gray from Peabody College, whose project was known as DARCEE. Today's academic preschools and kindergartens are close cousins of the models launched in the '60s. They also represent "moving down" the behaviorist-based curriculum that, in the 1960s, became so popular in elementary schools. The theory behind behaviorist programs is that positive reinforcement *beyond the satisfaction of accomplishing a personally meaningful task* is essential in shaping behavior—in this case, behavior that will help children "achieve" in school.

The traditional Montessori method, though it places great emphasis on respecting children, on children *doing*, learning through a self-paced discovery process, and on *intrinsic reward* (learning materials are self-correcting), and could not be called "academic," would still, many early childhood educational leaders think, fall into this broad behavior modification group because

• the choices are not the child's (there is a strictly sequenced series of activities, and though each child progresses on her own timetable, teachers maintain tight control of how space, time, and materials are used);

• cooperative and collegial planning on the part of the children, *pretend*-type play, playing, and conversation are strongly discouraged;

• play (spontaneous) and projects (group) are not as important a part of the program as are using the special (excellent) Montessori materials;

• there is a right answer to everything, including the correct way to use each clever and useful piece of Montessori equipment, which appears to be a reasonable idea, but does mean that creativity is not central to the program (for example, children are not usually free to use the materials in their *own* ways *in addition to* the correct way; to some "mainstream" early childhood people, this seems restrictive).

Teachers in both developmentally appropriate and academic programs need to be good at classroom management, but the former need to be good at guiding the group through participatory democracy, whereas the latter need to be good at managing in a more didactic and dictatorial manner (though sugarcoated and delivered tactfully). However, many child management techniques used by teachers are shared across the board. Both kinds of teachers manage their classrooms with small gasps of appreciative pleasure; encouraging comments; eyebrow Olympics; little smiles that wilt like cut flowers when a child's work or behavior is disappointing, followed by sad, censorious faces, and gentle blandishments; and, when necessary, looks that pin children to their repeated indiscretions and errors.

Moreover, because in the real world we rarely see either the developmentally appropriate or the academic preschool model in its pure form and at its best, and instead see the two models on a continuum from marvelous to mediocre or worse, the differences are not always as clearcut as they may appear here.

## Main areas of disagreement

There seem to be three major areas of disagreement between people who

prefer the academic preschool and people who prefer the so-called "developmentally appropriate." The disagreements center on:

1. How do children most effectively learn *at this age*? We've probably talked about this enough for now.

2. What is most important for children to learn at *this* age, whether they are in a program of one sort or another or at home?

3. What are the repercussions later in the child's school years, adolescence, and adult life of the academic preschool experience versus experience in a developmentally appropriate program? What is the purpose and point of what we unfortunately call "preschool"? (These years aren't pre-*anything* and shouldn't be considered as so, any more than college should be called "pregraduate school," or one's 35-year career should be termed the "preretirement period.")

Another intriguing topic is **why** so many teachers, parents, and others prefer the academic-style preschool, but we will have to defer this discussion till another time.

## *What is most important for children to learn at this age regardless of the setting they're in?*

Let's tackle this giant topic next, and touch upon some highlights.

The presence of high **self-esteem** correlates with school success, therefore it's a very important thing for children to learn at this age. (Moreover, *low* self-esteem correlates with all sorts of serious problems, such as dropping out of school, teen-age pregnancy, alcohol and drug abuse, teen-age depression, and teen-age suicide. If she thought about it, no educator would want to risk contributing to any child's low self-esteem.)

> **If a child doesn't desire the goal, the activity isn't motivational. If the child isn't motivated, she will probably not develop the habit of aiming at excellence.**

## Self-esteem

Self-esteem is generated in children in large part through the process of frequently meeting and mastering **meaningful** new challenges. (This, by the way, is a core concept of the Montessori method, which stresses positive regard for self as an autonomous learner.) A key concept here is **meaningful.** If we expect a young child to master tasks that are meaningless to her *as an individual*, she has little satisfaction or feeling of self-worth in doing the chore, even if she succeeds. Hence we are not fostering maximum feasible positive self-esteem, which *should* be one of our chief goals. (Nor, of course, are we achieving academic excellence with *this* individual child; she "succeeded" because the task was too easy for her! "Performing" that which is personally meaningless and poses no personal challenge produces neither a boost to self-esteem nor educational excellence. Why would good teachers give boringly too easy, meaningless work unless they had never reflected upon it, or believed that they had to, to keep their jobs?)

For intellectually gifted children, meaningless work can be quite destructive, as it tends to *lower* their self-esteem; they feel awkwardly out of place with their peers, who seem to be struggling, and wonder if there's something wrong with *themselves* because everything is such a breeze. For children gifted in other areas than the intellectual (e.g., music, art, athletics), the message of all these academic "activities" may be that *their* specialties are irrelevant. This isn't likely to boost children's self-esteem regarding their specialness. Teaching children to sing, "I'm Special," while ignoring (devaluing) their specialness, seems at best absurd, but it happens everyday. Though it may cause a flurry of controversy to say, it probably happens more commonly in academic programs because teachers aren't given time and a green light to explore individual children's *real* specialnesses with them.

It's possible that doing meaningless paperwork makes some children feel good *because they are pleasing an adult who believes the work is meaningful.* The child feels good because she is *being* good, not because it felt good to do the work itself. Being good, that is, pleasing someone you strive to please, can build self-esteem to a point. Being a pleasing, approved-of person surely must be a boost to self-esteem. But we've all heard tales about the son who became a physician only to please his father, or the daughter who married a certain man only to please her parents, and how hollow their lives became unless and until they collapsed and changed them so they were living in ways *they* found meaningful.

In later life—on the job—employed people do have to do certain things to please the boss, to get promoted, to keep the job, to earn the paycheck. But research tells us that *the most successful employees, managers, and CEOs claim to feel more rewarded by feeling they've done an excellent job at something they find meaningful than by any other kinds of "rewards,"* assuming that supervisors provide satisfying inclusion, reasonable recognition for successes, and supportive work climates in all senses of the word *supportive.*

As has many times been pointed out in *Young Children*, self-esteem is generated in children in large part through a process of frequently meeting and **mastering** meaningful new challenges. A key part of this concept is **mastering.** If we expect a young child to master tasks that are impossible for her *as an individual,* there is no satisfaction or feeling of self-worth in slugging away and slogging through the chore—because she's *failing.* Hence, again, with this child as with the child for whom the task is far too easy, we're not fostering maximum feasible positive self-esteem. (In less technological cultures, children are expected gradually to master all aspects of becoming adults of their gender in the community. All of it feels meaningful. All of it can be mastered. Developing *low* self-esteem and all the concomitant problems isn't as dire a likelihood lurking over children's shoulders as it is in complex contemporary America.)

Jerome Kagan, a professor of developmental psychology at Harvard, writes in

# Self-esteem is not taught. It's learned, largely through the way adults live with young children.

his fascinating book *The Nature of the Child:*

[A]s the child approaches her second birthday, she shows behavioral signs of anxiety if she cannot implement a behavior she feels obliged to display. The recognition that one cannot meet a standard regarded as appropriate provokes distress .... The child cannot ignore parental [and teacher/caregiver] standards because she is in a "closed" situation, dependent upon the care and instrumental help of [these adults]. The child accepts these standards as reasonable demands to be met [**whether or not they are**]. Additionally, the child recognizes that the parents, and many other children, have met these standards, and thus that they are within human capacity. It is not possible for the child to rationalize the standards away.

But if a particular child finds the standards too difficult to attain, she becomes vulnerable to distress. Some people may call this emotion shame; others, guilt; others, a sense of unworthiness. This emotion can generate a feeling of impotence either to cope with problems or to attract the approval and affection of others. The child believes that the self is not worthy of positive regard....

A central fact of modern, middle-class Western society is that standards of academic accomplishment are so high that many children fail to meet them. More important, there is no easy way for a child to do penance for this failure. There are no useful instrumental activities that the American child can engage in to prove his effectiveness, utility, or value. The average middle-class child is an object of sentiment with no useful economic role in the household. The situation contrasts sharply with the child in a rural village in a less developed community, who is aware that his work is of value to the family....

In Third World villages, where the standards set for children are relatively easy to meet (to cook, clean, gather wood, or take care of babies), children less often experience the distress of failure. (1984, pp. 266–268)

If a child is failing at most of the tasks we assign him, we aren't achieving academic excellence, either, because the beleaguered child is learning nothing

except that he "isn't a good student"; which he may, depending upon how many other areas he feels a failure in, interpret to mean that he "isn't a good *person.*" If schoolwork is one of the *few* areas in which the child sees that he continually can't do what he's expected to do (in other words, if he feels successful in most other parts of his life), the discouraging experience will probably only sour him on *school,* not on himself in every dimension.

But if the child is being burdened and blocked by other things of major importance going against him as well (for example, if he's the least liked, most parentally disparaged sibling, or if he's seriously disabled and from a very low-income family, yet in a predominantly middle-class school where there are few mainstreamed children with atypical needs), **another** low blow to his self-respect may simply add up to too much to bear, resulting in the crushing of any budding self-esteem he may have had.** Furthermore, many children misperceive what their parents mean: A child whose parents push for his academic success in preschool may think that the parents love *achievement* rather than *him.* Not knowing all the skeletons in every child's family closet or psyche, why would good teachers take a risk like this? Programs for 3-, 4-, and 5-year-olds include many children from low-income minority families. Exposure to the kinds of experiences school systems base later education upon is essential before the question of **mastery** ever arises. Whether or not academic preschools are best for this group of children has been extensively investigated; see, for example, the work of David Weikart. It seems paradoxical, but academic preschools are not the most helpful way for low-income children to achieve later academic success. The explanation lies, of course, in the maturation theories of Gesell (physical) and Piaget (mental).

A very important difference between *academic* preschools and kindergartens, and *developmentally appropriate* early childhood programs, revolves around the idea of **mastery:**

● The academic program places a great deal of emphasis on the necessity for each child to **master** predetermined subskills of reading, pre-spelling, and math. There is a corresponding emphasis on **testing.** Because of the extreme focus on mastering a set of adult-selected skills, all in one narrowly defined "academic" dimension of the child's total experience, **the child gets the unequivocal message that self-initiated "mastery" in all other areas (physical agilities, abilities, and feats including those involved in dancing; knowledge and talents in each of the arts including careful observation, reproduction, and appreciation; prowess in appreciating literature; delight and expertise in using mathematical ideas; "street wisdom"; being an exceptionally nurturing person) is unimportant,** of little value.

This may lower the amount of positive self-esteem the child derives from mastery in all nonacademic areas of his life. As previously mentioned, this is not uncommonly magnified in the minds of *gifted* children. In contrast,

• The so-called developmentally appropriate program places heavy emphasis on the necessity for each child of **choosing what he will "master";** and encouraging exploration—as well as mastery—in a wide variety of areas. When the child examines, investigates, messes around, tries out, tries on, develops interest in, develops enthusiasm for, he wins as many brownie points as when he "masters." In many programs, especially programs attended by children from low literacy, non-print-rich, low socioeconomic homes, teachers make sure that many materials and learning encounters involving conversation (language), good books (reading), drawing/talking/dictating stories as accompaniments, captions/labels/signs (writing, spelling, reading), letters, sounds, mathematical concepts, measurements, numerals, and so on are included in the daily free choice program. Teachers engage in activities featuring all this as helpful friends.

**Though there may be developmental screening and assessment "tests," there are no norm-referenced, standardized achievement tests. Exposure and comfortable familiarity are valued as much as "mastery"; digging deeply into a topic of interest with an enthusiastic teacher's help—pursuing educational excellence—is also valued as much as is "mastering" a specific body of knowledge (shallowly).**

In the developmentally appropriate program, it's assumed that mastery in

*all* areas of living, using *all* kinds of intelligences (musical intelligence, aesthetic intelligence, interpersonal intelligence, etc.), is valid and worthwhile. The child has many more arenas in which to develop positive self-esteem. It is not assumed, as it is in the academic program, that only academic mastery matters. Nor is it assumed, as it is in the academic program, that each child should be ready to master each academic item on more or less the same day of his life. Children are perennially exposed to the ingredients of academic life: They learn letters, sounds, numbers, shapes, and so on, each in his own way and each in his own time.

## Self-discipline

The existence of **self-discipline** in an individual is essential if educational excellence is to be a reality. **Healthy self-discipline** gradually grows as young children strive and struggle

• to manage the plethora of **age- and stage-appropriate tasks** encountered
— in play,
— in adult-started and -guided projects, and
— in the complicated social situations that continually crowd in upon our natural wish to do whatever we want whenever we want to; and

• to internalize the firm, fair guidance grown-ups and older children give. Out of all this each child develops personal standards and aspires to live up to them. If the young child is expected to manage a great many tasks which to a person of *this* age (3, 4, 5) and *this* stage (preoperational, possessed by magical thinking and an innate urgent need to move around, requiring opportunities to initiate, explore, discover, and individuate rather than always to capitulate) seem arbitrary, uninteresting, and very difficult (it's even very difficult for

young children to sit still!), *a great deal of stress comes along with the self-discipline.* This is **unhealthy self-discipline,** self-discipline achieved at much too high a health and mental health price. Of course, another reaction to mission impossible, familiar to us all, is to quit trying, a reaction resulting in "bad" behavior and poor report cards.

Anybody, a child too, can *occasionally* benefit from doing things that seem arbitrary, uninteresting, and very difficult. A little of this is "character building." It builds ability to adjust to what others want, creative coping skills, forbearance, capacity to tolerate frustration—in short, **self-discipline.** But more than just an occasional dose of expectations that are arbitrary, uninteresting, and too difficult **doesn't lead to self-discipline,** it leads to trouble. (We really should digress here to discuss all the things that children learn, not *in spite of* their tendency to move a great deal, but *through the medium of movement.* Oh me, oh my, there's so much to talk about that that will have wait till a later date!)

Lest anyone misunderstand, we hasten to state that all leading early childhood educators believe in discipline, because it's in a context of discipline that each child develops **self**-discipline. On this, as on many things, teachers in academic and developmentally appropriate programs for young children agree. Children need routines, rules, boundaries, behavioral expectations and standards, procedures, policies, limits … children need control. They need reasonable, age-appropriate control, and of course understanding. They need fair, firm discipline at home (both homes if the parents are divorced). They need it in child care settings. They need it everywhere else they spend significant amounts of time. As any child psychologist, child psychiatrist, psychiatric social worker specializing in family counseling, well-trained traditional nursery school/kindergarten ed-

---

**The goal is much more than for children to learn mere academics. We want each child to explore something of interest in considerable depth. This is learning how to learn with excellence.**

---

ucator, parent or caregiver whose credential is good success in rearing happy, emotionally well-balanced, productive children will tell us, *as Freud himself told us in book after book,* children left largely undisciplined, lacking guidance in slowly but steadily growing up, indulge their most primitive impulses greedily, devour the time and attention of beloved adults, whiningly demand the first turn, the longest turn, and the most turns, struggle for the best possessions, bite, sulk, howl, and throw half-hour raging tantrums. Many child development specialists are opposed to pressing and stressing children beyond their capacity to cope, but these specialists still strongly believe in child-guidance-style discipline. David Elkind, for example, professor of Child Study at Tufts University and one of the nation's best known proponents of today's "Don't Rush Them" school of thought, writes,

Children need and want help in controlling their impulses; if they are not called upon to control themselves, they use their behavior to control adults. Yet in fact it is scary to a child to have power over adults. Consequently, handed a power they did not want, did not need, and could not handle, such children [are] willful, domineering, given to temper tantrums, and on the whole abominable. (1981, p. xi)

Two things that are extremely important for children to learn at this age are positive self-esteem and healthy self-discipline, and neither is learned through gimmicks and techniques, or through alienating lectures. Whether these characteristics are better learned in academic or developmentally appropriate programs is a question worth pondering. One might guess the latter, because in the former, teachers are so distracted and driven by other objectives and directives that they may not be able to focus as fully on these two great big goals.

## For further reading

Bauch, J.P. (Ed.). (1988). *Early childhood education in the schools.* Washington, DC: National Education Association.

Biber, B. (1984). *Early education and psychological development.* New Haven, CT: Yale University Press.

Calkins, L.M. (1986). *The art of teaching writing.* Portsmouth, NH: Heinemann.

Council of Chief State School Officers. (1988). *Early childhood and family education: Foundations for success.* Washington, DC: Author.

DeVries, R., & Kohlberg, L. (in press). *Programs of early education: The constructivist view.* Washington, DC: NAEYC. (Original work published in 1987)

Elkind, D. (1988). The resistance to developmentally appropriate educational practice with young children: The real issue. In C. Warger (Ed.), *A resource guide to public school early childhood programs* (pp. 53–62). Alexandria, VA: Association for Supervision and Curriculum Development.

Gardner, H. (1983). *Frames of mind: Theory of multiple intelligence.* New York: Basic.

Glickman, C.D. (1981). Play and the school curriculum: The historical context. *Journal of Research and Development in Education, 14*(3), 1–10.

Hendrick, J. (1988). *The whole child: Developmental education for the early years* (4th ed.). Columbus, OH: Merrill.

Hill, P.S. (1987). The function of the kindergarten. *Young Children, 42*(5), 12–19. (Originally published in 1926)

Johnson, R. (1987). *Approaches to early childhood education.* Columbus, OH: Merrill.

Jones, E. (1989). *Emergent curriculum: Planning and letting go.* Unpublished manuscript, Pacific Oaks College, Pasadena, CA.

Kamii, C. (1982). *Number in preschool and kindergarten: Educational implications of Piaget's theory.* Washington, DC: NAEYC.

Kamii, C., & Joseph, L. L. (1989). *Young children continue to reinvent arithmetic—2nd grade: Implications of Piaget's theory.* New York: Teachers College Press, Columbia University.

Kamii, C., & DeVries, R. (1978). *Physical knowledge in preschool education: Implications of Piaget's theory.* Englewood Cliffs, NJ: Prentice-Hall.

Karnes, M.B., & Johnson, L.J. (1989). Training staff, parents, and volunteers working with gifted young children, especially those with disabilities and from low-income homes. *Young Children, 44*(3), 49–56.

Katz, L., & Chard, S. (1989). *Engaging children's minds: The project approach.* Norwood, NJ: Ablex.

McCracken, J.B. (Ed.). (1986). *Reducing stress in young children's lives.* Washington, DC: NAEYC.

National Association for the Education of Young Children. (1984). *Accreditation criteria & procedures of the National Academy of Early Childhood Programs.* Washington, DC: Author.

National Association for the Education of Young Children. (1985). *Guide to accreditation by the National Academy of Early Childhood Programs.* Washington, DC: Author.

National Association of State Boards of Education. (1988). *Right from the start.* Alexandria, VA: Author.

National Council for the Social Studies. (1989). Social studies for early childhood education and elementary school children preparing for the 21st Century: A report from NCSS task force on early childhood/elementary social studies. *Social Education, 53*(1), 14–24.

Nebraska State Board of Education. (1984). *Position statement on kindergarten.* Lincoln, NE: Author.

Oken-Wright, P. (1988). Show and tell grows up. *Young Children, 43*(2), 52–58.

Paasche, C.L., Gorrill, L., & Strom, B. (1989). *Children with special needs in early childhood settings.* Menlo Park, CA: Addison-Wesley.

Sawyers, J. K., & Rogers, C. S. (1988). *Helping young children develop through play: A practical guide for parents, caregivers, and teachers.* Washington, DC: NAEYC.

Southern Association on Children Under Six. (1986). *Position statement on quality four-year-old programs in public schools.* Little Rock, AR: Author.

Strickland, D.S., & Morrow, L.M. (Eds.). (1989). *Emerging literacy: Young children learn to read and write.* Newark, DE: International Reading Association.

## References

Bredekamp, S. (Ed.). (1987). *Developmentally appropriate practice in early childhood programs serving children from birth through age 8* (expanded ed.). Washington, DC: NAEYC.

Elkind, D. (1981). *The hurried child: Growing up too fast too soon.* Reading, MA: Addison-Wesley.

Kagan, J. (1984). *The nature of the child.* New York: Basic.

Kamii, C. (Ed.). (1990). *Achievement testing in the early grades: The games grown-ups play.* Washington, DC: NAEYC.

# WHAT'S MISSING IN CHILDREN'S TV

*A powerful medium of persuasion is failing its promise. The US Congress demands reform. Other nations watch in suspense. Cast your vote for the programs TV should show.*

## Peggy Charren

*Peggy Charren is founder and president of Action for Children's Television (ACT) and a Visiting Scholar in Education at Harvard University's Graduate School of Education. As former director of the Creative Arts Council of Newton, Massachusetts, she worked with theater and dance groups, artists, musicians, poets, and writers to develop programs for classroom enrichment.*

I LIKE CHILDREN'S TELEVISION.

It can offer our youngest viewers the opportunity to learn about a wide variety of places, people, occupations, ideas, life styles, and value systems, many of which will affect the way they will live the rest of their lives. It can help children to think, to question, to imagine, to create. It can introduce them to the stories of Anansi the Spider Man and Coyote the Trickster...the legong and bari dance of the children of Bali. It can teach them to value poetry and music, freedom of expression and peace. It can empower them to act to make their world a better place.

It *can* do all this...but is it *doing* it? I'm convinced that it's not doing nearly enough.

Children in the US today spend four hours a day watching TV, more time than they spend in the classroom, or in any activity except sleep. Many people worry about the effects of television on children.

They worry about incessant exposure to violence. Are children learning that aggressive behavior is an acceptable solution to problems?

What are the effects of TV's racial and sexual stereotypes?

How has TV's rapid-fire delivery affected children's ability to learn?

Some feel that TV is a plug-in drug and the only way to deal with it is to get rid of the set. I disagree. I like television.

People around the world feel the same way, as I heard repeatedly in a small town outside of Paris this fall at FIMAJ, the first international market for children's TV programming. It's interesting to note that many people in countries like France and Britain have not been concerned in the past about children's TV. Now, however, as their networks become more commercialized, these nations are beginning to understand what some of us in the US have been decrying for decades. And, although other countries have not developed the quantity of children's programming the US has, all of us gathered in France shared one problem—how to get the good stuff on the air.

I met people from several continents waiting with suspense for the outcome of US legislation intended to assure a certain amount of high-quality television for children. I have pushed this legislation for the same reason I started Action for Children's Television (ACT)—because TV is one of the most powerful, cost-effective instruments of education the world has ever known.

Unfortunately, it's often used to showcase violence, raunchy rock rhymes, dirty words, and sexual innuendo. Many adults, frustrated and angry with this television fare that children watch, want to censor it. But censorship is not the way to protect children's rights to entertainment and education on the TV screen. The right to express what some consider offensive speech is the price Americans pay for freedom of political speech. And we cannot afford to risk losing that freedom.

ACT is proud of the fact that it has never once in its 20-year history told a broadcaster to "take this program off the air because we don't like it." ACT supports a broadening, not narrowing, of television viewing options, and we believe that children and young adolescents are best served by programming designed especially for them, not by cleaned-up adult TV fare.

ACT wants each American child to grow up with the ability to thoughtfully determine his or her own individual understanding of right and wrong, based on the widest possible amount of information that parents, schools, and television can provide.

It's obvious that TV could be doing a lot more, but, as we'll see, the present profit-oriented environment of the television industry makes that especially difficult. That's why we're interested in hearing from you, the home or school viewer: What do *you* as a parent, teacher, or other adult TV watcher think is missing from children's TV? What type of educational programming do you feel is needed to balance the current fare?

The main link between the needs of American children and broadcasters' responsibility to the American public as a whole is the legal obligation imposed upon each American broadcaster to serve the public interest as defined in the US Communications Act of 1934. (See box, Why a New Bill.)

It is the responsibility of the broadcasting media to provide as broad a range of opinions as possible and to keep the public informed about all sides of a controversial issue. Of course, not all controversial topics are appropriate subjects for children's television. But a surprising number are, if they are handled in a manner suited to the age of viewers.

Playing against this opportunity is economic reality. American commercial cable companies, local stations, and national networks are corporations, with a responsibility to their shareholders to maximize profits. Maximum diversity of service to the television public does not usually go hand in hand with maximum profits. And the necessary compromise between diversity and profits is not easy to achieve; nor does it tend to favor the public interest.

Instead, with certain significant exceptions, commercial TV is used to educate children to behave as a market segment, to lobby for products they don't need, to consume instead of to save. Children are persuaded to buy what they want before they can know what they need.

Unlike adults, children do not zap the ads when they use a remote control device. The ads feature more children and better animation than the programs they interrupt. Children like commercials, and corporations know how to take advantage of this sad fact of TV life.

Research and common sense indicate that advertising to children is inherently unfair and deceptive. In fact a number of countries—including Belgium, Denmark, and Sweden—ban TV selling to children. Others—including Finland, France, and the Netherlands—have restrictions.

For-profit corporations try to make their trade names and products an integral part of the everyday life of consumers. They are particularly determined to reach young children, not just to increase current profits but to build brand identity for future sales. Brand-name preference persists over very long periods of time and adds enormous value to any consumer product. That's why the vice-president of Grey Advertising says: "It isn't enough to just advertise on television....You've got to reach kids throughout their day—in school, as they're shopping in the mall...or at the movies. You've got to become part of the fabric of their lives."

ACT has filed formal complaints against deceptive advertising practices with the Federal Trade Commission and the Federal Communications Commission, but as yet no action has been taken.

## HALF-HOUR COMMERCIALS

In an insidious variation some advertisers, toy manufacturers, and television producers have turned children's shows into half-hour ads for toys—GI Joe, ThunderCats, and other war-related product lines for boys; Day-Glo colored stuffed animals for girls. Hasbro even turned a plastic necklace, Charmkins, into a series.

During the 1980s, toy manufacturers turned more than 70 toys into TV series, blurring the distinction between editorial and commercial speech and creating a toy promotion bonanza for the advertiser.

Perhaps the most dangerous example of willingness to commercialize the environment of childhood is Whittle Communications' "Channel One," a daily 12-minute classroom newscast interrupted by four 30-second commercials. In return for guaranteeing that at least 92% of its students will watch these ads every day, each school that accepts the program receives free TV monitors for most of its classrooms.

The 4,700 schools that have said "yes" to this Trojan horse of a deal are ignoring some basic educational, moral, and legal tenets. Learning works best when you feel good about yourself. Teen counselors call it self-esteem. But advertising works when a felt need is created that only a product will satisfy. Advertising in a classroom emphasizes economic differences. It is outrageous to tell students to spend money on anything when so many live in poverty.

It is worth noting that some states, including California and New York, have banned "Channel One" in the classroom and more than 12,000 schools across the country have signed up for "CNN Newsroom," a daily, 15-minute, commercial-free newscast, applauded by educators and available without charge from Ted Turner's Cable News Network. The Discovery Channel's "Assignment Discovery" and The Christian Science Monitor's "World Classroom" are two other ad-free services.

But, despite the depressing picture I have painted, it is possible for American families to find terrific children's television, uninterrupted by sales pitches, on our TV screens.

One broadcasting entity that does make an effort to meet the needs of children is, of course, the Public Broadcasting Service. PBS, since its inception more than 20 years ago, has been a constructive noncommercial alternative to commercial television and has had a profound and positive impact on children's lives. PBS has pioneered much creative programming for young people—"Mister Rogers' Neighborhood," "Sesame Street," "3-2-1 Contact," "WonderWorks," and "Long Ago and Far Away"—and has made TV learning both in school and at home a high adventure. However, public television's limited resources must be used to serve adult audiences as well. We cannot rely solely on the public system to fill the children's programming gaps left open by commercial TV.

That's why people like Gerald Lesser, Harvard University professor of education and developmental psychology, are pursuing other avenues. Dr. Lesser recently met with producers, educators, and researchers from several nations looking for ways to cooperate in creating original news programming for children.

In the past Japan, Norway, Canada, and Britain, among others, have achieved varying degrees of success with children's news shows, while countries like Hungary and Yugoslavia are entering the field for the first time. Their hope is that international cooperation—sharing ideas and perhaps resources—will result in news shows that will appeal to children and hold their interest.

## CABLE AND CASSETTES
Educational and pay cable channels provide some engaging options without commercials for families that can afford the extra expense. In addition to the

# Action for Children's Television

Twenty years ago, I found that the children's TV programming available to my two young children did not offer them enough choice. I decided to do something about it. I started Action for Children's Television.

Although concern about television and children was widespread in 1968, there was no organized advocacy for change. I wasn't sure *how* to become a child advocate. I knew that I didn't want to use censorship tactics as a way to change television. Censorship meant fewer choices. We needed more choice, not less. I knew that many of my friends felt the same way.

So we took the first step. We began in a manner commonly referred to as grass roots—and it doesn't get much grassier than Newton, Massachusetts, a suburb of Boston. Meetings in my sitting room progressed to discussions in New York and Washington with TV executives and government representatives.

Today ACT is a public charity, with a paid staff of four, more than 100 volunteer representatives across the country, more than 10,000 contributing members, and the support of 150 major national associations, including health, education, and parent organizations and trade unions. We conduct business as a public company, with an outside board of directors, an annual audit, and an annual report. Our yearly budget is approximately $175,000.

Instead of censorship, ACT looks to the laws that regulate broadcasting as the vehicle for change. ACT's goal has been to increase viewing options for children and young teens, to get on that small screen the kind of choices one finds in a good children's library. Traditionally, ACT's program has involved two parallel sets of activities: (1) legal argument before regulatory agencies and (2) education of the public through the print and electronic press, outreach programs, publications, and private-sector advocacy.

ACT's strategies to broaden children's viewing options within the existing system are carried out simultaneously on several fronts:

1. Petition the FCC (Federal Communications Commission) to increase the amount of service that broadcasters are required to provide for young audiences, so that children and young adolescents will have more choice.

2. Work in support of affirmative action to bring more minorities and women into positions of power in the television industry, because this will help to eliminate racism and sexism from television programming.

3. Encourage increased funding of public television, which provides impressive noncommercial alternatives for children.

4. Educate broadcasters and cablecasters about the diverse needs of young audiences.

5. Encourage the development of alternative technologies, such as cable television and home video, which increase program choice for young people.

6. Educate parents to take responsibility for their children's television viewing experiences by carefully consulting the television schedule, by turning the TV set off more often, and by talking to children about what they watch.

7. Help teachers, school principals, pediatricians, dentists, and other professionals concerned with the welfare of children pay attention to the influence of television on young audiences.

8. Petition the Federal Trade Commission to eliminate deceptive advertising targeted to children, because America's free speech guarantees do not protect deceptive commercial speech.

These eight strategies do not encompass ACT's entire program. But they demonstrate that television reform does not have to mean censorship. It does not have to mean interference with program content. Instead, TV policymaking should focus on issues of choice, access, and education.—*P.C.*

# Why a New Bill

The public interest standard is defined by only a few words in the US Communications Act of 1934, a piece of legislation that charges the Federal Communications Commission to license each broadcaster to operate "in the public interest, convenience and necessity." These seven words are the hook upon which Action for Children's Television hangs its entire program for change. Without the public interest standard, Americans would lose their best legal argument for responsible television service.

More people want to broadcast than there are available frequencies; for each frequency the government selects the broadcaster who will best serve the public interest and gives that person only a short-term license, with the government keeping everyone else off the frequency. In exchange for this scarce privilege bestowed without charge, the broadcaster pledges to act as a trustee for all those kept off—to serve the public interest and show a government agency, the FCC, that it has done so in order to get its license renewed for another term.

Then in 1984 came deregulation.

Deregulation of broadcasting under the Reagan administration seriously hurt children and badly damaged the industry's capacity to serve their needs. TV rules were relaxed or eliminated. For example:

1. The number of stations or channels a single entity could own increased, resulting in giant megasystems with little community affiliation.

2. The length of time a channel must operate before it could be sold went from three years to zero, resulting in rapid turnover, with some stations up for sale twice within one year.

3. Limits on the amount of commercial time per hour were removed.

4. Stations were permitted to replace informative filings in the FCC at renewal time with a post card saying that they had served the public.

5. Stations were freed from the obligation to serve children with a "let 'em eat cable" attitude implied by the then FCC chairman, Mark Fowler.

These deregulatory policies caused stations to be perceived not as public trustees but as economic opportunities.

The Children's Television Act of 1990, recently passed by Congress and allowed to become law by President Bush, puts a limit on the number of minutes of ads per hour in children's programs and requires stations to air educational shows for children as a condition of license renewal. It also provides for a stable funding source for children's programming through a national endowment, although at this time specific funds have not been appropriated.

Admittedly, the number of ads permitted is too high and the program requirement is not very specific, but I believe that, with this law on the books, caring parents will find it easier to guide their children to a more nutritious TV diet.—*P.C.*

---

Disney Channel and Nickelodeon, there are children's programs worth watching on Showtime, HBO, the Discovery Channel, and the Learning Channel.

Home videocassettes solve the TV problem for many parents, providing for the first time easy access to music shows and TV versions of stories designed for young audiences.

But there is already a cloud on this promising horizon. Some children's videos contain commercials at the beginning, the end, and even in the middle of the tape.

If knowledge is power, what do we do about the fact that the new communications technology boom may work against the interest of the many US citizens who are poor? In a world where information is the prerequisite to responsible action, we cannot afford to divide the TV audience into informational haves and have-nots.

To increase choice for those who cannot afford costly new technologies, ACT recommends cable and satellite policies that reflect this concern. We are working with the American library system to encourage libraries to lend videos as they do books.

Another of ACT's current priorities (see box, **page 121**) is to promote a much higher level of television awareness in the home. Because most of children's TV viewing is done at home, helping young people make sensible viewing choices is ultimately up to parents. We try to encourage parents and children to take a second look at family TV habits: to talk together about the role television plays in children's lives and to find new ways to solve TV-related problems.

The role of television is not to replace families and teachers as the chief influence on children in our society. But television, viewed selectively and in moderation, can encourage children to discuss, wonder about, and even read about new things. Above all, it can lead them to ask questions.

As we set policies that will open the marketplace to new ideas and to the kinds of shows that are missing, we should keep in mind the section on mass media adopted by the General Assembly of the United Nations at the December 1989 Convention on the Rights of the Child. It says in part that mass media education should be directed to "the preparation of the child for responsible life in a free society, in the spirit of understanding, peace, tolerance, equality of sexes, and friendship among all peoples, ethnic, national and religious groups..." That's a meaningful prescription for the future of children's television.

# School-Age Child Care:

## A Review of Five Common Arguments

Mick Coleman, Bryan E. Robinson, and Bobbie H. Rowland

During the past decade, parents and educators have increasingly expressed concern over the potential safety and developmental risks associated with children in self-care, or the care of another child (Garbarino, 1984; Harris, Kagay, & Ross, 1987; Robinson, Rowland, & Coleman, 1986; 1989; Zigler & Ennis, 1988). One result has been a growing interest in school-age child care (SACC) programs.

Unfortunately, implementation of a SACC program is not always an easy task. Different values and beliefs can be held within any given community as to (a) whose responsibility it is to provide SACC; (b) the types of services that should be provided; and (c) how best to manage the day-to-day operation of the program.

In this article, the authors examine five common arguments that they have encountered during their SACC programming work over the past six years. Some of the arguments have come from parents, others from teachers, and still others from community leaders. Programming resources are also given to assist early childhood educators in addressing the arguments so that they might plan for the effective development and delivery of SACC services.

*Argument 1: There is no need for SACC programs. They have always existed.*

It is true that parents have for decades depended upon relatives, libraries, churches, park and recreation services, and youth clubs as informal sources of SACC. Unfortunately, these services are often unable to meet the growing demand for SACC (Coleman, Rowland, & Robinson, 1989). In some cases, the number of children requiring services is too great. In other cases, the type of services desired by school-age children and parents go beyond the training of the staff or the philosophy of the SACC services; rather, they require a wide range of services. As noted by one parent:

*I don't want my child in school all day. He needs to be a kid. He needs to play in a safe environment. The program did nothing more than*

*help him with his homework and give him books to read.*

The authors have also heard the opposite complaint, that a particular SACC program placed too much emphasis on recreation and too little emphasis on helping children complete homework assignments. In fact, there are many SACC options available, each having its own set of potential advantages and disadvantages (see Massachusetts Office for Children, 1988). Each educational facility must consider its own unique values, needs, resources, and barriers in deciding upon the implementation of a SACC program. This process should ideally include a community needs assessment, the results of which should provide guidance on developing a philosophical mission statement (e.g., educational, recreational, support, enrichment, protection), as well as operational policies (e.g., hours of service, schedules, staffing, finances, curriculum). The needs assessment survey need not be complicated. As noted in

*Mick Coleman is Assistant Professor, Child and Family Development, and Extension Human Development Specialist, University of Georgia, Hoke Smith Annex, Athens, Ga. Bryan E. Robinson and Bobbie H. Rowland are both Professor of Human Services, University of North Carolina, Charlotte, NC*

From *Day Care & Early Education,* Summer 1991, pp. 13-17. Published by Human Sciences Press, 72 Fifth Avenue, New York, NY 10011.

Table 1
*Developing a SACC
Needs Assessment Survey*

*Who*
- needs SACC? Consider:
  the age or grade of children.
  the sex of children.
  family income.
  the area of residence.
  the needs of children with exceptionalities.
- should staff the SACC program? Consider:
  child care providers.
  trained adult community volunteers.
  professional youth leaders (e.g., Camp Fire, 4-H, YWCA).
  college students.
  retired or substitute teachers.

*What*
- barriers might prevent parents from using SACC services? Consider:
  cost.
  transportation.
  hours of operation.
  overcrowded program.
  dislike of program policies (e.g., discipline).
  dislike of staff (e.g., not involved with children).
- barriers might prevent children

from using SACC services? Consider:
  dislike of activities (e.g., too "babylike").
  dislike of schedule (e.g., too rigid).
  dislike of staff (e.g., too authoritarian).
  too few children of the same age enrolled in program.
- activities would parents (and children) like in a SACC program? Consider:
  homework time.
  free play.
  snack.
  arts/crafts.
  recreational activities.
  safety education classes.
  drama.
  dance.
  tutoring in special classes (e.g., piano, computers).
  field trips.

*When*
- are SACC services needed? Consider:
  before school.
  after school.
  during teacher in-service days.
  during school vacation.
  during inclement weather.
  when child is sick.
  at night.

*Where*
- should SACC programs be located? Consider:
  local schools.
  recreation departments.
  youth club/agency sites (e.g., YMCA).
  churches.
  day care centers.

*How*
- satisfied are parents with their current SACC arrangement?
- satisfied are children with their current SACC arrangement?
- much are parents willing to pay for SACC services per week?
- many hours per day do children currently spend at home alone?
- many hours per day do children currently spend at home under the supervision of another school-age child?

*Why*
- provide SACC services?
  The answer to this question should (a) be based on an analysis of responses to the preceding questions and (b) guide SACC program developers in writing a philosophical mission statement, operational policies, curriculum guide, and job descriptions.

---

Table 1, the survey should revolve around a basic set of who, what, when, where, how, and why questions.

*Argument 2: School-age children are old enough to care for themselves.*

While school-age children may sometimes appear old enough to care for themselves, their growing independence should not be overinterpreted. School-age children still need adult guidance and support in order to successfully handle self-care situations that demand adultlike responsibilities. This point was recently discovered by one elementary-school teacher who lamented:

*I have three children in my class who go home alone every afternoon. "I don't want to go home alone," they cry. How can I help?*

One of the first questions that should be asked in a situation like this is whether the parents are fully aware of their child's fears. They may not be.

It is during the school-age years that children first begin to develop friendships and interests independent of their parents. Parents may subsequently place too much trust in their child's readiness to assume self-care responsibilities. Yet, the confident school-age child who left for school in the morning may, like the children encountered by the above teacher, become fearful later in the afternoon when faced with the prospect of returning home alone. Other children may react against their fear by acting out. Even children who enjoy their

newfound independence can quickly find themselves in situations for which they are unprepared due to a lack of self-care information, experience, and/or skills.

All children have the same sense of curiosity that can lead to accidents in the absence of adult supervision. Safety for children in self-care should thus be viewed as a developmental issue rather than a geographic issue. For example, children living in rural areas are sometimes more isolated than their peers living in urban areas and may thus be able to gain help in an emergency. Even parents of children living in "safe" middle-class neighborhoods cannot completely protect their children against the potential hazards associated with a self-care situation.

The safety risks associated with childhood behavior is perhaps best reflected in the fact that between twelve and fourteen million American children (or one in four) under age fifteen require medical attention due to accidental injury each year (National Coalition to Prevent Childhood Injury, 1988). These numbers are greater than for any disease, making injuries the number one health risk for American children under the age of fifteen.

Children in self-care may especially be at risk for in-home accidents. A recent study sponsored by the Whirlpool Corporation found that in 71% of all homes fitting the self-care category, children under age fourteen were using major home appliances on a regular basis, in many cases as part of their household chores (Project Home Safe, 1987).

Less is known about the social-emotional and psychological threats to children in self-care. Some studies report that children in self-care suffer from fear, anxiety, and loneliness, while other studies report that children in self-care are no different in their psychosocial adjustment from their peers under adult supervision (see reviews by Robinson et al., 1986, 1989).

Regardless of their child care arrangement, all children can benefit from learning in-home and out-of-home safety skills (e.g., responding to emergencies and strangers; time management; food safety). School-age child care programs represent an ideal situation in which to demonstrate safety skills, as well as give children the opportunity to practice safety skills. A list of safety curriculum resources is given at the end.

*Argument 3: Anyone can care for school-age children. Specialized training is not required.*

This is an argument also frequently heard in relation to preschool child care. However, in the case of SACC there is an added twist in that some educators may fail to make a clear distinction between the care and education of preschoolers versus that of school-age children. For example, at a recent workshop on guiding school-age children, one preschool teacher remarked:

*I do the same thing with my nine-year-olds in the afternoon that I do with my three-year-olds in the morning. I make them sit beside me and hold my hand when they misbehave.*

Apart from adopting a more positive strategy for guiding three-year-olds, this teacher's inability to see other options for guiding school-age children reflects a simplified mind-set of transferring the preschool day into the after-school program.

Effective preschool teachers do not necessarily make effective SACC teachers, since some adults relate better to certain age groups than others. It is thus unrealistic to expect all teachers of three-year-olds to understand or relate to nine-year-olds.

Regardless of their training or work experience, all SACC teachers should have a knowledge of the development of school-age children, their interests and needs. Armed with this knowledge, SACC teachers can plan an after-school schedule that takes into account the previous seven to eight hours of mental, sedentary school work in which children have been engaged. More specifically, the after-school schedule should provide children with maximum independence in choosing and implementing their own activities. A relaxed, flexible after-school schedule is also needed in which children select their own activities. Such a child-centered environment helps children to develop a sense of self-confidence and industry.

SACC teachers help children to develop real-life problem-solving skills by allowing them to negotiate their disagreements, assign meaning to their play activities, and solve dilemmas that arise from their play activities. Put another way, SACC teachers are most effective when they facilitate activities by asking challenging questions (e.g., "What do you think would happen if you used a different color?"), providing information (e.g., "John is using a *legend* to read the map"), and offering supportive suggestions (e.g., "Maybe your kite would fly higher if you tried a different type of paper. What do you think?"). In contrast, formal "teaching" methods transform the after-school program into an extension of the school day, denying children a change of pace and the opportunity to learn on their own.

SACC teachers should also consider the role of school-age children in a SACC program. It is inappropriate to assume that older school-age children are willing or able to help care for smaller children, a situation that can arise when the teacher is unsure of how to plan or implement school-age activities.

Older children do not enjoy the same types of activities or respond to the same types of guidance techniques as younger children. SACC teachers thus need specialized resources and training related to the development and facilitation of activities for school-age children. The staff training and activity resources listed at the end can help SACC teachers to learn developmentally appropriate approaches for working with school-age children of different ages.

*Argument 4. There is not enough money to pay for SACC.*

SACC programming can indeed be expensive, involving such major expenses as staff, utilities, educational materials, rent, transportation, snacks, and insurance. When confronted with costs, the authors are reminded of a simple but powerful statement made by a colleague when asked about the expense of implementing a SACC program. She replied, "We pay for what we value."

Paying for value should indeed be a central theme in developing SACC programs. Unfortunately, SACC budgets are sometimes developed with insufficient attention given to the types of materials and equipment preferred by school-age children or their use of these materials. School-age children are more likely than preschoolers to use large quantities of materials in creating more complex products; they are more likely to be attuned to commercial products advertised on television; they are accustomed to using more sophisticated (and expensive) equipment in their school classrooms; they use indoor and outdoor equipment that is different from that used by preschoolers; and they have more personalized interests and hobbies that require a wide range of materials (Meritt, 1988).

According to a national survey, the median weekly payment made by parents for child care for children between the ages of five and fourteen was $40.10 (U.S. Department Commerce, 1987). However, variation was found within the survey results, with payments going as low as $10-$19 per week and as high as $70 and over.

SACC programs may be supported by a combination of service fees and private and in-kind support, as well as local, state, and federal grants. Parent fees usually provide most of the operating revenue for SACC programs (Baden, Genser, Levine, & Seligson, 1982). Additional private support may come from individuals, foundations, businesses, or service organizations. In-kind support (e.g., rent, transportation, utilities, custodial service, staff) may come from cooperating agencies.

Fortunately, parents seem to be willing to pay for SACC services. According to one recent national survey, 59% of all parents were willing to pay for after-school educational programs, and 52% were willing to pay for after-school noneducational programs (Harris et al., 1987).

One current source of government support for SACC programming is the Dependent Care Planning and Development Grant (Office of Management and Budget, 1988). This grant provides for a variety of services in two broad areas: (a) resource and referral, and (b) direct SACC service delivery. Funds may be used to assist in the planning, development, expansion, or improvement of SACC services. Some states also have special grants available for SACC programming, such as the "Children's Trust Fund" (1989).

The respective House (H.R. 3) and Senate (S. 5) child care bills would provide additional financial support for SACC programming. The future

of these bills depends upon the House and Senate's reaching a resolution on differences between their respective bills, as well as the President's signing the compromise bill.

*Argument 5: Parents are more concerned with affordable SACC than quality SACC.*

In fact, and not surprisingly, parents want both. It is thus particularly frustrating when they sometimes find that they can have neither. As noted by one parent:

*I don't know what to do. My child refuses to go to the after-school programs that I can afford, calling them "baby-sitting." And those that she likes are too expensive.*

Developing affordable, quality SACC programs need not be difficult. The financial cost of operating a SACC program can be accommodated by networking with a local school and/or other community agencies. This arrangement allows for the sharing of materials, staff, and facility space. In fact, many of the most successful SACC programs in the nation have been conceived of and addressed as a community issue in which community resources are shared.

Likewise, developing a quality SACC curriculum is not difficult when we take into account the developmental needs of school-age children within the context of their typical day. After school, school-age children need time to refuel with a nutritious snack, time to let off steam through safe and interesting outdoor games, time to work on homework, time to socialize with peers, and time to pursue their own interests. As mentioned above, a developmentally appropriate SACC curriculum addresses these needs by providing a relaxed schedule and a child-centered environment. A number of organizations can supply SACC administrators and teachers with information on developing such an environment. Five such organizations include the following.

The School-Age Child Care Project
Center for Research on Women
Wellesley College
Wellesley, MA 02181

Project Home Safe
American Home Economics
    Association
1555 King Street
Alexandria, VA 22314

National Association for the
    Education of Young Children
1834 Connecticut Avenue NW
Washington, DC 20009-5786

Georgia School-Age Child Care
    Council
1340 Spring Street, Suite 200
Atlanta, GA 30309

University of Kentucky
College of Home Economics
Department of Family Studies
The Research and Development
    Center for School-Age Child
    Care and Early Education
102 Erikson Hall
Lexington, KY 40506-0050

## Conclusion

As interest in SACC continues to grow, educators are being looked to for guidance in the development and implementation of quality SACC programs that contribute to the growth and development of school-age children. The resources given in this paper are provided to assist educators in providing this guidance.

## References

Baden, R., Genser, A., Levine, J., & Seligson, M. (1982). *School-age child care: An action manual.* Boston: Auburn.

Children's Trust Fund. (1989). *Children's trust fund of Georgia.* (Available from Children's Trust Fund Commission, 10 Park Place South, Suite 410, Atlanta, GA 30303).

Coleman, M., Rowland, B. H., & Robinson, B. E. (1989). Latchkey children and school-age child care: A review of programming issues. *Child and Youth Care Quarterly, 18* (1), 39-48.

Dodd, C. (1989). *The new school child care demonstration act of 1989 (S. 457).* (Available from Senator Christopher Dodd, United States Senate, Washington, DC 20510).

Garbarino, J. (1984). *Can American families afford the luxury of childhood?* Unpublished manuscript, Pennsylvania State University, College of Human Development, University Park, 1984.

Harris, H., Kagay, M., & Ross, J. (1987). *The American teacher 1987: Strengthening links between home and school.* New York: Metropolitan Life Insurance Company.

Massachusetts Office for Children. (1988, January). *School-age child care technical assistance paper: Getting started.* Boston: Author.

Meritt, P. (1988, October). From one director to another: Tips on school age child care. *Child Care Information Exchange,* 26-28.

National Coalition to Prevent Childhood Injury. (1988). *Safe kids are no accident.* Washington, DC: Author.

Neugebauer, R. (1979, November). School age day care: Getting it off the ground. *Child Care Information Exchange,* 9-15.

Office of Management and Budget. (1988). *1988 catalog of federal domestic assistance.* Washington, DC: U.S. Government Printing Office.

Project Home Safe. (1987). *Whirlpool corporation study shows children regular appliance users.* Washington, DC: American Home Economics Association.

Robinson, B. E., Rowland, B. H., & Coleman, M. (1986). *Latchkey kids: Unlocking doors for children and their families.* Lexington, MA: Lexington.

Robinson, B. E., Rowland, B. H., & Coleman, M. (1989). *Home alone after school: Providing the best care for your child.* Lexington, MA: Lexington.

U.S. Department of Commerce, Bureau of Census. (1987, May). *Who's minding the kids? Child care arrangements: Winter 1984-85.* (Current Population Reports, Household Economic Studies, Series P-70, No. 9). Washington, DC: U.S. Government Printing Office.

Zigler, E., & Ennis, P. (1988). Child care: A new role for tomorrow's schools. *Principal, 68* (1), 10-13.

## Selected In-Home and Out-of-Home Safety Curricula

Bower, D. W. (1986). *Care of myself.* University of Georgia Cooperative Extension Service, Hoke Smith Annex, Athens, GA 30602.

Columbia Gas System. (1988). *How to be a key performer.* 200 Civic Center Drive, P.O. Box 117, Columbus, OH 43216-0117.

Corporation for Public Broadcasting. (1988). *What if I'm home alone?* 1111 16th Street NW, Washington, DC 20036.

Cyr, L. F., Holmes, V. J., & Kelly, J. M. (1987). *3 to 5, I'm in charge.* University of Maine Cooperative Extension Service, Roger Clapp Greenhouse, Orono, ME 04469.

Johnson, C., & Pinson, C. (1989). *When I'm in charge.* North Carolina State University Extension Service, P.O. Box 7605, Raleigh, NC.

Labensohn, D. (1986, June). *On my own and ok.* Iowa State University Cooperative Extension Service, Child Development Department, 103 Richards Hall, Ames, IA 50011.

Todd, C. M. (1986). *Operation safe kids.* University of Illinois Cooperative Extension Service, 547 Bevier Hall, 905 South Goodwin Avenue, Urbana, IL 61801.

## Selected Staff Training and Activity Resources

Arns, B. (1988). *The survival guide to school-age child care.* Huntington Beach, CA: School-Age Workshops Press.

Bender, J., Elder, B. S., & Flatter, C. H. (1984). *Half a childhood: Time for school-age child care.* Nashville, TN: School-Age Notes.

Blau, R., Brady, E. G., Bucher, I., Hiteshew, B., Zavitkovsky, A., & Zavitkovsky, D. (1977). *Activities for school-age child care.* Washington, DC: National Association for the Education of Young Children.

Dade County Public Schools. (1984). *Afterschool care activities manual.* Office of Vocational, Adult, and Community Education, 1450 NE Second Avenue, Room 814, Miami, FL 33132.

Fink, D. B. (1985). *An intergenerational adventure: A training curriculum for older adult caregivers working with school-age children during the hours after school.* Wellesley, MA: Wellesley College Center for Research on Women.

*Project Home Safe.* American Home Economics Association, 1555 King Street, Alexandria, VA 22314.

Rowland, B. H., Coleman, M., & Robinson, B. E. (1987). *School-age child care training manual.* Charlotte, NC: The Council for Children.

*School Age Connections Newsletter.* University of Illinois Cooperative Extension Service, 547 Bevier Hall, 905 S. Goodwin, Urbana, IL 61801.

*School Age Notes Newsletter.* School Age Notes, P.O. 120674, Nashville, TN 37212.

University of California Cooperative Extension. (1988). *4-H afterschool program manuals.* 11477 E. Avenue, Auburn, CA 95603.

# Tests, Independence and Whole Language

*Standardized tests often do more harm than good,
but is there an alternative? Here's what a noted
New Zealand educator has to say*

**BRIAN CUTTING**

Brian Cutting is Educational Director of Wendy Pye Limited, an international publishing consultant and book publisher based in Auckland, New Zealand.

66 *Whole language is not 'airy-fairy' and neither is whole language evaluation.* 99

Why should children fail? Is it their fault, or does it have more to do with the educational system?

It would seem difficult to blame the children themselves. After all, most of them learn to talk, with all of language's complexities, well before they go to school (even though their learning continues for some years after that). Why is this learning so successful? Why do children learn to talk so naturally, and with apparent ease? These are some of the contributing factors:

• No one expects children to fail—not the children themselves, not their parents, not even the politicians and administrators concerned with education policy.

• Children are responsible for much of their own learning. Parents don't teach them every day. There's no manual for learning to talk which says: *Step one, tongue movements; Step two, consonants; Step three, vowels.* If such manuals did exist, children would certainly be less successful.

• Children practice for a long time. In fact, we're happy to let them take up to three years before some concern is voiced. And we're tolerant and full of praise for their "mistakes," not even seeing them as mistakes, but (especially at the beginning stages of learning) delighting in their attempts to say words.

• There are no tests of talking. Everyone recognizes that children will learn different things, at different rates and in different ways. There are no tests, because children *do* learn to talk.

But imagine what would happen if someone decided that tests of talking were essential. A test would be designed, and talkers tested. For some children, the test items would be easy. These children would be ahead of the test. For some, the test items would match what they know—their stage of development. They would be fine. For others, the test items would be beyond their present competence. They, on the basis of the test, would fail.

What would happen to these failed talkers? Using the model given by learning to read, there would be remedial type classes where the children could practice all the things they didn't know. There would be exercises designed to improve their ability to pass the test, rather than on learning to talk (which the children were doing quite happily until they, and their parents, found out that they couldn't). These would be artificial exercises which someone had identified as important elements in the "learning-to-talk" process.

Even the most elegant of standardized tests of "talking" would show that some children were good (passed) and some children were bad (failed). In fact, there would be an outcry if such a test were given, because of the huge number of children who would be placed behind their more successful peers and who would be removed to attend specially funded "talking" programs.

If we really wanted to make learning to talk a non-success story, the easiest way would be to design tests that would set a standard which all children would be expected to reach. We all know that such procedures would be futile for children learning to talk. So why do we use similar procedures for children learning to read and write?

Apart from learning to talk, children have learned many things successfully. It's worthwhile asking how they learned to do all these things. Not from following a manual. Not from learning to do all the parts before trying the whole. Not from artificial exercises divorced from real contexts. And not from tests, which supposedly identify what children know and don't know about a task. (Unfortunately, tests don't free learners; they constrain learning to what test developers believe to be important.)

**Dismal cycle.** We can't treat children as if some will be winners and others failures, because gradually the children who fail (when they really thought they were doing quite well) will begin to associate learning with failure. After repeated failure, they'll see school as futile. Worse, they'll begin to see themselves as hopeless. They and their parents never question what the test is testing or how how well it tests. Why would any education system fail children in this way, almost guaranteeing that five-year-olds will become habitual failures, doomed to a dismal cycle of practice-test-remediation until the children end up in special education classes?

There has to be a better way and there is. The focus on independent learning implies that the focus should be on independent evaluation as well.

This personal assessment of individual learning is not haphazard or random. (Whole language is not "airy-fairy" and neither is whole language evaluation.) It is systematic, regular and thorough. It can be used by teachers to help individual children learn more effectively about reading. (Is this book too difficult? Which books would help most?)

This kind of assessment caters to children's individual needs, while providing teachers with the feedback needed to help their children become independent. It helps teachers learn about reading and changes their ways of thinking about *how* children learn to read. Evaluation should not be viewed as an isolated chore necessary to give a child some grade, but rather as a natural part of the daily class program—a part that is vital for successful teaching and learning.

**Proving failure.** The whole point of learning is to be independent. Independence can

never be achieved if children have been turned away from learning by repeated failure, no matter how lofty the goals of the original program. It always amazes me that we have to prove failure over and over again. Most adults couldn't face such a system, so why do so many adults seem to support such a system for children, even when they're aware of its consequences?

The recorded observations of reading behavior provide all the information needed to show parents that their children are making progress. They also allow teachers to show parents how they can help their children at home.

Is it too heretical then to ask if we need the tests, the workbooks and the reading materials associated with them? Is it so difficult to replace them with alternative methods of assessment which place the emphasis on individuals and observations?

By the way, I wonder whether the basal workbook test system survives not because of its educational value (which is a proven failure for so many children). I wonder whether it owes its resilience to administrators who don't really trust their teachers to provide effective learning through alternative models of learning like whole language.

**The upper grades.** There is often an assumption that real learning starts after children move on from the lower grades, that more formal education and evaluation procedures now become essential. No more play! Down to work! Well, such a system may work for the successes of the school system, but for those already disillusioned by repeated failure, more of the same will hardly prove to be the panacea they seek. Why continue a cycle of failure?

If the differences between children entering school are great, so are the differences between children entering a class at the beginning of the year. The implication for teachers is that, just as in the lower grades, independent learning should be the focus of classroom practice. It follows that evaluation should be as individualized as possible. Children's learning can't be constrained by the uniformity that testing brings. The emphasis on individuals and independent learning means that teachers have created classrooms where diversity is recognized and can exist.

If learning in the upper primary and middle school years is to change, teachers and children must be allowed independence from a set, inflexible program of teaching and testing. The principles of whole language learning can help teachers to provide more enjoyable and successful learning for

*"The focus on independent learning implies that the focus should be on independent evaluation as well."*

*" It always amazes me that we have to prove failure over and over again. "*

all their children. And, the same principles which guided evaluation in the lower grades should guide evaluation for older children.

A balanced approach to evaluation should continue, with emphasis placed on observations, listening to children read, individual responses of various kinds, the children's own evaluation of their learning. Tests just don't give the feedback needed for self-evaluation of learning. They only give feedback on success or failure.

**Worthwhile system.** Listening to children read (running records, miscue analysis) is essential. You cannot find out what your children really know about reading without doing this. No test can do it more effectively, so it's worthwhile to organize a system where you listen to children read on a regular basis.

There's no reason why you shouldn't extend the "listening" with an individual conference, getting children to read both orally and silently, and then questioning them to find out how to help them understand more (about both the book and the reading process itself).

Also, there's no reason why these individual conferences should not be in the form of informal prose inventories, both published and those made up by you. All you need to make your own inventories are books with a developmental, gradual sequence of difficulty. The information collected can be stored in cumulative records, which will provide all the valid evidence needed by the school and parents about a child's progress.

The responses children make about their learning is one of the most valuable ways of evaluating their learning. If they can read a

book and successfully turn it into a play, they have demonstrated their understanding of it. As they read independently, they can construct responses of many kinds to show how well they have understood what they read—information which is not available through other means.

If national comparisons need to be made, the standardized tests used should correlate with the teaching practice and assessment used in schools. Otherwise, the mismatch will guarantee failure for many learners.

It's difficult being a whole language teacher. You often have to work in a system which subverts your beliefs. You integrate language arts and then unravel the strands, teaching and testing tenses of verbs. You teach reading using whole contexts and marvelous materials, and you do worksheets on phonics because that is what will be tested. You evaluate learning by running records and observations (and even some diagnostic tests), only to have a standardized test tell you and your children—children you know are learning to read well, especially in terms of their competence— that they really are failures.

It's hard, but teachers and the parents of the children they teach must look for alternative ways of evaluating language learning, ways that move away from the tests and classroom practices that guarantee, for too many children, failure in school.

*I would like to gratefully acknowledge the contribution to this article made by Jill Eggleton, author of* Whole Language Evaluation *(available through The Wright Group).*

# Tracking Progress Toward the School Readiness Goal

*It's time to design new forms of school readiness assessment, forms that do not encourage tracking of students, narrowing the curriculum, or kindergarten retention.*

PENELOPE ENGEL

**Penelope Engel** is a Professional Associate of the Educational Testing Service, Suite 475, 1825 Eye St., N.W., Washington, D.C. 20006.

"By the year 2000 all children will start school ready to learn."[1]

The National Governors' Association (NGA) set this national school readiness goal at its meeting in February 1990. At first glance, the statement may appear to be a call for a nationwide school admissions test for 1st grade, but if you know what lies behind this sentence, you'll see that nothing could be farther from the truth. In fact, this statement helped focus public attention on the compelling arguments *against* group-administered school readiness tests.

Widely publicized in the literature, these arguments have been debated in numerous forums and forged into policy statements by at least a dozen education organizations. Three general premises emerge: group-administered pencil-and-paper readiness tests are inappropriate for preschoolers and lack sufficient validity for making school entry decisions (Meisels 1989, Meisels et al. 1989, NAEYC 1988); their use often has the effect of narrowing the preschool curriculum and making

it excessively academic (Shepard and Smith 1988, Bredekamp and Shepard 1989); and test scores, when used to deny school entry, contribute to the practice of kindergarten retention, which is counterproductive public policy (Shepard and Smith 1989).

At the NGA meeting, the President and the governors warned that an assessment for school readiness should *not* be developed for purposes of measuring progress toward the readiness goal, because of the danger that it could be wrongfully used to determine when a child should start school. "Other current indicators of readiness may serve as proxies," they noted, "and still others need to be developed."[2]

The governors suggested that new methods be developed using teachers' cumulative observations of children.[3] At a minimum, this would yield better information to improve learning. It could possibly produce meaningful data for policymakers as well.

## The Limitations of Proxy Measures

Figure 1 lists specific objectives toward meeting the readiness goal. These objectives concern provision of quality preschool programs, prenatal nutrition, and health care, as well as

the involvement of parents as their children's teachers. Policymakers will use "proxies," defined as indicators that do not measure children directly but that indirectly measure factors positively associated with readiness, in order to track national progress toward these objectives.

The National Center for Education Statistics (NCES) is now assembling these proxy data from various government-sponsored national surveys. These include national statistics on prenatal care; low birthweight babies; child nutrition; the percent of eligibles served by subsidized preschool programs; the supply, demand, and quality of preschool services; the kinds of learning experiences provided; the extent of parental involvement; and child retention in early grades. NCES will rely heavily on the National Household Education Survey, a planned triennial telephone survey to a national sample of households, for the ongoing tracking of the education-related information, including data on parents as their children's teachers.[4]

Proxies, however, are not adequate readiness measures. While appropriate now as an interim method for tracking progress toward the readiness goal, they are nonetheless insufficient for this purpose. They provide

## Fig. 1. National Goals For Education Readiness

**Readiness Goal 1: By the year 2000, all children in American will start school ready to learn.**

Objectives:
- All disadvantaged and disabled children will have access to high-quality and developmentally appropriate preschool programs that help prepare children for school.
- Every parent in America will be a child's first teacher and devote time each day helping his or her preschool child learn; parents will have access to the training and support they need.
- Children will receive the nutrition and health care needed to arrive at school with healthy minds and bodies, and the number of low birthweight babies will be significantly reduced through enhanced prenatal health systems.

an important piece of the puzzle by periodically informing us about factors, including essential services to children, that enhance early learning. But they do not tell us the extent to which our children have the requisite skills, attitudes, or behaviors they need and, therefore, what we need to know to help them succeed in school. Knowing the percentage of low birthweight babies each year is important, but this won't tell us why children aren't learning to read. Making high-quality preschool programs available to all needy children is unquestionably desirable; but paradoxically, to obtain good "proxy" data on the overall quality of such a program, you need an outcome measure of its effect on children.

The Office of Educational Research and Improvement (OERI) acknowledges "the proxy measures based on preschool enrollment, parental involvement, and characteristics of preschool programs do not suffice to make inferences about actual readiness to begin school."[5]

With good, and more direct, measures of children's behavior, we will know better, for example, if certain kindergarten teaching strategies are differentially effective for youngsters with limited English proficiency, a particular type of disability, or a certain learning style. If we increase funding or redesign a program, we need to know the effect of such changes. With only proxy data to report, we can say we doubled the budget and we're serving twice as many, but we can't say if the program made a difference in children's learning.

Real improvement in a child's readiness to learn and a teacher's readiness to teach is enhanced, not by having macro-level data on the national percent of eligible participants in a pro-

gram, but by understanding behavior within the personal microcosm of that teacher with that child, as they interact with parents and other children.

### The Fear and the Need

In discouraging the development of a national readiness test, the governors did the right thing. Their decision reflects concern in the professional community that national use of an inappropriate assessment, even if administered to only a sample of children, could lead to a highly academic preschool curriculum and ultimately to denying children the right to enter school with their age-mates.

Their decision is, in fact, only one of several recent behavioral and policy changes that discourage the use of school readiness tests. Several states have discontinued mandated kindergarten or early grade testing, and pre-K through 1st grade programs were recently granted a statutory exemption from Chapter 1 testing requirements. Further, informal, off-the-record communications with publishers reveal that sales of group-administered tests for the early and preschool grades have either remained flat or started to decline.

Assessment of young children, however, hasn't gone away, and it probably won't, because assessment—*good assessment*—is needed more than ever. In spite of the decrease in legislative requirements and a broad awareness of the dangers of misusing readiness tests, the pressure for "results" from states and districts for accountability purposes is increasing.

The Southern Regional Education Board (SREB), for example, now reporting annually on the progress of its 15 member states toward Year 2000 education goals, includes results of readiness assessments among the indi-

cators of progress toward its school readiness goal.[6] And as one measure of the quality of programs, SREB includes "the use of assessments or tests of readiness for young children."[7] Legislation introduced in the U.S. Senate in 1990 requires that all relevant data on school readiness be considered for inclusion in a national report card on the educational goals.[8] Good readiness measures are needed not only for accountability purposes, but also for diagnosing learning needs, planning appropriate interventions, and evaluating programs.

### A Call for Reform

Because of what Sharon Kagan, Yale University's Associate Director of the Bush Center in Child Development

> **Knowing the percentage of low birthweight babies each year is important, but this won't tell us why children aren't learning to read.**

and Social Policy, calls a "fortuitous collision of events," a unique opportunity is now present for a major national reform in the assessment of young children. Our increased need for information to help children begin to learn has combined with our heightened awareness of the failings of readiness tests, so that "the seeds are right for change."[9] Now is the time to invest in a reform of this country's school readiness assessment.

The reform should begin with an effort to separate school entry from readiness. Many other nations have specific school starting points. In Sweden, children start school at age seven; in Japan, West Germany, and Switzerland at six; in New Zealand at five; and in Britain and Australia as early as four. The concept of readiness, wrongly applied, can be used to keep the "unready" out and thus deny those who need it most an opportunity to engage in learning at school. The dangers of wrong school entry decisions, whether on the basis of test scores or not, and the increasing practice of voluntary retention by overzealous parents, would be greatly reduced if, at the established age, all children entered school, "ready" or not. As Meisels says, "If you're alive, you're ready to learn, no matter what the tests say."[10]

The next step of assessment reform should be to reach consensus on the expectations we have for young children. We need to know what we want to "ready" children and teachers *for*. That means defining the skills, behaviors, and attitudes children should learn and teachers should teach in the 1st grade of school. Perhaps some of our nation's best minds, most experienced teachers, and most knowledgeable parents—those who understand child development and its many dimensions, its wide variations and its spurts and starts—could reach consensus.[11] Perhaps the encroachment of increasingly higher levels of academic demands into the preschool and kindergarten could be reversed by publicly stating just what we expect *and do not expect* of 1st graders. The precursors to these expectations then could become our readiness indicators.

## A Kinder, Gentler Way
We need to develop better means of assessing children's readiness than group-administered readiness tests. The governors, in fact, suggested several strategies for states to use to improve assessments:

"Develop assessment systems for young children that reflect the ultimate goals of producing independent, creative, and critical thinkers. Train teachers to observe and assess children's work in different content areas, using methods such as portfolio systems, observational checklists, and cumulative sampling of children's work. Develop models to use teacher assessments of student proficiencies for reporting to parents and the public . . ."[12]

We know a good deal about assessing readiness from work already begun (Anderson 1987, NAEYC 1988, Meisels 1989, Meisels et al. 1989). This work tells us that, ideally, readiness assessments should:

● encompass the multiple dimensions of readiness, including cognitive, social/emotional, attitudinal, and physical/motor behaviors;
● be an ongoing process of observing a child, rather than a one-time snapshot;

● gather information on behaviors that children have had an opportunity to develop;
● provide data useful for instructional improvement—to help the teacher get ready for the child;
● be indirect measures of children—that is, recorded by an adult, rather than directly by a child on an answer sheet;
● be conducted in a natural setting that is comfortable, familiar, and nonthreatening to the child;
● be administered to individuals, one-on-one, or to very small clusters of children, but not to large groups;
● be designed so that children can respond by pointing, acting, doing, or manipulating;
● be conducted by someone who is properly trained and who can relate well to children;
● be scored to yield a profile along the various readiness dimensions;
● be used in a nonpunitive way—that is, not for sorting, tracking, or denial of school entry. This last point is most important.

## Promising Prospects
In this section, I want to highlight three examples of developmental work in progress that appear to offer particular promise: one is from the State of Georgia, one from a test publisher (CTB Macmillan/McGraw-Hill), and one from research scientist Samuel Meisels.

The State of Georgia has now produced a developmentally appropriate method for evaluating readiness called the Georgia Kindergarten Assessment Program (GKAP). This program represents a positive directional change from Georgia's 1988 group-administered, machine-scored, norm-referenced test used for making school entry decisions (which probably did more to advance readiness assessment reform in this country than all other causes combined).

GKAP is a homegrown individually-administered readiness assessment on which three times a year, teachers record children's behavior across five capability areas. A series of "structured assessment activities" involving children's use of manipulatives gives additional information on two of the dimensions. A videotape illustrates the expected behavior for standardization of teacher ratings. The process relies heavily on teacher judgment and

yields good diagnostic information; however, its value for accountability purposes is not yet clear. A mechanism has been designed, but not totally implemented, for aggregating data from classrooms, to schools, to districts, to the state. Teachers record *yes/no* data, but not a total score, for each child on each of the five capabilities, on scannable forms for automatic generation of totals. The new system has been very costly, and the price of maintaining it is not yet known. Further refinements need to be made and analyses conducted.

CTB Macmillan/McGraw-Hill has recently produced a "Developing Skills Checklist" for children aged 4 to 6, which is individually administered and is packaged in a kit with attractive manipulatives. For each child, teachers can generate a criterion-referenced diagnostic profile of performance in eight areas. These checklists produce normative scores on mathematical concepts and operations, language, memory, auditory skills, print concepts, and a prereading composite. National percentiles, stanines, and normal curve equivalents are provided for each scale for four time periods (spring of pre-K and fall, winter, and spring of kindergarten). Included in the process are a method for recording multiple observations throughout the year on seven clusters of social/emotional behavior and a mechanism for compiling group data. So far, researchers have found high internal consistency reliability, and a two-year predictive validity study is now under way.

Samuel Meisels, Professor of Education and Research Scientist at the University of Michigan, is currently developing and piloting in nine school districts a new three-part readiness assessment process consisting of (1) a comprehensive criterion-referenced checklist of developmentally-based classroom learning, completed by the kindergarten teacher for each child on three different occasions throughout the school year; (2) the compilation of a portfolio of samples of the progression of each child's work; and (3) a summative teacher report form for providing year-end comparative, and possibly scaled and aggregate, data.

These three efforts suggest that supportive, child-friendly, and learning-enhancing measures can also produce aggregate data for accountability to the public. Since the governors recommended that a readiness assessment *not* be developed to measure progress toward the national goal, the government will presumably seek methods for indirectly compiling information gathered by others, such as teachers or parents, who have observed the behavior of children. The efforts I have described suggest the kinds of data that might be compiled.

Educators need more information, however, to ensure that the data compiled are valid, reliable, and useful and that they are collected in a uniform and equitable manner. It is essential to assure that observation criteria are clearly specified, that representative samples of all categories of behaviors are observed, and that raters are consistent. Test developers must create effective methods for recording, compiling, analyzing, scaling, and reporting data. They must conduct field tests and validity studies to determine whether performance on a readiness assessment predicts success in school, and evaluate the usefulness of aggregate scores reported to policymakers.

Any new assessment method must be monitored for possible inappropriate uses, such as retaining preschoolers, tracking, narrowing, further academic loading of the curriculum, or "teaching to the test," and evaluated for practical considerations such as costs and time. Finally, test users should compare the overall value of a new assessment method with existing practices.

Having been instructed by the White House to develop "other" readiness measures, OERI should lead the way toward better school readiness assessment by underwriting the consensus-building process and sponsoring

needed research and development. Whether or not a method better than proxies is ever created for national monitoring, readiness assessment in this country needs to be reformed. We need a kinder, gentler way to measure.

---

[1]National Governors' Association, *National Education Goals*. A statement adopted by the members of the NGA in Charlottesville, Virginia, on February 25, 1990, p. 3.

[2]The White House, *National Education Goals*. Press release from the Office of the Press Secretary, January 31, 1990, p. 3.

[3]National Governors' Association, *Educating America: State Strategies for Achieving the National Goals*. Report of the Task Force on Education. (Washington, D.C.: NGA, 1990), p. 15.

[4]See B.J. Turnbull, (April 1990), "Readiness for School—Issue Brief." Washington, D.C.: Policy Studies Associates, and Office of Educational Research and Improvement (OERI), "Education Summit Follow-up, Special Set, 6/1/90," internal document, for a more complete delineation of all the proxy data sources mentioned here.

[5]OERI, Ibid., p. 4.

[6]J. D. Creech, (1990), *Educational Benchmarks 1990*. (Atlanta: Southern Regional Education Board), p. 6.

[7]Southern Regional Education Board, (1989), *Reaching the Goal of Readiness for School* (Atlanta: SREB), pp. 11–12.

[8]S.3095, The National Academic Report Card Act of 1990, introduced by Senator Jeff Bingaman on September 24, 1990.

[9]S. L. Kagan, (July 13, 1990), personal communication, The Bush Center in Child Development and Social Policy, Yale University.

[10]S. Meisels, (July 5, 1990), personal communication, Center for Human Growth and Development, University of Michigan.

[11]See National Association for the Education of Young Children, (1990), "Position Statement on Readiness," for a good discussion of what is meant by readiness.

[12]National Governors' Association, *Educating America: State Strategies for Achieving the National Education Goals*, Ibid.

### References

Anderson, L. W. (1987). "Comments on a National Assessment of School Readiness." In *The Assessment of Readiness for School: Implications for a Statistical Program—Report of a Planning Conference*. Washington, D. C.: Center for Education Statistics, pp. 27–36.

Bredekamp, S., and L. Shepard. (1989). "How Best to Protect Children from Inappropriate School Expectations, Practices, and Policies." *Young Children* 44, 3: 14–24.

Meisels, S. J. (1989). "High-Stakes Testing in Kindergarten." *Educational Leadership* 46, 7: 16–22.

Meisels, S. J., D. Steele, and K. Quinn. (1989). "Testing, Tracking, and Retaining Young Children: An Analysis of Research and Social Policy." A commissioned paper prepared for the National Center for Education Statistics, December 1989.

National Association for the Education of Young Children. (1988). "Position Statement on Standardized Testing of Young Children 3 through 8 years of age." *Young Children* 43: 42–47.

Shepard, L. A., and M. L. Smith. (1988). "Escalating Academic Demand in Kindergarten: Counterproductive Policies." *The Elementary School Journal* 89: 135–145.

Shepard, L. A., and M. L. Smith. (1989). "Academic and Emotional Effects of Kindergarten Retention." In *Flunking Grades: Research and Policies on Retention*, edited by L.A. Shepard and M.L. Smith. Philadelphia: The Falmer Press, pp. 79–107.

# Project Spectrum: An Innovative Assessment Alternative

By evaluating young children's strengths in many domains, not just language and logic, the Spectrum battery promises to give all children a chance to shine.

Mara Krechevsky

**Mara Krechevsky** is Project Director, Project Spectrum, Harvard Project Zero, Harvard Graduate School of Education, Longfellow Hall, Appian Way, Cambridge, MA 02138.

It's free choice time in the afternoon 4-year-olds' classroom at the Eliot-Pearson Children's School in Medford, Massachusetts. The class is participating in Project Spectrum, an innovative approach to assessment in early childhood. Hallie, not quite 4 years of age, is once again roaming from activity to activity, finding it difficult to concentrate on a task for longer than five minutes at a time. Her ever-patient teacher first tries engaging her in the art table project, then in experimenting with the siphons at the water table, and finally in playing hospital at the dramatic play area, all to little avail. Hallie is easily distracted; she becomes sillier as the hour wears on, making increasingly poor eye contact with the teacher and speaking in nonsense words.

With 20 minutes left until group time, Hallie's turn comes up for the week's Spectrum activity: the assembly task. This task involves taking apart and reassembling two food grinders. Successful completion of the activity depends on a combination of fine motor skills with visual-spatial and problem-solving abilities. Hallie's eyes light up expectantly upon seeing the first grinder, and she immediately touches the main fastener, which loosens the handle and inner mechanism. Within minutes, the grinder is completely disassembled, and Hallie begins to put the pieces back together, carefully figuring out the correct direction in which to turn each screw. She adopts a trial-and-error approach, her feet swinging excitedly up and down from her chair whenever she succeeds. She remains focused, persistent, and methodical throughout—correcting her own mistakes, oblivious to the rest of the class.

This anecdote illustrates the power of the Spectrum approach to assessment. Spectrum began in 1984 at Harvard and Tufts Universities as an attempt to reconceptualize the traditional linguistic and logical/mathematical bases of intelligence. Our first four years of research centered on identifying young children's distinctive cognitive and stylistic profiles. In addition to assessing linguistic and mathematical abilities, the Spectrum assessment battery examines mechanical, spatial, bodily, musical, social, and scientific abilities as well (see fig. 1).

In a political climate that places increasing pressure on educators to extend formal instruction downward and embrace a narrow view of scholastic readiness, Spectrum offers a developmentally appropriate alternative based on a broad view of the mind.

## A Rich Classroom Environment

The theoretical foundation of the project stems from Howard Gardner's (1983) theory of multiple intelligences and David Feldman's (1980) theory of development in non-universal domains. Although many early childhood educators still think in terms of children's progressing through broad, undifferentiated stages of universal development, Spectrum was designed to recognize variation in both children and areas of activity. Thus, the Spectrum model identifies domain-specific strengths in areas often not included in many Piagetian or neo-Piagetian approaches to education. Spectrum is based on the assumption that every child has the potential to develop strength in one or several content areas and that it is the responsibility of the educational system to discover and nurture these proclivities. Rather than building around a test, the Spectrum approach is centered on a wide range of rich activities; assessment comes about as part-and-parcel of the child's involvement over time in these activities.

As Figure 1 indicates, the Spectrum measures range from relatively structured and targeted tasks (for example, in the number and music domains) to less structured measures and observations (for example, in the science and social domains). These measures form one part of a rich classroom environment that is equipped with engaging materials, games, puzzles, and learning areas. The learning areas enable children to make initial explorations of materials related to the domains assessed by Spectrum, as well as offering follow-up activities. For example, after the storytelling task, children can be asked to create their own storyboards at the art area. The assessment activities are administered throughout the school year. Documentation takes a variety of forms, from score sheets and observation checklists to portfolios and tape recordings.

## A Look at Spectrum's Facets

Distinctive features of the Spectrum assessment system include:

1. *Blurring the line between curriculum and assessment.* By gathering information over time in the child's own environment, Spectrum effectively blurs the traditional division between curriculum and assessment. For example, teachers collect children's artwork in portfolios and observe bodily-kinesthetic abilities through a bi-weekly creative movement session. The traditional test setting of a small room with an unfamiliar examiner administering timed and standardized instruments, in the Spectrum view, provides too narrow and skewed a view of the child. In the Spectrum tasks, children's skills are integrated, rather than isolated. Thus, as we saw earlier, the assembly activity engages Hallie in an applied and meaningful task presented as part of her preschool curriculum.

2. *Embedding assessment in meaningful, real-world activities.* Rather than just focusing on skills useful in the school context, Spectrum uses the concept of adult *endstates* to focus its assessments on abilities relevant to achieving significant and rewarding adult roles. Examples of endstates include *naturalist*, *salesperson*, *singer*, *dancer*, and *social worker*. Thus, in the language domain, Spectrum examines a child's ability to tell stories or provide a descriptive account of an experience—valuable skills for novelists and journalists—rather than his or her ability to repeat a series of sentences. For Hallie, the applicable endstate is *mechanic*. In contrast to many standardized assessments, which might have Hallie copy shapes or block patterns, Spectrum provides her with a real machine to work on. This grounding of assessments in real-world activities ensures that the areas addressed are likely to be meaningful to the child, the teacher, and the child's family.

3. *Using measures that are "intelligence-fair."* Rather than viewing all

---

## Fig. 1. Areas of Cognitive Ability Examined in Project Spectrum

### Numbers

*Dinosaur Game*: Measures a child's understanding of number concepts, counting skills, ability to adhere to rules, and use of strategy.

*Bus Game*: Assesses a child's ability to create a useful notation system, perform mental calculations, and organize number information for one or more variables.

### Science

*Assembly Activity*: Measures a child's mechanical ability. Successful completion of the activity depends on fine motor skills and visual-spatial, observational, and problem-solving abilities.

*Treasure Hunt Game*: Assesses a child's ability to make logical inferences. The child is asked to organize information to discover the rule governing the placement of various treasures.

*Water Activity*: Assesses a child's ability to generate hypotheses based on his or her observations and to conduct simple experiments.

*Discovery Area*: Includes year-round activities that elicit a child's observations, appreciation, and understanding of natural phenomena.

### Music

*Music Production Activity*: Measures a child's ability to maintain accurate pitch and rhythm while singing and his or her ability to recall a song's musical properties.

*Music Perception Activity*: Assesses a child's ability to discriminate pitch. The activity consists of song recognition, error recognition, and pitch discrimination.

### Language

*Storyboard Activity*: Measures a range of language skills including complexity of vocabulary and sentence structure, use of connectors, use of descriptive language and dialogue, and ability to pursue a storyline.

*Reporting Activity*: Assesses a child's ability to describe an event he or she has experienced with regard to the following criteria: ability to report content accurately, level of detail, sentence structure, and vocabulary.

### Visual Arts

*Art Portfolios*: The contents of a child's art portfolio are reviewed twice a year and assessed on criteria that include use of lines and shapes, color, space, detail, and representation and design. Children also participate in three structured drawing activities. The drawings are assessed on criteria similar to those used in the portfolio assessment.

### Movement

*Creative Movement*: The ongoing movement curriculum focuses on children's abilities in five areas of dance and creative movement: sensitivity to rhythm, expressiveness, body control, generation of movement ideas, and responsiveness to music.

*Athletic Movement*: An obstacle course focuses on the types of skills found in many different sports such as coordination, timing, balance, and power.

### Social

*Classroom Model Activity*: Assesses a child's ability to observe and analyze social events and experiences in his or her classroom.

*Peer Interaction Checklist*: A behavioral checklist is used to assess the behaviors in which children engage when interacting with peers. Different patterns of behavior yield distinctive social roles such as facilitator and leader.

abilities through the window of language and logic, as most standardized tests do, Spectrum attempts to tap abilities directly, via their own particular medium. In the above anecdote, Hallie works directly with simple mechanical objects, rather than answering questions about how machines work. The music perception and production tasks of the assessment employ Montessori bells and simple songs, while the movement activities elicit both athletic and creative movement.

4. *Emphasizing children's strengths.* In contrast to many educational approaches, particularly those used with children at risk for school failure, the Spectrum assessment approach seeks to identify children's areas of strength and to construct their education as much as possible around those domains of competence. Giving children experience in their areas of strength might not only increase their sense of self-esteem but suggest ways to address areas that are not as strong. For example, to boost Hallie's language skills, she could be asked to dictate

---

**Spectrum's grounding of assessments in real-world activities ensures that the areas addressed are likely to be meaningful to the child, the teacher, and the child's family.**

---

instructions for disassembling a grinder or to tell a story about a machine she might invent.

5. *Attending to the stylistic dimensions of performance.* In order to capture fully a child's approach to a task, we soon discovered it was important to look not only at a child's cognitive skills but at certain stylistic features as well. "Working styles" describe how a child interacts with the materials of a domain, such as his or her persistence, attention to detail, and level of confi-

dence (see fig. 2). While some children exhibit the same working style across domains, others have styles that are much more content-specific. Such information has important implications for designing educational interventions. In Hallie's case, she revealed the capacity to become extremely focused and reflective when working in her area of strength.

In the Spectrum approach, all of the information collected on a child is compiled at year's end into a "Spectrum Profile": a short description, written in nontechnical prose, of the child's participation in the project's activities. The report addresses each child's areas of strength, either relative to himself or herself or to the child's peer group. Because of our belief that psychologists spend too much time ranking children and not enough time trying to help them, we also give concrete suggestions for follow-up activities that can be carried out at home or in the community. A "Parent Activities Handbook" suggests home activities that use inexpensive and easily acquired materials (for example, different ways to grow seeds, measuring and counting games, and so on).

## Early Research Results

Hallie's class was one of two Eliot-Pearson preschool classrooms that participated in the initial phase of Spectrum research. This phase focused on assessing individual children's cognitive and stylistic strengths. Preliminary results from the two classrooms suggest that the Spectrum system does indeed identify distinctive intellectual profiles in young children[1] (for a full report, see Gardner and Hatch 1989, Krechevsky and Gardner 1990). We also found some evidence that a child's strength in one area might facilitate performance in another. For example, one child demonstrated exceptional storytelling ability, yet generally refused to participate in creative movement. However, she moved with unusual expressiveness when presented with storyboard props as a stimulus during one of the movement sessions.

With regard to working styles, most children seemed to exhibit domain-specific configurations. Many were reflective and attentive to detail only in their areas of strength. However, some children demonstrated a more general working style, which at times worked to their disadvantage. For example, one boy approached every activity with his own agenda of ideas. Although in the less structured environment of the class he conducted many compelling experiments to test his hypotheses, he was unable to adjust to more structured task situations.

Preliminary follow-up data on children in the original Spectrum class indicate that strengths and working

---

**Fig. 2. Stylistic Features Examined in Project Spectrum**

Child is:
- easily engaged/reluctant to engage in activity
- confident/tentative
- playful/serious
- focused/distractible
- persistent/frustrated by task
- reflective about own work/impulsive
- apt to work slowly/apt to work quickly

Child:
- responds to visual/auditory/kinesthetic cues
- demonstrates planful approach
- brings personal agenda/strength to task
- finds humor in content area
- uses materials in unexpected ways
- shows pride in accomplishment
- shows attention to detail/is observant
- is curious about materials
- shows concern over "correct" answer
- focuses on interaction with adult
- transforms task/material

styles remained roughly constant one to two years later. Sometimes the particular combination of a child's areas of strength and working style determined whether or not a strength would re-emerge. One girl, who in preschool constantly sought the positive regard of her peers, spent a lot of

> **All of the information collected on a child is compiled at year's end into a "Spectrum Profile": a short description of the child's participation in the project's activities.**

time at the writing table because her language abilities were advanced for her age group. However, because she was not the most able in her group the following year, she devoted the majority of her free time to art activities. Thus, the language abilities identified earlier were less likely to resurface and develop.

Responses from parents indicated that the areas where they were most surprised to learn of strengths included music perception, mechanical ability, and creative movement. A number of parents in the follow-up found it very useful to have a written profile to which they could compare more recent views of their child. The area parents were most likely to encourage at the one-year follow-up was drama, perhaps because they saw it as an especially effective way to combine

ability in the language, social, and movement domains.

Currently, the Spectrum approach is being modified for use with children in kindergarten and 1st grade and for children who are more at risk for school failure. A broad-based Spectrum curriculum is being implemented in selected 1st grade classrooms with a large at-risk population in Somerville, Massachusetts. Children are being encouraged to develop their areas of strength in an apprentice-type model and to bring these strengths to bear on the established curricular goals of the 1st grade. We are administering pre- and post-tests to determine change in children's academic achievement, self-esteem, attitude toward school, and school adjustment.

## Their Place in the Sun

It may be important at this point to outline the disadvantages and the advantages of Spectrum. First, a pluralized model of intelligence runs the risk that achievement-oriented parents will push their children in 15 areas, instead of a few. Second, parents and teachers may be tempted to track a child prematurely into pursuing his or her area(s) of strength. Finally, parents outside the mainstream culture may not be as concerned with their children's performance in domains not valued by the traditional culture.

Nevertheless, the approach offers a number of benefits. The Spectrum battery exposes children to more domains than are typically included in early childhood assessments or curriculums. Spectrum also actively involves children in the assessment process. They collect their work for the art portfolios and tape their own stories and songs. Time is also set aside for children to reflect on the activities in general. The Spectrum approach can be used on many levels: as assessment, as curriculum, or as a powerful philosophical framework through which to view children and their particular sets

of strengths and working styles. In fact, the approach is as much a framework and set of ideas as it is a discrete program. Spectrum is currently being adapted for a variety of purposes by both researchers and practitioners in the field.[2] Because the approach takes individual differences seriously, it enables teachers to accommodate diverse populations and to individualize their curriculums. Moreover, because of its provision of many ways to demonstrate excellence, including ways that go beyond conventional scholastic success, Spectrum may be particularly suited for at-risk children. At best, the Spectrum approach promises to increase the chances for all children to find their place in the sun.

[1] Because of the small sample size, the results reported in this article should be regarded as tentative.

[2] We encourage these efforts and are interested in hearing from people who have tried to implement Spectrum. However, for reasons of logistics and limited resources, at present we cannot provide much in the way of support.

### References

Feldman, D.H. (1980). *Beyond Universals in Cognitive Development*. Norwood, N.J.: Ablex.

Gardner, H. (1983). *Frames of Mind: The Theory of Multiple Intelligences*. New York: Basic Books.

Gardner, H., and T. Hatch. (November 1989). "Multiple Intelligences Go to School: Educational Implications of the Theory of Multiple Intelligences." *Educational Researcher* 18, 8: 4–10.

Krechevsky, M., and H. Gardner. (1990). "The Emergence and Nurturance of Multiple Intelligences: The Project Spectrum Approach." In *Encouraging the Development of Exceptional Skills and Talents*, edited by M.J.A. Howe. Leicester, U.K.: The British Psychological Society.

*Author's note:* The work described in this article was supported by generous grants from the William T. Grant Foundation, the Rockefeller Brothers Fund, and the Spencer Foundation.

# Identification of Preschool Children with Mild Handicaps:

## The Importance of Cooperative Effort

Ronald L. Taylor, Paula Willits
and Nancy Lieberman

*Ronald L. Taylor is Professor of Exceptional Student Education and Paula Willits, Doctoral Student, Florida Atlantic University, Boca Raton. Nancy Lieberman is Preschool Coordinator, Broward County Public Schools, Florida.*

Public Law 99-457 was passed, in part, to assist school districts in providing appropriate services for preschool handicapped children. This mandate requires that school districts must identify and serve *all* preschool children who are handicapped, including those with mild handicaps. Identification of children who display minor speech/language, cognitive/learning or emotional/behavioral problems presents a unique challenge to the educator.

Because of the nature of the preschool population, traditional evaluation procedures used with school-age students will be largely ineffective and of questionable validity (Peterson, 1987). It is clear that school districts will have to make many modifications to their current assessment process. Among other changes, it will be necessary that preschool teachers

and child care workers become more involved in the initial identification of these children. In addition, the parent must become a more active participant throughout the evaluation process. A number of specific concerns must also be addressed, including those related to screening, planning the evaluation and interpreting/communicating evaluation results. The central theme of all these concerns is the need for a cooperative, coordinated effort.

## CONCERNS WITH SCREENING

Appropriate screening information enables school districts to make intelligent decisions about the need for further evaluation. It is probable that the individuals most directly involved with initial screening (at least on an informal basis) will be the preschool teacher/child care provider and the parents of the child (Lerner, Mardell-Czudnowski & Goldenberg, 1987). These individuals are in the best position to observe a child, gather pertinent information and make the appropriate referral. Another method in which a child might be referred is through

some formal screening effort by the school district or community agency. It is therefore important that communication and coordination be emphasized among teachers/parents, those involved with formal screening, and the school district evaluation team responsible for determining eligibility for preschool handicapped programs.

Another issue relates to making incorrect decisions at the screening stage. Most professionals agree that it is probably better to make a false positive than a false negative error (Peterson, 1987). This means that if there is any question, a child should be referred for further testing at this point. It is better to overidentify at the screening stage than to risk missing a child who would benefit from early intervention. The more in-depth evaluation procedures should help clarify which children truly need services. This also has implications for selection of the screening test to be used. Some instruments (e.g., the Denver Developmental Screening Test) lack sensitivity and subsequently tend to lead to false negative errors (Wolery, 1989).

## PLANNING
## THE EVALUATION

### How To Evaluate

Certain characteristics related to the typical preschool child will influence the choice of evaluation procedures. For example, it is typical for young children's behavior to be variable during the preschool years (e.g., Lidz, 1983; Paget & Nagel, 1986). Performance on any one day may not give a true picture of a child's abilities. In addition, a clinical testing setting is often a very unnatural, anxiety-producing one for a young child. Finally, typical preschool behaviors such as separation anxiety, fear of strangers and lack of compliance may contribute to the very real possibility of making false assumptions about a child's abilities or disabilities (Martin, 1986; Torrey & Rotatori, 1987).

As a result of these factors, it is important that the child be evaluated on more than one occasion. This is not limited to formal testing, but could and should include observation and informal evaluation. In fact, it is a good idea to observe or informally evaluate the preschool child prior to any formal testing. This information can be used to determine the appropriate procedures/instruments, as well as provide another "sample" of behavior on which to base decisions. Consistent with an ecological assessment model, it is preferable to observe the child in more than one setting to provide additional information.

Even after observing the child, selection of appropriate procedures can be problematic, particularly due to the general lack of acceptable standardized tests for this age range. It is extremely important to investigate a test's technical characteristics related to the preschool population (Sheehan, 1989). Were preschoolers adequately represented in the standardization sample? Is the test-retest reliability acceptable for this age group? Does the test have adequate predictive validity? Unfortunately, the majority of tests used with this population fail to meet acceptable criteria (Lehr, Ysseldyke & Thurlow, 1986). In addition, the choice of instruments should be made with the curriculum of the preschool program in mind; information collected during the evaluation should serve the dual purposes of determining eligibility and helping to plan educational programs (National Association for the Education of Young Children, 1988).

Administration of standardized tests is also challenging with young children. Preschoolers' short attention spans, lack of test wiseness, and normal fears and apprehensions due to unfamiliarity with the testing situation can make assessment sessions quite difficult (Lichtenstein & Ireton, 1984). Examiners must be allowed to adapt administration of standardized tests if needed. Of course, examiners should carefully document any procedural changes found necessary to get the child to respond.

With the limitations of formal testing, it is both necessary and beneficial to rely heavily on more informal procedures. Information from such procedures can help validate the formal test results and provide meaningful additional information. Again, the preschool teacher and/or parent will play a crucial role in providing this information. Such procedures might include use of developmental histories and interviews that will allow input from the parents. Also, language samples and observation of the child in both structured and unstructured settings will provide valuable data.

### What To Evaluate

It is necessary to determine the evaluation domains that must be assessed to meet local or state eligibility criteria. Although PL 99-457 does not require use of specific labels, many states have adopted a categorical approach similar to that used with school-age children (Sheehan, 1989). In Florida, for instance, mildly handicapped preschoolers must qualify for programs for learning disabilities, emotional handicaps, educable mental handicaps or speech/language impairments. By carefully analyzing eligibility criteria for programs that will serve preschool children, appropriate assessment areas can be determined.

If a categorical approach is used, parents and teachers must be informed that the label is not always permanent, but is the best descriptor of the child's needs at that time. In addition, parents must clearly understand that the instructional needs of two children with the same label may be the same or quite different (Sheehan, 1989).

### Whom To Evaluate

It is extremely important to involve the parent throughout the assessment process. Many instruments designed for preschool children use the parent as an informant. In addition, informal techniques such as interviews and developmental histories will require input from parents. Other significant family members should also be included when appropriate. In some families, for example, grandparents who assume primary child-rearing responsibilities might be in the best position to provide relevant information.

### Who Will Evaluate

One very important decision involves the choice of evaluators who will work with a given child and the manner in which they will operate. Among the possible evaluation models are the unidisciplinary, multidisciplinary, interdisciplinary and transdisciplinary models (Wolery & Dyk, 1984). In the *unidisciplinary* model, the child is evaluated by only one person. In the *multidisciplinary* approach, a team is used but communication is limited. There is more role-identification and increased communication in the *interdisciplinary* approach, while the most carefully planned, integrated model is the *transdisciplinary.*

In general, the more communication and cooperative planning among the team members, the better the evaluation will be. This might involve the child being simultaneously evaluated by a team consisting of a psychologist, a speech/language clinician, a teacher and appropriate therapists. Team members should be familiar with both their own areas of expertise and those of other team members. Determination of who comprises the team for a given child should be an individual decision based on referral/screening information, observational data and the evaluation domains that are subsequently identified.

### Where To Evaluate

Another decision that must be made is the choice of the evaluation setting. It is hoped that the child will be observed and evaluated in more than one setting (Peterson, 1987). Any formal testing may need to be scheduled in a large room that allows for gross-motor activities. If furniture is used (as opposed to testing on the floor), it should be age-appropriate (Paget, 1983).

### CONCERNS WITH INTERPRETATION/ COMMUNICATION

Interpretation of evaluation results becomes easier if multiple sources of information have been used to document behavioral and developmental trends (Florida Department of Education, 1989). A child's developmental strengths and weaknesses should become obvious if relevant procedures and instruments have been chosen for the evaluation process. What is not so obvious is how to convey that information both in written and oral form to parents and future preschool special education teachers (if the child is found eligible for services).

Parents may react with shock, fear, guilt or denial when confronted with negative information at post-evaluation meetings (Peterson, 1987). For these reasons, they should be informed at every step in the evaluation process. Team members should also realize that when a final "diagnosis" is stated, the parents may not be "taking in" the rest of what is being said during the meeting. The following suggestions may help ease a rather painful stage in the evaluation process (Biggs & Keller, 1982; Hooper, 1977):

1) First inform parents of four or five positive things about their child.
2) Encourage parents' questions and acknowledge their feelings.
3) If labels are required, remind parents of their transient nature at this age.
4) Inform parents of future re-evaluations.
5) Avoid technical terms and concepts; use everyday terminology.
6) Organize evaluation results in a logical fashion, with test scores and observations grouped to show patterns in the child's abilities and behaviors.
7) If possible, include another parent of a handicapped child as a team member to provide support and answer questions.

Along with orally presenting evaluation results to parents, evaluation team members must convey the child's results in written form. Final evaluation reports should be written in a meaningful way. One recommended format is the "translated report" developed by Bagnato (1980). Translated reports focus on the child's performance relative to specific preschool curriculum objectives. They are organized by developmental or functional domains, not by tests given. A child's developmental strengths and weaknesses are described in behavioral terms, linked to specific curriculum objectives with functional levels listed and

instructional needs delineated to facilitate development of an Individual Education Program. Quite specific recommendations are made for behavioral and instructional management.

Another approach that might be used is the *System To Plan Early Childhood Services* (Bagnato, Neisworth, Gordon & McCloskey, 1990). This approach provides a systematic method of linking screening, evaluation, program planning and progress monitoring. Results of the evaluation are presented in a meaningful way that addresses various service options.

### A PROPOSED MODEL

A number of "best practice" suggestions have been discussed. These include the following:

■ Make sure there is a link between screening and evaluation.
■ Gather information from the parent and the home environment.
■ Use multiple evaluators/evaluation sessions.
■ Consider child characteristics in test selection.
■ Observe/discuss the child prior to the formal evaluation.

The Broward County School District in Florida has developed a model of preschool evaluation that incorporates these best practice suggestions (see Figure 1). This approach minimizes the time needed to evaluate the child and maximizes the communication between team members. Two points should be made before the model is described. First, categorical labels (educable mentally handicapped, learning disabled, emotionally handicapped, speech and language impaired) are required for preschool children in Florida. Analysis of eligibility for those categories resulted in the nine evaluation domains noted in the model. Second, because Broward County is a large county, a transdisciplinary approach is feasible with an evaluation team

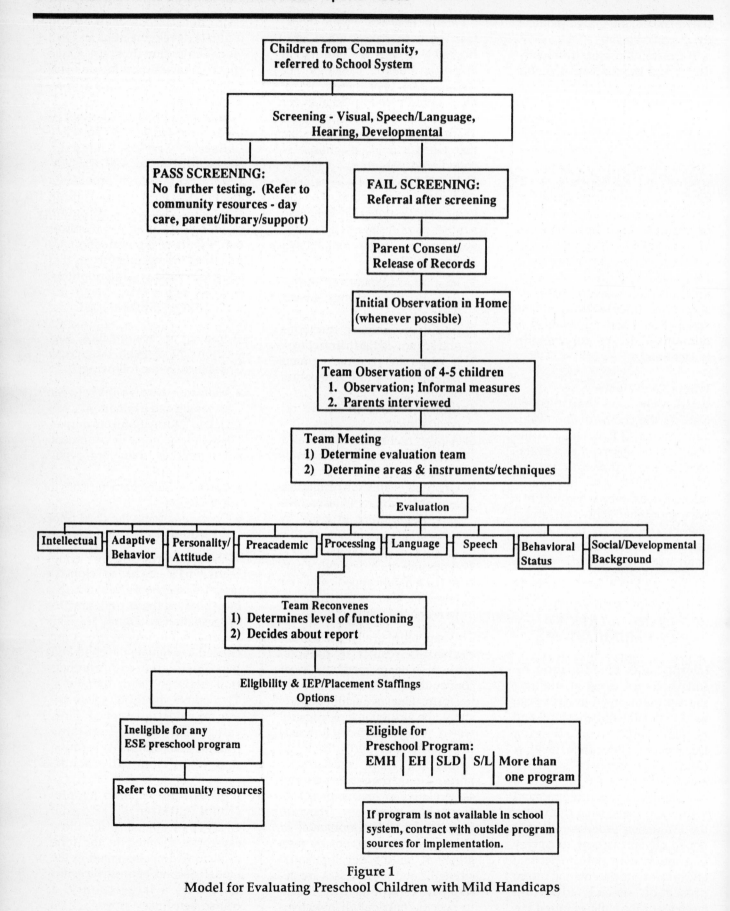

Figure 1
Model for Evaluating Preschool Children with Mild Handicaps

housed together within a school or center. Smaller districts might have to modify this model somewhat. The flowchart in Figure 1 can be divided roughly into three phases: screening, planning the evaluation and conducting the evaluation.

## Screening

With this model, initial screening procedures are conducted through Child Find Services. The process begins when groups of children who have been referred for screenings (usually from parents and preschool teachers) are gathered at one location and given individual vision and hearing acuity screenings, along with speech/language and developmental screening. Parents are immediately informed by screening team members as to whether further testing may be indicated; consent and release of records are obtained for those children who will continue to be evaluated.

Because it is important that the evaluation team be familiar with screening procedures to avoid duplication of effort, one person from the evaluation team is designated to mutually plan and coordinate the screening with the Child Find designee. Those individuals also share information with parents and preschool teachers about the services available and the characteristics of children who might qualify.

## Planning the Evaluation

Children who fail initial screenings are observed at home when possible by at least one evaluation team member. The child is then given a preliminary evaluation by a team consisting of a school psychologist, a speech and language clinician, a preschool special education teacher and any other appropriate professional. A developmental instrument (usually the Battelle Developmental Inventory) is used for this preliminary evaluation. While the child is being evaluated, the parent is interviewed. A team meeting is held once this information has been collected. Team members review all screening and preliminary evaluation information and determine the nature of the formal evaluation. Decisions made at this point are:

- Which team members will evaluate the child?
- Will the child be evaluated individually by the chosen members or simultaneously by the team?
- What domains need to be evaluated?
- What instruments/procedures should be used?

A formal assessment session is then scheduled if necessary. Because of the nature of the criteria for speech and language impairment, determination for eligibility for that category can be made at this point.

## Conducting the Evaluation

Once the decision regarding the nature of the evaluation has been made, testing is scheduled and conducted. After the evaluation, the team reconvenes to determine the child's levels of functioning and to write the final evaluation report. An eligibility staffing is later held with the parents to share evaluation outcomes and decide what placement options, if any, will be employed based on the child's results. Built into this system is a "transition reevaluation" prior to the child's entering kindergarten to update his/her developmental status and provide information for program changes if necessary.

This model highlights the importance of observing preschoolers prior to formal testing and emphasizes the importance of gathering as much information as possible from a variety of sources, including the family. It also emphasizes the practicality and efficiency of a team approach. Districts must be sure to choose a delivery system that does not result in delays in identification and placement for mildly handicapped youngsters. Pooling the knowledge of a variety of experts, while involving them in a cost-efficient, time-efficient system, works extremely well with the preschool population.

In summary, prekindergarten evaluation of mildly handicapped children is a multifaceted, specialized endeavor. Assessment of young children with mild handicaps requires a number of skills and procedures not involved when older youngsters are evaluated. Individuals from a variety of disciplines must be willing to share their expertise with a team of informed professionals, as well as parents. Special skills, creative thinking and patience are required to discover the developmental strengths and weaknesses of such very young children. It is imperative that educators and parents work together in a cooperative and coordinated fashion to meet that goal.

## References

Bagnato, S. (1980). The efficacy of diagnostic reports as individualized guides to prescriptive goal planning. *Exceptional Children, 46,* 554-557.

Bagnato, S., Neisworth, J., Gordon, J., & McCloskey, G. (1990). *System to plan early childhood services.* Circle Pines, MN: American Guidance Service.

Biggs, D., & Keller, K. (1982). A cognitive approach to using tests in counseling. *Personnel and Guidance Journal, 59,* 528-532.

Florida Department of Education. (1989). *Preschool assessment and training for the handicapped manual.* Tallahassee: Author.

Hooper, G. (1977). Parental understanding of their child's test results as interpreted by elementary school teachers. *Measurement and Evaluation in Guidance, 10,* 84-88.

Lehr, C., Ysseldyke, J., & Thurlow, M.

(1986). *Assessment practices in model early childhood education projects* (Research Report #7). Minneapolis: University of Minnesota.

Lerner, J., Mardell-Czudnowski, C., & Goldenberg, D. (1987). *Special education for the early childhood years* (2nd ed.). Englewood Cliffs, NJ: Prentice-Hall.

Lichtenstein, R., & Ireton, H. (1984). *Preschool screening: Identifying young children with developmental and educational problems.* Orlando, FL: Grune & Stratton.

Lidz, C. (1983). Issues in assessing preschool children. In K. Paget & B. Bracken (Eds.), *The psychoeducational assessment of preschool children* (pp. 17-28). New York: Grune & Stratton.

Martin, R. (1986). Assessment of the social and emotional functioning of preschool children. *School Psychology Review, 15,* 216-232.

National Association for the Education of Young Children. (1988). NAEYC position statement on standardized testing of young children 3-8 years of age. *Young Children, 44,* 42-47.

Paget, K. (1983). The individual examining situation: Basic considerations for preschool children. In K. Paget & B. Bracken (Eds.), *The psychoeducational assessment of young children* (pp. 51-62). New York: Grune & Stratton.

Paget, K., & Nagel, R. (1986). A conceptual model of preschool evaluation. *School Psychology Review, 15,* 154-165.

Peterson, N. (1987). *Early intervention for handicapped and at-risk children.* Denver: Love.

Sheehan, R. (1989). Implications of PL 99-457 for assessment. *Topics in Early Childhood Special Education, 8,* 103-115.

Torrey, C., & Rotatori, A. (1987). Assessment practices for young handicapped children. In A. Rotatori, M. Banbury, & R. Fox (Eds.), *Issues in special education* (pp. 38-54). Mountain View, CA: Mayfield.

Wolery, M. (1989). Child find and screening issues. In D. Bailey & M. Wolery (Eds.), *Assessing infants and preschoolers with handicaps* (pp. 119-143). Columbus, OH: Merrill.

Wolery, M., & Dyk, L. (1984). Arena assessment: Description and preliminary social validity data. *Journal of the Association for Persons with Severe Handicaps, 9,* 231-235.

# Preschool Classroom Environments

## That Promote Communication

Michaelene M. Ostrosky

Ann P. Kaiser

**Michaelene M. Ostrosky** *(CEC Chapter #46) is a Doctoral Student and* **Ann P. Kaiser** *(CEC Chapter #69) is Professor, Department of Special Education, Peabody College of Vanderbilt University, Nashville, Tennessee.*

Children learn what language *is* by learning what language can *do* (Bates, 1976; Hart, 1985). The function of language depends upon it's effects on the environment. An environment that contains few reinforcers and few objects of interest or meets children's needs without requiring language is *not* a functional environment for learning or teaching language.

Recent research suggests that environmental arrangement is an important strategy for teachers who want to promote communication in classrooms (Alpert, Kaiser, Ostrosky, & Hemmeter, 1987; Haring, Neetz, Lovinger, Peck, & Semmell, 1987). To encourage use of language, classrooms should be arranged so that there are materials and activities of interest to the children. In addition, teachers must mediate the environment by presenting materials in response to children's requests and other uses of language (Hart & Rogers-Warren, 1978). Creating such opportunities and consequences for language use through environmental arrangement can play a critical role in a child's language acquisition (Hart, 1985).

Both social and physical aspects of the environment set the occasion for communication (Rogers-Warren, Warren, & Baer, 1983). The physical environment includes the selection and arrangement of materials, the arrangement of the setting to encourage children's engagement, and scheduling of activities to enhance children's participation and appropriate behavior. The social environment includes the presence of responsive adults and children and the verbal and nonverbal social interactions that occur among the people in the environment. In addition, contingencies for language use, the availability of a communication partner, the degree to which adults preempt children's communicative attempts, and the affective style of the listener have an impact on children's language acquisition and production (Hemmeter, 1988).

As shown in Figure 1, the social and physical aspects of the environment are linked to communication when an adult mediates the physical environment in response to children's use of language. The adult links the child's language to the environment by ensuring that the child's communication attempts are functional and reinforced. As a mediator, the adult can use an incidental teaching process to model and prompt elaborated language in order to expand the child's current skills (Hart, 1985).

Environmental arrangement can en- courage children to initiate language as a means of gaining access to materials and getting help. By providing the materials requested by a child, the adult serves the important function of specifically reinforcing that child's use of language. In addition, the environmental arrangement supports the adult in attending to the child's interest and communication attempts, thereby increasing the likelihood that the adult will respond to the child's interest and provide materials contingently (Haring et al., 1987).

## Seven Strategies for Arranging the Environment

The basic goal of environmental arrangement is to increase children's interest in the environment as an occasion for communication. The environment is managed and arranged to promote requests and comments by children and to support language teaching efforts by adults. Using the environment to prompt language includes the following steps:

1. Focusing on making language a part of children's routines.
2. Providing access to interesting materials and activities.
3. Providing adult and peer models who will encourage children to use

language and respond to their attempts to do so.

4. Establishing a contingent relationship between access to materials or assistance and use of language.

The seven environmental strategies described here are designed to (a) increase the likelihood that children will show an interest in the environment and make communicative attempts and (b) increase the likelihood that the adult will prompt the use of language about things of interest to the children by providing clear and obvious *nonverbal* prompts for them to communicate. When the environment is arranged in this way, attractive materials and activities function as both discriminative stimuli and reinforcers for language use.

### Interesting Materials

Materials and activities that children enjoy should be available in the environment. Young children are most likely to initiate communication about the things that interest them. Thus, increasing the likelihood of children's interest

in the environment increases the opportunities for language use and teaching. Teachers usually know which toys and materials individual children prefer. However, a simple inventory of preferences can be taken at staff meetings or by systematically observing children's choices during free play. Parents often can provide information regarding their children's preferred toys and activities. Once toy preference has been determined, teachers can enhance interest in the environment by making such toys or materials available. For example, if a child enjoys bead stringing, various shaped and colored beads, noodles, and sewing spools could be made available. Identifying preferred activities and materials is especially important for a young child with severe disabilities. Variations in activities and materials must be carefully monitored to ensure that the child remains interested. For example, a child with severe disabilities who likes squeak toys may enjoy a variety of these toys but not like a Jack-in-the-box that makes a similar sound. Rotating the toys available at any given time is also a good way to make old toys more interesting; when they reappear they seem brand new!

### Out of Reach

Placing *some* desirable materials within view but out of reach will prompt children to make requests in order to secure the materials. Materials may be placed on the shelves, in clear plastic bins, or simply across the table during a group activity to increase the likelihood that the children will request access to them either verbally or nonverbally. These requests create opportunities for language teaching, since when children request a specific material they are also specifying their reinforcers (Hart & Rogers-Warren, 1978). Thus, a teacher who prompts language and provides the requested material contingent on the child's response effectively reinforces that response. The effectiveness of this strategy can be enhanced by showing the children materials, naming the materials, and then waiting attentively for the children to make requests. During snack time or before a cooking activity, a teacher can prompt children to make requests by placing the cooking materials across the table from them. Children with severe disabilities might gain access to these materials by point-

Figure 1. Social and physical aspects of the environment set the occasion for communication as the adult serves as the mediator in response to children's use of language.

ing or eye gazing, whereas more skilled children might be encouraged to use signs, words, or even complete sentences. Teachers must be careful not to frustrate students by placing too many communicative demands on them. A balance of requesting materials and playing independently is important in every activity.

## Inadequate Portions

Providing small or inadequate portions of preferred materials such as blocks, crayons, or crackers is another way to arrange the environment to promote communication. During an activity the children enjoy, an adult can control the amount of materials available so that the children have only some of the parts that are needed to complete the activity. When the children use the materials initially provided, they are likely to request more. Providing inadequate portions of an interesting and desirable material creates a situation in which children are encouraged by the arrangement of the physical environment to communicate their needs for additional materials. For example, during snack time, an adult can encourage requests by presenting small servings of juice or pieces of a cookie rather than a whole cookie. A child who enjoys watching the teacher blow bubbles can be encouraged to make requests if the teacher blows one or two bubbles and then waits for the child to request more.

When children initiate language with requests for more, the teacher has the opportunity to model and prompt more elaborate language as well as to provide functional consequences for the children's communicative attempts. For example:

Teacher: (Blows two bubbles and stops.)
Child: "More"
Teacher: "Blow more bubbles?"
Child: "Blow more."
Teacher: (Blows more bubbles)

## Choice Making

There are many occasions when two or more options for activities or materials can be presented to children. In order to encourage children to initiate language, the choice should be presented nonverbally. Children may be most encouraged to make a choice when one of the items is preferred and the other is disliked. For example, the adult may hold two different toys (e.g., a big yellow dump truck and a small red block) and wait for the child to make a verbal or nonverbal request. If the child requests nonverbally, the adult has the option of prompting the child to verbalize ("Tell me what you want") or simply modeling a response for the child ("Yellow truck"). Children's verbal requests can be followed with expansions of their language ("You wanted the yellow truck") or models of alternative forms for requesting ("Yellow truck, please").

## Assistance

Creating a situation in which children are likely to need assistance increases the likelihood that they will communicate about that need. The presence of attractive materials that require assistance to operate may encourage children to request help from adults or peers. A wind-up toy, a swing that a child needs help getting into, or an unopened bottle of bubbles are all examples of materials that can provide a nonverbal prompt to ask for help.

## Sabotage

Setting up a "sabotage" by not providing all of the materials the children will need to complete a task (e.g., paints and water but no paintbrush following an instruction to paint), or by otherwise preventing them from carrying out an instruction, also will encourage them to make requests. This environmental strategy requires children o problem solve and indicate that something is wrong or missing. They must first determine what is needed, and this initial discovery may require prompts from an adult. The missing materials are cues for the children to communicate that something is not right or that additional materials are needed. Sabotage is an effective prompt for language when the cues are obvious and children's cognitive skills are sufficiently developed to make detection of the missing material easy and rapid. Sabotage should be carried out in a warm, engaging manner by the teacher; the episode should be brief and never frustrating to the child.

## Silly Situations

The final environmental strategy is to create a need for children to communicate by setting up absurd or silly situations that violate their expectations. For example, an adult who playfully attempts to put a child's shoes on the adult's feet may encourage the child to comment on the absurd situation. During snack time, an adult can set up an absurd situation by placing a large piece of modeling clay or a colored block on a child's plate instead of a cracker, then waiting expectantly for the child to initiate a verbal or nonverbal request.

Children develop expectations for the ways things should be in everyday environments. They learn routines and expect that things will happen in a particular order. When something unexpected happens, they may be prompted to communicate. Of course, children must *have* expectations before the expectations can be violated. Thus, use of this strategy must be tailored to the individual skills of the children and to their familiar routines. For example, a child who always stores articles of clothing and materials in a specific "cubbie" will probably notice when an adult places a silly picture over it; a child who does not consistently use a specified "cubbie" would be unlikely to notice and respond to such a change in the environment.

## Making the Strategies Effective

To make these seven environmental strategies work, the teacher must follow the student's lead. The teacher must notice what the child is interested in, establish joint attention on the topic of interest, and encourage the child to make communicative attempts. By monitoring the child's interest and identifying which materials and activities the child enjoys, an adult can select the ones that will best serve as reinforcers for language.

The nonverbal cues that accompany the environmental arrangement strategies should be faded over time so the child is responding more to things of interest in the environment and less to the adult's cues (Halle, Marshall, & Spradlin, 1979). For example, it may be necessary at first for teachers to shrug their shoulders, raise their eyebrows, and tilt their heads, while extending their hands containing different toys, in order to direct children's attention to the environment and to the opportunity for choice making. As children become more skilled at initiating requests, fewer and less obvious nonverbal prompts should be given.

The use of environmental strategies must be tailored to each child's cognitive level and responsiveness to the environment. For example, putting a coat on a child backward and waiting for the child to communicate that something is wrong may require additional prompts if the child is unable to problem solve at this level. For environmental strategies to be effective, they must be geared to each child's level and they must cue communicative responses that are emergent in the child's repertoire.

## Conclusion

How adults respond to children's communication attempts when they are elicited by environmental arrangement is extremely important. Immediate feedback and access to the desired material or requested assistance, as well as a positive affective response, are essential consequences for communication attempts. As in all applications of naturalistic teaching processes, these episodes should be brief, positive, successful for the children, and designed to reinforce the children's use of language and their social engagement with adults (Hart & Rogers-Warren, 1978).

## References

Alpert, C. L., Kaiser, A. P., Ostrosky, M. M., & Hemmeter, M. L. (1987, November). *Using environmental arrangement and milieu language teaching as interventions for improving the communication skills of nonvocal preschool children.* Paper presented at the National Early Childhood Conference on Children with Special Needs, Denver, CO.

Bates, E. (1976). Pragmatics and sociolinguistics in child language. In O. M. Moorehead & A. E. Moorehead (Eds.), *Normal and deficient child language* (pp. 411–463). Baltimore: University Park Press.

Halle, J., Marshall, A., & Spradlin, J. (1979). Time delay: A technique to increase language use and facilitate generalization in retarded children. *Journal of Applied Behavior Analysis, 12,* 431–439.

Haring, T. G., Neetz, J. A., Lovinger, L., Peck, C., & Semmell, M. I. (1987). Effects of four modified incidental teaching procedures to create opportunities for communication. *The Journal of the Association for Persons with Severe Handicaps, 12,*(3), 218–226.

Hart, B. M. (1985). Naturalistic language training strategies. In S. F. Warren & A. Rogers-Warren (Eds.), *Teaching functional language.* Baltimore: University Park Press.

Hart, B. M., & Rogers-Warren, A. K. (1978). Milieu language training. In R. L. Schiefelbusch (Ed.), *Language intervention strategies* (Vol. 2, pp. 193–235). Baltimore: University Park Press.

Hemmeter, M. L. (1988). *The effect of environmental arrangement on parent-child language interactions.* Unpublished master's thesis, Vanderbilt University, Nashville, TN.

Rogers-Warren, A. K., Warren, S. F., & Baer, D. M. (1983). Interactional bases of language learning. In K. Kernan, M. Begab, & R. Edgarton (Eds.), *Environments and behavior: The adaptation of mentally retarded persons.* Baltimore: University Park Press.

*The development and dissemination of this paper were partially supported by Grant No. G008400663 from the Office of Special Education and Grant No. G008720107 from the National Institute for Disability and Rehabilitation Research. The authors are grateful to Cathy Alpert and Mary Louise Hemmeter for their contributions in the development of these environmental arrangement strategies.*

# Parental Feelings

*The Forgotten Component When Working
with Parents of Handicapped Preschool Children*

**Richard M. Gargiulo
and Stephen B. Graves**

*Richard M. Gargiulo is Professor,
Department of Special Education, The
University of Alabama at Birmingham.
Stephen B. Graves is Assistant Pro-
fessor, Department of Curriculum and
Instruction.*

Educators are becoming increasingly aware of the importance of parental participation in the education of young handicapped children. The idea of involving parents in the educational decision-making process is experiencing a rebirth due to the recent enactment of the preschool mandate P.L. 99-457, the Education of the Handicapped Act Amendments of 1986. This federal initiative directs local education agencies to serve children, ages 3 to 5, who are developmentally delayed or "at-risk" for future problems. Youngsters who, for instance, were born premature, manifest Down syndrome, suffer from fetal alcohol syndrome or have parents who are mentally retarded will be provided early educational experiences.

Like its predecessor P.L. 94-142, parental involvement constitutes a significant element of this new legislation. Although both of these enactments recognize parents' rights to be involved and actively participate, schools by and large have exhibited little sustained effort in working with parents or soliciting their assistance in the instructional process (Schulz, 1987). This is truly unfortunate, for research suggests that parent participation can oftentimes be the difference between program success and failure (Mandell & Fiscus, 1981; Swick, 1987).

## An Arena for Conflict

The education of the preschool child with special needs does not fall within the exclusive jurisdiction of the early childhood professional; parents are an important and necessary part of the team (Graves & Gargiulo, 1989). Yet, according to Gallagher and his colleagues (Gallagher, Beckman, & Cross, 1983), the history of parent-professional relationships is gloomy and counterproductive. Barriers frequently exist between parents and educators. These obstacles to partnerships may result from actions on the part of professionals. Some workers consider parents more of a nuisance than a resource (Seligman & Seligman, 1980). Teachers have occasionally blamed parents for causing, or at least not preventing, their child's disability (Seligman, 1979). Gargiulo (1985) observed that some professionals are opposed to parent involvement and, therefore, are reluctant to share responsibilities and allow meaningful participation.

Parents frequently view their interactions with professionals as adversarial. Roos (1978) asserted that professionals have mishandled parents. Perhaps the most demeaning and devastating trait of professional people, according to Schulz, is the tendency to deny parents' expertise and knowledge about their own child (1987, pp. 117-118).

In all fairness, impediments to collaboration can be a product of the parents' behavior. Professionals do not have a monopoly on negative attitudes (Schulz, 1987). Parents, on occasion, can be demanding, uncooperative, overly dependent, defensive and hostile. Some parents criticize professionals for not recognizing their child's disability earlier, while others have even accused the professional of causing the handicap (Gargiulo, 1985). Kraft and Snell (1980) identified four types of parents frequently encountered by school personnel: the blame-oriented parent who regularly calls attention to shortcomings in the school; the invisible parent who takes no initiative and fails to respond to messages; the supercooperative parent who continually abuses the teacher's time; and finally, the pseudoexpert parent who knows more about education than the teacher.

Given this arena of mutual distrust, antagonism and suspicion, it is easy to understand how relationships between professionals and parents fail to develop.

## Understanding Parental Reaction to Exceptionality

Fortunately, in many situations, parental status has changed from one of mere recipient of services to that of active participant. In addition, there have been recent appeals for early childhood professionals to view parents as program partners (Graves & Gargiulo, 1989; Peterson, 1987). Although currently professionals are more sensitive to the contributions of parents, one critical component is frequently absent from discussions on working with parents of exceptional children. Rarely is consideration given to how parents *feel* about being the mother or father of a child with a disability. Parental reaction to exceptionality can significantly influence the parent-professional relationship. Many of the behaviors and actions exhibited by parents, such as those identified herein, are the direct result of the parents' interpretation of what exceptionality means to them and their son or daughter.

> **When professionals are able to demonstrate empathy as well as respect for the parents' perspective of exceptionality, misinterpretation of parental actions diminishes.**

Parental reaction to a handicapping condition is highly individualistic. Each parent will respond in his or her own way. Helping professionals will, therefore, encounter parental conduct that varies along a continuum of emotional responses. Stage models, such as those developed by Opirhory and Peters (1982) and Gargiulo (1985), are useful for explaining parental behavior. Workers, Gargiulo (1985) contends, who view feelings such as denial, anger, grief, guilt and shame as necessary, normal and perfectly legitimate human responses to a crisis are in a good position to understand parents and effectively interact with them.

When professionals are able to demonstrate empathy as well as respect for the parents' perspective of exceptionality, misinterpretation of parental actions diminishes. Parents who refuse early intervention services, fail to keep appointments or seek second opinions, for example, should not be condemned or criticized. Rather, these behaviors should be seen as natural and an indicator of the parents' degree of acceptance of their preschooler with special needs. The parents' level of involvement and extent of participation is a gauge of their location on the acceptance continuum.

Stage models are beneficial for understanding parental responses to exceptionality. Yet, the needs of the parents reflect not only their ability to cope but also the developmental needs of the child (Schulz, 1987). Professionals must be cognizant of this and customize their interactions with parents to meet these changing needs. For example, the demand placed upon the professional who has the responsibility of informing parents that their son or daughter is handicapped is most likely different from the counsel required of a teacher who is dealing with parental fears and concerns as the youngster makes the transition from a preschool program to public school.

Parents will also recycle their feelings. Stages that were previously navigated will reappear and demand attention. This review of prior feelings is usually in reaction to specific events in the life of the child or the family, such as the beginning of a new school year or the birth of a sibling. Recapitulation is normal. Professionals should be prepared for it. Additionally, both parents may not necessarily be at the same stage of acceptance. As noted previously, exceptionality frequently means different things to mothers and fathers. Individuality of response should be accepted as well as respected. Not only do parents commonly traverse the continuum separately, they do so according to their own timetable.

## Suggestions for Working with Parents

The following list of nonprioritized hints is designed to facilitate an effective and meaningful relationship with parents of young children with handicaps.

■ Explain terminology. Many parents have no previous experience with exceptionality. This may be their first exposure to a disability label. The parents' conceptualization of cerebral palsy or mental retardation is most likely different from that of the professional.

■ Parents will frequently exhibit negative feelings when confronted with the news that their son or daughter is handicapped. Workers need to send a message that it is okay to have these feelings. They need to be acknowledged and then understood.

■ Teachers must listen! If one wishes to discover the parents' agenda and wishes concerning their child, active listening is of critical importance. Effective helpers want to know what the parent is thinking as well as feeling.

■ Use a two-step process when initially informing parents that their child requires special educational services. After sharing diagnostic information, it is strongly suggested that professionals allow parents time to comprehend and absorb what they have been told. The parents' affective concerns must be dealt with prior to proceeding with matters such as intervention recommendations, treatment regimens and strategies or duration of services. These issues should be addressed in a follow-up

interview as the parents' emotional state permits.

■ Keep parents informed. Use a variety of two-way communication techniques. Be as positive as possible when discussing a child's performance. Demonstrate respect, concern and a sincere desire to cooperate.

■ Be accountable. If you agree to assume certain responsibilities or gather information for the parent, be certain to follow through. Accountability demonstrates to the parents that they can depend on you. Trust, consistency and dependability significantly increase the chances for an effective relationship.

■ Recognize that diverse family structures and parenting styles will influence parent participation. In some circumstances, the responsible or concerned individual may not be the child's biological parent. Therefore, respect the parent's right to choose his or her level of involvement. Turnbull and Turnbull (1982) urge professionals to tolerate a range of parent participation matched to needs and interest.

## A Final Thought

Today, parent participation is a right, not a privilege. While professionals may encounter parents with so much emotional and attitudinal baggage that it prohibits real dialogue with them (Gorham, 1975), it is the professional's job to find ways, rather than excuses, of involving parents (DeWert & Helsel, 1985). Successful early intervention efforts require that parents and professionals collaborate as equals. The ultimate beneficiaries of this partnership will be our young children with special needs.

## References

DeWert, M., & Helsel, E. (1985). The Helsel family today. In A. Turnbull & H. Turnbull (Eds.), *Parents speak out* (2nd ed.) (pp. 101-106). Columbus, OH: Charles Merrill.

Gallagher, J., Beckman, P., & Cross, A. (1983). Families of handicapped children: Sources of stress and its amelioration. *Exceptional Children, 50,* 10-19.

Gargiulo, R. (1985). *Working with parents of exceptional children.* Boston: Houghton Mifflin.

Gorham, K. (1975). A lost generation of parents. *Exceptional Children, 41,* 521-525.

Graves, S., & Gargiulo, R. (1989). Parents and early childhood professionals as program partners: Meeting the needs of the preschool exceptional child. *Dimensions, 17,* 23-24.

Kraft, S., & Snell, M. (1980). Parent-teacher conflict: Coping with parental stress. *The Pointer, 24,* 29-37.

Mandell, C., & Fiscus, E. (1981). *Understanding exceptional people.* St. Paul, MN: West.

Opirhory, G., & Peters, G. (1982). Counseling intervention strategies for families with less than the perfect newborn. *The Personnel and Guidance Journal, 60,* 451-455.

Peterson, N. (1987). *Early intervention for handicapped and at-risk children.* Denver: Love.

Roos, P. (1978). Parents of mentally retarded children—misunderstood and mistreated. In A. Turnbull & H. Turnbull (Eds.), *Parents speak out* (pp. 13-27). Columbus, OH: Charles Merrill.

Schulz, J. (1987). *Parents and professionals in special education.* Boston: Allyn & Bacon.

Seligman, M. (1979). *Strategies for helping parents of exceptional children.* New York: Free Press.

Seligman, M., & Seligman, P. (1980). The professional's dilemma: Learning to work with parents. *Exceptional Parent, 10,* 11-13.

Swick, K. (1987). *Perspectives on understanding and working with families.* Champaign, IL: Stipes.

Turnbull, A., & Turnbull, H. (1982). Parent involvement in the education of handicapped children: A critique. *Mental Retardation, 20,* 115-122.

# Guiding Behavior

Adults who live and work with young children on a daily basis often report great satisfaction and fulfillment when developmental progress is observed. There is also considerable ambivalence and strain when children act differently than adults would like or expect. Certainly, children's behavior is not always easy or pleasant to deal with due to their fundamental immaturity, inexperience, and childlike ways of perceiving the world. Coupled with these realities, many people feel there has been a widespread societal breakdown in disciplined behavior in both children and adults. Accordingly, discipline and guidance are common discussion topics for adults who share young children's environments.

Heated, unproductive arguments may occur if adults do not realize that the broad concept of discipline suggests varied meanings and strategies for different people. For some adults, discipline means punishment—swift, painful, and involving fear, coercion, or isolation from peers. But researchers and observers of young children have clearly shown that punished, coerced, and isolated children feel humiliated, lose self-esteem, and fail to develop coping strategies to handle future problems.

For early childhood educators, discipline means guidance. It involves the following steps: first, understanding typical child development and examining one's attitudes about children; second, preventing certain behaviors through monitoring the daily schedule and room arrangement; third, redirecting and modifying undesirable behavior; fourth, modeling and explaining more acceptable, appropriate, or mature behavior; and fifth, using reasoning with children and teaching them verbal skills for peer interaction. Discipline, in this connotation, means steadily building self-control so children can develop positive self-esteem, respect for the needs of others, and gradually move toward healthy independence and problem-solving skills that they may draw upon in future situations.

Any program or plan for guiding behavior must focus on young children. So an appropriate beginning of guidance and discipline is an understanding of the concept of self-esteem. What was once thought of as a singular element of children's development that could be enhanced through use of catch phrases, praise, or stickers is now considered quite complex. Self-esteem involves an inner sense of acceptance and value as well as outer-directed self-regulation and evaluation. Early in life, children begin developing an actual self along with their conception of self. These two dynamics are shaped by others and can at times be in conflict. This is why an attempt to address a child's low self-esteem with words of praise may prove ineffective.

When self-esteem is viewed as both a personal and social interaction, the role of early childhood educators becomes significantly more important than artificially bolstering a child through a particular situation with a smiley-face sticker. It is a process of leading the child to a valued and realistic identity. This process begins with showing respect for children's well-being. In day-to-day transactions, it means acknowledging that children deserve the space to be themselves, make their own decisions, do their own work. At the same time, since children are dependent, respect includes assuming responsibility for nurturing their growth and development. The long-term goal is to foster confidence, initiative, and sociability in children. These can best be accomplished when discipline is regarded as a learning experience and respect is maintained even in difficult circumstances.

In devising a plan for guiding behavior, a teacher is concerned with both validating children's feelings and heightening their awareness of the feelings of others. It takes careful communication to guide children in negotiating problems while affirming all parties. When to intervene in a situation or when to allow natural consequences takes thought and skill. If they understand the causes of frustration and aggression in children, such as unnecessary waiting, crowding, insufficient play materials, or poor curricular planning, teachers can made changes so that children's self-esteem and control are supported in healthy ways.

As with all areas of early childhood education, a high-quality, effective plan for guiding behavior does not arrive prepackaged for the teacher's immediate use. Guiding and disciplining is hard work, requiring careful attention to individual children and differing situations. Teaching young children to negotiate problems is largely a mental and verbal process. Mastery of authentic and humane guidance techniques takes time reflecting on ethical principles, refining strategies, and seeking the best emotional climate.

### Looking Ahead: Challenge Questions

Why is it important to establish an atmosphere of respect during the early childhood years?

What are ways teachers can demonstrate their respect for young children?

How do teachers enable children to analyze situations before problems occur?

What communication skills are helpful to use in assisting young children to negotiate problems?

During the preschool years, what abilities are involved in developing self-control?

How can teachers promote self-control in early childhood settings?

What are the behaviors that might indicate a young child is under pressure?

# How Well Do We Respect the Children in Our Care?

## Stacie G. Goffin

*Stacie G. Goffin is Assistant Professor, Early Childhood Education, University of Missouri - Kansas City.*

Children are spending increasingly larger proportions of their early years in group settings outside their homes. Statistics abound describing the quantity of mothers currently in the workforce. Interest in early childhood education, however, is more than just the result of increasing maternal employment. There are other crucial statistics.

• Twenty-five percent of all children—47% of black children, 40% of Hispanic children and 10% of white children—are born into and spend their lives in poverty (Halpern, 1987).

• One in five children who entered 1st grade this past fall is at risk of becoming a teen parent, and one in seven is at risk of dropping out of school (Children's Defense Fund, 1988).

• The decreasing number of future workers means every potential employee needs to be competent and skilled.

In combination, these changing demographics and social circumstances have focused attention on early childhood care and education as a solution to welfare reform, teenage pregnancy, female employment and future labor needs. Noticeably absent from this list of public policy concerns, however, is the well-being of children. This omission points to the low priority the general public gives to issues associated with quality. Quality issues argue the validity of children's well-being in the present and contrast with the current focus of arguments supporting early childhood education in terms of future returns.

As early educators, however, we cannot side-step the issue of quality; we need to become more reflective about the "treatment" children are receiving. We can begin by asking the question, "How well do we respect the children in our care?"

As defined by the *New Scholastic Dictionary of American English* (Kessen, 1981), the term *respect* has the following meanings: to be mindful of; to pay attention to; to show consideration and esteem for; to avoid intruding upon; and to avoid violating. Based upon this definition, respect can be both a noun and a verb. As a noun,

respect can be a result or outcome of our interactions with children; it can also be a description of our behavior, as in "respectful." The major focus of this discussion, however, is on respect as a verb—as an action word. As early educators, we show our respect *for* children by what we do *with* children.

To answer the question just posed, the various meanings of respect have been amplified in relation to daily interactions with children and their families. They have been used repeatedly to describe 12 active (and knowingly overlapping) categories that frame the ways early childhood educators can display their respect, or disrespect, to children. The intent is to provoke thinking about the meaning and impact of our actions with and for children.

## TWELVE ACTIVE WAYS TO RESPECT CHILDREN

### Action #1: Showing respect for childhood

The idea of childhood as a separate, developmental period is a relatively recent cultural invention; in fact, it is only several hundred years old (Kessen, 1979; Postman,

1982). Yet, many recent writers have expressed concern that the idea of childhood as a separate developmental period is disappearing (see, for example, Postman, 1982). This implies we have been guilty of intruding into and violating this unique period of growth.

In early childhood settings, examples of this kind of disrespect include ignoring the ways children learn through play and expecting them to learn in ways similar to older children. In addition to being inappropriate, when the curriculum focuses on skills and knowledge children supposedly need for later schooling (e.g., lining up, coloring within the lines, learning pre-skills), children's future development is being emphasized as more important than their current well-being. As a result, childhood becomes merely a stepping-stone to future stages of growth rather than a meaningful time for development in its own right.

Disrespect for childhood is also expressed in the frustration and outbursts of anger many adults display when children "act their age," instead of conforming to adult standards. The term *childish* has acquired a negative, rather than positive, connotation.

Early childhood teachers and caregivers are frequently praised for their patience. When they display their patience because children have failed to meet inappropriate expectations, however, they reveal misunderstandings about child growth and development (Weber-Schwartz, 1987). Those who understand children accept "childish" behavior like negativism, for example ("No! Me do it!"), as developmentally appropriate behavior for 2-year-olds. Even though respectful adults will want to help 2-year-olds learn other ways of expressing their feelings, they also recognize that children behave differently from adults because of their maturational level and inexperience.

Consequently, respect for childhood requires paying attention to and showing esteem for the characteristics of childhood—such as activity, impulsiveness, curiosity, learning through exploration—and then organizing teaching and learning to reflect these understandings. To quote Weber-Schwartz (1987), "Because I accept what *is*, I put energy into effective teaching, not into struggling against the reality that children are children" (p. 53, italics in original).

### Action #2: Responding with sensitivity to children's individuality

Respectful actions in this category go beyond respect for childhood. They acknowledge the unique characteristics of individual children and the ways their uniqueness is revealed in decisions, choices, preferences and styles of responding to and interacting with objects and people. To show consideration for these qualities requires we support and encourage these characteristics as worth nurturing. Too often, children's personal ways of responding are viewed as interference with an adult's prepared plans or as misbehavior, rather than as evidence of a child's individuality or personal perceptions of the situation.

Commitment to children's individuality requires accepting and supporting children's personal goals and values as worthwhile. Early childhood settings that primarily function in whole groups and emphasize adult-prescribed learning offer limited opportunities for children to personalize learning through making their own decisions, acting as initiators of their own learning or pursuing their own interests. Yet, it is these flexible opportunities that encourage and support individuality and personal growth. In contrast, heavy doses of group instruction and standardized curriculum encourage and support conformity.

Being mindful of children's in-

dividuality also occurs when adults actively listen to children even though their comments may seem trivial. It is reflected in greetings and dismissals recognizing children's arrival and departure, in interesting alternative activities for children who are not interested in the adult-chosen activity and, most important, in consideration of children's individual ways of acting their age.

Admittedly, we cannot always be flexible in response to children's individuality, but we can give more consideration to how well we are accommodating children's needs and interests. Because we adults have more authority than children, it is easy to expect children to adjust to adult preferences; it is less easy to remind ourselves that it is often more supportive and growth-enhancing if we adjust to the individuality of children.

### Action #3: Developing nurturing relationships with children
### Action #4: Using adult authority with wisdom to facilitate children's growth into caring adults

Adults are bigger and stronger than children. They have more experiences and greater skills. Consequently, the power relationship between children and adults is unequal and unbalanced in favor of adults. The critical issue for children is how adults choose to use their authority. Dreikurs and Solz (1964) use the term *social equality* to describe an optimum relationship between children and adults. In this type of relationship, adults recognize that even though children are dependent upon them and have less knowledge and fewer skills, they are still entitled to respect as human beings.

This respect, however, does not suggest that adults should abdicate their responsibilities toward children. Because children are dependent upon us and are less knowledgeable and skillful, we must assume responsibility for nurturing and fostering their

## Table 1
### Early Educator Responses to the Question:
### "How Well Do We Respect the Children in Our Care?"

I show my respect when:
- I listen to what a child has to say.
- I take time for a child when I'm very busy.
- I play with children.
- I color a picture with children.
- I recognize accomplishments.
- I allow children to settle disputes between themselves.
- I listen to a special song.
- I show interest in a child's project.
- I make eye contact.
- I encourage their viewpoints.
- I allow them to make choices.
- I try to arrange a schedule to be accommodating to a parent.
- I allow for privacy.
- I try to respond with words and actions to a child's uniqueness.
- I call children by their names.
- I know how to say "no."
- I encourage independence.
- I respond to their questions.
- I allow a child to talk uninterrupted.
- I respect a child's choice of friend and play equipment.
- I allow children to make mistakes.
- I realize their individuality.
- I am flexible.
- I allow them to disagree.
- I care for their property.
- I allow transition time.
- I listen to a child's problem and realize how upsetting the situation can be to a child.
- I talk to children as people.
- I give each child a chance to communicate.
- I ask a child for his/her solution to a problem.
- I value their opinions.
- I remember that play is of great importance in each child's life.
- I prepare myself well for class so I don't have to "waste" children's time.

I am somewhat disrespectful when:
- I do not take a child's opinion seriously.
- I avoid an issue a child felt needed immediate attention.
- I use time out.
- I leave the children alone.
- I walk away from a child while he/she is crying.
- I don't stop to listen.
- I respond with "uh-huh."
- I use a "baby-talk" tone of voice with younger children.
- I use angry words under stress.
- I cut their conversations close.
- I finish a task for them to hasten time.
- I forget to follow through on something I promised.
- I answer a question for them with a strange adult present so they are more articulate or seemingly more socially acceptable.
- I spend physical time with a child but am emotionally distant from the situation.
- I behave impatiently.
- I use sarcasm.
- I shout.
- I physically force a child into a situation in which he's uncomfortable.
- My expectations are too high.
- I rush children.
- I don't take care of myself physically or emotionally.
- I call them names; e.g., dumbbell.
- I show frustration because their needs interfere with my schedule.
- I focus on children's bad behaviors.
- I belittle their feelings.
- I sneak up on a child doing wrong.
- I ignore them.
- I stop a child who is really interested in a project.
- I don't allow a child to explain why or how a friend got hurt, or how an accident occurred.

*Note:* Thanks to all the early educators who shared their thoughts; their own wording has been used as much as possible.

---

growth. This is where wisdom comes in! Nurturing children's development into caring adults requires not only respect for childhood and a child's individuality, but also knowledge and understanding about child growth and development.

Furthermore, despite our frequent acknowledgment of the importance of children's emotional development, since the 1960s this aspect of growth has become a stepchild to cognitive (which often means academic) development. Yet, a nurturing relationship is the basis for child development. It is a necessary foundation for children's growth into caring human beings, as well as their relationships with peers and adults.

In fact, intellectual development and socio-emotional development are inseparable. They can be separated only for purposes of theory, pedagogy and research. This understanding requires adults to be as responsive to children's social-emotional needs as to their intellectual demands.

### Action #5: Considering how day-to-day practices influence children

Children learn not only from *what* they are taught, but also from *how* they are taught. They learn from how the day is arranged, how the environment is organized and how others try to teach them. As early childhood educators, we need to become more sensitive to

the cumulative impact of our daily interactions with children, including intrusions into their play and activity, usurpation of their decision-making abilities and lack of attention to their feelings. Table 1 lists a sampling of responses to the title question from early childhood practitioners. Their answers highlight the day-in, day-out interactions that reveal respect, and unintended disrespect, for children.

We need to facilitate children's involvement in personally meaningful activities and experiences. The demands of group living can be softened by allowing children to make meaningful decisions and providing more opportunities for them to pursue their individual interests. We want to minimize the times we unnecessarily or unthinkingly forget to pay attention to children's interests and preferences.

One of the most challenging aspects of early childhood education is trying to understand a child's perspective about an experience. Lack of sensitivity to children's individual ways of making sense of their experiences often leads adults to impose their own ways of organizing and interpreting experiences (see, for example, Paley, 1986; Suransky, 1982).

For example, in one early childhood setting, a group of 4-year-olds sat cross-legged on the floor in a circle, watching as their teacher lifted a pencil, a beanbag and three baby-food jars out of a bowl and then set them on a mat. The teacher announced, "Many of these things have been on the earth for a long time." She held up a baby-food jar of soil and said, "LAND has always been here as far as we know." She returned the jar to the mat and lifted up another jar filled with water, saying, "WATER has always been here as far as we know." She set the jar back on the mat and held up the last jar (which appeared empty) and said, "AIR has always been here as far as we know." She placed the jar back on the mat and asked, "Can you see anything else that has always been here?" Antoine called out excitedly, "The bowl!!"

The teacher answered, "No. MAN made the bowl. Someone INVENTED the bowl. Can anyone think of something in our room that someone made?" Antoine raised his hand and shouted, "Horses on the wall!" The teacher pointed to the teacher-prepared horses decorating the wall above the blackboard. She asked, "What about the horse on the farm? Where did it come from?" Antoine announced excitedly, "Horses!!" The teacher smiled at Antoine and asked again, "Where did they *come* from—did man make them or did God make them?"

This teacher appeared unaware that her way of thinking about these concepts differed from Antoine's. From Antoine's point of view, the experience probably helped him to learn self-doubt and how to "play the circle-time game." It is likely he also learned that right answers are arbitrary, since his reasoned thinking was consistently corrected. It is unlikely, however, that he learned much about the distinctions between natural and manmade materials, which appears to have been the teacher's objective.

It is equally important to pay attention to children's needs in our scheduling and organizing. Too often we feel that responding to children's needs (e.g., to receive affection, to be first in line, to take more time) interferes with classroom routines or that being tough while children are young, better prepares them for a harsh world later on. In reality, it is just the opposite. By responding to children's needs, we strengthen their abilities to accept themselves and to cope with difficult circumstances.

Sensitivity to children's perspectives is seen when adults try to understand children's thinking, their needs, preferences and reactions. Failure to consider the impact of our day-in, day-out living arrangements with children underestimates the daily impact of teacher-child interactions and can undermine children's opportunities to develop their individuality.

**Action #6: Recognizing discipline as a learning experience for children and viewing mistakes as potential learning opportunities**
Discipline is frequently confused with punishment; its purpose is often mistakenly limited to stopping inappropriate behavior. Discipline, however, describes the guidance provided to help children understand adult expectations and develop control from within. It is an ongoing process of guiding children's development.

When children and adults cooperate with each other, classroom life proceeds smoothly. When children do not comply with a teacher's request, the result is usually a discipline encounter. The term *encounter* highlights that the outcome desired by the teacher is not shared by the child, reminding us that children are active decision-makers (Goffin, 1987). These disagreements often result in conflict between teachers and children.

It is this aspect of discipline that has received the most discussion and unfairly earned discipline the one-sided reputation of being negative and unpleasant. Still, the important point is that discipline in general, and discipline encounters in particular, are both learning experiences for children. The ways teachers and caregivers structure these daily experiences clearly reveal their consideration and esteem for children.

A major characteristic of adult-child relationships is the discrepancy between the power and authority of children and adults. We intrude upon children when we use our authority and power to coerce them (most easily characterized by the phrase "Because I said so, that's why!") to fulfill our needs (for order or schedule, for example) without being mindful of their needs, interests and individuality. Respectful adults carefully use their power and authority to help children learn appropriate behaviors and inner controls in ways that show consideration for their feelings and developing capabilities; for example, by acknowledging feelings, providing explanations and linking behavior with rational consequences.

**Action #7: Acknowledging children's competencies**
**Action #8: Organizing a curriculum that provides children with interesting things to think about**
We often fail to be mindful of what

children are capable of doing. There is a tendency to narrowly focus on skills and information children do not yet possess. As a result, some early childhood educators see their major responsibility as teaching children the next item in a series of learnings. This emphasis, however, fails to show esteem for children's capabilities. Learning experiences should be organized as extensions and elaborations of children's current interests and understandings—the basis for meaningful learning.

Research reveals that children are much more capable than we have credited them (Bruner & Harste, 1987; Donaldson, 1978; Gelman, 1979). It is demeaning, as well as boring, to have weekly units on fragmented skills or topics such as the color *blue*, the shape of a circle or the letter *C*. It is also frequently meaningless. A 4-year-old, working to create an octopus by gluing precut construction paper tentacles on a yellow circle of paper, turned to his teacher standing nearby and asked, "What am I making?" "Octopuses," the teacher responded. "Why?" he followed up. "Because," the teacher replied, "the letter we're learning about is *O* and octopus begins with it." "Oh," he said as he returned to his gluing.

Children are entitled to activities and experiences that are engrossing and that permit the teacher to challenge their thinking. Learning is more than memorizing labels and making associations between objects. Esteem for children demands we pay attention to their abilities and provide meaningful, relevant and interesting ways for them to expand their understandings. It also requires talking *with* children (instead of *at* them) by attending to what they are doing and asking questions related to their actions.

As the following anecdote clearly reveals, we dominate the learning process when our teaching primarily focuses on what *we*

think children ought to know, regardless of its relationship to their current interests and activities.

During a circle-time activity, the teacher flashed picture cards to the seated children. "And, what is this?" she asked. "A boat," children shouted. "Where does it go?" A child interjected, "Teacher, I rode a boat on my vacation." Another child yelled, "I did, too." "I have a boat at my house," a third child contributed. The children then began talking with each other, sharing comments like: "We went to Disney World on our vacation … We went to Colorado." "Quiet!" the teacher shouted. "Now, I said quiet. That's enough about vacations; you can talk about that at free time. We have to get through this."

> **Research reveals that children are much more capable than we have credited them.**

**Action #9: Supporting and strengthening parents in their childrearing responsibilities**
Many children spend the majority of their waking hours with their teachers and caregivers. It is easy, therefore, for early childhood educators to lapse into a possessive attitude about the children in their care. This feeling is often heightened by tensions between parents and teachers/caregivers surrounding differing views on issues such as values, discipline, the importance of play and a child-centered curriculum (see Galinsky, 1988). These tensions are perhaps inescapable in any relationship where two unrelated adults care about the well-being of the same child. Still, it must be remembered that it

is parents who have made an unending commitment to their child, and it is with their parents that children are most emotionally intertwined.

Parenting is becoming respected as a challenging as well as highly personalized family enterprise. Parent programs based upon these premises are being called family support programs (Weissbourd, 1983). These programs strive to strengthen parenting by being responsive to parents' individuality and respecting the responsibilities they have assumed as parents.

We can show our support to parents in four ways: 1) by acknowledging the challenge of parenting, 2) by coming to know parents as individuals with their own personalities and family circumstances that help define their parenting, 3) by using these understandings to avoid judgmental interpretations of parents and their decisions, and 4) by acting as advocates for the parent-child relationship (Goffin & Caccamo, 1986). By strengthening and supporting parents in their parenting role, we show consideration for the importance of family in a child's life and express esteem for the challenge of parenthood.

**Action #10: Acknowledging the expertise needed to be a professional in early childhood education**
**Action #11: Speaking out on behalf of early childhood education as a profession**
The status of those who care for children is a leading indicator of how society views childhood and shows esteem for children. In general, society expresses limited interest in other people's children and therefore has little regard for those who do (Grubb & Lazerson, 1988). Society's attitude toward child care and caregivers, in particular, reveals the still dominant assumption that parents—mothers in particular—should be held totally responsible for the daily care

and education of their own children. This viewpoint encourages a custodial approach to child care outside the home.

As the number of women in the workforce and concerns for quality education increase, however, the importance of supplementing parents' responsibilities is gaining greater acceptance. We know the importance of our jobs and the contributions we make to children and their families. We know we are both underpaid and undervalued. But too many of us are also uninformed and undereducated about how to fulfill our responsibilities as early childhood educators.

For example, after beginning an afternoon kindergarten session with a 20-minute whole group handwriting exercise, a teacher announced, "Every day, after we have writing, we will have Center Time. Who knows what Center Time is?" "Well," the teacher answered, "if you went to preschool, they probably called it Play Time. And what is the difference between preschool and kindergarten? One is like babysitting and one is real school. And we are in real school here and we do real work, but sometimes we think play is learning, too."

This is a significant time in the history of early childhood education. The field is rapidly expanding. Simultaneously, early childhood educators are attempting to upgrade their status and compensation. Yet, at the same time, we are trying to convince many of the "outsiders" entering the field, as well as those already within our ranks, that early childhood education has a distinctive, professional knowledge base.

Knowledge of child development and early childhood education informs our practice and assures young children of programming specific to their needs and interests. It also provides a rationale for fending off the inappropriate expectations held by those unfamiliar with the issues unique to early childhood education (Goffin, 1989). More clearly articulating our purposes and convincing educational decision-makers and others about the unique characteristics of early childhood education remain two of our major professional challenges.

**Action #12: Speaking out on behalf of children's needs to parents, school administrators, business and community representatives, and policymakers**

Recent political and economic events have sensitized us to the realization that children's issues are not above politics. Policies made by business and government structure many of the decisions early childhood educators make for children and the kinds of experiences children live.

As early educators, we experience, either directly or indirectly, the personal stories behind the statistics. Our relationships with parents create the opportunity to release parents' power on behalf of their own as well as other children (Goffin, 1988). Our relationships with the community place us in a unique position to inform others about the needs of children and families. Our knowledge and experiences enable us to help policymakers better understand the lives of their youngest constituents. Therefore, we are violating our responsibility to children when we fail to act on our beliefs and to share our knowledge with others.

Advocacy on behalf of children is a critical vehicle for actualizing our commitment to children. It is a necessary component of an expanded vision of the role of the early childhood educator.

It is important to recognize that advocacy includes, but is not limited to, political activity. Everyone can participate in personal advocacy (Goffin, 1988). When we personally reach out or speak out to others and, by our interpersonal actions, try to help children and their families achieve needed or desired outcomes, we are performing personal advocacy. Personal advocacy takes advantage of opportunities to use our expertise on behalf of children and families.

A child care director's presentation to architects and a church committee about the importance of low windows in children's classrooms—despite her uncomfortable feelings of "exceeding her proper limits"—demonstrates personal advocacy. This director spoke out on behalf of children's needs for light and an aesthetically pleasing environment, despite her discomfort and anxiety. Her personal advocacy efforts resulted in differently designed, more appropriate classrooms for children.

Early childhood educators are among those who speak on behalf of others' children, not just their own. Our caring cannot be restricted to classrooms if we truly want to improve the lives of children.

## Conclusion

This article began by emphasizing respect as an action word. It was suggested that educators show their respect *for* children by what they do *with* children. The 12 categories just described, however, reveal that showing our respect requires we go beyond our interactions with children. Esteem for childhood requires not only respectful actions with children but respectful actions on their behalf.

**References**

Bruner, J., & Harste, H. (1987). Introduction. In J. Bruner & H. Harste (Eds.), *Making sense: The child's construction of the world* (pp. 1-25). New York: Methuen.

Children's Defense Fund. (1988). *A children's defense budget FY89: An analysis of our nation's investment in children.* Washington, DC: Author.

Donaldson, M. (1978). *Children's minds.* New York: W. W. Norton & Company.

## 4. GUIDING BEHAVIOR

Dreikurs, R., & Solz, V. (1964). *Children: The challenge.* New York: Dutton.

Galinsky, E. (1988). Parents and teacher-caregivers: Sources of tension, sources of support. *Young Children, 43*(3), 4-12.

Gelman, R. (1979). Preschool thought. *American Psychologist, 34,* 900-905.

Goffin, S. G. (1987). Introduction. In S. G. Goffin & S. Vartuli (Eds.), Classroom management in new context: Teacher as decision-maker [special issue]. *Dimensions, 15*(4).

Goffin, S. G. (1988). Putting our advocacy efforts into a new context. *Young Children, 3*(3), 52-56.

Goffin, S. G. (1989). Developing an early childhood research agenda: What can we learn from the research on teaching? *Early Childhood Research Quarterly, 4,* 187-204.

Goffin, S. G., with Caccamo, J. (1986). *In partnership with parents.* Jefferson City, MO: State Department of Elementary and Secondary Education, Division of Special Education.

Grubb, N. W., & Lazerson, M. (1988). *Broken promises: How Americans fail their children.* Chicago: University of Chicago Press.

Halpern, R. (1987). Major social and demographic trends affecting young families: Implications for early childhood care and education. *Young Children, 42*(6), 34-40.

Kessen, W. (1979). The American child and other cultural inventions. *American Psychologist, 34,* 815-820.

Kessen, W. (1981). (Ed.). *New scholastic dictionary of American English.* New York: Scholastic, Inc.

Paley, V. G. (1989). On listening to what children say. *Harvard Education Review, 56*(2), 122-131.

Postman, N. (1982). *The disappearance of childhood.* New York: Delacorte.

Suransky, V. P. (1982). *The erosion of childhood.* Chicago: The University of Chicago Press.

Weber-Schwartz, N. (1987). Food for thought: Patience or understanding? *Young Children, 42*(3), 52-54.

Weissbourd, B. (1983). The family support movement: Greater than the sum of its parts. *Zero to Three, 4*(1), 8-10.

# Nurturing Success

*Positive ways to build self-esteem in your children*

## PATRICIA H. BERNE
## WITH EVE BERNE

*Dr. Patricia H. Berne, a former nursery school teacher, is now a practicing clinical psychologist in Washington, D.C. Her book,* Building Self-Esteem in Children, *and her work with the National Council for Self-Esteem have nurtured and encouraged teachers, parents, and children across the country.*

*Eve Berne, Patricia Berne's daughter, is a former day-care teacher and assistant director. She is currently special projects consultant for a child-care resource and referral center in Cambridge, MA.*

I remember talking with a friend of mine, Sally, the mother of five children. One day as we sat together on the beach and watched our children play, Sally told me she had a very wise uncle. She thought he was wise because he had given her the most important piece of advice about raising children. Naturally, I asked her what that advice was. She said her uncle's words were: "The most important thing you can give children, more important than any material thing you might be concerned about, is a sense of self-confidence." Furthermore, he had told her, if she could give her children confidence in themselves, they would be able to get all the other things they needed for themselves.

As we sat on the beach and thought about Sally's uncle's words and our children played together in front of us, I know we wished very much, as most parents do, to give our children self-confidence.

As a mother, teacher, and counselor, I have spent much of my effort and thought building self-esteem in children, because self-esteem seems to be the foundation of self-confidence. Perhaps both words describe the same quality.

Self-esteem doesn't mean overconfidence. When you have self-esteem, you know yourself and accept yourself with your limitations; you are not ashamed of your limitations but simply see them as part of the person you are, perhaps as a boundary you're challenged to expand.

**Children's self-esteem grows when they know you care enough to be with them.**

## 4. GUIDING BEHAVIOR

In the first years of a child's life personal feelings of esteem are directly related to the people closest to him or her. When the people are nurturing and the environment they create offers opportunities for success, the child is well on his way to a healthy self-image.

Children who feel good about themselves take part in healthy relationships. They are open to new ideas and eager to share their own. Their confidence enables them to face challenges, cope with disappointments, and enjoy successes. These are children who are anxious to discover and share the wonder of life.

Success nourishes self-esteem. As children grow, they expand their perception of the people who influence them from family members to other caregivers. This gives special meaning to the people in an early childhood environment. In this setting children can experience success in their relationships with others (feeling loved and lovable, giving and receiving affection, building friendships); and in their abilities to relate as skillful, competent, and capable people.

In contrast, low self-esteem interferes with a child's ability to learn and to relate well to others. In some children, feelings of inadequacy surface in bossy and aggressive behavior. This may cause other children to become submissive and unsure.

These feelings show how a negative self-image affects a child and those around him. If he is perceived as a ''difficult child,'' his behavior can start a cycle in which everyone involved shares a loss of esteem because each person shares a part of the frustration.

The nurturing environment you create and the supportive, caring relationships you build with your children will provide them with a strong foundation for future success. Here are some ways to reinforce and build self-esteem in your children throughout the year.

## Building Positive Relationships

One of the first steps in developing children's self-esteem is to establish good relationships with them. Relationships that are mutually loving and caring, honest, and supportive create an atmosphere for healthy human growth. Here are some principles that focus on building such relationships with children.

■ **Create an atmosphere of trust.** The tone of your voice, your belief that each child is worthwhile and unique, and the care you take to kneel and speak to each child at eye level are immediate indicators to children that you are someone they can trust. In addition to using words and gestures to affirm that you care and value children, make sure your physical setting supports this attitude.

Some children feel valued when they can accomplish certain things by themselves, such as choosing between activities, returning toys to low-level shelves, and reaching for an intriguing book. Others feel important when they can be assured of structured activity. A teacher-directed collage project with a lot of materials to choose from can fulfill the needs of a child who is hesitant to make choices, while still enabling him to grow.

For some youngsters, noise, activity, and large numbers of people can be overwhelming. A quiet corner with a soft couch and fluffy pillows offers a welcome and safe retreat.

■ **Help children say goodbye.** Often at the beginning of the year, children create dropping-off rituals as a way to say goodbye to their parents. One youngster used the mail slot in the classroom door as a special, final place to touch his father's hand. Other children may run to the window to say goodbye. Respecting and supporting these goodbye routines communicates to children that you understand and value their relationships with family members.

■ **Keep children informed of the day's activities.** Let children know what their choices are when they arrive in the morning. Prior to transitions, keep them informed as to what will happen next. Notify them when cleanup time approaches so they will have ample time to complete the activities in which they are involved. Each day take advantage of snacktime to talk about what is scheduled for the rest of the day. There is comfort in predictability, and predictability helps children feel in control and capable.

■ **Be available to children.** When you agree to be available to a child, let the child know you are available specifically for him for this period of time. This

# 10 Principles of Self-Esteem

**1.** Children feel more confident in a setting that is conducive to their feeling cared for and valued.

**2.** Children's self-esteem grows when they know you care enough to be with them.

**3.** A moment's reflection about the wording of a question can make a significant difference in a child's self-esteem.

**4.** Children are enhanced by the network of people, things, and events that make up their lives. When you accept children in their network, you accept them completely.

**5.** Growth in self-esteem is connected with children's acceptance of their right to have strong feelings.

**6.** In a trusting and nonjudgmental atmosphere, self-esteem can grow.

means giving that child your *full* attention. Children appreciate not only your availability but also your undivided attention. When you spend time alone with a child, whether it's for five minutes or five hours, you're giving that child quality time. That helps build self-esteem because your attention to him affirms his value to you.

■ **Keep questions open-ended.** Keep your requests open-ended and invitational, for example, "Would you like to join us in playing this game? If you're not sure, I can ask you again in a few minutes." Always give children another chance to choose. They are still learning the art of making choices.

Instead of speaking to a child in an accusing tone ("You forgot to put the blocks away," which translates to "You betrayed my trust"), use an invitational approach ("Did you forget to put the blocks away? It's easy to forget things like that. Would you like some help?").

Try to put yourself in the child's position as you pose questions and suggestions. Avoid setting up a situation where a child is forced to express judgment about a fellow pupil. By asking, "Do you want to play with Darlene?" you may be putting the child in a position where he feels an obligation to please you — the acceptable answer in this case being, "Yes." Or, it may be that the child doesn't mind playing with Darlene but has no interest in what she is doing. Instead, phrase questions with a focus on the task or the toy, for example, "Darlene's using the blocks. Would you like to use them, too?" You're now giving the child a free choice — no strings attached for the child or the teacher.

■ **Remember names and details about children.** Especially at the beginning of the year, it builds self-esteem in children when you care enough to remember not only *their* names, but the names of their pets, their family members, places they told you about, and other significant details about them. Familiarity with concrete names shows you were really listening and you really understood. When I work with children, I like to remember stories they tell me, including some of the details. I like to mention these stories to them at a later date when some statement comes up that triggers my memory. Remembering such details indicates to children that their lives were real to me and that I found these details important.

■ **Be nonjudgmental.** To a child, embarrassment translates into humiliation — picturing oneself as worthless, incompetent, and unlovable. Suppose a child accidentally spills something at snacktime. Ease any embarrassment the child might feel and help maintain self-esteem by being casual and matter-of-fact. "Oh, I have problems pouring, too. Let's clean it up together."

The goal is to remedy mistakes and accidents inconspicuously. If you notice a child has wet his pants, take him aside quietly and say, "Let's change your pants. We keep extras here because this happens to other children, too." Your acceptance, along with a smile and gentle voice, conveys nonjudgmental acceptance. The more sensitive you are to each child's feelings the safer he will feel.

■ **Find ways to share laughter.** Relationships are usually more inviting if children expect they're going to be fun, and maybe even funny. But using humor effectively requires special sensitivity toward each child.

For example, reaching a withdrawn child through humor means understanding what he may be sensitive to and what he might think is funny. Then, telling an appropriate story from the mouth of a friendly, funny puppet can establish the beginnings of a positive and enjoyable relationship.

Laughter can also be a healing force.

For some children, exaggerating a situation until it can be laughed at helps heal the wounds of embarrassment. Help children to understand that everyone makes mistakes and laughter can be healthy, helpful, and healing.

Remember, too, when you enable a child to see himself as an entertaining person, someone people enjoy being with, you contribute to his healthy self-esteem. Acknowledge a child's sense of humor and help him feel good about himself for making you and others laugh and smile.

> **"The most important thing you can give children, more important than anything material, is a sense of self-confidence."**

## Dealing with Strong Emotions

Many children don't express strong emotions such as fear, sadness, anger, or loss, for fear of being overwhelmed by their emotions. These feelings are then repressed but don't go away unless they are dealt with. Other children express these feelings through emotional outbursts. They do not always know why these outbursts happened and are often embarrassed afterwards. It is important for children to have appropriate outlets for these sometimes overwhelming feelings. Here are some ways to help your children express them in healthy ways.

■ **Acknowledge a child's right to strong emotions.** Feelings are real experiences. When adults deny that children have a legitimate right to strong feelings, they are denying the children's sense of themselves as capable of being thinking, discriminating, evaluating, and honest persons. I remember one child who had been bitten by another in a nursery school. Although the skin was

---

**7.** Success comes from acknowledging the positive in a nonevaluative way.

**8.** Humor can be a great antidote for low self-esteem, especially when children want to get out of their depressed state quickly.

**9.** Children's self-esteem grows when they know that you want to share something you value with them.

**10.** Self-esteem thrives on success. The bridge you build for the child can provide a successful "crossing."

---

not broken by the bite, the teeth marks were clearly visible, and the child was crying. The teacher said to the child, "You're not hurt." As the child continued to cry, the teacher kept on insisting the child was not hurt.

My concern here was that the child's sense of reality was being denied. Of course the child wanted the teacher's attention, and in fact may have been more scared or angry about the bite than hurt. Instead of simply insisting, "You're not hurt," the teacher could have reflected on some of the possible feelings that were present, for example, "Maybe you're scared. Maybe you're angry. Maybe you'd like me to comfort you." Instead, the child was told *what he wasn't feeling,* which left a kind of vacuum in his sense of reality. He was being told he had no right to cry. As adults, we don't have to agree with a child's view of a situation, but we can still acknowledge the child's right to his feelings.

■ **Provide appropriate outlets for children's strong feelings.** Some children hear phrases such as, "Don't be afraid," or "Don't be sad," so often that they perceive experiencing these strong emotions, especially anger, as something akin to being bad. Others become champions of denial, not even recognizing that they are angry.

■ **Reassure frightened children with concrete facts.** When a child is very frightened about an event, your calm

**"Nothing is as**

**effective in**

**building self-**

**esteem as success.**

**It even has the**

**power to reverse**

**a child's negative**

**self-image."**

tone, informational statements about what is predictable, and any reference you can make to what he knows to be true will be reassuring. One teacher slowly brought a sobbing child close to her and quietly asked him to breathe along with her. As children learn patterns to help them calm down, they feel more in control of their lives, strong emotions don't seem so frightening, and their esteem is enhanced.

## Inviting Success

Nothing is as effective in building children's self-esteem as success. It even helps to reverse a child's negative self-image. The suggestions that follow offer ways for you to build success into children's lives by finding their existing interests and capitalizing on previous successes.

■ **Acknowledge children's accomplishments.** It's easy to forget to notice when a child does something well after the first time, for example, "Kim, you were able to put all those cans back on the shelf by yourself again today. You know, that's really great."

Giving children concrete examples of past successes is another way to build their feelings of confidence. When inviting children to learn a new skill, base your interaction on a skill that was already learned. For instance, when a child seems reluctant to use a new addition to the art table — a big container of glue — the teacher can remind the child of something he already knows about: "Do you want to try using this glue with me? Yesterday you painted at the easel, so you already know how to use a brush. The pot of glue is like a pot of paint and you can use this brush to spread it on the paper. Let's try it together."

■ **State the positive without evaluating.** Recognize what is positive and successful in a child's work or behavior, then acknowledge it by describing what you see and how you feel. Whenever possible, avoid evaluating children, their behavior, or what they do, even if your evaluation is favorable. Most typical evaluations include "right," "wrong," "good," "bad," "better," and "worse." Instead of evaluating children or their work, I have found it more success-

ful to *describe.* For instance, when children draw pictures and show them to me, instead of saying, "It's a good picture," I talk about the details of the picture. In this way the child knows that I am looking at the picture in depth. Sharing reactions to the picture encourages an interaction in the relationship, which enhances self-esteem. The same applies when children show me other things they've accomplished or made. I talk about the effort they put into the work, the choice of materials, colors, and shapes. All this is a validation and affirmation of them, not merely an evaluation of their product.

■ **Share something that belongs to you.** By allowing children to hold and touch something you have worn, you are sharing with them something you have chosen for yourself. A favored item of mine was a necklace, the pendant of which was a magnifying glass. I'd take it off and hand it to a child. He could use it to examine his skin, fingernails, clothing, or anything else that occurred to him. This magnifying glass often bridged difficult beginnings with a new child. Sometimes it even went overnight to some child's home.

## Lighting the Spark

Be aware that whatever you do, you are modeling certain behaviors. Children imitate as well as draw conclusions from what they observe. As a teacher and caregiver of young children, one of your most important privileges is to invite into the world the miracle of human growth and the unique spark that is a part of every child. Within this spark lives the hidden potential in a child, waiting to be realized over a lifetime — the abilities to relate; to love and be loved; to feel alive and powerful; to be able to trust and feel compassion; to be playful and curious; to forgive mistakes and take risks; and to live a full, emotional life.

What you do to build self-esteem in each child this year not only affects that child today, but builds a foundation to nurture a person who can one day have a positive influence in the world. You *can* make a difference in a child's world.

*Portions of this article were excerpted from* Building Self-Esteem in Children *by Patricia H. Berne and Louis M. Savary (The Continuum Publishing Co., 1981).*

# Children's Self-Esteem
# The Verbal Environment

## Marjorie J. Kostelnik, Laura C. Stein and Alice P. Whiren

*Marjorie J. Kostelnik, Laura C. Stein and Alice P. Whiren are faculty members in the Department of Family and Child Ecology, Michigan State University, East Lansing.*

Young children continually gather information about their value as persons through interactions with the significant adults in their lives (Coopersmith, 1967; Swayze, 1980). This process begins in the home but very quickly extends to the educational settings in which children participate. Thus family members, caregivers and teachers serve as the mirror through which children see themselves and then judge what they see (Maccoby, 1980). If what is reflected is good, children will make a positive evaluation of self. If the image is negative, children will deduce that they have little worth; they are sensitive to the opinions adults have of them and often adopt these as their own.

In the classroom, teachers convey either enhancing or damaging attitudes that frequently are manifested in what they say to children and how they say it. Such manifestations may or may not be the result of conscious decisions on their part. Yet teacher verbalizations are a key factor in the degree to which children perceive themselves as worthy and competent or the opposite (Kostelnik, Stein, Whiren & Soderman, 1988). Consider the following scenario:

Imagine that you are invited to visit an early childhood program in your community. You arrive early and are asked to wait in the classroom until the youngsters return from a field trip. Surveying your surroundings, you notice brightly colored furniture comfortably arranged, sunlight softly streaming through the windows, children's art work pleasingly displayed and a large, well-stocked aquarium bubbling in a corner. You think to yourself, "What a pleasant environment for children."

Just then, a child bursts into the room sobbing. She is followed by an adult who scolds, "Maria, stop that bawling." As the other youngsters file in, you hear another child exclaim, "When do we get to take our projects home?" An adult snaps, "Why can't you listen. I just said they stay here until tomorrow."

Your favorable impression is ruined. Despite the lovely physical surroundings, the way in which adults are talking to children has made the setting uninviting. You wonder whether children could ever feel good about themselves under such circumstances. What you have overheard has made you privy to an invisible but keenly felt component of every program—the verbal environment.

## THE VERBAL ENVIRONMENT

Adult participants in the early childhood setting create the verbal environment. Its components include words and silence—how much adults say, what they say, how they speak, to whom they talk and how well they listen. The manner in which these elements are enacted dictates children's estimations of self-worth. Thus verbal environments can be characterized as either positive or negative.

## 4. GUIDING BEHAVIOR

### Characteristics of the Negative Verbal Environment

Negative verbal environments are ones in which children are made to feel unworthy, incompetent, unlovable or insignificant as a result of what adults say or do not say to them. Most practitioners can readily identify the most extreme illustrations: adults screaming at children, making fun of them, swearing at them or making them the target of ethnic slurs. Yet there are less obvious, more common adult behaviors that also contribute to negative verbal environments:

1) *Adults show little or no interest in children's activities because they are in a hurry, busy, engrossed in their own thoughts and endeavors, or tired.* Whatever the reason, they walk by children without comment and fail to acknowledge their presence. When standing near children, they do not talk with them and respond only grudgingly to children's attempts to initiate an interaction. In addition, grownups misuse time designated for interaction with children by talking more with their colleagues than the youngsters. Rather than paying attention to children, most of the adult's time is spent chatting with other adults. Children interpret these behaviors as obvious signs of disinterest.

2) *Teachers pay superficial attention to what children have to say.* Instead of listening attentively, they ask irrelevant questions, respond inappropriately, fail to maintain eye contact or cut children off. Occasionally they simply ignore the communication altogether, saying nothing, thus treating the children as if they were not present.

3) *Adults speak discourteously to children.* They interrupt children who are speaking to them, as well as youngsters who are talking to one another. They expect children to respond to their own requests immediately, not allowing them to finish what they are doing or saying. Their voice tone is demanding, impatient or belligerent; they neglect such social courtesies as "Excuse me," "Please" and "Thank you." In addition, their remarks often make children the butt of a group joke. Young children attend as much to the sarcastic tone of voice as to the meaning of words and are not able to appreciate the intended humor.

4) *Teachers use judgmental vocabulary in describing children to themselves and others.* Typical demeaning labels include "hyper," "selfish," "greedy," "uncooperative," "motor mouth," "stubborn," "grabby" and "klutzy." Adults say these words directly to children or to another person within the child's hearing. In either case, youngsters are treated as though they have no feelings or are invisible or deaf.

5) *Staff members actively discourage children from talking to them.* They tell children that what they are doing or saying is uninteresting or unimportant and that they should be doing or talking about something else. Thus youngsters hear admonishments like: "All right, already! I'm sick of hearing about your troubles with Rhonda; find something else to talk about." Or, "I don't want to hear one more word about it. Not one peep!" Sometimes adults put children off by saying, "Hush," "Not now" or "Tell me about it later." The "later" seldom comes.

6) *Grownups rely on giving orders and making demands as their number-one means of relating to children.* Their verbalizations consist of directions ("Sit in your chair") and admonishments ("No fighting," "Everybody get your coats off and settle down for lunch," "Stop fooling around"). Other comments that are positive in tone or content are relatively scarce.

7) *Adults ask questions for which no real answer is expected or desired.* Typical queries might include: "What do you think you're doing?" "Didn't I tell you not to stomp in the mud?" "When will you ever learn?" Regardless of how chil-dren respond, their answers are viewed as disrespectful or unwelcome. Children soon learn that these remarks are not a real invitation to relate to the adult.

8) *Caregivers use children's names as synonyms for the words "no," "stop" or "don't."* By barking out "Tony" or "Allison" as a reprimand, adults attack the essence of the child's being, thereby causing children to associate the most personal part of themselves with disapproval and rejection. When using this tactic adults fail to describe the objectionable behavior or to clarify the reason for the negative tone of voice, thus leaving children with the notion that something is inherently wrong with them as persons.

9) *Teachers use baby talk in giving information or directions.* Instead of clearly stating, "Ruth and Toby, please put the puzzles in the puzzle rack," adults confuse and demean children by saying, "We need to put the puzzles in the puzzle rack," when they have no intention of assisting. Other kinds of baby talk involve using the diminutive form of a name (*Jackie* instead of *Jack*), even though the child and the parents prefer the other. These may be combined in particularly exaggerated ways, as when one caregiver pursed her lips and squealed in a high pitch, "How are we today, Jackie? Shall we quit crying and ride the horsie?" Such messages define children as powerless and subservient; these statements are never used between persons of equal status.

10) *Adults dominate the verbal exchanges that take place each day.* They do all the talking and allow children little time to respond either to them or their peers. Feeling compelled constantly to query, inform or instruct, they bombard children with so much talk that youngsters have few opportunities to initiate conversations on topics of their own choosing. This leaves children feeling rushed and unsatisfied.

All of the preceding verbal behaviors convey to children adult attitudes of aloofness, disrespect, lack of acceptance and insensitivity. Such encounters tend to make children feel inadequate, confused or angry (Hoffman, 1963). A different set of circumstances exists in programs characterized by a positive verbal environment.

## Characteristics of the Positive Verbal Environment

In a positive verbal environment, adult words are aimed at satisfying children's needs and making children feel valued. When speaking to children, adults focus not only on content but also on the affective impact their words will have. Adults create a positive verbal environment when their verbal exchanges with children have the following attributes:

1) *Adults use words to show affection for children and sincere interest in them.* They greet children when they arrive, take the time to become engaged in children's activities and also respond to their queries. In addition, they make remarks showing children they care about them and are aware of what they are doing: "You've been really working hard to get the dinosaur puzzle together." "You seem to be enjoying that game." They laugh with children, respond to **their humor and tell children they enjoy being with them.**

2) *Adults send congruent verbal and nonverbal messages.* When they are showing interest verbally, they position themselves near the child at a similar height from the floor, maintain eye contact and thoroughly pay attention. Other actions, such as smiling or giving a pat, reinforce praise and words of positive regard. Incongruent messages, such as following through on a limit while smiling or pinching a child's cheek hard while giving praise, are avoided.

3) *Adults extend invitations to children to interact with them.* They may say, "Here's a place for you right next to Sylvia" or "Let's take a minute to talk. I want to find out more about your day." When children seek them out, grownups accept the invitation enthusiastically: "That sounds like fun." "Oh good, now I'll have a chance to work with you."

4) *Teachers listen attentively to what children have to say.* They show their interest through eye contact, smiling and nodding. They encourage children to elaborate on what they are saying by using such statements as "Tell me more about that" or "Then what happened?" Moreover, adults pause long enough after making a comment or asking a question for children to reply, giving them time to gather their thoughts before responding. Such reactions make children feel valued and interesting.

5) *Adults speak courteously to children.* They refrain from interrupting children and allow them to finish what they are saying, either to the adult or another child. The voice tone used by adults is patient and friendly, and social amenities such as "Please," "Thank you" and "Excuse me" are part of the verbal interchange.

6) *Adults use children's interests as a basis for conversation.* They speak with them about the things youngsters want to talk about. This is manifested in two ways. First, they follow the child's lead in conversations. Second, they bring up subjects known to be of interest to a particular child based on past experience.

7) *Adults plan or take advantage of spontaneous opportunities to talk with each child informally.* In the course of a day, children have many chances to talk with adults about matters that interest or concern them. Eating, toileting, dressing, waiting for the bus, settling down for a nap and just waiting until the group is called to order are treated as occasions for adult-child conversation. Adults do not wait for special, planned time to talk with youngsters.

8) *Teachers avoid making judgmental comments about children either to them or within their hearing.* Children are treated as sensitive, aware human beings whose feelings are respected. Discussions about children's problems or family situations are held in private between the appropriate parties.

9) *Adults refrain from speaking when talk would destroy the mood of the interaction.* When they see children deeply absorbed in activity or engrossed in conversation with one another, staff members allow the natural course of the interaction to continue. In these situations they treat silence as a sign of warmth and respect and refrain from too much talk at the wrong time.

10) *Grownups focus their attention on children when they professionally engage with them.* They put off housekeeping tasks and personal socializing so that they are fully available for interaction with children. When possible, adults involve children in maintenance tasks and interact with them. In a positive environment, adults are available, alert and prepared to respond to children.

## Importance of a Positive Verbal Environment

Positive verbal environments are beneficial both to the children and the adults who participate in them. In such an atmosphere, children get the message that they are important. This enhances their self-perceptions of competence and worth (Openshaw, 1978). Additionally, children's self-awareness increases as they have opportunities to express themselves, explore ideas and interact spontaneously with other children and adults (Kostelnik et al., 1988). These conditions also increase the likelihood that youngsters will view the adults in the program as sources of comfort and support. As a result, adults find it easier to establish and maintain rapport with the children. This in turn makes youngsters more receptive to the social learnings adults wish to impart to them (Baumrind, 1977; Katz, 1977). These include rules, customs and how to get along with other people.

In sum, adult behaviors that characterize a positive verbal environment are synonymous with those commonly cited as representing warmth, acceptance, respect and empathy (Coletta, 1977; Gazda, 1977; Rogers, 1961). All four of these components contribute to the relationship-building process and provide the foundation for constructive child growth and development.

### Establishing a Positive Verbal Environment

Few helping professionals would knowingly act in ways that damage children's self-esteem. Observations of early childhood settings, however, show that frequently adults unintentionally slip into verbal patterns that produce the negative verbal environment described here (Kostelnik, 1978, 1987). Recent interviews with day care, Head Start, preprimary and elementary school teachers point to three common reasons why this occurs (Kostelnik, 1987):

• Adults fail to consciously consider the impact their words have on children.

• Adults get caught up in the hurried pace of the job and think they cannot take the time to have more positive verbal interactions with the children.

• Adults are not used to thinking before speaking and, as a result, say things they do not really mean and talk in ways they do not intend.

Over the years it has become increasingly clear that positive verbal environments do not happen by chance. Rather, their crea-

tion is the result of purposeful planning and implementation. Those who are successful in their efforts first recognize the characteristics of the positive verbal environment and then incorporate the corresponding behaviors into their interactions with children. The steps for achieving these results are listed below:

1) *Familiarize yourself with the features of both positive and negative verbal environments.* Reread the guidelines presented here. Think about situations from your experience that illustrate each one.

2) *Listen carefully to what you say and how you say it.* Consider how children may interpret your message. If you catch yourself using habits that are poor, correct them on the spot. Ask colleagues to give you feedback about how you sound, or carry a tape recorder with you for a short period of time as a means of self-observation.

3) *Make a deliberate decision to create a positive verbal environment.* Select one characteristic and think of how to integrate it into your daily routine. Practice such simple strategies as using children's names in positive situations, showing your pleasure in their company or inviting children to elaborate on what they say. Try these techniques one at a time, until they become second nature to you. As you become more proficient, gradually increase the number of techniques you use.

4) *Keep track of the positive verbal behaviors that you use.* Ask a colleague to help you identify positive verbal characteristics and determine how often you use them. As you substitute more positive approaches to verbal interaction for the negative ones, you will have a record of your success. Self-improvement is easier to recognize when short evaluations are carried out periodically.

5) *Give recognition to other staff members who are attempting to improve the verbal environment for children.* Words of approval and en-

couragement are as important to adults as they are to children. Progress toward any goal is made easier when others recognize both effort and achievement.

What adults say to children conveys to them messages of competence or inadequacy. Through their verbalizations teachers create a climate in their classroom that is called the verbal environment, a key factor in the degree to which children develop high or low self-esteem. Such environments are characterized as either positive or negative. Continual exposure to a negative verbal environment diminishes children's self-esteem, whereas exposure to a positive verbal environment enhances children's self-awareness and perceptions of self-worth. To ensure that the verbal environment is a positive one, teachers should consider carefully what they say to children and make purposeful attempts to follow the guidelines cited in this article. The outcome of these efforts is a classroom in which children feel good about themselves and see the teacher as a positive presence in their lives.

### References

Baumrind, D. (1977). Some thoughts about childrearing. In S. Cohen & T. J. Comiskey (Eds.), *Child Development: Contemporary Perspectives.* Itasca, IL: F. E. Peacock.

Coletta, A. J. (1977). *Working together: A guide to parent involvement.* Atlanta: Humanics.

Coopersmith, S. (1967). *The antecedents of self-esteem.* Princeton, NJ: Princeton University Press.

Gazda, G. M. (1977). *Human relations development: A manual for educators* (2nd ed.). Boston: Allyn & Bacon.

Hoffman, M. L. (1963). Parent discipline and the child's consideration of others. *Child Development 34,* 573-595.

Katz, L. G. (1977). What is basic for young children? *Childhood Education* 54(1), 16-19.

Kostelnik, M. J. (1978). *Evaluation of a communication and group management skills training program for child development personnel.* Unpublished doctoral dissertation, The Pennsylvania State University.

Kostelnik, M. J. (1987). *Development practices in early childhood programs.* Keynote Address, National Home Start Day, New Orleans, LA.

Kostelnik, M. J., Stein, L. C., Whiren, A. P., & Soderman, A. K. (1988). *Guiding children's social development.* Cincinnati, OH: Southwestern.

Maccoby, E. E. (1980). *Social development—Psychological growth and the parent-child relationship.* New York: Harcourt Brace Jovanovich.

Openshaw, D. K. (1978). *The development of self-esteem in the child: Model interaction.* Unpublished doctoral dissertation, Brigham Young University, Provo, UT.

Rogers, C. R. (1961). *On becoming a person.* Boston: Houghton Mifflin.

Swayze, M. C. (1980). Self-concept development in young children. In T. D. Yawkey (Ed.), *The self-concept of the young child.* Provo, UT: Brigham Young University Press.

# SOLVING PROBLEMS TOGETHER!

**ADAPTED FROM *KEEPING THE PEACE* BY SUSANNE WICHERT**

*"My tower won't stay up!" "It's my turn to use the blocks!" "I don't have anywhere to play!" Whether a child experiences frustration with a situation or with another child, resolving a dilemma nonaggressively incorporates problem-solving skills. Whether this process involves children working things out on their own or the skillful intervention of an understanding adult, the components of nonaggressive conflict resolution—cooperation, communication, and empathy—do much more than enhance children's self-esteem. They form the basis of important coping skills that encourage the participants to want to cooperate more fully and enable them to do so. These are skills on which children can build for a lifetime.*

## YOUR PHYSICAL ENVIRONMENT

The amount of unresolved conflict in any setting can be reduced by creating an environment where people feel comfortable, valued, free to express their feelings, and assured of getting what they need. Your setting can also help children engage repeatedly in the communication and problem-solving skills that foster cooperative conflict resolution. Take a look at your environment. Make sure your setting allows children to:

● **Function with the maximum degree of independence.** When children are able to do many things for themselves, alone or with the help of another child, their self-esteem is enhanced, and you can spend time observing, supporting, and guiding.

● **Function at low stress levels.** Physical factors such as noise level, visual clutter, use of color, and space/child ratio influence stress levels. (This includes stress on adults as well.)

● **Be as comfortable as possible.** Does your setting help to establish a strong link between family members and your program with places where a parent or other family member and child can be together comfortably for a while? Does your setting have "retreat" spaces for children and adults who need time to be alone during the day?

## SUPPORTIVE INTERACTION

The daily role adults play can help children develop the wide array of attitudes and skills necessary for cooperative conflict resolution, and, in turn, reinforce children's self-confidence so they can handle even more difficult situations. Here's an example:

*On a bright, sunny morning after three days of rain, the*

*preschoolers were glad to be playing outside again. Kudra was carefully scooping up a pile of wood chips and carrying them to his "mountain." Andy and Joan were so involved in their game they barely noticed when Joan ran right through Kudra's mountain, or that Kudra called angrily after them.*

*Their teacher, who had seen what happened, called Andy and Joan to her: "I think Kudra has something he needs to tell you." She walked with them over to Kudra, who was restoring his pile, and said, "Kudra, I think you had something you wanted to tell Joan."*

*"You ran right through my mountain and wrecked it!"*

*"Sorry!" Joan yelled as she hurried back to the game.*

*The teacher asked them to wait, saying, "I think we have a little problem," and gathered them into a huddle. "Kudra, can you tell Joan and Andy how you felt?"*

*"I didn't like it."*

*Then she turned to Joan and Andy. "Let's go over here and see if we can think of a way you can keep from running into Kudra again." They went a small distance away from Kudra, who continued his play, and the teacher asked, "What do you think the problem was?"*

*Andy responded, "Joan wrecked Kudra's pile and he didn't like it."*

*Joan interjected, "Well, it wasn't all my fault. Andy was chasing me!"*

*"Tell Andy that, and then maybe the two of you can figure out what you need to change about your game to keep it from happening again." The teacher waited while the two children worked through some ideas. When they turned back to her they suggested that they could run in an area where there were no other children.*

*"That's a good idea! It's great that you worked the problem out."*

The process illustrated in the scenario achieves a number of things. Kudra was given an opportunity to state the problem to Andy and Joan in a setting where his right to express his feelings was validated. Andy and Joan got a very clear message that what another child has to say is important and they have an obligation to listen. In the process of finding a solution, their teacher asked Joan and Andy to define the problem and made sure they understood that Kudra's feelings were the result of their actions. In this case, she allowed them to try out their solution. If there was still a problem, she could then go to them and say, "Your idea was a good one, but it doesn't seem to be working," and engage the children in continued discussion.

### Considering Feelings and Predicting Consequences

Like curiosity, empathy occurs naturally in children. However, it varies from child to child, often influenced by the responses of adults who are important in their lives. A child's curiosity is enlivened when we respond patiently to questions and when we ask questions intended to make that child think about why something might be. In much the same way, we can strengthen a child's ability to respond empathetically.

"Empathy training" involves enabling children to begin to make decisions about their behavior on the basis of understanding its consequences. Learning about consequences requires that we talk with children about them and

give children opportunities to predict them. Look again at the story of Kudra, Andy, and Joan and how the teacher might have handled it had she decided to intervene at an earlier point:

*Realizing that Andy and Joan were so intent on their game that they probably wouldn't notice Kudra building a mountain nearby, the teacher stopped them to explain: "Your game looks like a lot of fun, but it doesn't seem like you're looking where you're running. That might cause a problem. What do you think?"*

*The children weren't sure, so the teacher continued: "The last time you went around the climber, I noticed that you came pretty close to Kudra. How do you think he feels when you come by him fast and close?"*

*"It might be kind of scary," Andy volunteered, and Joan added, "Yeah, he might be afraid we'll bump him."*

*"Mmmm... what do you think he would tell you about how it makes him feel?" asked the teacher.*

*"Bad," came the answer from both the children.*

*"He looked kind of sad before," said Andy.*

*The teacher responded, "I think so, too. You can tell a lot about how people feel by what their faces look like, can't you? I'm glad you noticed. Now, how do you think you can change your game so that Kudra will feel comfortable, too?"*

In this case, the teacher didn't wait for the consequence but chose to give the children an opportunity to try to predict what might happen. This strategy is very useful because even though we acknowledge that people can learn from mistakes, they can also learn without having to make them. Predicting consequences gives children practice in analyzing situations before problems occur.

### Understanding Responses

It is also important to give children opportunities to understand situations from the point of view of others. Children can learn tolerance and understanding of individual responses through discussions and from the kind of behaviors adults model. Here is an example:

*Three-year-olds Jon and Lena were very close friends, often inseparable during the day. One morning Jon arrived earlier and waited eagerly for Lena. When she came in the door with her father, he ran to her, grabbed her, and hugged her with a great amount of energy. Lena clung to her father's leg, frowning. After a few days, with no sign of change in this routine, the teacher decided to approach Jon about it. Rather that tell him not to run to Lena, she decided to help him figure out the problem. The next morning, after he made his usual run, she took him aside. "You like Lena a lot, don't you?" she asked.*

*Jon nodded.*

*"It's pretty hard for you to wait for her to come to school, isn't it?"*

*Jon nodded again.*

*"When she finally comes, it seems like you want to run right over to her and give her a big hug..."*

*"Yeah, and I want her to come play with me."*

*"Have you noticed what she does when you do that?"*

*"Yeah, she holds on to her dad. Sometimes she says mean things to me."*

*"Why do you think that is?"*

*"Maybe she doesn't want me to hug her?"*

*"I think you're right. Why do you think that is? She likes to give you lots of hugs other times."*

*"I don't know."*

The teacher decided that she should help explain. *"Well, you know how when you first come in the morning, sometimes you like to be alone with your mom for a little while? You like to take your time to say goodbye, and you want time to get a hug from her?"*

*Jon nodded.*

*"I think maybe Lena wants to take some time like that with her father. When you run over to her she may feel like you aren't giving her that time. I know that you're excited to see her, but do you think you could give her that time? If you keep playing when she comes in, she'll probably come over to you when she's ready. Do you think you might like to try that tomorrow? I could help you if you want."*

In this situation, the teacher helped Jon understand what Lena's response meant and also validated his feelings in a way that related to an experience he'd had. Then she explained to Lena (when Jon was there) what Jon would be doing. The next day she helped Jon remember, and after Lena said goodbye to her father, engaged both of them in a conversation encouraging Lena to tell Jon how she felt, and asking Jon to share his feelings, too.

Applied consistently, this process of validating children's feelings and helping them understand the feelings of others ultimately enables children to work out situations by themselves. Self-esteem is enhanced as children begin to feel more in control of their lives. However, in order for the process to work, the adults involved need to help one another — if one is engaged in a discussion with children, another covers the group. This cooperation is a type of modeling; and modeling concern, honesty, respect, and thoughtfulness for one another makes it possible for these attitudes and qualities to grow.

## COMMUNICATION SKILLS

Negotiation means communication, and clear communication involves a number of skills. The common element running through all of these skills is a person's ability to focus on what's going on for the other person involved, and to respond to it. As you work with children, remember that this is a process — a developing skill.

### Focusing Attention

When you encourage children to talk to one another, help them make sure the other person is listening. Model appropriate behaviors by getting down to children's level, using their names to make sure you have their attention, and remaining focused on them while you speak.

Children may also have difficulties focusing on the person who is talking *to* them, so move everyone to a place where there will be few distractions. Let children know that you will help if they have trouble getting someone's attention. (You can simply go with the child and say, "Ellen has something she needs to tell you.") Then let the children take it from there.

### Hearing and Being Heard

You may need to help children put their problems into words — stating why they are upset *and* what they want the other person to do. Here are some familiar examples with possible clarifications. A child might say:

"I won't be your friend anymore!" which could translate into, "I don't like it when you grab things from me. Please give it back."

"I never get to go on the swing!" might be, "Can I have a turn next?"

"You're mean!" might translate to, "I don't want you to chase me."

One sentence you can use frequently is, "Tell me (him/her) what it is that you want (need)." With smaller children you might say, "Use words to tell me (him/her) what you want (need)." Once the problem is stated in these terms, the solution is usually close at hand. Your involvement helps get children into the habit of saying what they mean.

### Understanding Body Language and Facial Expressions

During the normal course of a day there are many opportunities to comment on facial expressions or body language. Observations such as, "He certainly looks angry, doesn't he?" and "Her face looks very sad. What do you think might be making her feel that way?" help children to understand some of the nonverbal ways people communicate. If a child responds with, "I don't know," encourage her to ask how the other person is feeling.

## NEGOTIATING PROBLEMS

As you guide children through negotiating problems, remember that your primary purpose is to encourage communication and keep them focused on coming to a resolution. Help the problem-solving proceed with the following steps: 1. focusing and calming; 2. giving attention to everyone involved; 3. helping children clarify and state the problem; 4. involving them in bargaining, resolving, and/or reconciling; 5. looking for a way to prevent the problem from continuing; and 6. affirming the process.

Children's abilities can be broken down into three skill levels — high adult intervention, minimal adult intervention, and letting children take charge. The following are examples to illustrate the particular kind of adult involvement required for each one.

### High Adult Intervention

At this level, the adult helps define the problem and models language:

*Maria was busy doing a puzzle when Sean came over and took a piece from the table. He had to reach over Maria's arm to try to make it fit. Their teacher was alerted when each child was trying to take the piece from the other. Sensing that they wouldn't be able to resolve the problem without help, she moved closer and knelt down, saying quietly, "Excuse me. Will you please hand me the puzzle piece?"*

*The children let go, both talking at once, upset and in loud voices. She gently touched both of them, saying, "You'll both have a turn to talk. Let's all take a deep breath and be quiet for a minute."* **(focusing and calming)**

*She turned to Sean. "I'm going to ask Maria to talk first, but you'll have a turn, too. It will help a lot if you don't interrupt her." Then she turned to Maria and asked, "Would you tell me what the problem is?"*

*Maria explained, with Sean interrupting on several occasions. The teacher assured him that he would have a turn to talk and went back to listening to Maria. Then Sean* was given an opportunity to explain the problem. *(During this kind of exchange, the child "placed on hold" inadvertently hears the other child's perspective.)* **(attention to all children concerned)**

After the teacher heard both sides, she stated the problem in clear and simple terms: *"So the problem is that Maria didn't like it when Sean took the puzzle piece from the puzzle she was working. And Sean wanted to help Maria work the puzzle. Is that right?"* **(clarification)**

Then she turned to Sean and said, *"Tell Maria what you wanted when you took the puzzle piece."* *(If a child isn't able to come up with the language, the teacher could model it. She might say, "Do you want to tell her that you want to help her with the puzzle?" or "Why don't you ask her if she would like some help with the puzzle?" If the other child doesn't want any help, making a face at the prospect and saying nothing, the teacher can model the language: "Tell him that you don't want any help right now.") In this case, Maria turned to Sean and said, "I don't want any help right now," and he responded, "Okay, I'll get my own puzzle."* **(resolution)**

If Sean didn't come to his own resolution, the teacher could still support Maria in her decision to work alone, and help Sean find an alternative choice of play. After going through a discussion like this, the most the adult usually needs to say about the initial grabbing might be a comment such as, *"It's a good idea to ask people if they want help."* **(prevention)**

The teacher closed this interaction by acknowledging the part the children played in resolving the problem. *"You did a great job talking to each other (not interrupting each other, listening to each other, etc.)."* **(affirmation)**

## Minimal Adult Role

This is the same situation but at this level the children are able to use their own language to define the problem. However, they still need an adult to help clarify and model.

*Maria is doing the puzzle when Sean comes over and takes a piece. She turns to him and says, "I'm doing this puzzle."*

*He answers, "But I know where this one goes!"*

*"No!"* she says as she pushes his hand away. *He continues to try to fit the piece in and the teacher comes over. "It looks like you have a problem. Would you like some help?"* *(Because the children are not really agitated, her statement is sufficient for **calming**.)*

*Maria looks at the teacher and says, "He won't give me back my puzzle piece."*

*"Tell him what you want."* **(attention)**

*"I want you to give me back the puzzle piece."*

*(The teacher makes sure Maria has Sean's attention and is speaking so he can hear.)* **(clarification)**

*"But I just wanted to help her do the puzzle."*

*"Then you need to tell Maria what you wanted and ask her if she would like some help."* He does, and Maria

answers, *"I don't want any help. You can do the puzzle when I'm done."* **(resolution)**

## Children Taking Charge

At this level, children are able to go off by themselves to solve the problem. Encourage the transition to this level by suggesting they go to a specific area, assuring them that their play spot will be saved, and letting them know you're available to help. Be sure to ask the children to come tell you their solution (so you can make sure it's mutually satisfying and affirm their process). Back to Maria and Sean...

As before, Sean has taken a puzzle piece, reached over Maria's arm, and tried to fit it in the puzzle. Maria tells him that she is doing the puzzle herself, and he responds that he knows where this piece goes. Maria says, *"No!"*

The teacher judges that the children will probably not take the initiative to remove themselves from the table to work out the problem, so she goes over and suggests, *"It looks like you two are having a problem. Would you like me to save your places while you go to the couch to work it out?"*

The children decide they would and proceed to the couch. They return shortly, and Maria tells the teacher, *"We've decided that I'm going to do the puzzle alone, and then we're going to do one together."*

The teacher asks Sean, *"Is that okay with you?"*

He nods and she tells them, *"I'll bet it felt good to work that out all by yourselves. Great job!"*

Obviously the process of resolving a situation will not always go as smoothly as illustrated in these examples. Sometimes children need more practice, are moving from one skill level to another, or are having a stressful day. As you assist, remember that the most difficult part of helping children negotiate can be resisting jumping in. Keep in mind that even though a solution may seem perfect to you — it is still *your* solution.

Cooperative conflict resolution is a process that reflects the intertwined relationship between self-esteem, tolerance of differences, understanding feelings, creative problem-solving skills, and the ability to interact nonaggressively. When you join in this process, you provide children with opportunities to develop positive self-concepts, encourage the development of caring behaviors, teach children to express and value their own feelings and the feelings of others, and show children how to resolve conflicts in nonviolent ways. What could be more important? . . .

We all want children to grow up with a strong sense of values that will enable them to be fair and kind. Part of this growth is learning to understand feelings—their own, and those of others—and being able to express those feelings. This ability, just like the ability to solve problems and cooperate, can be learned through practice and experience. You'll find additional activities and important information in *Keeping the Peace: Practicing Cooperation and Conflict Resolution with Preschoolers* by Susanne Wichert.

# The Tasks of Early Childhood:
# The Development of Self-Control —
# Part II

Four-year-old Tommy felt mad that Jonah was hogging the big building blocks. He stood nearby, feeling more and more disgruntled. Just a week ago, his teachers had carried out a group discussion about hitting and hurting. No one was supposed to hit, even if you were mad. The group had discussed other ways to express their feelings. They had talked about telling a child what you wanted, or getting a teacher to help you out.

Alice Sterling Honig
and Therese Lansburgh

*Alice Sterling Honig teaches at Syracuse University in the Department of Child and Family Studies, College for Human Development, in Syracuse, NY. She is an editorial board member of* Day Care & Early Education. *Therese Lansburgh is Chair of the Maryland Committee for Children and an advocate for families and children at the state and national levels.*

*But Tommy got so frustrated. Impulsively, he clenched his fist and raised his arm above his head. Ms. Ida glanced over and looked straight at him with a reminding look. "I wasn't going to hit him. I was only just raising my arm, Ms. Ida," Tommy*

*protested. She smiled encouragingly and helped Tommy find another activity to interest him.*

*Nine-month-old Natalie was restless and whimpering, feeling so hungry she was ready to start hard crying. She needed her bottle and she needed it right away. But Ms. Mollie was not quite ready. She was just finishing a diaper clean-up and was washing her hands. She called softly over to reassure Natalie. Hearing her caregiver's reassuring tones, Natalie brought her fist up to her mouth. She managed to get some fingers into her*

*mouth and suck vigorously. She was able to calm herself and keep in control for a few minutes until her caregiver came over with a bottle of milk and a lap to snuggle Natalie while feeding her.*

*Three-and-one-half-year-old Deanna was in a crowded shopping mall with her parents. They needed to buy many more items than those on their list, and the shopping trip was growing very long and tiring for their little girl. Papa said, "Deanna, we did not realize that we would need to buy so many extra things, and that our*

From *Day Care & Early Education*, Summer 1991, pp. 21-26. Published by Human Sciences Press, 72 Fifth Avenue, New York, NY 10011.

*shopping trip would take this long. We're sorry. Thank you for being so patient."* The little girl acknowledged her father's courteous explanation and apology and sighed, *"Well, I guess it was necessary."* Her father smiled with pride — at her forbearance and her big vocabulary for such a little girl.

The children described above were practicing a precious skill — the skill of *self-control*. In a time when crime levels are soaring, and many persons heedlessly hurt others horribly with assault, rape, and murder, the personal attributes of self-control are particularly important. The sophisticated conscience of an adult may take years a-building. But the building blocks begin in early childhood. Self-control is a good signpost that moral development is proceeding well for young children.

## What Is Self-Control?

Self control in the preschool years is expressed in the ability to:

Trust and cooperate with adults.
Delay the gratification of immediate needs or wants for a little while.
Find internal ways to be more patient without blaming or hurting others.
Channel angry impulses so that words instead of fists are used.
Think about and empathize with upset feelings of others.
Balance rights with responsibilities.
Find ways to cheer up even when things go wrong.
Take turns.
Recognize other's rights as well as one's own.
Find inner ways to keep from whining or falling apart into temper tantrums despite frustrations.
Modify the frequency and intensity of unacceptable actions according to situational needs, even when teachers or parents are not present.

All societies have rules regarding acceptable or unacceptable behavior for children beyond infancy. Parents and other caregivers in the culture teach children what is permitted (toileting on a potty; blowing your nose in a hanky; asking for a turn with a toy) and what is disapproved (wiping one's nose on one's hand; whacking a peer so you can grab a toy).

When children are very young, adults often maintain strong *external* controls over child behavior. Adults scoop up a toddler who may be ready to bop another baby over the head with a toy. They use scolds, or they distract and refocus the little one. They repeat simple rules over and over. Sometimes they arrange environments to *prevent* conflicts of interest or will when a toddler will get too frustrated and then burst into a temper tantrum or act out angrily. Often *proactive* discipline techniques are used to prevent loss of self-control. For example, a wise parent (knowing that sitting a child in the grocery cart while Papa shops in a crowded store may well end up in a cranky scene, with the child demanding sweets at the checkout counter) often brings along an apple or a few crackers to head off the child's loss of emotional control.

As a preschooler grows, her or his behavior seems to be more and more maintained by *internalized* standards of conduct, particularly when authority figures are not around to say, "No!" Consider the young toddler who moves with fascination toward the wall plug into which a tempting lamp cord is plugged. As she approaches and wants to reach to pull out the cord or poke a finger into the plug, she says to herself, "No, no, no plug" and toddles sadly away. She is well along in the process of developing self-control.

Such behavior begins very early with the help of skilled caregivers who understand the individual differences in children and the seesawing that a child will go through while learning more mature emotional behavior.

## Flexibility of Control: Our Goal for Children

Self-control is not easy to learn. Young children have strong needs and few cognitive skills for understanding why they have to wait for a turn or to take others' needs into account.

Sometimes caregivers are so anxious to "civilize" young children that they teach a rote technique like saying, "I'm sorry," without helping a youngster to develop more awareness of others' rights or awareness of the effects of hurtful actions.

Four-year-old Vern had hit a child just a few minutes ago. The teacher had quietly and firmly restated classroom rules about hitting. Now he again raised his fist angrily, about to hit another child. The teacher swiftly moved over and knelt in front of him, looking him directly in the eye. "Vern, what are you going to do with your hands?" she asked. He was silent. "You were about to hit someone," the teacher said. "That makes me feel angry. We just talked about what hands are for. And hands are not for hitting or hurting someone. Now, you tell me, Vern, what are hands for?" "For hugging … for playing with toys," Vern answered tentatively. "OK, then, when you feel angry, Vern, what could you do?" the teacher inquired. "I could hug somebody," Vern rejoined. The teacher looked at him. "Vern, I was feeling so angry with you when you went to hit someone that I didn't want to hug you. When you are feeling angry, do you really want to hug someone?" Vern shook his head no. The teacher continued, "When I am angry with you, do I hit you?" Vern said, "No, never." The teacher pursued, "Vern, what *am* I doing with you?" Vern replied, "Talking." "Yes," agreed the teacher, "And what could *you* do when you are feeling angry?" "I could talk," suggested Vern.

Some adults place very high demands for obedience, polite behavior, and neatness on young children, so that the children feel anxious and overcontrolled. Such children may be fearful of using finger paint or playdough because they have been taught that getting messy is something strongly disapproved of by their special adults. Some preschool children have difficulties with constipation because they have been made too fearful about a possible mess in their pants.

On the other hand, some adults bring up little children without the firm guidance, clear rules, and social expectations necessary to assist young children into more socially acceptable interactions. Such children may act rudely, gallop wildly, kick or hit others, and be heedless of other children's or the teacher's needs and rules in the preschool classroom. Neither *overcontrol* nor *undercontrol* is a desirable outcome. Overcontrolled children often act rigid and joyless, not spontaneous. They may be highly anxious, or critical of other children's misbehavior. Undercontrolled children may lash out aggressively or crumple into temper tantrums and whining at the slightest frustration, or they may be easily led into mischief by more dominant peers. *Ego resiliency* refers to flexibility of controls (Honig, 1985), a highly desirable goal for children.

## Factors That Influence Self-Control

What factors influence the development of *knowledge* of what is permissible and what is prohibited, of what situations require patience and a willingness to wait? What factors influence children's *ability* to wait, to use words instead of fists, to take others' feelings into consideration, to cooperate instead of defy or cry? Parental child-rearing techniques and the child's cognitive level are probably the most important influences, but other factors come into play, too. Inherited capacities, cultural and religious norms and practices, child-care-setting characteristics, peer interactions (such as bullying or friendliness), and teacher support for prosocial learnings in the classroom are also important influences in shaping children's development of self-control (Honig, 1982).

Babies learn only gradually *what* they must control about their strong emotional responses and *when* and *how* they are expected to control them. Learning self-control begins early. By four months, a baby picked up for nursing may strain and fuss a bit, but she can wait for a few minutes until her caregiver is ready to begin the feeding. She no longer yowls immediately or loudly in response to pangs of hunger when her caregiver has picked her up. She has begun already to learn self-control.

### Differences in Temperament

Some children are born more easygoing. Some have a more cheerful mood, and some are more cautious (Thomas and Chess, 1981). Helping easygoing children develop self-control can be easier than working with children whose temperaments are more triggery or impulsive, or who have a low tolerance of any sort of frustration.

Some toddlers have a predisposition to shyness. They stay close to an adult when taking a walk in the neighborhood around the child care center. Others may try to dash madly off down the street. Some are frightened by new experiences, tend to comply with adults, and seem more obedient. Thus, some children may appear self-controlled, but their temperamental fearfulness is what impels their "good" behavior.

### Age and Maturity

Just as they differ in the timing and skill with which they develop motoric competence in walking, running, and climbing, children differ in their ability to learn the task of self-control. Some adults have inappropriate expectations about when a child will be able to handle disappointment, anger, frustration, or jealousy more maturely. Children who are expected to develop adult-desired self-control in too many areas too soon, before they are ready, may become overly solemn, sullen, and sneaky, or defiant and noncooperative.

### Mastery of Other Emotional Tasks

Children who have developed a basically trusting and secure relationship with their caregivers, who feel that their actions bring results and that they are *willing to try* (Honig and Lansburgh, 1990) are more likely also to develop a sense of personal responsibility for their own actions. Such children learn to influence others in positive ways as friends. They also feel confident enough so that they can have influence over their own internal impulses. Those with little basic trust in the positive regard of their caregivers or those in whom severe threats and punishments have damaged the will to try may be too discouraged to tackle the work of controlling their impulsive, disapproved behaviors toward others. Grown-ups have dominated them, and they do not see that their own internal efforts at control can be successful.

## Parental Methods of Teaching Self-Discipline and Control

Parents and caregivers differ in their ways of socializing and disciplining children. They vary in their ability to "read" a baby's signals. Caregiver beliefs and skills in socializing children are crucial determinants of how successful a young child will be in developing self-control. *Socialization* means learning how to behave in ways approved by your family and culture. For example, during the first year of life, infants gradually learn to obey an adult's firm "no-no" for touching dangerous objects, such as a sharp pair of scissors or an unprotected electrical plug.

Some adults have unrealistic expectations too early that a baby can understand the meaning of "No" or "Quit that!" Often, a baby is bewildered and frightened by the sharp tone and the anger and threat in the adult's voice. Suppose a baby in a high chair is curious about what has happened to the toy he just pushed off the edge of the table top. Where could it be? Curiously the ten-month-old lifts his body to peer over the edge. "Cut that out!" says the caregiver sharply. Startled, the baby bursts into tears. His behavior was interpreted by the adult (unaware of how the baby is figuring this situation out) as deliberate and willful disobedience of the rules for staying in one's seat.

When teachers and parents understand developmentally what task a very young child is trying to accomplish, they may not be so overcontrolling. Finding a positive way to say, "Sit down, honey. Your toy fell down on the floor and I will get it for you. Sit down nice and safe, please!" will be more helpful than undecipherable warnings and prohibitions that cause a baby to freeze but do not lead to either understanding or inner controls.

Some discipline techniques work better than others at helping children develop self-control. Researches have shown that *power-assertive* discipline that involves physical punishment or threats of physical punishment, in particular, leads to defiance and lack of mastery of aggressive actions. Even though they may temporarily stop "misbehaving," these children have been given a strong example of how to lose self-control and to use external power to get others to do what they want!

Some types of discipline have been found far more likely to lead to compliance and self-control. Where *inductive discipline* is used by parents, toddlers begin early to self-monitor and to avoid actions for which they have internalized the rules (Hoffman, 1977). What are inductive methods? They include *reasoning with children* and *explaining the reasons for rules*, rather than using forceful commands, punishments, or threats. Children who have been brought up with parents who use firm rules, give explanations, have high expectations of approved behavior, and are positively and genuinely committed to their child's welfare are more likely to internalize controls. Baumrind (1977) has called this kind of parenting "authoritative" in contrast to either "permissive" or "authoritarian" (dictatorial) disciplining.

Authoritative caregivers are *for* their children. They are warm and nurturant, yet they have high expectations of their children. They are firm in not accepting unacceptable behavior, are effective in disciplining, and explain clearly the reasons why they discipline as they do. Permissive caregivers act in a nonpunitive way, but they let unacceptable behavior go on without dealing with it, and they do not require the child to learn to behave more responsibly and maturely.

Lara came home from the day care and told her mother, "It's OK to hit. You just don't know. It's OK to hit, 'cause when we hit in the day care, Miss Kathy doesn't do anything to anybody."

When adults do not firmly stop bullying or do not notice scapegoating, then they are supporting the continuation of social patterns that do not promote self-control, positive socialization, or optimal peer interactions. Authoritarian patterns are also nonproductive. If a child is required to accept forceful discipline and an adult's authority as absolute, that child can become more nervous, more stressed, and more likely to act out insecurity and resentment by aggressive or aggrieved actions toward others.

## Research on Self-Control

Toddlers who have had secure attachments to a nurturant, responsive parent do not fall apart or give up when faced with a difficult tool-using task. Sroufe (1979) found that such toddlers, when faced with challenging tasks, were more able to maintain self-control; they persisted longer without temper tantrums and were more likely to enlist their parents' support in struggling to solve the tool-using tasks which were too hard for them to solve on their own. In contrast, other mothers gave orders but not helpful assistance to their toddlers. They had been insensitive to their children in infancy. These children gave up easily, were unable to maintain self-control, became oppositional, and had more temper tantrums.

The securely attached infants who had exhibited more self-control in the tool-using tasks as toddlers were rated at five years of age, by their preschool teachers as highly ego-resilient, self-reliant, and moderate in self-control. The children who had been insecurely attached in early infancy, and who had been poor at self-control as toddlers under the stressful task conditions in the laboratory, were rated either as much more undercontrolled or overcontrolled. Thus, research has significantly linked self-control to early patterns of infant-parent attachment.

Longitudinal studies follow chil-

dren over several years. In one such study at the University of Minnesota, 120 children aged three to seven years were given an attractive toy for a short period of time and were then told to stop playing with it (Masters and Binger, 1976). Almost half of the two-year-olds were able to inhibit their impulses when their parents asked them to stop playing with the attractive toy. The percentages of self-control rose dramatically with age, most sharply between two and three years of age. When the children were followed over time, self-control proved to be quite a stable individual characteristic. That is, the children who had good control at age two made greater progress later in self-control.

A talking-clown box was used with 70 four-year-old boys and girls by Patterson and Mischel (1976) to tempt children off-task. The preschoolers were warned that the clown box might tempt them to stop working at their pegboard task, and in that case they would lose an opportunity to play with attractive toys after the pegboard work and would be allowed to play only with broken toys.

Groups of children were taught verbalizations that they could repeat to the clown box in order to help them control the temptation to give up working and thus forfeit the reward they desired. The first group were helped to resist temptation by concentrating on the promised reward. The researcher suggested that they say to themselves, "I want to play with the fun toys and Mr. Clown Box *later*." In the second group the children were to say to themselves, "I'm going to look at my work." Children in a third group were told they could say anything they wanted to themselves to help them avoid looking at the clown box. A nursery rhyme or something else irrelevant was suggested to the fourth group, and the fifth group received no instructions. Children in the first and second groups — those for whom the later reward was emphasized and those who were helped to plan in detail how to ignore Mr. Clown — worked longer at the pegboard task than those children who has less specific plans or no plan. Thus, some self-instructional plans of what to say to yourself are more helpful than others in boosting children's ability to resist temptations that can distract them from their tasks.

At what point, while a child is misbehaving, does a caregiver need to intervene? Some boys in one research study were stopped just before they reached for a forbidden toy. Others were not stopped until after they had touched the toy (Walters, Parke, and Cane, 1965). Adult prevention *prior* to the unacceptable behavior was more effective: The boys in that group demonstrated greater self-control in resisting temptation later when they were left alone with the forbidden toy.

In stress research, self-control has proved to be a factor, along with high self-esteem, problem-solving skills, and higher empathy, that allows children to cope when they live highly stressed lives. Fourth- to sixth-grade urban children who proved resilient despite many stresses were found to have more internalized controls and more realistic expectations for self-control in mastering stressful life conditions (Parker et al., 1990).

## Teacher Techniques for Promoting Self-Control

What can caregivers do to promote self-control in early-childhood educational settings? Researches suggest first that a warm, personally attentive, genuinely focused relationship with a child will increase that child's self-esteem and chances of trying harder to control impulses toward disorganization or hurtfulness toward others.

The *teacher is a powerful role model.* If a caregiver shouts, acts very irritated, or blows up at naughtiness, then children are being given a message that it is OK to have a short fuse and lose control.

Teachers can stay near a child who has difficulty in mastering forbidden actions. If an adult is nearby and caring and supportive, the child who may have a strong urge to act out aggressively by sweeping the frustrating puzzle pieces off the table or hitting a

peer will get prompt signals from the teacher. The teacher will keep the classroom and the children safe and secure. The child does not have to explode or act out in anger and fright. A calm, supportive, and alert teacher nearby serves as a beacon of security (Wolfgang, 1977).

**Prevention Helps**

When children are overtired or teased or feel that others have unfairly received more than their share, they may more easily act out. Teachers need to make sure that fair access to toys and materials is provided. Overcrowding, as when too many children are in a small block corner, can trigger out-of-control use of blocks as pretend guns or throwing toys, which results in hurt children and hurt feelings. Thoughtful planning and judicious use of space as well as resources both help children maintain good self-control in play.

*Reasoning with children,* as well as providing understandable explanations of regulations, promotes children's development of notions of what is acceptable and what is expected. Such *inductive techniques* promote self-control far more than overcontrolling, critical, or overly permissive methods.

*Bibliotherapy* is a helpful aid. Teachers need to choose books that tell stories about animals or children who are in difficult, stressful, scary, or frustrating situations where the characters try hard not to use mad feelings or angry outbursts and do try to use more reasonable ways to solve their problems. Children identify with such story characters.

*Good plans to remember rules and reasons* boost self-control. Teachers can help children think of good plans to help themselves remember rules against hitting. Caregivers can give children words to say that will aid them in controlling impulsivity. One preschooler ran and ran in the long hallways of his center located in a church basement. He would yell out, "Yo-yo, come and play with me," to a four-year-old girl he liked very much. The teacher explained to Yolanda that

she could keep working on her puzzle, and tell her friend, "I'm busy working on my puzzle. You come here and do puzzles with me." This verbal scaffolding helped Yolanda not to dash off and run aimlessly as well as helped lure her playmate into a more constructive activity.

*Refocus children on appropriate interactions* and activities. If children's play seems to be veering toward a loss of self-control, the caregivers need to step in judiciously and redirect the children. Adults can use firm suggestions. With toddlers, distraction and luring the toddler into more appropriate activities help support positive play while preventing inappropriate behaviors.

If a child has totally lost self-control and is kicking and yelling, a caregiver may need to hold that child firmly so that the child cannot pose a danger to others. The teacher can reassure the child, "I will not let you hurt others or yourself. You can get back into control. I will help you. You are feeling very upset. I will hold you so you feel safe until you can get calm again and get back into control."

*Use encouragement and admiration* when children are showing good self-control. Specific praise helps. Admire a child who has struggled to use words instead of fists. In the child care setting, express appreciation when children have been patient even though the lunch delivery was delayed. Children need to know that their special persons, their teachers, value their struggles to work toward self-control, an important foundation for classroom cooperation and compliance.

### References

Baumrind, D. (1977). Some thoughts about childrearing. In S. Cohen and T. J. Comiskey (eds.), *Child Development: Contemporary perspectives.* Itasca, IL: Peacock.

Hoffman, M. L. (1977). Moral internalization: Current theory and research. In L. Berkowitz (ed.), *Advances in experimental social psychology,* Vol, 10. New York: Academic Press.

Honig, A. S. (1982). Prosocial development in children. *Young Children, 37*(5), 51-62.

Honig, A. S. (1985). Research in review: Compliance, control, and discipline. *Young Children,* Part 1, *40*(2), 50-58; Part 2, *40*(3), 47-52.

Honig, A. S., and Lansburgh, T. (1990). The tasks of early childhood: Part I. The will to try. *Day Care and Early Education, 18*(2), 4-10.

Masters, J.C., and Binger, C.C. (1976, Sept.). *Inhibitive capacity in young children: stability and development.* Paper presented at the annual meeting of the American Psychological Association, New York.

Parker, G. R., Cowen, E. L., Work, W. C., and Wyman, P. A. (1990). Test correlates of

stress affected and stress resilient outcomes among urban children. *Journal of Primary Prevention, 11,* 19-35.

Patterson, C. J., and Mischel, W. (1976). *Self-instructional plans and children's resistance to temptation.* (ERIC Document Reproduction Service No ED 141-679).

Spaner, S. D., and Jordon, T. E. (1973). *Analysis of maternal antecedents to locus of control at age 60 months.* (ERIC Document Reproduction Service No. 087 555).

Sroufe, L. A. (1979). The coherence of individual development. *American Psychologist, 34* 834-841.

Thomas, A., and Chess, S. (1981). The role of temperament in the contribution of children to their own development. In R. M. Lerner and N. A. Busch-Rossnagel (eds.). *Individuals as producers of their own development.* New York: Academic Press.

Walters, R. H., Parke, R. D., and Cane, V. A. (1965). Timing of punishment and the observation of consequences to others as determinants of response inhibition. *Journal of Experimental Child Psychology, 2,* 10-30.

Wolfgang, C. H. (1977). *Helping aggressive and passive preschoolers through play.* Columbus, OH: Merrill.

# A is for Apple, P is for Pressure—
## Preschool Stress Management

**JANAI LOWENSTEIN**

*Janai Lowenstein is codirector of the Conscious Living Foundation in Drain, OR 97435.*

*"Why, preschoolers don't need stress management. They don't have stress! All they have to do is play and grow up." The person responsible for this statement had no daily contact with or knowledge of the dynamics involved in a child's reality. While the sources of stress may differ—for example, a child may be stressed from learning how to share toys while mom and dad are plagued with financial concerns—all individuals, whether adults or children, experience stress. We develop our patterns of stress response when we being life and interact with the environment around us.*

Although children learn about stress in much the same way that adults do, the physical aspects are more important to them. From the onset, their learning has to be tactile; they need to see, touch, hear, and feel their way through stress signs in order to fully understand the concepts of stress management. They are accustomed to learning about themselves in relationship to their environment outside their bodies: tie shoes to prevent tripping; wear a raincoat when it is raining, and so on. Therefore, a structure must be built to bridge a child's internal experience with the external environment for greater understanding of self.

By teaching preschoolers how to make healthy choices for themselves regarding their own behavior, teachers and parents give children a foundation for building self-care and self-confidence. Helping children develop an internal frame of reference will increase their self-control in dealing with life's ongoing stressors rather than allow them to feel victimized by blaming those stressors for how they think, feel, and act. Children can polish their skills by practicing during stressful events and as a result, gain self-esteem. Without skills for handling stress, they are more apt to wallow in confusion, self-doubt, and self-pity, and depend on external stimuli for temporary gratification.

Two basic concepts must be established through teaching modalities to firmly set the groundwork for teaching stress management skills:
1. Understanding how the mind, body, and emotions work together; and
2. Realizing that there are appropriate and inappropriate levels of relaxation and tension.

Since learning, adaptability, curiosity, and implementing new skills with self and the environment are at a premium for readiness in the preschool years, children in this age range can easily be taught stress management skills. However, applying and reinforcing these skills in daily occurrences creates the real potential for practical use over the life span. To teach stress management skills and to apply stress management techniques, teachers must recognize stress signs. As children become aware of their own stress signs, they can prevent unnecessary tension and assume more responsibility for their own psychophysiological health.

### Recognizing Stress

In most instances, stress signs are easily monitored in children. By knowing a child's normal state of being (body language, ways of expression, eye sheen, eating and sleeping habits, ways of interacting with others, and playing behaviors) it is easier to notice changes. For example, withdrawal or frequent acting out, restlessness during the day or night, destruction of objects, nightmares, biting nails, jiggling hands and feet, abrupt body movements, changes in vocal tones and energy levels, cold hands/feet, irritability, lack of concentration, extra body tension (e.g., twitching, stiff shoulders) can all be signals that something is not right. However, deviations in a child's normal range

This article is reprinted with permission from the *JOPERD* (Journal of Physical Education, Recreation & Dance), February 1991, pp. 55-58. *JOPERD* is a publication of the American Alliance for Health, Physical Education, Recreation and Dance, 1900 Association Drive, Reston, VA 22091-1599.

of behaviors can also mean there is a new stage of growth or an illness setting in. Such deviations also could be indicative of nutritional deficiency, allergy or physical ailment, all of which are stressors themselves. One of the benefits gained in the analysis of this unknown sea of stressors and signals is the fact that as children learn to recognize their own stress signs, they learn more about themselves.

Another point to remember is that if there is stress in the lives of

> ## If there is stress in the lives of the adults who care for the child, there will undoubtedly be stress signs in the child.

the adults who care for the child, there will undoubtedly be stress signs in the child because he or she is an integral part of the system, whether at home, school, or elsewhere.

Beyond normal stress, "superstress" is sweeping the land and children are not forgotten in its wake. Our culture is filled with cancer producing food additives, water-air-land-sun polluting toxins, disintegration of the family system, soaring economic pressures upon the working classes, lack of reality in television programming, and rampant drug use. Consequently, what were once considered stress-related illnesses for adults are now infiltrating very young bodies. Professionals in the medical field agree that an increasing number of young children are suffering from tension migraine headaches, ulcers, eating and sleeping disorders, hyperactivity, nervous disorders, blood sugar imbalances,

violence and suicides, and depression and apathy.

### What Teachers Can Do
Teachers at all levels must teach and use basic stress management skills in the classroom. Demonstrate the difference between appropriate and inappropriate levels of tension and relaxation. For example, show children which groups of muscles it is necessary to tighten while carrying a chair or heavy object across the room. Let them do it, then discuss the experience. Next, demonstrate how you would look if you tensed those same muscles while talking with a friend. Again, let the children experience it to feel and know for themselves. Assign partners and let the children role-play with each other.

Between activities requiring focused attention, choose one emotion at a time to explore. For example, suggest everyone (including you) make an angry, tense face and body; make angry sounds, stomp around with angry movements, even dance an angry dance. Point out that the mind, body, and emotional feelings always work together. To do a thorough job, the children should notice how their angry thoughts and emotions create body tension. Next, have children do the same for a totally different emotion such as happiness, noticing again how the mind, body, and emotions work together. Let the children understand that it is impossible to have angry thoughts and a happy body or feelings. They should also pay attention to the fact that they are in control of changing everything inside them! By playing with the spectrum of emotions in this way, children can become aware of their internal body signals, telling them which emotion is in place at any given time. It is much harder to lose control when an internal reference point is in place.

### Exploring Stress through Role-Playing
Nonverbal role-plays can be used to help children exaggerate a situation

with their bodies. This type of activity facilitates an increased awareness internally for personal stress signs. Begin by first role-playing an emotion. Show facial tension, body tension and movement. Let the children guess what emotion you are depicting and which of your body parts are tense. Ask them what kinds of thoughts you were having, too. It is important to reinforce the mind/body/emotional connection frequently.

An energizing way to reinforce the concepts of tension/relaxation, emotional awareness and mind/body coordination is to explore a jungle with the children right in your own living room, backyard, or school gymnasium. Simply ask children to join you in becoming an angry ape, sad snake, tense tiger, happy hyena, cowardly kitten who can turn into a courageous cat, or any combination of tense and relaxed animals. Act out each animal, making appropriate noises and body motions. Children are enthusiastically creative when they can learn through their own fun experiences.

Find other modes of reinforcement that can meld into the stream of activities already established. If children already stretch occasionally, vary the stretching pace through emotional awareness (e.g., excited stretch, slow and sad stretch, etc. ). If it is rainy outside and there's a need for stress-relief from lack of exercise, children can do some jealous jumping in place, some happy arm swinging, and nervous body jitters.

When eyes are dazed, attention span is scattered, and yawns dot the classroom, allow the children to drift into right brain activity with a relaxation exercise emphasizing health, history, or science fiction exploration. The quickest way for children to enter a deep state of relaxation and simultaneously release some tension, is to tell them to put lots of hard, tight, tense spots all over their bodies. Tell them to hold tension everywhere while you count to five. Look for scrunched up faces, contorted torsos, tightened toes, and shallow breathing movement. Demonstrate how to do it first. While they are all tense, have them pay attention to the fact that they are holding their breath. Then instruct them to release all the tension at once, letting out deep sighs of relief. If time allows, use imagery by having the children close their eyes while you guide them on a fun, relaxing journey to a rainbow planet, another time in history, or to magical woods where you can encourage them to feel good about themselves. When children are relaxed, with eyes closed, it is easy to reinforce the lessons of the day by reviewing them briefly.

In everyday interaction with children, it is important to integrate stress management concepts into normal activities. First, develop a language system to fit your needs and the activities you are already engaged in with the children. Speak more about emotions, where you feel tense inside, what your thoughts are like, and the fact that you need to take a deep breath when you are upset.

Help children become more aware of stressful situations and make healthier choices by saying, "Gee, Bobby, your shoulders look pretty tight and tense. And your forehead looks wrinkled like something is bothering you. What are you feeling and thinking right now?" As the role model, you may need to share how you feel when you tense similar areas. Provide a body outline for the child to use, coloring body parts that feel hard and tense or simply marking them with an "X." This provides a tactile mode of expression and reinforcement in the child's internal awareness as well as improved ability to communicate clearly about his or her internal world.

In addition, create space on the agenda for children to personally share what causes stress or tension in their lives. Lists (words or pictures) can be made and group discussions can be facilitated. Role-

plays can be generated for awareness, expression, and creative problem-solving once children understand the basic concepts of stress management.

When a few minutes are available, children can close their eyes and slowly, deeply, breathe rainbow colors into their bodies. (They can color this later to show you what they look like when they help themselves feel good by filling themselves with different colors or rainbows.) Also, if difficulties arise helping a child discover which emotion he or she feels, choosing a color that rep-

> *Create space on the agenda for children to personally share what causes stress or tension in their lives.*

resents the feeling inside his or her body can help. Follow through with artwork if appropriate. Help children to breathe fun colors into the body parts that were tense after processing uncomfortable situations.

### What Parents Can Do
Parents can teach and role-model basic stress management skills easily in the home. They can also reinforce skills being taught in preschool or day-care, or suggest to their child-care administrators that these concepts be taught if they are not presently utilized.

All the aforementioned techniques can be introduced in the home setting with one or more children. If only one child is present, puppets can be used to enhance group discussions. Puppets are also handy in any young children's group to prompt discussions and

understanding as well as to reinforce concepts. A fun, tactile exercise for teaching the difference between tension and relaxation is easily facilitated if a rock and sock are available. Place a rock in one of the child's hands, a soft sock in the other. Model the exercise yourself as you explain how to tighten body parts to make them hard like the rock, then take a deep breath and relax individual body parts to make them soft like the sock. Start with the face, tensing and then relaxing, and progress all the way down to the feet, one body part at a time. Be sure to use the words "tight, hard and tense," referring to the rock and "soft, calm and relaxed," referring to the sock.

Children frequently are so subjectively caught in their emotional turmoil that they have little or no understanding of what they are projecting into the world around them, let alone what their appearance is to others. A portable mirror is an unpopular tool (from the child's point of view) to use during outbursts of emotion caused by anger, jealousy, frustration or the like. Have this self-reflector easy to reach, but out of the child's sight, then raise it up to meet the child's eyes right in the middle of the tantrum or experience you want the child to see. This reflection can teach children more about themselves than any number of words. However, it will be important to explain why this is being done and ask children at the appropriate moment what they have seen and learned about themselves. Another dynamic tool is to role-play a child's emotional outburst. After this, ask the child to display the way he or she sees you expressing yourself when upset. Stress management reinforcement is a two-way street!

### The Breath of Life
Whether working with children at home, school, the playground, in the grocery store or in a car, there is one central key that can provide magic in this process for all parties concerned…the breath of life! All

relaxation skills have one true core: deep, even, slow breathing. Just as tension can create more tension in any situation, deep breathing can render speedy healing to an ailing body, mind, or emotions, as well as provide self-control in the midst of anxiety and chaos. Make a game of checking heart rates by placing hands on chests to feel fast or slow heartbeats.

Take deep breaths every time the cuckoo clock strikes or a telephone rings. Make it fun and easy to integrate! Have hand-check games: touch each others' hands to see if they are warm, which generally indicates relaxation, or cool, indicative of internal arousal.

Educating children about life has always been a major responsibility of a society in any given time. If we want our most precious resource, children, to survive whatever is ahead in our super-stressed world, they must have the tools made available to them to cope with daily stressors. Their own internal resources are waiting to be tapped, the resources they will have with them through every step in life's journey. Without these basic life skills, they will have difficulty making healthy choices for their own well-being. By knowing themselves, they can choose right actions over wrong actions, feel good enough about themselves to be content without substance abuse, and know how to prevent stress-related illnesses. They will also be able to communicate clearly, to respect others because they respect themselves, and be able to nurture healthy relationships. Most of all, they will care. It is easy to incorporate stress management skills into children's lives, as easy as remembering that A is for Apple, P is for Pressure.

---

## The Role of Art in Stress Management

In both home and school settings, artwork can prove to be an invaluable tool for awareness, expression, and reinforcement. Preschoolers who can understand the spoken word and hold a crayon can use colors on paper to express their feelings if given instructions and opportunities to do so. The artwork of an angry child will present quite a contrast to that of a child who is feeling content. Use the artwork as a media to help young children learn to label, understand, and talk about their emotions. Place a variety of colored sheets done by children on the refrigerator or a wall and ask them what feeling each sheet has.

Once again, create every opportunity that can possibly be woven into life's scheme. Have body outlines available for children to color regarding their internal experiences, thus providing a steady stream of tactile bridging between their inner and external worlds. The body outlines become a self-made mirror for the children, and provide adults with a means of helping the children to help themselves.

A note of caution regarding use of the body outlines: When children first begin learning about what is going on inside their bodies, a common response to the question "Where do you feel tight or tense inside?" is "Everywhere." Unfamiliar with their own internal geography, it will be important for you to either ask questions about body parts, one at a time, and/or be firm in telling the child to choose one or two body parts that feel tighter or harder than any other parts.

# Curricular Applications

- **Creating and Inventing (Articles 37–40)**
- **Content and Process (Articles 41–44)**

Unlike the job of a secondary teacher who concentrates on one academic area, the job of an early childhood teacher is to meet the needs of a young child in many different areas. Hendrick (1990) looks at the child as five different selves that combine to form the whole child. It is the job of the teacher of young children to plan developmentally appropriate activities to meet the physical, emotional, social, creative, and cognitive selves of the young child. Only then can the curriculum truly be centered on the children and appropriate for their growth and development.

Contrary to popular opinion, greater professional expertise and effort are required to plan, monitor, and evaluate a play-based cooperative learning program for young children (which provides activities that encourage healthy development of the five selves of the child) than a program that is teacher-directed and contains many sit-and-

listen activities. There are many commercial kits and packaged curriculum guides that can be purchased that suggest everything from activities for group time on a particular day to dittoed sheets for the children to color for "creative art." The problem with these teaching aids is they are generic and do not meet the developmental needs of children of varying levels or in one specific program, but are intended for all children in general. Teachers who plan localized curricula and have an understanding of the life-styles of the children in their class are better able to develop a true working relationship with the young children in their care and their families.

With more and more subjects being required in the elementary school the integration of subjects allows for more flexibility in planning and for more unity in the total curriculum. Lynda C. Greene's article, "Science-Centered Curriculum in Elementary School," provides a look at how school districts in California are capitalizing on localized curricula to integrate science along with many other subjects required. Curriculum webbing, which uses the concept of broad themes, enables children to see the relationships between topics and to bring cohesiveness to the activities and materials available in the classroom.

The time children spend in appropriate large muscle development is time well spent when one reads the numerous research studies detailing the inferior physical condition of children in America today. As noted above, teachers often are so focused on planning for the brief choice time each morning, which often centers on creative and cognitive activities, that gross motor development is left to the 30 minutes of free time spent running around on a poorly equipped and unsafe playground. The National Survey of Playground Equipment in Preschools concludes that preschool playgrounds are dangerous and require much-needed attention to improve the quality of experiences children gain while outside.

Playing with materials and language is the way the young child conquers the world of objects and symbols and constructs knowledge about their properties. Part of the teacher's role is to provide information to parents on the benefits of play in the young child's development. Thus, developing a philosophy for and implementing an early childhood program that focuses on the developmental needs of young children requires, in addition to time and money, a thorough knowledge of how to select play materials and media for children of differing ages, abilities, and backgrounds. It also means teachers are responsible for sharing with parents the ways in which their children spend their day and the activities in which they participate. If the only concrete evidence parents receive of their child's day are pictures done at the easel or collages made from stickers, chalk, and feathers, they will continue to see art as the only creative endeavor in which their child can participate and not see the value in blocks, puppets, movement, or music. Teachers must show they appreciate and value creative endeavors made with nonexpendable as well as expendable materials.

Section B, *Content and Process*, contains four new articles. The section starts with "The Many Faces of Child Planning" that details ways in which children indicate their plans for the day, and to what degree they outline how they will spend their time. Teachers often devote a great deal of thought and attention to planning activities, arranging the environment, and selecting materials in which the children can participate and use during free choice, discovery, or work time; but they never give thought as to how to present the choices or how to assist the children in planning for and beginning their day.

When children begin to communicate through print, they are embarking upon one of the most challenging yet rewarding skills one can develop. The five-year-old child who makes a sign for his bedroom door that states, "Ples Do Nit Lat Clay in My Ram. Love, Clark," should be encouraged to continue to put words on paper, not discouraged from creative writing by being told to only use words he knows how to spell correctly. Teachers who are aware of steps children take in emergent literacy recognize the unique skills children bring to the reading process and capitalize upon their eagerness for learning and their insatiable appetite for encouragement while they are learning. The article "Writing in Kindergarten: Helping Parents Understand the Process" provides answers to commonly asked questions along with charts that show examples of children's writing at various stages of development.

**Looking Ahead: Challenge Questions**

What do young children actually learn by playing? How can play materials be evaluated for their contribution to children's development? What are the developmental characteristics of play?

How can teachers demonstrate to parents and children that all types of creative endeavors are valued?

What are the benefits of invented or temporary spelling in assisting the child to become literate?

What needs to be done to make many of the playgrounds in America today safe for all children to use?

What are the different types of planning one would be most likely to observe in preschool children?

How has the switch to a science-centered curriculum benefited elementary school children?

How is the process of learning to read and write connected? What can facilitate this process in the classroom?

# Learning to Play: Playing to Learn

Pauline Davey Zeece and Susan K. Graul

Have you ever heard comments such as "In this program we focus on learning — *not* playing" or "Is this a day care program where children learn or play?" At a time when the importance of early life experiences has gained public attention, there is the temptation to overlook or at least misunderstand the value and importance of play.

*Pauline Davey Zeece and Susan Graul are at the Department of Human Development and the Family, University of Nebraska - Lincoln, Lincoln, NE.*

For many decades, play has been considered an integral part of childhood (Rubin, Fein, & Vanderberg, 1983; Smilansky, 1968). As such, it serves vital functions by integrating and balancing all aspects of human functioning (Rogers & Sawyer, 1988). Through play, young children gain mastery over their bodies, discover the world and themselves, acquire new skills, and cope with complex and conflicting emotions (Bruner, 1972; Papalia & Olds, 1986; Rubin et al., 1983; Vygotsky, 1976). This makes play an important part of early childhood programming. Play is one of the most effective ways children learn about their ever-changing world.

In a historical overview, Christie (1985) concluded that caregivers' and teachers' attitudes toward their role in children's play have changed since the 1960s. Before 1960, adults assumed not only that play was trivial, but that interference in children's play

was not beneficial (Sutton-Smith, 1986). However, Smilansky's 1968 study provided evidence that play training impacted on the quality of children's play and enhanced various areas of their cognitive development. It was gradually accepted that intervening in children's play could be beneficial to children in many ways.

## Importance of Play

### Defining Play

Exact definition of *what* constitutes children's play appears to be more difficult to determine than recognition of *when* children are actually playing. Although a universal agreement on the definition of play has not yet been established, Rubin and colleagues (1983) identified six criteria from the research literature that characterize children's play behavior:

1. *Play is intrinsically motivat-motivated.* Children play because they want to and not because they are required by adults to act in certain ways. Thus, the motivation for engaging in

play behavior comes from the child, rather than the adult (Gottfried, 1985; Rogers & Sawyer, 1988).

2. *Play involves attention to the means rather than the end.* Because behavior during play is most often spontaneous, children's play may begin as a make-believe trip to the moon, change to racing cars, and end in making spaghetti. The focus of play is on the activity rather than the end product.

3. *Play is dominated by the child.* Children gain a sense of mastery and self-worth in play because they are in control. When playing, children can become a mommy or a monster, a dancer or a doctor, or even a child care teacher! In addition, objects may perform magic (e.g., "This is my shield, no one can get me now" or "My doll can fly").

4. *Play is related to instrumental behavior.* Children may appear to "shoot" a gun when they pick up a block and yell "bang." Actually, they are only pretending to shoot. The key to this characteristic of play is pretense. Pretense helps to widen chil-

From *Day Care and Early Education*, Fall 1990, pp. 11-15. Published by Human Sciences Press, 72 Fifth Avenue, New York, NY 10011. Reprinted by permission.

dren's perspectives and lessen their egocentrism (Grusec & Lytton, 1988).

5. *Play is not bound by formal rules.* Unlike games, the flexibility of real play allows young children to change rules as they interact. A stool may be a table one minute and a bed the next. In the first instance, the "rule" of play would dictate children to eat from the stool; in the second instance, they would sleep on it.

6. *Play requires active participation.* Unlike daydreaming, play requires children to move and create. Thus, behaviors are considered play only when children engage in them actively.

In addition to these six criteria of play, there are several developmental characteristics of young children's play which impact on their overall growth.

## Understanding Developmental Characteristics of Play

*Play stimulates children's thinking.* The value of play can be conceptualized in cognitive terms (Butler, Gotts, & Quisenberry, 1978). To study the relationship between thinking and play, Smilansky (1968) developed one of the most widely used descriptions of children's cognitive levels of play. Accordingly, it was proposed that children's activities are directly related to the way they think as they play. Thus, activities may be categorized by cognitive levels which include functional, constructive, and dramatic play, as well as games with rules.

In *functional* play, children use their bodies to practice and test their physical limits and to explore the immediate environment. Children try a wide variety of new actions through the use of imitation. Even very young infants engage in functional play as they first entertain themselves with things as simple as watching their own hands move. Later, children engage objects as they use their bodies in this kind of play. Functional play consistently occurs in solitary and parallel social play situations and declines as children get older (Hetherington, Cox, & Cox, 1979; Rubin, Maroni, & Hor-

nung, 1976: Rubin, Watson, & Jambor, 1978).

*Constructive* play is the most common form of cognitive play activity used by preschool children (Rubin et al., 1983). Children manipulate objects to construct or create. From manipulating materials, children learn various uses for them. By learning to use materials effectively, young children see themselves as the creators of events. This gives them a sense of confidence in themselves and a feeling of power in an otherwise adult-controlled environment.

*Dramatic* play begins around the age of two. It includes role playing and/or make-believe activities (Rubin et al., 1983). For example, a child may pretend to be a firefighter, a chef, or a cat. When such activities are supported, dramatic play develops social tendencies in children and allows them to act simultaneously as actors, observers, and participators in a common endeavor (Smilansky, 1968).

The most sophisticated form of dramatic play is sociodramatic play, which emerges around three years of age. This play depends on the child's ability to talk and provides for the re-creation of real-life happenings. Children assume roles they have learned from experiences with adults and other children. Many experts believe that participation in sociodramatic play is critical to cognitive, as well as social, development (Golomb & Cornelius, 1977; Rubin et al., 1983; Smilansky, 1968).

The fourth kind of cognitive play is *games with rules.* This play typically does not begin until children are school-aged and continues through adulthood. Children must be able to control their behavior, actions, and reactions to play games with rules effectively (Piaget, 1962; Rubin et al., 1983). This may explain why preschoolers so often cry, pout, or even cheat when they try to participate in formal games with stringent rules.

*Play enhances language development.* The effects of play on verbal cognition and language development are found throughout the research lit-

erature (Levy, 1984; Rubin et al., 1983). For example, Bruner (1983) found that children use some of the most complicated grammatical forms of speech while playing. Play also provides a safe way to try out new words and phrases and to experiment with their meanings and usage.

Play promotes the acquisition of verbal forms of interpersonal contacts which precede thought and writing (Garvey & Hogan, 1973). Children learn not only the words but the nuance of language that is so important in human communication. They enjoy playing with the sounds and rhythms of language and connecting these to the words and reactions of others.

*Play provides an arena for social learning.* In play, the way children group themselves among their peers is referred to as the *social level of play.* As children become older and more mature, their play becomes increasingly more complex, and the social level of their play changes (Johnson, Christie, & Yawkey, 1987; Parten, 1932; Rogers & Sawyer, 1988; Smilansky, 1968). In social play, activities may be ordered from those which require the least amount of involvement to those which require the most. There is an increase in interactive play as children become older.

Infants' first social play usually involves interacting with an adult. In this play, each participant is intently involved with the other. The adult and infant exchange sounds and smiles in a turn-taking system which is sometimes called the beginning of social conversation (Rogers & Sawyer, 1988). As infants become older (i.e., between 6 and 18 months), they spend less time with adults and more time with objects (Rogers & Sawyer, 1988). Around the age of two and through the preschool years, children become increasingly involved in social play with peers. Through social play, preschool children are eventually able to repeat their own behavior, understand and imitate their peers' behavior, get the attention of others, and engage in social interaction (Rogers & Sawyer, 1988; Smith & Vollstedt, 1985).

More than a half century ago, Parten (1932) developed one of the most elaborate categorizations of children's social play. Based on observations of children in free play in a nursery school setting, Parten arrived at six play categories: solitary, parallel, associative, cooperative, unoccupied, and onlooking.

In *solitary* play, children play alone and independent of those around them. They play with materials that are different from those used by other children in the immediate playing area. The key to this play rests in the notion that children center their interest on their own play when they play alone (Parten, 1932).

Closely related to this type of play is *parallel* play. In parallel play, children play independently with similar objects and side by side with other children. They do not attempt to play with other children or to control those who came into or leave the play area. However, the activities that children choose in parallel play naturally bring them closer to other playing children (Parten, 1932).

Children interact with one another in *associative* play. They engage in similar, if not identical, activities, but there is no clear division of labor or organization. Children do not impose their individual ideas on the group, and each child plays as he or she wishes. Yet there is overt recognition by the playing children of common interests and relationships (Parten, 1932).

In *cooperative* play, one or two children assume the role of leader. This encourages a marked sense of belonging or not belonging to the group. Leaders control the play by directing and assigning roles and telling other children what needs to happen in the play (e.g., "I'll be the dad and you be the baby" or "That can't be the car; the car only runs here"). Play leaders change frequently, just as play itself changes. Thus, children may take on a variety of responsibilities or roles as they engage in cooperative play (Parten, 1932).

Finally, young children may not always be directly involved in play. In-stead, they may stand back and watch other children play or may simply watch anything that happens to be of interest to them at a certain time (Rogers & Sawyer, 1988). This kind of play is referred to an *unoccupied* or *onlooking* play behavior. The onlooking child spends time watching others play; the unoccupied child participates in a variety of nonplay behaviors (Parten, 1932).

*Play allows for testing of feelings and emotions.* As young children learn to play, they learn social rules and test the limits of permissible behavior without getting into trouble (Grusec & Lytton, 1988). They are able to make "mistakes" without punishment and to interpret the reactions of others in safe ways.

In play, children also learn to deal with emotionally overwhelming experiences by re-creating them in their minds and play (Erikson, 1963). For example, children may play monster when they are afraid of the dark, tiny baby when they are anxious about the arrival of a new sibling, or child care provider when they are unsure of a change in child care arrangements. Additionally, play affords young children a safe way to say such things as "I hate you" or "Go away!"

Play also allows an avenue for the expression of positive feelings and emotions. Children may re-create happy times and special events; they may become their own heroes or heroines. In such sociodramatic play, children explore new roles and are helped to see things from others' point of view. They begin to understand the needs and feelings of others by acting these out in their play.

## Optimizing Children's Play: The Adult Role

Although children may play without adult intervention, the quality of their play may be enhanced by adults. This occurs best when adults understand that play is learning for children, advocate for play in early childhood education programming, model play for children, and create an environment that optimizes play experiences.

*Understanding That Play Is Learning for Children.* One of the most effective ways to enhance children's play is to understand the critical role it assumes in all areas of development. As they play, children use their minds and their senses to explore and learn. They make meaningful and exciting discoveries: banging pan lids together creates sounds or echoes; being the "boss" is difficult at times; building high structures with small blocks is tricky; finishing the last piece of a difficult puzzle is wonderful. Children learn when they play — and they learn in ways that will ideally sustain them throughout their entire life. Understanding all of this creates an attitude of support for play in young children's lives. Play is learning for children.

*Advocating the Importance of Play to Others.* Advocacy for play begins with accurate information about its effect on children. If parents, providers, and policymakers are not well informed, young children may be pushed to excel in "academics" (i.e., flashcards and worksheets) at the expense of developmentally appropriate learning (Bredekamp, 1986; Elkind, 1986). But with accurate information about the role of play in development, programs and curricula may be developed and implemented in ways which foster optimal growth. Children need adults to advocate for the importance of play.

*Modeling Play for Children.* The need to play continues throughout the life span. Although the props and language of play may change as children age, the goal of play is similar for all living beings. Play functions as a release of feelings and an avenue for learning. It acts as a mechanism by which affective and cognitive energies may be renewed. When adults engage in the play of children, they commit to a mutual and unique sharing with the children entrusted to their care.

Thus, modeling play becomes an important job for adults. Children may need adults to help them initiate play or to enter a play group. They may require encouragement to negotiate the language or rules of play. Others may need to play with adults. However, it is important that adults not interfere with or dominate spontaneous play behaviors. Thus, modeling entails an understanding of developmental and individual differences in children, as well as insight into the situations which surround their play.

*Creating an Environment Conducive to Play.* Greenman (1988) suggests that an environment is an ever-changing system. More than the physical space, it includes the way time is structured and the roles people are expected to play. It conditions how children and adults feel, think, and behave; it dramatically affects the quality of living. A well-conceptualized environment is critical to children's play. Therefore, it ideally provides children with opportunities for decision making, motor, social, and cognitive skill development (Weinstein & David, 1987).

There are many ways adults can contribute to the development of an effective play environment for young children. Some of these include:

1. *Using a variety of play materials.* The environment should include a variety of materials (e.g., puzzles, blocks, play dough, and books), with the quantity of materials great enough so children need not wait to begin playing. Children in transitional and nonplay behavior often become bored or restless. Age-appropriate variety and quantity of materials reduce the opportunities for off-task behavior.

2. *Ensuring accessibility of toys.* Toys located on low, open shelves create an atmosphere where children are free to move about the room without total dependence on adults. If children feel in control of their playing environment, they begin to become independent in their actions and to develop an internal ability to act autonomously.

3. *Promoting diversity in play.* Children enjoy engaging in a variety of activities with each one, ideally leading to developmental gain. To foster a variety of interests and play behaviors, children need access to art

materials, dramatic play props, blocks, and manipulative toys.

Art materials (e.g., scissors, markers, crayons, scraps of paper and materials, collage materials, glue, and tape) should be out and accessible to children at all times. Providing this opportunity encourages children to be creative on their own timetable. It supports the notion that art is creation and not craft.

Dramatic play props should be changed frequently and related to children's real-life experiences. It may be useful to store dramatic play materials in easily movable prop boxes whose contents can be continually added to over time. These different props allow children to role play a variety of life experiences and to determine how these experiences affect them.

The block area is one of the spaces in which dramatic play is most likely to occur. Ideally, it should be filled with interesting props to complement block play. Children enjoy being challenged with many blocks. Thus, it is better to rotate a large set of blocks and props between two groups or programs than to divide the blocks into smaller sets.

Providing children with three-dimensional objects to manipulate enhances their interest in and curiosity about the world. Children seek more information about objects they are allowed to touch, compared to those they are not allowed to touch. Thus, question asking among young children can be maximized by the thoughtful placement of manipulatable objects in children's environment. The use of such material does not need to be limited to a table or counter. Many children enjoy playing on the seat of a chair, an overturned box, or even the floor. The trick is to conceptualize all areas in an environment as potential, usable space.

4. *Structuring traffic patterns.* Environments need to provide not only a variety of play materials, but also a variety of play spaces organized to define play areas. An environment should have open spaces for such things as block building and other

construction; small and cozy places for reading books, talking to a friend, or being alone; and clearly defined areas for manipulative, art, and dramatic play. Traffic patterns should allow children to have a sense that what they are doing will not be interrupted or destroyed by passing children and adults.

5. *Allocating time effectively.* Transition times should be minimal between play activities. Planning for children should be built around their need to play, rather than using play to "fill in" gaps in planning. Young children require long periods of time to play because it often takes them awhile to organize and begin their play activities. Without considerable blocks of time to play, children may not be able to follow through to the end of their play activity.

6. *Facilitating a positive atmosphere.* The environment includes not only physical and temporal components, but also interpersonal ones. When adults demonstrate mutual regard for one another and communication is positive, the feeling within the environment will be one of support and encouragement for everyone. When relationships between adults break down, children may sense tension or stress. This may make it difficult for children to communicate, create, and play constructively.

## Conclusion

Quality play is not a luxury but a necessity in the lives of young children. With adult support, children's play becomes a catalyst for optimal growth and development. Play contributes to learning and cognitive maturity as children consolidate what they know with what they are learning as they play. Indeed, children play to learn as they learn to play!

## References

Bredekamp, S. (Ed.). (1986). *Developmentally appropriate practice.* Washington, DC: National Association for the Education of Young Children.
Bruner, J. (1972). The nature and uses of immaturity. *American Psychologist, 27,* 687-708.

# 5. CURRICULAR APPLICATIONS: Creating and Inventing

Bruner, J. (1983). Play, thought, and language. *Peabody Journal of Education, 60,* 6-69.

Butler, A., Gotts, E., & Quisenberry, N. (1978). *Play as development.* Columbus, OH: Charles E. Merrill.

Christie, J. F. (1985). Training of symbolic play. *Early Child Development and Care, 19,* 43-52.

Elkind, D. (1986). Formal education and early childhood education: An essential difference. *Phi Delta Kappan,* pp. 631-636.

Erikson, E. (1963). *Childhood and society.* New York: Norton.

Garvey, C., & Hogan, R. (1973). Social speech and social interaction: Egocentrism revisited. *Child Development, 44,* 565-568.

Golomb, C., & Cornelius, C. (1977). Symbolic play and its cognitive significance. *Developmental Psychology, 13,* 246-247.

Gottfried, A. (1985). Intrinsic motivation for play. In C. C. Brown & A. W. Gottfried (Eds.), *Play interactions: The role of toys and parental involvement in children's development* (pp. 45-52). Skillman, NJ: Johnson & Johnson.

Greenman, J. (1988). *Caring spaces, learning places.* Redmond, WA: Exchange Press.

Grusec, J., & Lytton, H. (1988). *Social development: History, theory, and research.* New York: Springer-Verlag.

Hetherington, E. M., Cox, M., & Cox, R. (1979). Play and social interaction in children following divorce. *Journal of Social Issues, 35,* 26-49.

Johnson, J. E., Christie, J. F., & Yawkey, T. D. (1987). *Play and early childhood development.* Glenview, IL: Scott Foresman.

Levy, A. (1984). The language of play: The role of play in language development. *Early Child Development and Care, 17,* 49-62.

Papalia, D., & Olds, S. (1986). *Human development* (3rd ed.). New York: McGraw-Hill.

Parten, M. B. (1932). Social participation among pre-school children. *Journal of Abnormal and Social Psychology, 24,* 243-269.

Piaget, J. (1962). *Play, dreams, and imitation in childhood.* New York: Norton.

Rogers, C., & Sawyer, J. (1988). *Play in the lives of children.* Washington, DC: National Association for the Education of Young Children.

Rubin, K. H., Fein, G. G., & Vanderberg, B. (1983). Play. In E. M. Hetherington (Ed.), *Handbook of child psychology* (pp. 693-774). New York: Wiley.

Rubin, K. H., Maroni, T. L., & Hornung, M. (1976). Free play behaviors in middle- and lower-class preschoolers: Parten and Piaget Revisited. *Child Development, 47,* 414-419.

Rubin, K. H., Watson, K., & Jambor, T. (1978). Free play behaviors in preschool and kindergarten children. *Child Development, 49,* 534-536.

Smilansky, S. (1968). *The effects of sociodramatic play on disadvantaged preschool children.* New York: Wiley.

Smith, P., & Vollstedt, R. (1985). On defining play: An empirical study of the relationship between play and various criteria. *Child Development, 56,* 1042-1050.

Sutton-Smith, B. (1986). The spirit of play. In G. Fein & H. Rivkin (Eds.), *Reviews of research: The young child at play* (Vol. 4). Washington, DC: National Association for the Education of Young Children.

Vygotsky, L. S. (1976). Play and its role in the mental development of the child. In J. Bruner, A. Jolly, & K. Sylva (Eds.), *Play — Its role in development and evolution* (pp. 537-554). New York: Basic Books.

Weinstein, C., & David, T. (1987). *Spaces for children: The built environment and child development.* New York: Plenum Press.

# *"Put Your Name on Your Painting, But... the Blocks Go Back on the Shelves"*

## David Kuschner

*David Kuschner, Ed.D., is Associate Professor of Early Childhood Education at the University of Cincinnati. He has done research and writing in the area of children's play and material use.*

My daughter's schoolwork has covered our refrigerator door for the past six years. During these six years, there has been a change in what she brings home from school as evidence of the day's activities. For the two years she was at the child care center, all that we saw were various forms of artwork: scribbles and beginning scenes done with tempera paints, broad washes of color applied with little fingers, and tissue, yarn, and glitter stuck together with gobs of glue. Then, starting in kindergarten, a shift occurred: Worksheets began to be mixed in with the artwork. Instead of pieces of paper with her own inventions expressed on them, we saw pieces of paper with somebody else's inventions, but with our daughter's connecting lines, colored in shapes, and traced letters. In first grade, the ratio of worksheets to artwork began to change in favor of worksheets, and now in third grade, when she pulls her "work" out of her backpack to show us, the pile of papers is mostly worksheets of one kind or another.

When I think about those art projects and worksheets, I do so both as a parent *and* as an early childhood educator. As a parent, I have been familiar with all of my daughter's teachers and classrooms: The teachers have been good and the environments rich and stimulating. Children in those classrooms were doing much more than just art projects and worksheets. As a teacher educator, I spend time in early childhood programs from preschool through third grade and I see children playing with blocks and puzzles, creating elaborate make-believe scenes, reading and listening to stories, engaging in language play, testing themselves on the playground, and negotiating relationships with their peers. While I am sure that the same activity has been occurring in my daughter's classrooms, the only "evidence" I have had about what my daughter does during her day has been the art projects and the worksheets, the portable products of some of the day's activities.

I also know that an emphasis on the importance of play for children's development is a part of our profession's long history and tradition. Our textbooks suggest how best to foster all types of children's play and our profession's major position statement, *Developmentally Appropriate Practice in Early Childhood Programs Serving Children From Birth Through Age 8* (Bredekamp, 1987) reinforces and supports these suggestions. The important voices of our history, from Froebel and Montessori

**Expendable materials such as paper and clay easily become permanent objects that children own and parents too are proud of. Nonexpendable materials such as blocks and dramatic play props are used with creativity but impermanence. A child does not "own" the blocks in the way she "owns" a painting.**

From *Young Children*, Vol. 45, No. 1, November 1989, pp. 49-56. Copyright © 1989 by David Kuschner. Reprinted by permission of the author.

through James Hymes and David Elkind, have continually emphasized the need to provide opportunities for children to play. We also need to show children we value their play, in all its forms. Why, then, do we have worksheets dominating so many of our first grade classrooms and now creeping down into many of our kindergarten programs? Why, as a parent, have I had only art projects and worksheets as tangible evidence of my daughter's school life?

## Teacher's differential responses to children's forms of play

Consider the following two observations of children at play in a typical preschool or kindergarten. We'll begin with *Ralph, the artist.*

During free time, Ralph chooses to paint at one of the easels. He is very definite about whether his paper should be placed horizontally or vertically on the easel and about the colors he wants to use. As he paints you can observe how he uses empty space in his painting and how he knows that shades of color can be created by blending paints together.

When Ralph is finished, he brings a teacher over to see what he has done. After a minute or so of admiring nods and interested questions, the teacher asks Ralph if he wants to put his name on the painting and then hang it on the line so that it will dry and he will be able to take it home. Ralph agrees, signs his name, finds a spot on the drying line, and runs off to find something else to do in the room.

Now consider the activity of *Jamie, the block player.*

As soon as activity time begins, Jamie makes her way over to the block area. After a few minutes, her block structure begins to take some shape: She is building a zoo. Soon Ryan comes over and joins in the construction. He adds to the structure by erecting more enclosures for the plastic animals Jamie has gathered from the toy shelf. Once

they place their animals in the zoo, they become animal trainers and zoo keepers, giving orders to and caring for their beasts.

About 40 minutes after Jamie had first started to build, a teacher walks over and watches for a few minutes. She asks the two zoo keepers a few questions, expresses her admiration for how well they built their zoo, and then tells them that it is time to clean up because snack time is approaching. Together they quickly put the blocks back on the shelves and the animals back into their boxes. Jamie and Ryan then join their classmates on the carpet for a story.

In each of these play episodes, children were involved in meaningful activity. Both types of play are vitally important for children's development. There are, however, important differences between the ways in which the teachers responded to the ending of each play episode.

## Expendable and nonexpendable materials

In order to understand the differences between the teacher behaviors with the artist and the block players it is first necessary to think about the materials the children were using. I previously described a framework for thinking about children's material use (Kuschner & Clark, 1976, 1977) that in part consists of analyzing the *nature* of the materials in question. Blocks, for example, are rigid, three-dimensional, often natural in color, and are usually symmetrically balanced. Paints, on the other hand, are colored, fluid, essentially two-dimensional, and applied with some sort of applicator (e.g., brush, finger) to some sort of surface (e.g., paper, table). This type of analysis highlights a very important difference between blocks and paints: Blocks are *nonexpendable* materials, paints are *expendable* materials.

Expendable materials—crayons, paints, paper, glue, tape, and glitter—will be used up by the chil-

dren. These materials are bought, used, and replaced. Materials that are expected to have a relatively long, functional life—blocks, puzzles, books, manipulative toys, and role-playing props—fall into the nonexpendable category. When a hundred dollars or so is spent on a set of blocks, the assumption is that the blocks will get years of use. Toys do break and puzzle pieces do get lost, but for the most part the expectation is that nonexpendable materials will have a long "shelf life."

Understanding this distinction helps make us aware of the socially determined constraints placed upon the use of various materials. The child who is encouraged to cut colored paper into the shapes he wants, glue the shapes onto construction paper in any design he wants, and then use markers he chooses to color the design is definitely not encouraged to make the same choices with units from the block set. Even though he may need a block of a particular shape for the farm he is building, he is not encouraged to take a block piece to the woodworking bench and cut it into that shape, nor is he encouraged to take a piece to the art area to paint it the color he needs.

*A sense of ownership and permanency.* This distinction not only suggests constraints on what children can do with materials but also suggests ways in which the behavior of *teachers* is influenced by the type of material children are using. Think again about the observations of Ralph and Jamie and how the teachers related to the endings of the play episodes. In the case of Ralph, the teacher helped him attach a sense of ownership (writing his name on the painting) and permanency to the activity (taking the painting home). In the case of Jamie, as interested in the block play as the teacher might have been, she did not encourage Jamie to sign her work (as a sculptor might), nor did she suggest that the zoo structure could have any permanent existence (certainly not to be taken home). What the teacher did do was to remind Jamie that her creation had to be dismantled and that the blocks needed to be put back on the shelves to be used another day by other children.

We all have some typical responses to the endings of children's play, and these responses differ *depending* upon the type of play it is and the type of material involved. If the child is playing with expendable materials—materials that result in a product the child can possess—we tend to focus on whether or not she has completed what she was doing. If the child is playing with nonexpendable materials—materials that belong to the classroom and need to be used again by other children—we tend to focus on the return of these materials to their storage places.

***Understanding the messages we send.*** Our typical differential reponses to children's play may be sending some unintended messages to both children and parents about the relative value of different types of play. Since all parents don't necessarily believe that play is important (Almy, Monighan, Scales, & Van Hoorn, 1984; Rothlein & Brett, 1984; Ramsey & Reid, 1988), we need to be aware of how our responses to children's play do and do not reinforce its value. As Rivkin (1986) writes, "In considering their interactions with children during play, teachers have to be simultaneously aware not only of developmental stages, but also of their own attitudes and values" (p. 214).

Consider the very language we use to talk about different types of children's play. What Timmy is doing at that table is *playing* with puzzles, while Juan and Alicia dressed up as firefighters are engaged in make-believe, role, and sociodramatic *play.* But Jerome over at the easel is doing his art*work,* and Nicole sitting at the table drawing lines between objects printed on a piece of paper is doing a *work*sheet. When Jerome and Nicole are fin-

ished, they will put their *work* in their cubbies to be taken home at the end of the day. When Alicia and Juan are finished the teacher may ask them if they had a good time *playing* firefighter and will remind them to put the props away. Jerome and Nicole's *work* may be displayed for parents' night and put in folders to be shared at parent-teacher conference time. Our language and actions regarding children's activity can socialize children into adult conceptions of the differences between work and play, thus suggesting which type of activity is more important (Suransky, 1982; Klein, Kantor, & Fernie, 1988). Spodek (1986) suggests that children's interests and what *they* believe is important may be influenced by the value messages sent by adults: "Children's interests, however, do not grow naturally from the child but rather are influenced by the social context in which the child functions... needs do not arise naturally but are related to elements that adults value" (p. 33).

***The importance of ownership and permanency.*** We shouldn't underestimate the power of having names attached to activities. When a name is connected to something a child has done, a sense of pride may be fostered and a valuing of the activity engendered. Beardsley and Zeman-Marecek (1987) capture this power as they answer their question, "What's in a name?"

As children progress through preschool experiences that allow them to explore the power of language in a social context, no symbol, no word emerges more powerfully than the child's own name. A 3- or 4-year-old who is encountering his first school experience finds that in this

world of many peers, his name—that ordered progression of letters that means him—takes on heightened significance. At home, he may be the only small person; what is his is obvious by its size and child-appeal. In the classroom, there are many small people; teachers can help the young child realize that what he *has* and what he *does* become uniquely recognizable by using the powerful label of his name. (p. 162)

The sense of permanency is also important because it can set the stage for children's reflection about their activity. When the product of a child's activity lasts past the immediate time of the activity, the child can literally and figuratively sit back and consider what he has done. He can reflect on the reasons for why he did it in the way he did and consider how he might change it or do it differently next time. When there is tangible evidence of the activity to reflect upon, there is the opportunity for revision and the evolution of activity that revision embodies.

Children are assisted in the reflection and revision process by teachers, peers, and parents who ask questions or make statements about what they have done. Asking children about their intentions, the materials they used, and the difficulty they might have had carrying out their intentions can help children focus on their activity. Asking children about how they plan on changing, modifying, or revising their activity can help them understand the relationship between what they have done now and what they might do in the future. High/Scope has incorporated such reflection under its "Plan-Do-Review" curriculum organization (Hohmann, Banet, & Weikart, 1979), and Was-

**The policy of cleaning up all materials should sometimes be set aside to honor children's creations. An intricate Lego™ truck or block zoo is worth looking at and talking about for a day or so.**

serman (1988) has proposed a "Play-Debrief-Replay" instructional model for elementary science curriculum. Wasserman suggests that the debriefing process is important because it helps children "extract meanings from their experiences" (p. 233).

## How to attach ownership and permanency to all types of play

There are a number of ways in which teachers can help children attach a sense of ownership and permanency to all forms of their play.

**Use photography to capture interesting activity.** Photography is a wonderful way to capture the excitement of children's activity. I walked into a kindergarten once to find the teacher taking a picture of a large group of children standing behind this massive block structure sprawling across the carpet. All of the children had contributed to the

building and every face was beaming.

Display photographs on walls, send them home to parents, or organize them into albums. I worked with one program that compiled albums depicting a year's worth of play and activity. The parents loved to look through these albums and often would order reprints of particular pictures. You can use photographs as story starters to encourage children to describe, both orally and in writing, what they had been doing.

Show slides, films, and videos at parent nights as a way of explaining what the goals and curriculum of the program are and as a terrific way of valuing all forms of children's play. Parents enjoy watching their children, as do the children themselves. Film and video, although more costly, offer the advantage over prints and slides of including sound and the dynamic aspect of children's activity.

Marietta Lynch

*Some children can guess-spell their own signs, labels, or captions. Others can copy them. Any child can dictate. Good preschool, kindergarten, and primary grade teachers have been integrating play, print, self-esteem building, and documenting children's school successes since our profession took shape 100 years ago.*

**Send notes home to parents.** Teachers should find efficient and effective ways of sending home written notes about children's play. Keep pads of paper close by so that you can make quick notes when you witness something interesting. (It is important to remember that this "something interesting" doesn't have to involve concrete activity. It may have been some language play or the resolution of social conflict.) I have known teachers who wore aprons with pockets to hold a pad and pencil just to make the note-taking process easier. Other teachers have created and duplicated notepaper with such starter sentences as, "You should have seen what _____ did today!" (Of course, such notepaper should only be used to communicate positive happenings!) Write the note when you see the interesting episode and leave it in the child's cubby or mailbox for him to take home or for his parent to find at arrival or departure time—a time during which a great deal of parent-school communication often occurs (Herwig, 1982). Share the note with the child to let him know that you noticed and valued what he had been doing. He will then have the pleasure of anticipating his parent finding the note.

**Attach signs to the products of children's activity.** I have seen teachers very effectively attach a sense of ownership and permanency to children's activity by helping the children make a sign to identify the product as theirs. When Jamie and Ryan spent 40 minutes constructing their zoo, instead of taking it down, the teacher could have helped them print a sign saying, "Jamie and Ryan carefully built this zoo together. Please do not disturb." Such a message serves a number of functions. A sense of ownership is attached to the activity. A sense of valuing is communicated because the teacher took the time to help the children make the sign. By placing the sign in front of the structure, some permanency is established—the sign serves as a bit of protection for the zoo itself. And, of course, the children are exposed to the functional power of the printed word in a very meaningful context, an experience important for the development of literacy (Schickedanz, 1986).

**Create a "favorite toy" display.** If some tabletop, cabinet top, or bookshelf space is available, it can be reserved for children to have their favorite *school* toy displayed with their name in front of it, much as artwork is often displayed. Displaying these toys or materials shows the child herself, other children, and parents that the activity represented by the toy is valued and that even though the toy or material cannot go home and doesn't *belong* to the child, the type of play supported by the toy is just as important as play that does result in products that can be sent home. As Levin and Klein (1988) suggest, the school environment can be used to foster communication between parents and children.

**Have the children write about what they do.** Encourage children, when developmentally appropriate, to write or dictate stories and descriptions about what they have been doing. This not only attaches ownership and permanency to the activity but again supports the development of reading and writing. These stories can be displayed on walls, made into books, or sent home. The stories and the process of creating them can also be part of the "plan-do-review" format as described in the High/Scope curriculum (Hohmann, Banet, & Weikart, 1979).

**Rethink attitudes about cleanup.** There is one last—and very important—suggestion as to how we can help children understand the importance of all of their play activity: Rethink our sometimes compulsive approach to cleanup time. It is true that some early childhood programs suffer from

constraints on the use of physical space—somebody else is going to use the space after the children leave and therefore all materials need to be put away. In addition, sometimes space is limited and parts of the classroom must serve multiple functions. Even with these constraints, we need to reflect upon the rules we create to manage the transitions from activity to activity. We tend to get caught up in what comes next as opposed to focusing on what the children are doing at the moment. There are probably more opportunities than we realize to let the products of children's activity remain visible for awhile. It may take some coordination with other teachers or custodians. By suggesting to the children that their efforts can have some permanence beyond the moment, we let them know that we found what they were doing then at least as interesting as what everyone is supposed to be doing next. As Ramsey and Reid (1988) write, "teachers can plan flexibly so that rigid schedules and routines do not disrupt the flow of play" (p. 233).

## Valuing all of children's play

The six suggestions just described do not comprise an exhaustive list. Undoubtedly, teachers have already found many more ways to attach a sense of ownership and permanency to the wonderful variety of children's play activity. We need to continue to find ways of doing so if we want to make sure that the message we send to children, parents, and other professionals is the one we intend: Play, in *all* of its forms, is what children do and is the way children grow, learn, and develop.

## References

Almy, M., Monighan, P., Scales, B., & Van Hoorn, J. (1984). Recent research on play: The teacher's perspective. In L. Katz (Eds.), *Current topics in early childhood education* (Vol. 5, pp. 1–25). Norwood, NJ: Ablex.

Beardsley, L. V., & Zeman-Marecek, M. (1987, February). Making connections: Facilitating literacy in young children. *Childhood Education, 63,* 159–166.

Bredekamp, S. (Ed.). (1987). *Developmentally appropriate practice in early childhood programs serving children from birth through age 8* (exp. ed.). Washington, DC: NAEYC.

Herwig, J. E. (1982). Parental involvement: Changing assumptions about the educator's role. In *How to involve parents in early childhood education* (pp. 6–30). Provo, UT: Brigham Young University Press.

Hohmann, M., Banet, B., & Weikart, D. (1979). *Young children in action: A manual for preschool educators.* Ypsilanti, MI: High/Scope.

Klein, E. L., Kantor, R., & Fernie, D. E. (1988). What do young children know about school? *Young Children, 43*(5), 32–39.

Kuschner, D., & Clark, P. (1976, November). *A framework for analyzing children's interactions with materials.* Paper presented at the annual conference of the National Association for the Education of Young Children, Anaheim, CA.

Kuschner, D., & Clark, P. (1977). Children, materials, and adults in early learning settings. In L. Golubchick & B. Persky (Eds.), *Early childhood education* (pp. 122–127). Wayne, NJ: Avery Publishing.

Levin, D.E., & Klein, A. (1988). What did you do in school today? Using the school environment to foster communication between children and parents. *Day Care and Early Education, 15,* 6–10.

Ramsey, P., & Reid, R. (1988). Designing play environments for preschool and kindergarten children. In D. Bergen (Ed.), *Play as a medium for learning and development* (pp. 213–239). Portsmouth, NH: Heinemann.

Rivkin, M. S. (1986). The educator's place in children's play. In G. Fein & M. Rivkin (Eds.), *The young child at play: Reviews of research, Volume 4* (pp. 213–217). Washington, DC: NAEYC.

Rothlein, L., & Brett, A. (1984). *Children's, teachers', and parents' perceptions of play.* Coral Gables, FL: University of Miami. (ERIC Document Reproduction Service No. ED 273 395)

Schickedanz, J. A. (1986). *More than the ABCs: The early stages of reading and writing.* Washington, DC: NAEYC.

Spodek, B. (1986). Development, values, and knowledge in the kindergarten curriculum. In B. Spodek (Ed.), *Today's kindergarten: Exploring the knowledge base, expanding the curriculum* (pp. 32–47). New York: Teachers College Press, Columbia University.

Suransky, V. (1982). *The erosion of childhood.* Chicago: University of Chicago Press.

Wasserman, S. (1988). Play-Debrief-Replay: An instructional model for science. *Childhood Education, 64,* 232–234.

# The State of American Preschool Playgrounds

JOE L. FROST
LOUIS E. BOWERS
SUE C. WORTHAM

Joe L. Frost is the Parker Centennial Professor at the University of Texas at Austin, Austin, TX 78712. Louis E. Bowers is a professor of physical education in the Department of Physical Education at the University of South Florida, Tampa, FL 33620. Sue C. Wortham is an associate professor in the Division of Education at the University of Texas at San Antonio, San Antonio, TX 78285.

How safe are our nation's playgrounds? Playgrounds for children are the subject of growing interest throughout the industrialized world, particularly in the United States. Two major reasons exist for this: (1) Evidence that play contributes to child development—social, cognitive, affective, motor—is accumulating at an accelerating rate, and (2) a growing awareness of preventable hazards on playgrounds. In the United States, these hazards, frequently resulting in child injuries or fatalities, are increasingly the basis for legal litigation.

Although some members of the general public believe that play is frivolous, wastes children's time, and detracts from academic success, little controversy exists among play scholars as to its overall value for child development.

Similarly, the issues of whether playgrounds are hazardous, and to what extent hazards exist, are being resolved. Data collected from hospital emergency rooms show that the number of playground injuries grew from about 118,000 in 1974 to more than 200,000 in 1988. "About 60% of all playground equipment-related injuries (for both public and home equipment) are a result of falls to the surface below the equipment... nine out of ten of the serious injuries" resulted from falls to the surface (U.S. Consumer Product Safety Commission, 1990, p. 1). Since most of these injuries were to young children (ages three to six) it is particu-

> **The worst of the lot are accidents waiting to happen, sterile in play value, and essentially unfit for children's play.**

larly important to examine the safety of preschool playgrounds.

Recently published, the results of the first national surveys of American public elementary school playgrounds (Bruya & Langendorfer, 1988) and American public parks playgrounds (Thompson & Bowers, 1989) revealed an overall pattern of antiquated design, hazardous conditions, and poor or absent maintenance.

In the National Survey of Playground Equipment in Preschool Centers (Wortham & Frost, 1990) 349 centers located in 31 states were examined. Centers were randomly selected from lists of all state licensed centers within the area. Surveys were conducted by 62 trained early childhood and physical education professionals.

### Survey Results: Equipment and Provisions' Play Value.

In evaluating results of the survey, two major factors were considered; play value and safety. The preschool outdoor environment that is rich in play value takes into account the developmental needs of the age groups involved. Three through five-year-old children engage in several types of play: exercise, dramatic (make-believe), constructive, and organized games. In addition, their play is affected by complexity, novelty, creative and problem-solving potential, and aesthetic qualities of equipment and materials.

The preschool survey revealed that a broad array of equipment, portable materials, and other provisions were available to young children. The permanent, fixed, equipment on a typical playground included one or more swings, slides, balance beams, overhead ladders, rocking apparatus, and climbers. Fewer than 20 percent of the playgrounds included see-saws and merry-go-rounds.

Among the portable materials, tricycles were most often available, with an average of about three per playground. Loose tires, sand, wagons, barrels and loose boards (building material, stacking blocks) were available, in descending order, ranging from about two tires per playground to about one barrel or board to every three playgrounds. Building materials and tools were absent on most playgrounds or from adjacent storage facilities.

Most playgrounds included grassy areas for organized games, accessible water, sand play areas, hard

This article is reprinted with permission from the *Journal of Physical Education, Recreation & Dance,* October 1990, pp. 18-23. JOPERD is a publication of the American Alliance for Health, Physical Education, Recreation and Dance, 1900 Association Drive, Reston, VA 22091.

surfaces for games and man-made shade structures. Storage, adjacent to or on the playground, was absent at over half of the sites. This is a critical omission, since convenient storage is essential to the provision of play materials for children's dramatic and constructive play and for organized games.

Cars and boats for dramatic play, water and earth (digging) play areas, and natural areas (plants, gardens) were found on fewer than one-third of the playgrounds. Toilet facilities, provisions for animals, and amphitheaters were found at only a few centers.

*Playground Equipment: Safety.*
*Swings.* There were 554 swing structures and 1,455 swing seats on the 349 playgrounds surveyed. About one-third (191) of the swing structures were designed for younger children (infants and toddlers) and 13 percent (194) had swivel suspensions to support tire swings. Hazardous elements were common, including 73 metal or wood seats, which constituted five percent of total swing seats. The United States Consumer Product Safety Commission (1981, p.8) guidelines recommend that seats be "constructed of light-weight material such as plastic, canvas, or rubber." Support structures were not firmly anchored on 45 swings; 21 percent of the structures had sharp corners, edges and projections; moving parts were in poor repair on 24 percent of the structures. Only 11 percent had barriers (e.g., low fences) to keep children from running into the path of swings.

The survey identified 531 slides or about 1.5 per playground. One hundred ten (110) of these were wide slides (over 3' wide). Six percent (34) of the slides had broken or missing parts; 18 percent (94) had sharp corners, edges, or projections; 16 percent (85) were not firmly anchored; 50 percent (264) had no deceleration chute at the slide exit.

*Climbers.* Combining all climbing equipment, the survey found that 16 percent were not firmly anchored; nine percent had unsecured or loose parts; ten percent had open holes at the end of pipes; 15 percent had sharp edges or protrusions; 39 percent lacked a guard rail around the highest platform; 44 percent contained openings between 4 1/2" and 9" that could entrap children's heads or necks. In addition, over 13 percent of the climbers were over eight feet in height and 24 percent were over seven feet high.

*Merry-go-rounds.* Among the 72 merry-go-rounds identified in the survey, 35 percent were not securely anchored; 60 percent had parts that were not securely fastened; 14 percent contained sharp edges and protrusions. Very hazardous conditions included open areas in the base around rotation post (16%); shearing actions in mechanism under the

## Play's Contributions to Child Development

**The evidence that play contributes to child development is impressive. Sources reveal that play *promotes cognitive development* (Sutton-Smith, 1967, 1977; Piaget, 1962; Saltz & Brodie, 1982; Fein, 1979; Saltz, 1980; Bruner, 1972; Bruner, Jolly & Sylva, 1976). Play *promotes social development* (Shure, 1981; Ladd & Mize, 1983; Eisenberg & Harris, 1984) and *leads to discovery, verbal judgment and reasoning*. It is also important in *developing manipulative skills, imaginative art, discovery, reasoning and thought* (Isaacs, 1933; Pepler & Ross, 1981). Play with objects *results in divergent production or expands uses for objects* (Sutton-Smith, 1968; Goodnow, 1969; Dansky, 1980b) and *improves problem-solving* (Sylva, 1977; Smith & Dutton, 1979; Dansky & Silverman, 1973; Eisenberg & Harris, 1984). Play *enhances language* (McCune-Nicolich, 1981; Schirmer, 1989).**

**Culture arises in the form of play (Huizinga, 1950). From a therapeutic perspective, play is *a means for overcoming fears* (Klein, 1932; Isaacs, 1933; Axline, 1947; Erikson, 1950). *Motor abilities are formed through play* (Bennett, 1980; Seefeldt, 1984; Staniford, 1979) and *playgrounds enhance motor development* (Gabbard, 1979; Myers, 1985).**

**Play training for children enhances imaginative play (Smilansky, 1968; Feitelson & Ross, 1973; Smith & Sydall, 1978), *enhances creativity* (Feitelson & Ross, 1973; Dansky, 1980a), *enhances language development* (Vygotsky, 1967; Lovinger, 1974; Saltz, Dixon & Johnson, 1977), and *enhances group cooperation* (Rosen, 1974; Smith & Sydall, 1978). Finally, *play training for teachers improves their interaction with children during play* (Busse, Ree & Gutride, 1970; Wade, 1985).**

base (seat) of the device (9%); gear boxes that could crush fingers (4%).

*Rocking equipment.* The 175 pieces of rocking equipment (primarily spring-mounted animal seats) included the following hazards: 67 percent were not firmly anchored; 17 percent had missing parts; pinching was possible in 47 percent of the devices.

*See-saws.* The 76 see-saws identified in the survey included: 56 percent that were not firmly anchored; 40 percent with internal moving parts accessible to fingers; 28 percent with loose joints or fasteners; 26 percent with sharp corners or projections. Only 19 percent included cushioned impact devices between the end of see-saws and the ground.

*Surfacing.* A wide range of surfacing material was found under and around playground equipment, including loose materials (sand, pea gravel, mulch), commercial surfacing and hard surfaces (packed earth, asphalt, concrete), and grass. Only the loose materials and commercial playground surfacing meet CPSC guidelines for safety. Less than half (48%) of the material under swings (sand, pea gravel, commercial matting) met this requirement; 53 percent of the material under slides and 63 percent under climbers met the requirement. The survey did not ascertain whether the acceptable materials were in a properly maintained condition ( 8" to 12" deep under and around equipment). Two of the authors participated in the surveys in about a dozen states. None of the playgrounds they surveyed met common guidelines for depth and maintenance of surfacing material.

### Implications: Play Value

Overall, most of the preschool playgrounds surveyed were developmentally sterile and lacking in play value. The major emphasis, judging from equipment and materials available, was on exercise or motor activity. The equipment for such activity was essentially the same as that provided

---

> *Tricycles were the most frequently available portable materials available on playgrounds.*

---

for older children at public schools and public parks. Since play is the primary vehicle for learning and development (intellectual, social, physical) in the early years, it is essential that all preschool playgrounds include a broad, rich selection of age/size-scaled equipment for motor development and portable materials (with storage) and other provisions for dramatic play, constructive play (with proper supervision), and organized games. In addition, the well-designed environment will feature nature areas, amphitheaters, toilet and drinking facilities, and places for gardening and animal care.

The availability of infant-toddler play areas and appropriate equipment designed especially for infants and toddlers was difficult to determine from the survey. Infants were served at many of the centers surveyed, but data on numbers of infants and toddlers served compared to older preschool children were not available. Smaller equipment for younger children was found on almost half of the playgrounds, and only 36 percent of the playgrounds had large and small equipment separated.

There were other indications that provisions for infant and toddler play were included on the preschool playgrounds. Tricycles, push and pull toys, small vehicles, balls, and materials for sand and water play were available at many of the sites surveyed.

Survey results indicate that some provisions are being made for the youngest children on preschool playgrounds. However, it appears

that designers of these playscapes do not understand the developmental differences between infants and toddlers and older children. Many of the playgrounds surveyed included opportunities for play experiences for younger children, but few of the play environments that served infants and toddlers provided for their unique play needs. The inclusion of smaller equipment and a sprinkling of toys seemed to be the norm, rather than providing environments designed specifically to enhance emerging physical, social, language, and cognitive skills in children between the ages of birth and three years.

### Safety

The overall results show that preschool playground equipment is smaller in size and better maintained than public school equipment (Bruya & Langendorfer, 1988) or public park equipment (Thompson & Bowers, 1989) and the array of equipment and materials is more varied. However, this finding only intensifies the concern for safety at school and park playgrounds: overall, the safety of preschool play equipment is unconscionably bad. All three locations feature playgrounds that are remarkably consistent with the antiquated 1928 guidelines of the National Recreation Association (1928). The worst of the lot are accidents waiting to happen, sterile in play value, and essentially unfit for children's play.

Four fundamental factors contribute to the hazardous state of playgrounds: (1) design of equipment, (2) zoning (arrangement) and installation of equipment, (3) maintenance, and (4) play leadership or supervision.

Given the current state of preschool playgrounds, school administrators should conduct careful evaluations of existing playgrounds, using professional expertise, followed by the development of a master plan replacing or rebuilding their playgrounds. Selection of equipment and related activities are guided by the master plan.

Much of the playground equipment now available from manufacturers and distributors violates CPSC safety guidelines. An analysis of equipment in the 1989 catalogs of 24 national companies showed that only three companies had "no violations." Nine additional companies had "limited violations" or "some violations." Twelve companies, or half of those surveyed, advertised play equipment with "extensive violations" or "extreme violations" (Frost, 1990). This analysis used catalog photographs, equipment specifications, and firsthand inspection of equipment. The original analysis by the author was verified in blind analyses by two additional playground specialists. The violations found in playground equipment catalogs included head entrapment areas, open base merry-go-rounds, excessive heights (up to 16'), heavy, rigid swing seats, and pinching/crushing mechanisms. Consequently, consumers should seek expert help and/or secure copies of CPSC guidelines and related professional literature to guide equipment selection.(See references for relevant literature.) A growing number of play equipment manufacturers/distributors are studying play and play environment research and are making dramatic improvements in their equipment. Such companies are valuable sources of playground assistance.

Once equipment has been selected, it must be properly installed. Some manufacturers provide directions for installation of their equipment. It is wise to secure experienced installers and require that they sign written confirmation that the equipment is installed according to manufacturer and CPSC guidelines. For additional security, the manufacturer's representative should inspect the installation and certify proper installation.

It is the rare preschool that provides regular, comprehensive maintenance for the playground, or that

provides staff training for playground supervision. The maintenance program should include the selection or development of a safety checklist (see Thompson, Bruya & Crawford, 1990), regular inspection of equipment and grounds, and prompt, thorough repairs. Teachers, administrators and custodians should receive annual training about playground safety and supervi-

> *Almost half of the climbing equipment had openings that could entrap a child's head.*

sion. They, in turn, should conduct safety sessions with children, including playground walk-throughs, discussions, and examples of safe and unsafe play practices. Staff training can begin with workshops staffed by play specialists, literature reviews, and visits to model playground programs.

Playgrounds are an essential component in the educative process for preschools. They contribute to child development and to academic goals such as language and reading. The play value of playgrounds is complemented by playground safety. The National Survey of Playground Equipment in Preschools concluded that preschool playgrounds are in a state of general disrepair and, overall, they are hazardous. Those concerned with preschool playgrounds should reevaluate their playgrounds, taking into account equipment design, safety, installation, maintenance, and supervision. The safety issue is of sufficient concern to involve school administrators, regulatory agencies, and legislators. Such groups, working with professionals in play, child development, physical education, and design, can collectively rebuild American playgrounds

and ensure that they meet the developmental needs and safety requirements of young children.

### References

Axline, V. (1947). *Play therapy.* Boston: Houghton Mifflin.

Bennett, C. (1980). Planning for activity during the important preschool years. *Journal of Physical Education, Recreation & Dance, 15*(7), 30-34.

Bruner, J. S. (1972). The nature and uses of immaturity. *American Psychologist, 27,* 687-708.

Bruner, J. S., Jolly, A., & Sylva, K. (Eds.) (1976). *Play: Its role in development and evolution.* New York: Penguin.

Bruya, L.D., & Langendorfer, S.J. (Eds.). (1988). *Where our children play: Elementary school playground equipment.* Reston, VA: American Alliance for Health, Physical Education, Recreation and Dance.

Busse, T., Ree, M., & Gutride, M. (1970). Environmentally enriched classrooms and the play behavior of Negro preschool children. *Urban Education, 5,* 128-140.

Dansky, J.L., & Silverman, I.W. (1973). Effects of play on associative fluency in preschool-aged children. *Developmental Psychology, 9,* 38-43.

Dansky, J. L. (1980a). Cognitive consequences of sociodramatic play and exploratory training for economically disadvantaged preschoolers. *Journal of Child Psychology and Psychiatry, 20,* 47-58.

Dansky, J.L. (1980b). Make believe: A mediator of the relationship between free play and associative fluency. *Child Development, 51,* 576-579.

Eisenberg, N., & Harris, J.D. (1984). Social competence: A developmental perspective. *School Psychology Review, 13,* 267-277.

Erikson, E.H. (1950). *Childhood and society.* New York: Norton.

Fein, G. (1979). Play in the acquisition of symbols. In L. Katz (Ed.), *Current topics in early childhood education.* Norwood, NJ: Ablex.

Feitelson, W., & Ross, G.S. (1973). The neglected factor—play. *Human Development, 16,* 202-223.

Frost, J. L. (Summer, 1990). Playground equipment catalogs: Most can't be trusted for safety. *Texas Child Care Quarterly*. Austin, TX: Corporate Child Development Fund of Texas and Texas Department of Human Services.

Gabbard, C. (1979). *Playground apparatus experience and muscular endurance among children 4-6*. (ERIC Document Reproduction Service, SP 022 020; ED 228190).

Goodnow, J. J. (1969). Effects of handling, illustrated by use of objects. *Child Development, 40,* 201-212.

Huizinga, J. (1950). *Homo Judens: A study of the play element in culture*. London: Routledge & Kegan Paul.

Isaacs, S. (1933). *Social development in young children: A study of beginnings*. London: Routledge & Kegan Paul.

Klein, M. (1932). *The psychoanalysis of children*. London: Hogarth.

Ladd, G., & Mize, J. (1983). A cognitive-learning model of social-skill training. *Psychological Review, 90,* 127-157.

Lovinger, S.L. (1974). Sociodramatic play and language development in preschool disadvantaged children. *Psychology in the Schools, 11,* 313-320.

McCune-Nicolich, L. (1981). Toward symbolic functioning: Structure of early pretend games and potential parallels with language. *Child Development, 52,* 785-797.

Myers, G.D. (1985). Motor behavior of kindergartners during physical education and free play. In J.L. Frost & S. Sunderlin (Eds.), *When children play*. Wheaton, MD: Association for Childhood Education International.

National Recreation Association (1928). *Report of committee on standards in playground apparatus*. New York: National Recreation Association.

Pepler, D.J. & Ross, H.S. (1981). The effects of play on convergent and divergent problem solving. *Child Development, 52,* 1202-1210.

Piaget, J. (1962). *Play, dreams and imitation in childhood*. New York: W.W. Norton.

Rosen, C.E. (1974). The effect of sociodramatic play on problem solving among culturally disadvantaged children. *Child Development, 45,* 920-927.

Saltz, E. (1980). *Pretend play: A complex of variables influencing development*. Paper presented at the Annual Meeting of the American Psychological Association.

Saltz, E., & Brodie, J. (1982). Pretend-play training in childhood: A review and critique. In D.J. Pepler & K.H. Rubin (Eds.), *The play of children: Current theory and practice*. New York: S. Karger.

Saltz, E., Dixon, D., & Johnson, J. (1977). Training disadvantaged preschoolers on various fantasy activities: Effects on cognitive functioning and impulse control. *Child Development, 48,* 367-368.

Schirmer, B.R. (1989). Relationship between imaginative play and language development in hearing-impaired children. *American Annals of the Deaf, 134,* 219-222.

Seefeldt, V. (1984). Physical fitness in preschool and elementary school-aged children. *Journal of Physical Education, Recreation & Dance, 55* (9), 33-40.

Shure, M.B. (1981). Social competence as problem solving skill. In J.D. Wine and M.D. Smye (Eds.), *Social Competence* (pp. 158-185). New York: Guilford Press.

Smilanski, S. (1968). *The effects of sociodramatic play on disadvantaged preschool children*. New York: John Wiley.

Smith, P.K. & Dutton, S. (1979). Play and training in direct and innovative problem solving. *Child Development, 50,* 830-836.

Smith, P.K., & Syddall, S. (1978). Play and non-play tutoring in preschool children: Is it play or tutoring which matters? *British Journal of Education Psychology, 48,* 315-325.

Staniford, D.J. (1979). Natural movement for children. *Journal of Physical Education and Recreation, 50*(8), 14-17.

Sutton-Smith B. (1967). The role of play in child development. *Young Children, 22,* 361-370.

Sutton-Smith B. (1968). Novel responses to toys. *Merrill-Palmer Quarterly, 14,* 151-158.

Sutton-Smith, B. (1977). Play as adaptive potentiation. In P. Stevens (Ed.), *Studies in the anthropology of play*. Cornwall, NY: Leisure Press.

Sylva, K. (1977). Play and learning. In B. Tizard & D. Harvey (Eds.), *Biology of play*. London: Heineman.

Thompson, D., & Bowers, L. (Eds.). (1989). *Where our children play: Community park playground equipment*. Reston, VA: American Alliance for Health, Physical Education, Recreation and Dance.

Thompson, D., Bruya, L.D., & Crawford, M.E. (1990). In S.C. Wortham and J.L. Frost (Eds.), Maintaining play environments: training, checklists, and documentation. *Playgrounds for Young Children: American survey and perspectives*. Reston, VA: American Alliance for Health, Physical Education, Recreation and Dance.

U.S. Consumer Product Safety Commission (February 26, 1990). *Focus projects on playground surfaces—transmittal of hazard analysis*. United States Government memorandum. Washington, DC: U.S. Consumer Product Safety Commission.

Vygotsky, L.S. (1967). Play and its role in the mental development of the child. *Soviet Psychology, 12,* 62-76.

Wade, C. (1985). Effects of teacher training on teachers and children in playground settings. In J. Frost (Ed.), *When children play*. Washington, DC: Association for Childhood Education International.

Wortham, S.C., & Frost, J.L. (Eds.). (1990). *Playgrounds for young children: American survey and perspectives*. Reston, VA: American Alliance for Health, Physical Education, Recreation and Dance.

# Emergent Literacy:

## How Young Children Learn to Read and Write

New insights into how children learn to read and write are changing— dramatically—the teaching of literacy.

**Dorothy S. Strickland**

**Dorothy S. Strickland** is State of New Jersey Professor of Reading, Rutgers University, Graduate School of Education, 10 Seminary Place, New Brunswick, NJ 08903.

Judy, aged 4, and Mikey, aged 5, are huddled close together looking at a picture storybook. Mikey begins to "read" to Judy. He is self-assured as he turns each page, his face displaying the knowledge of someone very familiar with the text. Although the words he utters are not always exactly those appearing in the written text, his rendering is an extraordinarily close approximation. Moreover, the meanings conveyed by Mikey are consistently appropriate, as are his intonation and style of storybook reading.

Judy notices that Mikey's attention seems rooted to the pictures and asks, "Mikey, what are all those black marks at the bottom of the page for?"

With unwavering confidence, Mikey answers, "Oh, those are for people who can't read the story from the pictures."

Anecdotes such as this one have been told many times, most often as cute vignettes describing a child's view of the world. However, recent research on young children's literacy development has shed new meaning on these stories. Researchers investigating children's explorations into reading and writing now regard stories like this one of reading "imitation" as highly significant demonstrations of literacy learning. Although early childhood educators have always been aware that young children enter school with a remarkable knowledge of oral language, it is only recently that awareness of their written language has received serious attention.

Current investigations build on the work of John and Evelyn Dewey (1915/1962), who contrasted the functional, meaning-driven learning that children engage in before they enter school with "the practices of the schools where it is largely an adornment, a superfluity and even an unwelcome imposition" (p.2). More recently, the work of Marie Clay (1982) has provided the foundation for new ways of studying and thinking about early literacy. Teale and Sulzby (1989) outlined the distinctive dimensions of the new research. Among its chief characteristics, they found:

● The age range studied has been extended to include children 14 months and younger;

● Literacy is no longer regarded as simply a cognitive skill but as a complex activity with social, linguistic, and psychological aspects;

● Literacy learning is perceived as multidimensional and tied to the child's natural surroundings, so it is studied in both home and school environments.

**Literacy is no longer regarded as simply a cognitive skill but as a complex activity with social, linguistic, and psychological aspects.**

### New Perspectives

The study of literacy learning from the child's point of view has given us new insights into how young children learn to read and write.

*Learning to read and write begins early in life and is ongoing.* When two-year-old Josh rushed to his Mom with the newspaper in his hands and shouted, "Peanut, peanut," she was puzzled at first. After noticing the advertisement for his favorite brand of peanut butter, she was both surprised and pleased at the connections he was making. Young children who live in a "print-rich" environment are constantly observing and learning about written language. Most of their learning occurs as a natural part of their daily lives, not as something rare or mysterious.

*Learning to read and write are interrelated processes that develop in concert with oral language.* The old

Dorothy S. Strickland, "Emergent Literacy: How Young Children Learn to Read and Write," *Educational Leadership*, Vol. 47, No. 6, March 1990, pp. 18-23. Reprinted with permission of the Association for Supervision and Curriculum Development.

belief that children must be orally fluent before being introduced to reading and writing has been replaced with the view that the language processes—listening, speaking, reading, and writing—develop in an interdependent manner. Each informs and supports the other. Recognizing the value of informal activities with books and other print materials, one teacher in an urban program for four-year-olds sets aside a short period of time each day especially for "book browsing." Children are encouraged to find a book they like and a comfortable place to read. They may read alone or with a friend. Book browsing usually follows a read-aloud session. The teacher uses this time to observe children as they recreate renderings of stories read to them. Children discuss and argue about their favorite pictures and characters. The teacher is amazed at how these children, most of whom have rarely been read to at home, have become so absorbed with literature. They constantly make connections between the content in books and related discoveries inside and outside the classroom. And, not surprisingly, the books that have been read to them are also their favorites for independent browsing.

## Young children who live in a "print-rich" environment are constantly observing and learning about written language.

*Learning to read and write requires active participation in activities that have meaning in the child's daily life.* Participating in listing all of the items needed to prepare a particular recipe, for example, can be an important literacy event for a young child. Helping to check off each item as it is purchased and then used in the recipe makes oral and written language come together through an activity that has current meaning for the child. This immediacy makes the activity much more meaningful than one that serves merely as preparation for something to be learned in the future.

*Learning to read and write involves interaction with responsive others.* As parents, caregivers, and teachers become increasingly aware of the importance of young children's attempts to write, they take time to listen to the stories and messages evoked by scribbling, which may be intelligible only to the writer. One kindergarten teacher shared her amusement as she recalled how an eager writer confidently began to share a story elicited from an entire page of scribbling. After a few minutes of reading, the youngster stopped abruptly and in an apologetic tone exclaimed, "Oops, I wrote that twice!"

*Learning to read and write is particularly enhanced by shared book experiences.* Family storybook reading plays a special role in young children's literacy development, and researchers have learned much through observations of this familiar ritual. Sharing books with young children has long been recognized as a crucial aid to their language and literacy development and as a socializing process within families. Teachers and caregivers can further support this process when they use "big books" to encourage children to participate in reading. These allow children to see the print as the story is being read to them at school in much the same way they do when being read to at home. The highly predictable language and storylines of these picture storybooks permit groups of youngsters to "read along." Saying aloud the repeated refrains and rhymes with the reader helps give them a sense of what it means to be a reader.

### Traditional Perspectives
Traditionally held views about reading and writing differ fundamentally from the concept of emergent literacy. Although learning to speak is accepted as a natural part of the maturation process that doesn't require formal instruction, the mastery of reading and writing has been considered an arduous learning task, requiring a period of intense readiness. Only after children were thoroughly primed with the necessary prereading skills was "real" reading instruction begun. "Getting them ready" consisted largely of direct instruction in learning letter names, letter-sound relationships, and a vari-

## Content of interest and importance to children is the basis for learning language, learning through language, and learning about language.

ety of visual-perceptual tasks. The task of learning to write waited until reading was well underway. Children were considered literate only after their reading and writing began to approximate adult models.

In contrast, an emergent literacy curriculum emphasizes the ongoing development of skill in reading and writing and stresses participation in literacy activities that are meaningful and functional from the child's point of view. In operation, here is how the two viewpoints might look in a kindergarten classroom.

### Old Ways Versus New
Teacher A has spent considerable time planning a program that will ensure her students are ready for the 1st grade curriculum. Preparing them for the reading program is of particular interest to her, since that is a high priority of the parents and of the 1st grade teachers. The entire year has been blocked out so that each letter of the alphabet is given equal time for in-depth study.

Using a workbook as her guide, she teaches the children the names of the letters of the alphabet, their corresponding sounds, and how to trace them in upper and lower case. The children play numerous games and engage in a variety of activities based on each letter. *All* of the children go through *all* of the activities in the order prescribed by the workbook, regardless of their previous knowledge. Reading instruction takes place during a specified time each day, and except for occasionally reading a story aloud, the teacher does very little to make literacy connections beyond that time.

Since kindergarten children are

thought to be incapable of and uninterested in writing, the teacher makes no provision for it in the curriculum. She gives workbook unit tests periodically. These closely resemble the nationally normed readiness test that will be given at the end of the year. The tests help Teacher A to identify those children who may be falling behind. Although she tries to give these children extra help, the very nature of the program allows little differentiation of instruction.

Thus, children who fail to catch on early keep falling farther and farther behind. By the end of the year, they either repeat kindergarten or are assigned to transition classes. Even those children who do well on the standardized test must often repeat the phonics program in 1st grade—this is a consequence that has baffled both Teacher A and the 1st grade teachers.

Teacher B relies heavily on the classroom environment to prompt student involvement with literacy. There is an inviting reading center filled with books within reach of the children. Most of the titles are familiar, since the books have already been read aloud. A writing center is also available with plenty of writing tools, paper, magnetic letters, and an alphabet chart at the eye level of the children. Children are encouraged to use these centers daily. Printed materials are everywhere. There is a message board where they record important news and reminders each day, and personal mailboxes made of milk cartons encourage note writing. Teacher B values scribbles, pictures, and beginning attempts at spelling as engagement in the writing process.

Adorning the walls are numerous charts depicting graphs, poems, lists, and other important information related to the theme currently under study. Read-aloud time occurs at least twice each day. Stories, poems, and informational books are shared. Books with highly predictable language and storylines are stressed, since they encourage group participation and independent rereading in the reading center.

Although Teacher B has definite goals regarding the concepts and skills she wishes to foster, she sees no need to organize them hierarchically or to introduce them in isolation. Rather, the print environment and related activities are carefully orchestrated to allow children to build on what they already know about literacy, refine it, and use it for further learning. Although a unit of study about bugs might lead to a poem about a busy buzzy bumblebee and an opportunity to discuss the letter *b*, the emphasis is not placed on merely matching letter to sound but on helping children gain an understanding of a pattern in their language—that certain letters and sounds are often related.

Teacher B looks for evidence of these understandings and assesses learning through observation and analysis of children's independent reading and writing and through their participation during storytime. She is distressed when what she has documented about a child's knowledge is not always revealed on a standardized test.

In this classroom, literacy learning is not relegated to a specific time of day. Rather, it is integrated into everything that occurs throughout the day. Most important, content of interest and importance to children is the basis for learning language, learning through language, and learning about language.

It is important to recognize that both Teacher A and Teacher B are caring, concerned professionals. Each is a fine example of the theoretical framework from which she operates. Teacher A operates from a traditional readiness framework, in which the teacher is both keeper and dispenser of knowledge. Her lesson plans are segmented and preorganized into what are thought to be manageable bits and pieces, dispensed in small increments over a specified time. All children receive the same instruction, and little use is made of the knowledge about language that children bring with them to school.

Teacher B sees her role as that of facilitator of children's learning. The classroom environment is structured so that certain events are very likely to occur. Learning stems as much from these incidental literary events that occur by virtue of living within a print-rich environment as from the numerous daily activities planned to involve children in oral and written language. Teacher B expects differences in the way children respond to the activities she plans. She carefully monitors their responses and plans accordingly. She emphasizes helping children build on

## Child, teacher, and parent should celebrate each new learning by focusing on what is known rather than what is lacking.

what they already know in order to make connections to new learning.

### Issues for Instruction
The move toward full-day kindergartens and programs for four-year-olds has prompted increased concern for developmentally appropriate instruction. Many schools are addressing this concern by implementing programs reflecting an emergent literacy perspective.

Not surprisingly, interest in emergent literacy has brought with it a host of issues. The issues reflect the problems schools face as they attempt to serve a younger population and, at the same time, change perspective on a host of long-held beliefs. Issues that predominate are those related to the place of writing and invented spelling, the development of skills, assessment, and continuity.

*Writing and invented spelling.* Because the importance of paying attention to young children's writing is a relatively recent concern, teachers and parents often feel uneasy about how they should respond to children's scribbles, strings of letters, and one-letter words. Traditional writing lessons have been associated with neatness, correct spelling, and proper letter formation. Teachers need to learn as much as they can about the early spellings that children produce independently. Encouraging children to scribble and invent their own spellings does not lead them to think that phonetic spelling is systematically being taught; they are aware that their inventions may not conform to adult norms. The children know that, as with other areas of their development, they are simply functioning as young learners moving gradually toward adult standards. Child, teacher, and

Learning to read and write requires that children participate in activities that have meaning in their daily life. Learning must be interesting and important to the child. (United Nations photo by John Isaac)

parent should celebrate each new learning by focusing on what is known rather than what is lacking. Providing daily opportunities for varied experiences with literacy is the best assurance that children will begin to demonstrate what they know about writing and spelling as they compose stories and messages. Spelling errors should never be allowed to interfere with the composing process.

*The development of skills.* As educators, we must be careful not to give parents the impression that we are anti-skills; we are not. Rather, we need to help them see the differing ways that skills are developed through an emergent literacy perspective: not as an accumulation of information about a task but embedded within the child's growing ability to actually do the task. For example, children learn letter names and the sounds they represent as a part of the purposeful reading and

writing they do, not as a set of meaningless fragments of information. Stress is placed on helping children think with text and helping them to become independent learners. Unfortunately, poor and minority children—who would benefit most from holistic approaches that require them to think with text and encourage them to become independent learners—are often the least likely to get this type of instruction.

*Appropriate assessment.* Although standardized tests have undergone severe criticism as screening devices and evaluative measures of young children's literacy, they unfortunately continue to be highly regarded by some policy makers as definitive evidence of young children's learning (Chittendon 1989). Challenges regarding the assumptions underlying such tests, particularly the narrowness with which literacy is defined, raise serious ques-

tions about their use (Valencia & Pearson 1987). Children's initial explorations with literacy involve a variety of experiences with books and print, which may be used for assessment. Among these are their knowledge of print conventions, their understandings about the relationships between letters and sounds (invented spellings), and their growing interest in listening to and making sense of stories. Standardized tests tap but a few of these. Yet, even as early as kindergarten, standardized test results are used to make important decisions about placement, retention, and promotion.

The integration of assessment and instruction is fundamental to an emergent literacy perspective. Increased reliance on systematic observation, record keeping, and analysis of children's classroom participation and work products and less reliance on standardized tests are the hallmarks of student evaluation and teacher planning.

*The need for continuity.* Continuity in the early grades is critical. Children who are supported by an emergent literacy curriculum in the prekindergarten and kindergarten years, only to be faced with a subskills approach in 1st grade, will not only be confused, they will be unable to demonstrate what they do know about literacy. Collaborative curriculum decision making with teachers and administrators within a particular school and with those in the early childhood centers that feed into them is essential. In addition to supporting articulation between schools and grades within a school, educators must help parents understand new approaches to literacy that may be outside their experience. Children benefit from consistency in their lives. They function best when the adults they care about most reflect a comfortable harmony in their expectations and beliefs.

*References*

Chittendon, E. (1989). "Assessment of Young Children's Reading: Documentation as an Alternative to Testing." In D. S. Strickland & L. M. Morrow (Eds.) *Emerging Literacy: Young Children Learn to Read and Write.* Newark, Del.: International Reading Association.

Clay, M. (1982). *Observing Young Readers.* London: Heinemann.

Dewey, J. and Dewey, E. (1915/1962). *Schools of Tomorrow.* New York: Dutton.

Teale, W. and Sulzby, E. (1989). "Emergent Literacy: New Perspectives." In D. S. Strickland and L. M. Morrow (Eds.). *Emerging Literacy: Young Children Learn to Read and Write*, pp. 1-15. Newark, Del.: International Reading Association.

Valencia, S. and Pearson, P. D. (1987). "Reading Assessment: Time For a Change." *The Reading Teacher*, 40, 726–733.

---

**Resources on Emergent Literacy**

Bissex, G. (1980). *GNYS AT WRK: A Child Learns to Write and Read.* Cambridge, Mass.: Harvard University Press.

Clay, M. (1975). *What Did I Write?* Portsmouth, N.H.: Heinemann.

Ferreiro, E. & Teberosky. (1982). *Literacy Before Schooling.* Portsmouth, N.H.: Heinemann.

Genishi, C. & Dyson, A.H. (1984). *Language Assessment in the Early Years.* Norwood, N.J.: Ablex.

Hall, N. (1987). *The Emergence of Literacy.* Portsmouth, N.H.: Heinemann.

Harste, J., Woodward, V. & Burke, C. (1984). *Language Stories and Literacy Lessons.* Portsmouth, N.H.: Heinemann.

Holdaway, D. (1979). *The Foundations of Literacy.* New York: Ashton Scholastic.

Schickedanz, J. A. (1986). *More Than the ABC's: The Early Stages of Reading and Writing.* Washington, D.C: NAEYC.

Strickland, D. S. & Morrow, L. M. (Eds.) (1989). *Emerging Literacy: Young Children Learn to Read and Write.* Newark, Del.: International Reading Association.

Taylor, D. & Strickland, D. (1986). *Family Storybook Reading.* Portsmouth, N.H.: Heinemann.

Teale, W. & Sulzby, E. (Eds.). (1986). *Emergent Literacy: Writing and Reading.* Norwood, N.J.: Ablex.

Temple, C. A., Nathan, R. G., Burris, N.A. & Temple, F. (1988). *The Beginnings of Writing.* Boston, Mass.: Allyn and Bacon.

—Dorothy S. Strickland

# The Many Faces of Child Planning

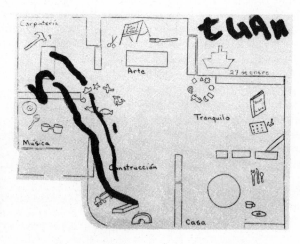

Mary Hohmann

High/Scope Educational Consultant

**C**hild planning has a central role in the High/Scope Preschool Curriculum. (At "planning time," a regular part of the High/Scope daily routine, each child discusses what he or she wants to do that day. At "work time," which follows planning, children carry out their stated plans.)

Through these daily experiences with planning, children learn to articulate their ideas and intentions. They develop a sense of control over their own actions and learn to trust their inner resources. Child planning also enhances the "learning potential" of the play that grows out of it. Motivational research suggests that children's intrinsic motivation to learn is greater in activities that they select themselves. In addition, specific research on the High/Scope Curriculum suggests that the play resulting from planning is more complex and challenging than unplanned play.

## Children's Plans: What to Expect

There are many good reasons, then, to encourage children to plan. As adults who wish to support child planning, we need to know **what to expect from young planners.** This article discusses some of the many possible forms that child plan-

ning can take and the implications for teachers and caregivers working to support child planning. Over the years, we've become increasingly aware of the range and variety of children's plans as we've observed planning time in many different High/Scope settings: in preschools, Head Start programs, day care settings, and home visit programs. From observational research conducted in High/Scope Curriculum programs, we've also learned about the planning process. Many of the insights about planning reported in this article come from a study conducted by C. Berry and K. Sylva of the plan-do-review process in British classrooms.

One dimension of child planning that most of these observers have noted is that **plans can be both verbal and nonverbal.** When asked what they would like to do, some young children respond by pointing, looking at a friend or toy, or simply going to one of the work areas and beginning to play. Other children respond in single words ("Cars," "Hammer"), phrases ("Over there by David"), brief sentences ("I want to make something for my mom"), or whole paragraphs ("First me and Lena are gonna' play dentist again. I'm being the dentist and she's the little girl. I'm gonna'

Reprinted from *High/Scope ReSource*, Spring/Summer 1991, pp. 4-6. Copyright © 1991 by High/Scope Press.

give her some special stuff so her mouth don't hurt"). Adults who value child planning are careful to acknowledge and support all plans that children make, whether or not they are expressed in words.

**Children's plans also vary in focus and complexity.** Based on their classroom observations, Berry and Sylva classified the plans children made into three different types: vague, routine, and elaborated plans.

**Vague plans** are minimal plans. In response to a question about what they are going to do, children just barely indicate a choice or beginning point, e.g., "Go over there," "House area," "Make something." Children who make such ambiguous plans seem to have an unclear picture in their minds of what they actually want to do. We have noticed that these children often end up doing one of three things: (1) going to a safe, unoccupied spot, picking up something like a doll or stuffed animal, and intently watching other busily engaged children; (2) wandering from place to place to explore the room and materials; or (3) seeking out an adult to join and follow them as they move about. Such children may be telling us: "I need to take in all the possibilities before I decide what to do or I want to do something really safe before I risk something new."

**Routine plans** are simple, specific plans in which children identify an activity, process, or material as their beginning intention, e.g., "Play with blocks," "Cutting-lots," "Computers." These children seem to have a clear picture in mind of themselves engaged in a particular experience or with a specific material. They know how they want to begin and generally get started right away, unless someone else is using the materials they had in mind.

**Elaborated plans** are more complex plans in which children mention an activity, process, or material as a beginning point, state a goal or out-

come, and also mention one or more steps or materials needed to carry out their intentions. Here are some examples of elaborated plans:

- "Make a Robin Hood hat. With a feather, a real one like Michael's."

- "Use the Construx. Make a telephone truck with a very tall ladder. And I think I'll put a cab for the driver. And balancers on the sides so it won't tip over."

These children have a more extensive mental picture of what they want to accomplish and how they will go about doing it. They are generally quite persistent in pursuing their original intentions in spite of problems that arise along the way. Another dimension of child planning often noted by experienced caregivers is that **children's plans may be perfunctory or real.** Children are usually enthusiastic about planning. Adults can hear this enthusiasm in the tone of children's voices as they plan, and see it in their bodies as they lean forward eagerly to describe their ideas. There are times, however, when this enthusiasm is missing. Even though a child may clearly state an intention, he or she seems to be just "going through the motions" of planning.

A perfunctory plan is a signal that something is impeding or delaying planning. Perhaps the child cannot make a genuine plan until she shares an upsetting experience that happened on the way to school. Or a child may be waiting for someone: "Sometimes Noah just says something, anything, at planning, because I think what he really wants to do is play with John, who hasn't arrived yet." When adults are alert to the possible reasons behind a halfhearted plan, they can respond by discussing the child's concerns; suggesting to Noah, for example, that he wait until his friend comes and then make a plan.

Another variable that affects the kinds of plans children make is their experience with the planning process. Observant adults recognize that **children's plans change over time** as children become familiar with available materials and playmates and their own ability to make choices and follow through on them. Children's plans usually become increasingly verbal as time passes; they also become more focused and complex. In a 1984 study of the development of the planning process in young children, W. Fabricius reported, for example, that most 3-year-old children can keep a goal in mind, but generally work toward it one step at a time. They deal with problems as they encounter them, rather than anticipating and planning for them. Between the ages of 3½ and 5½, however, Fabricius reported that children gradu-

COREY

scissors
Tijeras

paper
papel

I'm going to work in the rincon del arte. Make a fur pillow for my ~~mother~~ mom

# Setting the Stage for Child Planning

**W**herever children plan in an early childhood program — in the living room, on the playground, in the art area, under the table — the setting has an impact on the quality of children's plans. Here are three key principles of arranging a setting for child planning.

**Stability.** Planning flourishes in a stable setting, so keep the adult, the other children in the planning group, and the physical setting fairly constant. When changes are to be made, alert children in advance: "Tomorrow, Becki's mom is spending the day with us, so there will be three planning groups instead of just two. Becki, Sandy, and Will from our table, and Devon and Mel from Bob's table will meet with Becki's mom. Everybody else will plan in their regular groups."

**Visibility.** Conduct planning in a space where children can see all the materials, places, and people available to them. This makes it easier for them to imagine what they will do. The younger the children, the more they need to be able to see the materials they are planning to use. In some early childhood settings — particularly in home day care, for example — children may not be able to see all the play spaces and materials as they make their plans. Adults can compensate for limited visibility in various ways: by touring the play spaces with children before planning, by bringing some of the available materials to the planning setting, or by planning in different parts of the center from time to time so that different materials are visible.

**Intimacy.** Planning is basically an intimate exchange between a child planner and a supportive adult in which the child indicates an intention and a way of acting on it, and the adult enters into a dialogue with the child about this plan. Since planning with a group of children involves a series of these one-to-one conversations, the smaller the group of children sharing their plans with an adult, the more intimate and unhurried is the planning exchange. In their study of the High/Scope plan-do-review process, Berry and Sylva found that children in smaller, more intimate, planning groups tended to make more detailed plans. They found that in planning groups of 1–4 children, 60 percent made detailed plans, while in planning groups of 8–10 children, only 15 percent made detailed plans. To explain these findings, they speculated that "staff become more concerned in larger groups with 'getting through' and not losing the attention of the group than in the quality of each child's plan."

Of course, in programs in which larger planning groups are a necessity, adults should be aware that encouraging children to make complex plans is *not impossible* in a larger group, only *more difficult.* Though the adults will need to engage the attention of the group (for example, by using role play, songs, games, tours, or chants), the focus should be on the individual child's plan. Adults can create an intimate atmosphere by listening attentively to the child's plan and using other one-to-one planning strategies. Another way to deal with the problem of too-large planning groups is to stagger the planning schedule: planning intensively with three or four children at a time, as they arrive in the morning. When adults are convinced of the importance of in-depth planning for each child, they usually find creative ways to make it happen.

# Two Steps to Success

*Planning involves a series of highly personal, individual conversations that occur in a group setting. The following steps take into account both the group and individual aspects of planning.*

**Step one: Engage the attention and interest of the planning group through a game-like activity, a special task, or challenge.** For example, children might explore a collection of new materials; take a guided tour of the center in a make-believe vehicle; use special props or materials while making a plan; use pantomime, drawing, or writing to plan; participate in games or role play to decide whose turn it is to plan next (e.g., "Today we'll pass the planning pillow. When the music stops, whoever has the pillow will plan next").

**Step two: Engage in one-on-one exchanges with each child.** Talk about his or her plan. Talk to the child at his or her own level. Create an intimate, unhurried atmosphere by showing the child your genuine interest in his or her plan, and by listening and observing attentively as the child expresses an intention. Encourage the child to talk further about his or her plan by commenting or asking questions about materials, space, sequence, prior related work, and other details. Deal sensitively with any concerns that may be impeding planning.

---

ally gain the ability to plan a multistep course of action, foreseeing problems and ways of dealing with them before they launch into action. For example, a 5-year-old might incorporate anticipated problems in her plan: "I'll make a bird house. I'll use the big cardboard blocks for the walls, but I'll need a big enough board or something else for the roof. If there isn't a piece of wood big enough, maybe a piece of cardboard will work."

## Adult Support for Planning

Children's plans, then, come in a wide variety of forms. The range of strategies adults use to support child planning is just as wide. Here we discuss just a few of the most important support strategies adults can use. We don't focus on **group** planning strategies — ways of engaging the interest of the entire planning group as each child takes a turn to plan — but on **individual** planning strategies — ways of enhancing the conversation with each child about his or her intentions. (For some examples of group planning strategies, see "One-to-One Planning Strategies" sidebar.)

One of the primary ways you can make these individual conversations more meaningful is to **listen attentively as the child states an initial plan.** Rushing through planning can cause children to feel hurried and anxious. After you question a child about his or her plan, it is important to pause and give each child ample time to respond. Whatever the child says or does tells you something important and suggests ways you might respond. Listen and observe for both nonverbal and verbal planning. If the child's communication is nonverbal, you may want to restate it in words or engage the child in a dialogue to clarify his or her intentions. Listen also for vague, routine, and elaborated plans to gain some idea of how well the child is able to picture the desired action sequence. Then think of ways you might help him or her foresee it more completely. Listen for perfunctory plans and deal sensitively with the issues behind them, reassuring children who are not ready to plan that it's okay to wait for a while.

Once children have indicated a plan in some way, the next step for adults is to **encourage children to develop their plans further.** At this point it makes some sense to distinguish between two groups of planners, nonverbal/vague planners and routine/elaborate planners. Interestingly enough, Berry and Sylva's research suggests that adults tend to question the first group extensively; the second, hardly at all. In their analysis, adults tend to keep after the vague or nonverbal planners until they arrive at a more complete picture of what they might do, but pass up the opportunity to converse with and question children who have the potential for thinking through and articulating quite elaborate plans. It's important to remember that *all* children need the opportunity to expand on and clarify their plans — even those who've stated an initial intention fairly clearly. There are many ways adults can encourage children to develop their ideas further. For example, they can talk with children about where they will work, the materials they will use, the sequence of their actions, and other details, and they can discuss the child's prior related work.

Is there time for a thoughtful planning conversation with each child? Yes, there is. First, even though such conversations take longer than a routine question-and-answer exchange (e.g., "What are you going to do?" "Play with blocks"), they don't take that much longer. In fact, thoughtful planning conversations often go rapidly, because they are intense and full of the unexpected. In addition, when adults converse

attentively with children about their plans, children are generally able to get started with less adult help — because many potential problems and choices have already been dealt with. This leaves the adult free to focus on conversations with other children about *their* plans. In this sense, in-depth planning with each child is a group management tool, since well-conceived plans generally lead the planner to a focused and appropriate set of actions.

*Note: For more information on the research cited here, see Berry, C. F., & Sylva, K. (1987, unpublished),* The plan-do-review cycle in High/Scope: Its effect on children and staff *(write Carla Berry, Chicago AEYC, 410 S. Michigan Ave., Chicago, IL 60605); and Fabricius, W. V. (1984, doctoral dissertation),* The development of planning in young children *(available from UMI, 300 N. Zeeb Rd., Ann Arbor, MI 48106).*

# Writing in Kindergarten

## *Helping Parents Understand the Process*

### Kathleen A. Dailey

*Kathleen A. Dailey is Assistant Professor, Elementary Education Department, Edinboro University of Pennsylvania and Kindergarten Teacher, Miller Research Learning Center (campus laboratory school).*

As a parent, how would you react to this work from a kindergarten child? Would you respond in the following manner?

"I can't believe Miss Davis let Tommy bring home a paper with so many mistakes."

"Doesn't she take time to spell the words for the children?"

"Shouldn't Tommy learn to make the letters correctly first?"

"How will he learn to spell correctly if she lets him spell like that?"

"He doesn't even know how to read yet and they expect him to write!"

Many parents may have this initial reaction, especially if the teacher has not prepared the parents for such work. Research in homes and schools suggests that the writing process of the child can be enriched by communication between teachers and parents. When parents first encounter the idea of writing programs for kindergartners, they need to be educated about the program. The following research-based answers to some of the most common questions are helpful in orienting kindergartners' parents to an early writing program.

**Figure 1.** *The flowers are coming out of the ground.*

### How does my child learn to read and write?

Literacy, the process of learning to read and write, begins at home long before children enter school (Ferreiro & Teberosky, 1982; Hall, 1987; Schickedanz, 1986). This process does not officially begin at a particular age; rather, it develops as children gain experience with language and print. The two processes, reading and writing, develop simultaneously.

A variety of activities, which can be a part of daily living in many homes, enhance literacy development. Children learn purposes for reading and writing as the parent and child sing a lullaby, share a picture book, make a shopping list or write a telephone message. Many children *read* environmental print, such as the names on cereal boxes and restaurant signs. Likewise, children learn how a book *works* and realize that print conveys meaning as they partake in a variety of experiences with books. As 2-year-old Ryan sits propped on his mother's lap with a book, she points to the cat and says, "What's that?" "Ki-Ki," says Ryan. Young Ryan gathers meaning from the pictures and the dialogue with his mother. With increased book knowledge, he comes to understand that the black marks on the page tell a story as well as the pictures.

At the same time, children begin

to experiment with different forms of writing that meet their needs and interests. Children may begin to copy letters and words from books, to write lines of squiggle or letters or to ask an adult to make models of letters for them. Children may write the names of family members and spellings of common objects. Writing interests may further develop as children choose to write letters, send postcards to friends, cast their superhero as the main character of their story or write a poem based on a favorite story, such as *In a Dark, Dark Wood* (Melser & Cowley, 1980) (see Figure 2).

The kindergarten reading program should be an extension of reading and writing that began in the home. It should help young children draw upon their past experiences to increase their understanding of how reading and writing function for specific and meaningful purposes (Dyson, 1984; Hall, 1987; Teale, 1982; Teale & Sulzby, 1989).

### Do drawing and scribbling help my child learn how to write?

Children's first attempts at authorship are frequently accompanied by a drawing. Drawing is an integral part of the writing process because it is a way for children to plan and organize their written text (Dyson, 1988; Strickland & Morrow, 1989). A drawing can tell a story that written words cannot yet convey for the young child. Parents should accept their children's drawings and encourage them to talk about these drawings. Some researchers encourage parents and teachers to write down what children dictate so they can see their own speech put into words.

Young children will frequently scribble. Scribble drawing takes on a circular form. As children intend these marks to be writing, the scribbles take on a linear, controlled form. A page full of scribbles may be a letter to Grandma or a restaurant menu. When asked to *read* this message, the child may first glance at the picture then point

to the scribbles as he or she relays the content of the written work. As the child's print awareness increases, these scribbled marks become more refined and take on the characteristics of print (see Figures 3 & 4).

### How can I encourage my child to write at home?

Research indicates that children engage in literacy events more in the home than in school (Schickedanz & Sullivan, 1984). This evidence supports the importance of parents as writing models. Observational studies of young children reveal that adults involved in writing behaviors such as writing a letter, making a grocery list or writing a check are often a stimulus for a child's early attempts to write (Lamme, 1984; Schickedanz & Sullivan, 1984; Taylor, 1983). When chil-

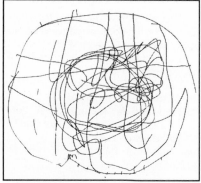

**Figure 3.** *Random scribbling*

**Figure 2.** *Poem based on the story,* In a Dark, Dark Wood
*On a dark, dark path*
*In a dark, dark house*
*On a dark, dark stair*
*In a dark, dark room*
*Boo! Ha-ha-ha*

**Figure 4.** *Controlled scribbling*

dren see adults writing for a variety of purposes, they discover ways in which writing is useful and meaningful.

Parents can create an environment that accepts and values writing by providing their children with many tools for writing. A variety of unlined paper and many different writing tools (markers, pencils, pens or chalk) are important materials for this craft. Children enjoy a variety of writing media. They may like the feel of writing letters or words in a tray of sand, pudding or jello. They may write using a computer or typewriter. Rich (1985) suggests using a "writing suitcase" as a portable writing station. The suitcase is filled with paper, markers, crayons, plastic letters and stencils. The child has access to the suitcase, is responsible for its contents and is free to add new items. The child is an active learner in the process. The writing that is produced is limited only by imagination.

**Aren't paper-and-pencil activities, like workbook pages, the best way of learning to read and write?** Children learn through direct participation in meaningful activities. When that learning is a complex process (like reading) rather than a skill (like tying shoes), it is even more important that the conditions of meaningful participation be met. Music is a good analogy. If we want young children to develop their musical abilities, we begin with enjoyment, not worksheets on musical notation. We accept their early efforts as well, realizing that the toddler who bounces in rhythm to a popular song may become a dancer or the child who pounds on a xylophone may play a musical instrument someday.

Reading programs that *teach* children to *read* and *write* through the use of dittos and workbook pages reflect practices that are developmentally inappropriate for young children (Elkind, 1986) for at least two reasons. First, the child's needs are not taken into consideration when the emphasis is on *every* child doing the same thing at the same time. Manuel has recognized the *M* at the beginning of his name and on the McDonald's sign since he was 3 years old. Manuel can write his own name and the word *MOM*. Manuel brings

**Table 1**

**THE ASSOCIATION BETWEEN LANGUAGE DEVELOPMENT AND WRITING DEVELOPMENT**

| Language | Writing | Spelling |
|---|---|---|
| Babbling | Random scribbling | |
| Holophrase—one word utterance is used to express a complete thought: "Mama" means "Mommy I want to get up." | | One letter spelling—one or two letters represent entire sentences or phrases: *H* = This is my house. |
| Repetition | Controlled scribbling—the same forms or the same letters are repeated as the child progresses toward mastery of that form. | Writing the same letters or words in order to attain mastery |
| Expanded vocabulary of frequently used words | | Incorporation of conventional spellings with invented spellings |
| Grammatical rules are applied to speech. "I want up." replaces "Me up." | | Transitional spelling—using simple rules to spell |
| Overgeneralization—internalization of grammar rules, but applied to more cases than those in which they work: "He runned after me." | | Overgeneralization—reliance on rules applied in previous spellings, yielding errors due to inconsistencies of the language. "LETUS" (lettuce) |
| More precise speech | | More precise spelling |

Adapted from Lamme, 1984.

home a paper with neatly circled *Ms*. As he hands the paper to his father, Manuel replies, "It was boring!" Molly completed the same paper yet is unable to tell you the letter name. The way and manner in which children learn varies for each individual. Approaches that may be effective for one child may be ineffective for the next.

Second, workbook writing directs the focus away from the child. "When worksheets and phonics lessons are given to young children all the initiative comes from the teacher. When this happens, teachers unintentionally prevent children from developing their own natural initiative" (Willert & Kamii, 1985). On the other hand, activities such as drawing and writing about a trip to the zoo, reading alphabet books and enjoying songs and fingerplays about sounds and letters allow children to take an active role in learning to read and write.

**I have difficulty figuring out what my child has written. How can I better understand what she writes?**
The writing of children develops in overlapping stages that parallel language development (Table 1).

As children make the transition from scribbling to more conventional forms of writing, they may represent their written work with a random ordering of letters such as *mTEo* to represent house. This is followed by stages that reveal the child's understanding of letter-sound correspondence, which is a first step toward reading (Chomsky, 1971). These stages are referred to as "invented spelling" because children apply what they know about sounds and letters to their early writing. It is common, however, for children to be in several stages of spelling development at once and revert to earlier stages as they experiment with writing. The stages of invented spelling development are shown in Table 2.

These early attempts are systematic even though the spelling is unconventional (Richgels, 1987), as shown in the spelling of *monster*, *grass* and *class* (Table 2). This systematic process enables children to take control of their learning and become independent writers.

**Should I correct my child's written work?**
When a child says "ba" for bottle, parents understand what the child

is trying to say and accept the pronunciation at the child's stage of development. Spelling development should be treated similarly. Early writing contains many words spelled unconventionally because children experiment with written form at particular stages of development. Children need models who are supportive and patient. When Jane asks, "Mommy, do you spell *tree*, T-R-E?" her mother responds, "That's the way it sounds, but that's not the way it is spelled. It's *T-R-E-E*." This response tells children that there are conventional spellings, but we also accept the way they spell. Criticism of misspelled words makes children fearful of making mistakes. Under these conditions, research shows that they write less and less well, sticking with *safe* known words. What is worse, they learn to dislike writing because they see it as a test rather than as a means of creative expression.

Parents may help children sound out words or spell words for them, but at the same time provide materials that foster independence in writing. Picture dictionaries provide children with an early reference tool. Parents need to show children how the dictionary is set up and how to locate words using the alphabet and picture cues. Parents can help children compile their own personal dictionary of frequently used words, such as objects in the home or names of family members. A set of words on cards serves the same purpose (Ashton-Warner, 1965). An accompanying illustration may help the child use the word cards independently. Understanding spelling development and fostering independence in writing through positive and nurturing practices are essential to a child's healthy attitude toward writing.

**My child will write letters correctly one day and reverse them the next. Is that normal?**
When parents of young children see a backwards *S* or *2*, they often

### Table 2
### THE DEVELOPMENT OF INVENTED SPELLINGS

| Stage 1 | Use of initial consonant to represent an entire word | M for monster<br>G for grass<br>C for class |
|---------|-------------------------------------------------------|----------------------------------------------|
| Stage 2 | Initial and final consonants serve as word boundaries | MR<br>GS<br>CS |
| Stage 3 | Inclusion of medial consonant; awareness of blends; may divide blend | MSTR<br>GRS<br>CALS |
| Stage 4 | Initial, final and medial consonants and vowel place-holder. Vowel is incorrect | MESTR<br>GRES<br>CLES |
| Stage 5 | Conventional Spelling | MONSTER<br>GRASS<br>CLASS |

Adapted from: Gentry, 1981; Graves, 1983; Lamme, 1984 & Strickland & Morrow, 1989.

worry that their child has a learning disability. Actually, such reversals are very prevalent in kindergarten, 1st and 2nd grade. It is common for children to experiment with reversed writing. Sometimes letters are reversed; sometimes they are placed upside down. These characteristics, including a tendency to write in any direction, are all related (Schickedanz, 1986). Children need practice with directionality and the orientation of printed symbols. Until children have attained consistency in left-to-right and top-to-bottom orientation and formed a mental image of what the letter *b* looks like, for example, they may continue to reverse written symbols. "All exploration is perfectly normal; it is a healthy sign that children are investigating print, getting used to it and figuring out how it works" (Marzollo & Sulzby, 1988, p. 83). If a child consistently reverses written symbols beyond 2nd grade, a parent may want to seek advice. Generally, however, reversals are not a cause for concern at an early age.

### What should I look for in my child's writing program?

"Everywhere I look, I see children's written work," comments a visitor to the kindergarten classroom. This atmosphere reflects one in which young writers have been experimenting with different types of print since their first day of school. Each time children sit down to write, they increase their knowledge of written form just through the act itself. At the writing center, children are working in their journals or writing a story. Writing, however, is not limited to one area of the room. In the block area, Erin made a sign that says *CASO* (castle). In the kitchen area, Patrick posted the special food for the day, *APLS* (apples). Meanwhile, the post office clerk is busy delivering letters addressed to Santa Claus (see Figure 5).

Young children's writing, speaking and action are closely re-

**Figure 5.** *Letter to Santa Claus*
*To Santa Claus*
*You are nice.*
*Get me a present.*
*I would like a Barbie.*
*I like you.*

lated. Early writing is not only a paper-and-pencil activity, but also a social process. In her observation of children, Dyson (1981) comments, "I saw no quiet, solemn-faced scholars, struggling to break into print. Rather, I saw (and heard) writers using both pencil and voice to make meaning on the empty page" (p. 777). In a writing environment one may observe children engaged in the following activities:

- Asking each other for help
  *How did you spell tyrannosaurus?*

- Planning and creating
  *I'm going to put brontosaurus in the water.*

- Rehearsing ideas
  *My brontosaurus will be eating plants.*

- Questioning each other about their products
  *What is your dinosaur doing?*

- Sharing and reading their work to each other
  *The Brotsrs is RunIng AWAW.* (*The brontosaurus is running away.*)

- Evaluating their work
  *That was a long sentence. I'll have to make more room on the paper next time.*
  
  (Adapted from Lamme, 1984)

In a quality kindergarten writing program, the child's teacher serves as model and facilitator of the writing process, providing the

children with an environment rich in opportunities to use and create written materials (Rich, 1985). The teacher observes children write, confers with them and accepts their work. "Teachers who grow writers in their classrooms also regard pieces of writing as growing things to be nurtured rather than as objects to be repaired and fixed" (Bissex, 1981).

### What does the teacher do during the writing conference with my child?

The writing conference serves as a personal and meaningful interaction between the child and the teacher; both are learners in the process. Early in the school year, Ms. Hart established a routine for writing conferences. She chose the couch area as a comfortable place where the children can share their written work. Chris knows that his conference with Ms. Hart is every Tuesday. As the other children in the class continue to write, Chris takes his folder, journal, personal dictionary and a pencil and sits with Ms. Hart on the couch. This time together provides Ms. Hart with insights into Chris's writing abilities.

Throughout the writing conference, Ms. Hart asks questions that guide the process (Table 3). This format eventually allows the children to go through the same process independently as they reflect on their own writing. She focuses on the child throughout the conference, allowing the child to take the lead. Through careful observation of written work, the teacher assesses what the child already knows about written language. She may notice, for example, that a child uses letter-sound correspondence correctly for *D* when writing *dog* (*DG*) but confuses *B* and *P* when spelling *boat* (*PT*). She may have the child write for her during the conference to observe the process firsthand. Ms. Hart keeps detailed records of the child's progress and makes teaching recommendations based on specific needs.

## 5. CURRICULAR APPLICATIONS: Content and Process

### Conclusion

Parents and teachers need to recognize that ". . . every child who can talk has the capacity to learn to write and also to seize upon its possibilities with enthusiasm" (Smith, 1981, p. 792). Parents and teachers have the responsibility to create an environment for children that develops confidence and success in writing. When parents and teachers understand the processes underlying writing development, they can help children participate in meaningful home and school activities that promote its growth. Thus, home and school partnerships built upon communication and understanding provide children with a firm foundation for successful writing experiences.

Acknowledgment: The author gratefully thanks Mary Renck Jalongo for her assistance in reviewing this article.

### References

Ashton-Warner, S. (1965). *Teacher*. NY: Simon and Schuster.

Bissex, G. (1981). Growing writers in classrooms. *Language Arts, 58,* 785-791.

Chomsky, C. (1971). Write first, read later. *Childhood Education, 47,* 296-299.

Dyson, A. H. (1981). Oral language: The rooting system for learning to write. *Language Arts, 58,* 776-791.

Dyson, A. H. (1984). N spell my grandmama: Fostering early thinking about print. *The Reading Teacher, 38,* 262-270.

Dyson, A. H. (1988). Appreciate the drawing and dictating of young children. *Young Children, 43*(3), 25-32.

Elkind, D. (1986). Formal education and early childhood education: An essential difference. *Phi Delta Kappan, 67,* 631-636.

Ferreiro, E., & Teberosky, A. (1982). *Literacy before schooling*. London: Heinemann.

Gentry, J. R. (1981). Learning to spell developmentally. *The Reading Teacher, 34,* 378-381.

Graves, D. (1983). *Writing: Teachers and children at work*. Portsmouth, NH: Heinemann.

Hall, N. (1987). *The emergence of literacy*. Portsmouth, NH: Heinemann.

Lamme, L. L. (1984). *Growing up writing*. Washington, DC: Acropolis.

Marzollo, J., & Sulzby, E. (1988). See Jane read! See Jane write! *Parents, 63*(7), 80-84.

Melser, J., & Cowley, J. (1980). *In a dark, dark wood*. San Diego, CA: The Wright Group.

Rich, S. J. (1985). The writing suitcase. *Young Children, 40*(5), 42-44.

Richgels, D. J. (1987). Experimental reading with invented spelling (ERIS): A preschool and kindergarten method. *The Reading Teacher, 40,* 522-529.

Schickedanz, J. (1986). *More than the ABC's: The early stages of reading and writing*. Washington, DC: National Association for the Education of Young Children.

Schickedanz, J. A., & Sullivan, M. (1984). Mom, what does U-F-F spell? *Language Arts, 61,* 7-17.

Smith, F. (1981). Myths of writing. *Language Arts, 58,* 792-798.

Strickland, D., & Morrow, L. M. (1989). Young children's early writing development. *The Reading Teacher, 42,* 426-427.

Taylor, D. (1983). *Family literacy—Young children learning to read and write*. Exeter, NH: Heinemann.

Teale, W. H. (1982). Toward a theory of how children learn to read and write naturally. *Language Arts, 59,* 555-570.

Teale, W. H., & Sulzby, E. (1989). Emergent literacy: New perspectives. In D. S. Strickland & L. M. Morrow (Eds.), *Emerging literacy: Young children learn to read and write* (pp. 1-15). Newark, DE: International Reading Association.

Willert, M. K., & Kamii, C. (1985). Reading in kindergarten. Direct vs. indirect teaching. *Young Children, 40*(4), 3-9.

---

### Table 3
### INAPPROPRIATE AND APPROPRIATE RESPONSES
### USED DURING WRITING CONFERENCES

| Inappropriate Responses | Appropriate Responses |
|---|---|
| "Allison, will you read this? I can't figure out what it says." | "What are you writing about Allison?" |
| "What is it?" | "Tell me about your picture." |
| "Can't you write about something else besides the zoo?" | "Do you like writing about the zoo?" |
| "Tomorrow, I think you should write about our field trip." | "What do you think you will write about next?" |
| "The next time I want you to figure out how to spell these words by yourself." | "Allison, how did you go about writing this?" |

Adapted from Graves, 1983.

# Science-Centered Curriculum in Elementary School

*A promising model for elementary schools makes science meaningful to students by connecting content in engaging ways with other subjects in the curriculum.*

LYNDA C. GREENE

**Lynda C. Greene** is an Educational Consultant, 124 Felton Dr., Menlo Park, CA 94025.

While construction was under way on the permanent home for Laurel Wood School in the rapidly growing Salinas City School District, Vicki Ogborn's 1st grade students were housed in an adjacent portable building. Recognizing a unique learning opportunity, Mrs. Ogborn embraced the new school's development as the subject of a year-long theme—Bit by Bit—Building It Together—through which her students carefully observed and learned from the construction process.

Starting with design and planning, students developed scale drawings of their bedrooms with the help of their parents. Later, they produced blueprints in their classroom. Soon the 1st grade room was filled with an array of building materials—wooden blocks, legos, tinkertoys, and toothpicks—as students constructed their own designs. Next, they studied rocks and soil and experimented with core sampling. Then, while the soundproofing was being installed in the new school, they explored the properties of sound. Language arts was also woven into the theme. After reading *The Three Little Pigs,* the children made models compar-

ing houses made of straw, sticks, and bricks. *Mike Mulligan and His Steam Shovel* served as a springboard for students to write and illustrate their impressions of the construction process.

Finally, as the building was being landscaped, the 1st graders learned about plants. (See fig. 1.)

Mrs. Ogborn's yearlong theme provided a meaningful structure to connect

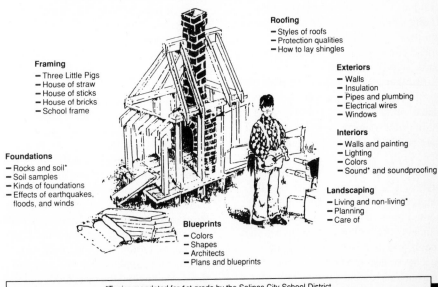

### FIGURE 1

### BIT - BY - BIT: BUILDING IT TOGETHER

Vicki Ogborn's 1st Grade Theme, Laurel Wood School, Salinas City School District

**Framing**
- Three Little Pigs
- House of straw
- House of sticks
- House of bricks
- School frame

**Foundations**
- Rocks and soil*
- Soil samples
- Kinds of foundations
- Effects of earthquakes, floods, and winds

**Blueprints**
- Colors
- Shapes
- Architects
- Plans and blueprints

**Roofing**
- Styles of roofs
- Protection qualities
- How to lay shingles

**Exteriors**
- Walls
- Insulation
- Pipes and plumbing
- Electrical wires
- Windows

**Interiors**
- Walls and painting
- Lighting
- Colors
- Sound* and soundproofing

**Landscaping**
- Living and non-living*
- Planning
- Care of

*Topics mandated for 1st grade by the Salinas City School District.

her students' learning in all subject areas. Clearly, they learned that science is all around them—a part of their everyday lives—and will view their completed school with a special perspective.

## Science as the Curriculum Centerpiece

This inventive 1st grade curriculum demonstrates the fundamentals of the Mid-California Science Improvement Program (MCSIP), based on Susan Kovalik's integrated, thematic learning model (Kovalik 1986). The project got its start in 1987, when the David and Lucile Packard Foundation looked at the status of science education in Monterey County's elementary schools. A survey of 350 teachers in 7 districts yielded predictable findings: teachers felt that they did not have the training required to teach science, the access to appropriate materials, nor the strategies for integrating science into their overcrowded days. These and others findings are consistent with those reported in Science for All Americans, published by the American Association for the Advancement of Science (AAAS, Rutherford et al. 1989). As a result of this preliminary research, MCSIP was initiated in 1987, with a grant from the Packard Foundation. The first year, 60 teachers in 11 schools joined the program.

The project's purpose is to assist and support elementary school teachers in implementing science education, on a daily basis, for all students as an integral part of the educational program. Using a hands-on, application-oriented approach, the project emphasizes a balanced curriculum, including physical, earth, and life sciences.

Another aspect of the program's philosophy is that a classroom should be a place marked by trust and respect. That is, in order to learn, students must feel safe and be free of fear, anger, and anxiety. Cooperative learning and carefully planned groupwork are used extensively. The program also stresses the importance of meaningful content presented in an enriched environment. Students often choose their own assignments and materials, allowing the teacher to accommodate a range of learning styles and abilities. Finally, MCSIP acknowledges that learning

> # The program actually turns the tables on the design of the school day, making science the ingredient that unites all other subjects.

takes time and that each child learns at his or her own pace.

## An Integrated, Thematic Approach

The program asks each teacher to develop a theme for the year, identifying major components for each month. The newly approved California Science Framework advances this strategy of themes as its first recommendation (California State Department of Education 1990). Such an approach provides a scaffold to unite the entire curriculum, avoiding the common fragmentation that occurs with separate, unrelated subject areas. The diversity of the themes—which blend science, language arts, social studies, mathematics, and fine arts—illustrates the creativity of the teachers. They include:

- The World Beneath My Feet
- A Shovelful of Dirt
- All Around You—Between, Below, Beyond
- Keepers of the Earth
- California, the Edge
- Magic, Marbles, and Motors: The Many Faces of Motion

Unlike other improvement programs, MCSIP does not ask teachers to add yet another subject to an already jam-packed day. Instead, the program actually turns the tables on the design of the school day, making science the ingredient that unites all other subjects.

Students read and write about science. Working in groups, they investigate and solve problems requiring measurement and computation. They learn about the innumerable applications of science to the world beyond the classroom and the exciting associated career opportunities.

Finally, the fine arts complement and reinforce the thematic approach, as students express their understanding through art, music, and movement. The yearly theme, which is displayed in the classroom, represents a year's worth of work and learning that showcases science as the fully integrated centerpiece of the curriculum.

## Teacher Training and Coaching

The success of the project is attributable in part to the well-planned training and the subsequent coaching that occurs in the classrooms. Each summer, during an intensive two-week training institute, teachers learn effective strategies for teaching science, study science content appropriate to their grade levels, and develop highly personalized, integrated science curriculum based upon the themes of their choice. Scientists from the University of California, Lawrence Hall of Science, and San Jose State University helped develop the science content portion of the training.

As teachers design activities, project staff urge them to strive to include all levels of thinking: knowledge, comprehension, application, analysis, evaluation, and synthesis. By the end of the institute, teachers have developed their themes for the year, and they receive a stipend to purchase science materials.

When they return to school in the fall, teachers are supported by the school principal and their fellow MCSIP teachers. In addition, MCSIP staff provide continuous staff development and classroom coaching. Program coaches visit each school at least twice a month to demonstrate lessons, observe the teachers in action, or provide consultation. The impact of the summer training is evident back in the classrooms, where renditions of Bloom's Taxonomy and references to Hart's (1983) ``brain-compatible'' theories of learning are displayed at all grade levels. To reinforce their summer learning and further develop their skills, teachers attend periodic training sessions.

## Early Evaluation Findings

With the assistance of the Stanford University School of Education, an early evaluation of the project was conducted. Evaluators measured the attitudes of students and teachers and assessed the program's impact on the science achievement of the participating students. At the end of the second year, students' achievement showed substantial and statistically significant gains.

Developed by the National Assessment of Educational Progress (1987), test items covered biology, physical science, earth science, and an NAEP area called the "process of inquiry." Of the students taking part in the project, 78 percent improved their scores, exceeding the NAEP nationwide figures and leading one evaluator to conclude that "MCSIP proved to be successful in improving student achievement in science" (Okamoto 1989).

In the spring of the project's third year, the Packard Foundation invited James Rutherford, Director of AAAS's Project 2061, to visit some project schools and classrooms. Rutherford concluded that MCSIP had "unusual promise," which was "quite possibly of significance nationally." Specifically, he commented on:

> The insightful use of science, substantive science, as the conceptual focus for instruction in reading, arithmetic, social studies, and other subjects.

> An approach to changing the attitudes, skills, and knowledge of elementary teachers that promises to be more than superficial and fleeting, that seems to foster teacher creativity, and that may be affordable. (Rutherford 1990)

### Impressions from the Classroom

Aside from the more formal findings, the effectiveness of MCSIP can be seen in the classrooms of project teachers.

For example, on one such visit, I observed young scientists in Janet Conn's 1st grade class at Flood School in the Ravenswood School District as they gingerly retrieved earthworms from their muddy containers. At last "Michael Jackson," a particularly recalcitrant worm, was located by the probing finger of a delighted child. Placing the specimen between two paper towels, one wet and one dry, she watched to see which surface "Michael" preferred. Armed with a magnifier, she searched for attributes Mrs. Conn had described earlier.

These children were studying science

**Students work cooperatively in small groups helping each other, learning from one another, and sharing the joy of discovery.**

through the theme, Over in the Meadow. Like her fellow project teachers, Mrs. Conn provides direct instruction in science and then orchestrates opportunities for her students to hypothesize, experiment, draw conclusions, and record their observations on such topics as: the senses, weather, rocks and soil, nutrition, birds of prey, life underground, metamorphosis, new life, and plants. Students work cooperatively in small groups helping and learning from one another, and sharing the joy of discovery.

The program has proven to have broad applicability over its four-year existence. Both teachers and principals report its success with educationally disadvantaged students as well as those identified as gifted. In addition, language differences have not been a barrier to the project teachers. In fact, project staff have found that real-world, firsthand science activities have actually accelerated the rate of language acquisition, particularly for bilingual students. For example, at Virginia Rocca Barton School in Alisal, 1st grade teachers Paula Tielsch and Esther Bench have teamed to provide a bilingual program for their students. Using the theme Every Creature's Home Is a Castle, they've devised techniques that make science accessible and exciting to all students.

### Enthusiastic Principals and Teachers

Principals and teachers alike are delighted about the project's effects. Henry Karrer of Alisal School feels that it helped turn his school around by giving his staff an opportunity to reorganize

their curriculum and rethink their entire approach to teaching. At Bayview School in the Santa Cruz City School District, Principal Don Kavanaugh sees MCSIP as "a way to provide staff development for teachers that will have a lasting effect." He finds the coaching invaluable because project "coaches have been able to work on what each teacher needs and wants."

After the first year, participating teachers met with an independent evaluator, who assessed the project using California's program quality review criteria for science. The evaluator noted that "virtually every teacher reported a dramatic increase in the amount of science instruction time as a result of MCSIP." She added that "most teachers [exhibited] an increased sense of comfort with science and a desire to know more science so as to better teach it to the students" (Sandman 1988). Teachers themselves report that they are teaching science more often and in more depth.

Regarding teachers' attitudes toward teaching science, project leaders and principals have seen a notable shift from one of fear and reticence to one of openness and enthusiasm. In several instances, principals feel that, with the support of MCSIP, struggling teachers have grown into accomplished educators. Teachers' informal comments reinforce these findings. One teacher, who was ready to abandon teaching before she became involved with MCSIP, says that the project saved her career. As a result of the project, Vicki Ogborn, the 1st grade teacher described at the beginning of the article, reappraised not only her students' abilities but her own as well. Her subsequent enrollment in geology and conceptual physics at the local college was particularly notable in light of the fact that she had always avoided science courses during her own education because she thought they were too difficult.

### A Beacon for Science Reform

The Mid-California Science Improvement Program is a beacon for the reform of science education at the elementary level.

The dedicated program staff and participating teachers and principals have developed a model for other educators to consider as they seek to improve the teaching of science in their locales.

**5. CURRICULAR APPLICATIONS: Content and Process**

Now entering its fifth year, MCSIP has trained and assisted 300 teachers in 30 schools throughout a dozen school districts in 5 counties. Two districts in Monterey County—Alisal and Santa Cruz—have adopted MCSIP districtwide and serve as models of the program, welcoming visitors from other districts. A new school, now under construction in Alisal, will eventually become a demonstration school.

MCSIP's strong partnership combines the power of the schools, private support, and university resources to improve both the content and methodology of science instruction. Starting with a clear understanding of the obstacles to effective science instruction, the project offers intensive staff development, comprehensive curriculum development, and long-term financial and professional support to enable schools to achieve lasting change. Further, the project acknowledges that change takes time and that the innovators need consistent and useful support. Finally, MCSIP has infused science into the lives of hundreds of children making it an integral part of their learning for the entire school year. In its efforts to achieve scientific literacy for all students, the project has proved its merit with a wide range of students representative of California's schools of tomorrow.

**The project's strong partnership combines the power of the schools, private support, and university resources to improve both the content and methodology of science instruction.**

## References

Kovalik, S. (1986). Teach for Success: An Integrated Thematic Approach to Teaching Science. Village of Oak Creek, Ariz.: Susan Kovalik and Associates.

National Assessment of Educational Progress. (1987). Learning by Doing. Princeton, N.J.: Educational Testing Service.

Okamoto, Y. (1989). "Evaluation of the 1988-89 Mid-California Science Improvement Program." Stanford, Calif.: Stanford University.

Rutherford, F. J., et al. (1989). *Science for All Americans.* Washington, D.C.: American Association for the Advancement of Science.

Rutherford, F. J. (May 1990). Letter to the David and Lucile Packard Foundation.

Sandman, B. (1988). "Report on the Mid-California Science Improvement Program." Prepared for the Packard Foundation, Los Altos, Calif.

*Author's note:* The development of this article was supported by the David and Lucile Packard Foundation.

# Creating a Reading/Writing Environment

**Beverly D. Stratton and**
**Martha C. Grindler**

*Department of Early Childhood Education and Reading,*
*Georgia Southern University, Landrum Box 8083, States-*
*boro, GA 30460-8083*

## ABSTRACT

This article describes a project implemented at Marvin Pittman Laboratory School with students in grades 1–4. Photography in conjunction with the Language Experience Approach was used to stimulate the students' thinking and writing skills. Word processing, via the Apple computer, was used as students generated language about their photographs. Ultimately, a book of photographs with accompanying text was compiled. This project allowed students to engage in purposeful reading, writing, and thinking because the published book served as a means of personal communication. Motivation was provided through the use of photographs and word processing. Comprehension was built in since the natural language of the learner was used. Most importantly, children were given an opportunity to share something of importance—themselves.

In order to master spoken language, children need to produce it themselves, comprehend its use by others, and have experiences using language in meaningful, functional ways. Children learn about *spoken* language when they are involved in its use, when it has the possibility of making sense to them. In the same way, children will try to understand *written* language by being involved in its use in situations where it makes sense to them and where they can generate and read language (Smith, 1988).

Writing begins with the will to say something to someone else (Temple, Nathan, Burris, & Temple, 1988). According to Balajthy (1989), students need opportunities to share creatively meaningful communication about themselves with others. Implementation of the Apple/Polaroid Language Experience Approach (A/PLX), an exciting, innovative extension of the language experience, does just that. This approach can be used with preschoolers, with students K–12 in remedial and/or enrichment programs, and in adult literacy programs. It is considered a holistic approach because it is based on the whole language model of literacy which develops reading skills naturally through meaningful, functional use of language. Preliminary data suggest that this approach, which uses the student's natural language and environment, can increase sight vocabulary on pre–post test measures, can dissipate hostility toward reading and school, can create eager, willing learners, and can enhance parental involvement in reading/school.

## THE PROJECT

An important aspect of teacher preparation is to provide prospective teachers with opportunities to work with individuals and small groups of students. The Apple/Polaroid Language Experience Approach (A/PLX) is an exciting extension of the language experience approach. (The concept of Polaroid Language Experience [PLX] is credited to Louis A. Oliastro in a Head Start program in Pennsylvania). A/PLX combines aspects of the language experience approach, photography, and word processing. This teaching/learning experience was designed to provide prospective teachers with an opportunity to interact with individual elementary students utilizing a "structured" reading/writing format.

Undergraduate college students enrolled in the Teaching of Reading were introduced to the A/PLX approach to reading/writing instruction. They were instructed in the use of the 40-column version of the *Magic Slate* word processing program. A pair of college tutors was assigned to work with an elementary grade student from the college's laboratory school. The elementary student had been identified by their classroom teacher as being able to profit from individualized instruction. The college students worked with the elementary students for approximately fifty minutes two times weekly for eight weeks.

## 5. CURRICULAR APPLICATIONS: Content and Process

Why A/PLX? The Apple/Polaroid Language Experience idea is a simple, relatively inexpensive, structured approach which can be quickly conveyed to "novice" teachers. Language experience uses the existing language and background experiences of the learner to develop reading, writing, listening, and speaking skills. Photography, another form of communication, is used to improve observational skills, to stimulate children's thinking through the use of a visual stimulus, and to serve as a vehicle for sharing information and communication with peers and with adults. Word processing, via the Apple computer, is considered a life skill that provides an individual with an efficient, effective means to communicate in writing. Studies indicate that the use of word processing encourages students to talk more, plan more, think more, and write and read more (Bradley, 1982; Collins, 1983; Kurland, 1983; Stromberg & Kurth, 1984).

### THE PROCESS

The first step in the process was to explain to students that together, the college tutor and the elementary student would take some photographs that would be made into a book about themselves. It was important to ascertain individual student interests and to cooperatively decide on the subject or topic for the book's content. Five to six photographs were taken for the first book. Other photographs can be added in the future.

Once a decision was made on the subject or topic of the book, the photographs were taken the way one normally takes photographs. It is important that the student be the center of attention. Photographers need to follow directions given with the Polaroid Sun camera to insure good photographs.

After all the photographs were taken, the students sequenced them—that is, the students decided which pictures would appear first, second, etc., in their individual books. This sequence was used to assist the students in writing the story line for their books.

Once the students had sequenced the photographs, these photographs were used to stimulate students' thinking and writing skills. As students generated language about the photographs, they typed their stories into the computer using *Magic Slate*, a 40-column version word processing program. The versatility of word processing allows the text to be read back immediately, stored on disk, and printed out for the students. Stories can be reloaded during subsequent sessions, encouraging students to write, edit, and rewrite their original creation. Introducing computers into the language classroom seems to increase almost automatically the amount of student cooperation, though teacher encouragement and modeling are vital to the successful development of these new attitudes toward learning (Balajthy, 1989).

Rewriting and editing required students to make judgments about syntax, semantics, and whether the written account can be understood by others. Editing also provided an opportunity for students to develop a practical application of the dictionary as they checked the spelling of words in order to make their finished copy similar to "book" writing. Ultimately, a book of photographs with accompanying text was compiled. The copy was clean, legible, and professional-looking.

A word bank of vocabulary words used in the story was developed. We utilized *Make-A-Flash* flashcard program from Teacher Support Software. Word activities were implemented to drill words, thereby adding them to individual students' sight vocabularies. Word banks offer many opportunities for instructional activities. They can be used as a personal dictionary when composing new stories, for learning/practicing alphabetizing skills, and to play word-matching, visual, and auditory discrimination games. To develop comprehension skills, they can be used in classification games asking such questions as, "Which is a color word? A word which shows action? A word which names a place?" Word banks are a rich resource for use in the teaching of reading.

### IMPLEMENTATION IN THE CLASSROOM

We learn to read by reading and to write by writing. The A/PLX approach is an attractive way to engage children in active participation of the reading-writing process. It is through practice that children become experts. The A/PLX approach is based on the premise that children can learn to read best by engaging in their own writing.

Whole Language proponents advocate learning from the familiar. Young and older children are egocentric and enjoy talking about themselves and their interests, i.e., that which is familiar. The personal photographs create a purpose for writing and ultimately a purpose for reading.

Motivation is often the key to successful learning and teaching. Children's increased motivation to write and their pride in the finished products is very motivational for teachers as well. Students are proud of the professional look of their books and are eager to share them with parents and friends. Typically, student contributions to the class library are the first ones to be checked out.

The A/PLX approach guarantees two things: increased language use (an essential part of reading readiness) and improved self-concept (another important contributor to reading success). Children are anxious to begin their projects and then to share what they have created.

Too often, computer use in the classroom has been criticized because many software programs resemble electronic workbooks. The A/PLX activity allows children to engage in purposeful reading, writing, and thinking. It serves as a tool to communicate.

One problem to anticipate is the amount of time that the children have access to the computers. Teachers must work out a management system in which project time is divided between word processing, photographing, and organizing the materials. Allowing the children to become involved in this planning is advantageous. And the final product is very much worth the energy invested.

## SUMMARY

Research indicates that learning about reading cannot be separated from learning about writing (Smith, 1988). The Apple/Polaroid Language Experience Approach is an exciting extension of the language experience approach which combines photography, a form of communication, and word processing skills. It is considered a holistic approach because it is based on the whole language model of teaching literacy which develops reading skills naturally through the meaningful, functional use of language. The approach offers something for all students, regardless of the mode(s) through which they learn best since all modes are incorporated:

- the learners use the auditory mode when stories are read aloud and/or when a speech synthesizer is utilized;
- the kinesthetic (motor) and tactile (touch) mode when they write and type the stories, and
- the visual mode with photographs and when they read the stories.

Motivation is provided through the use of photographs and word processing via the computer. Comprehension is built-in since the natural language of the learner is used. Children are given an opportunity to share something of importance—themselves.

## REFERENCES

Balajthy, E. (1989). *Computers and reading: Lessons from the past and the technologies of the future.* Englewood Cliffs, NJ: Prentice Hall.

Bradley. V. (1982). Improving students' writing with microcomputers. *Language Arts, 59,* 732–743.

Collins, A. (1983). *Learn to read and write with computers* (Reading Ed. Rep. No. 42). Champaign: University of Illinois at Urbana-Champaign.

Kurland, D. M. (1983). *Software for the classroom: Issues in the design of effective software tools* (Tech. Rep. No. 15). New York: Bank Street College of Education, Center for Children and Technology.

Smith, F. (1988). *Understanding reading* (4th ed.). Hillsdale, NJ: Lawrence Erlbaum Associates.

Stromberg, L. J., & Kurth, R. J. (1984). *Using word processing in composition instruction.* Paper presented at the annual meeting of the American Reading Forum, Orlando, FL.

Sunburst (1984). *Magic Slate* [Computer software]. Pleasantville, NY.

Teacher Support Software (1988). *Make-A-Flash* [Computer software]. Gainesville, FL.

Temple, C., Nathan, R., Burris, N., & Temple, F. (1988). *The beginnings of writing* (2nd ed.). Boston: Allyn and Bacon.

# Reflections

Americans enter the mid-1990s in need of jobs and prosperity. Waves of recession have left people talking about how to strengthen the national economy. Election issues revolve around education and training, technology, and trade.

On personal levels, Americans need restoration of their relationships. Racial animosities and disrespect are leading to increasing problems. While state-supported segregation may have ended, discrimination continues. Election issues address racism and protection of all peoples.

As unemployment grows and community relations rupture, America's families are shaken. Parents find themselves without meaningful work and an income that pays for groceries. Communities become fearful places for children who want to play with friends. Increasing poverty puts more and more mothers and young children at risk for the basics of life. And crime is the only economy left in some places.

A stagnant economy means state and local governments make cuts in education and public services, which affect all families with young children. Fortunately, new federal legislation will help offset some of these cuts. Money will go to safe and affordable child care, Head Start, and increased health care for pregnant women and young children. Child immunizations and shelter against homelessness will be provided increased funding. The tragedy is that the recession robs these programs of significant increases.

In the face of steadily rising poverty and violence, some national values are in danger of being forgotten. They need to be rediscovered and taught to children. At the heart of lessons learned from life is the premise that democracy is not a spectator sport. It is built from initiative and hard work.

America's educational goals for the year 2000 are intended to ensure that all future citizens will have the knowledge and skill to do the hard work of democracy. The goals and objectives for our nation address the current achievement gap among groups of students. If America is to prosper in the future, no social, racial, or cultural group can be left to underachieve. This can be accomplished only by massive educational support that focuses on success for all.

Bleak economics and insecure politics of the nation are determining the future course of early childhood education. We may not know how to cure these national ills, but we must continue to make a compassionate effort to protect and educate the new generations most deeply affected by current conditions.

## Looking Ahead: Challenge Questions

What lessons have we learned from the 1980s that could make the future better for young children?

In what ways have young children's lives improved over the last two decades?

What could be the long-term effects of day care on children?

How can parents become more informed about the quality of care for their child?

How should the high turnover rate of child care teachers be addressed?

What must early childhood educators do to prepare young children for the year 2000?

What skills will be needed to be a productive citizen in the future?

# Unit 6

# The Day Care Generation

Pat Wingert
and Barbara Kantrowitz

**M**eryl Frank is an expert on child care. For five years she ran a Yale University program that studied parental leave. But after she became a new mother two years ago, Frank discovered that even though she knew about such esoteric topics as staff-child ratios and turnover rates, she was a novice when it came to finding someone to watch her own child. Frank went back to work part time when her son, Isaac, was 5 months old, and in the two years since then she has changed child-care arrangements *nine* times.

Her travails began with a well-regarded daycare center near her suburban New Jersey home. On the surface, it was great. One staff member for every three babies, a sensitive administrator, clean facilities. "But when I went in," Frank recalls, "I saw this line of cribs and all these babies with their arms out crying, wanting to be picked up. I felt like crying myself." She walked out without signing Isaac up and went through a succession of other unsatisfactory situations—a babysitter who couldn't speak English, a woman who cared for 10 children in her home at once—before settling on a neighborhood woman who took Isaac into her home. "She was fabulous," Frank recalls wistfully. Three weeks after that babysitter started, she got sick and had to quit. Frank advertised for help in the newspaper and got 30 inquiries but no qualified babysitter. (When Frank asked one prospective nanny about her philosophy of discipline, the woman replied: "If he touched the stove, I'd punch him.") A few weeks later she finally hired her 10th babysitter. "She's a very nice young woman," Frank says. "Unfortunately, she has to leave in

May. And I just found out I'm pregnant again and due in June."

That's what happens when a *pro* tries to get help. For other parents, the situation can be even worse. Child-care tales of woe are a common bond for the current generation of parents. Given the haphazard state of day care in this country, finding the right situation is often just a matter of luck. There's no guarantee that a good thing will last. And always, there's the disturbing question that lurks in the back of every working parent's mind: *what is this doing to my kids?*

The simple and unsettling answer is, nobody really knows for sure. Experts say they're just beginning to understand the ramifications of raising a generation of youngsters outside the home while their parents work. Mothers in this country have always had jobs, but it is only in the past few years that a majority have gone back to the office while their children are still in diapers. In the past, most mothers worked out of necessity. That's still true for the majority today, but they have also been joined by mothers of all economic classes. Some researchers think we won't know all the answers until the 21st century, when the children of today's working mothers are parents themselves. In the meantime, results gathered so far are troubling.

Some of the first studies of day care in the 1970s indicated that there were no ill effects from high-quality child care. There was even evidence that children who were out of the home at an early age were more independent and made friends more easily. Those results received wide attention and reassured many parents. Unfortunately, they don't tell the whole story. "The problem is that much of the day care available

> **Child care has immediate problems. But what about the long-term effect it will have on kids?**

in this country is not high quality," says Deborah Lowe Vandell, professor of educational psychology at the University of Wisconsin. The first research was often done in university-sponsored centers where the child-care workers were frequently students preparing for careers as teachers. Most children in day care don't get such dedicated attention.

Since the days of these early studies, child care has burgeoned into a $15 billion-a-year industry in this country. Day-care centers get most of the attention because they are the fastest-growing segment, but they account for only a small percentage of child-care arrangements. According to 1986 Census Bureau figures, more than half of the kids under 5 with working mothers were cared for by nonrelatives: 14.7 percent in day-care centers and 23.8 percent in family day care, usually a neighborhood home where one caretaker watches several youngsters. Most of the rest were in nursery school or preschool.

Despite years of lobbying by children's advocates, there are still no federal regulations covering the care of young children. The government offers consumers more guidance choosing breakfast cereal than child care. Each state makes its own rules, and they vary from virtually no governmental supervision to strict enforcement of complicated licensing procedures for day-care centers. Many child-development experts recommend that each caregiver be responsible for no more than three infants under the age of 1. Yet only three states—Kansas, Maryland and Massachusetts—require that ratio. Other states are far more lax. Idaho, for example, allows one caregiver to look after as many as 12 children of any age (including babies). And in 14 states there are absolutely no training requirements before starting a job as a child-care worker.

Day-care centers are the easiest to supervise and inspect because they usually operate openly. Family day care, on the other hand, poses big problems for regulatory agencies. Many times, these are informal arrangements that are hard to track down. Some child-care providers even say that regulation would make matters worse by imposing confusing rules that would keep some potential caregivers out of business and intensify the shortage of good day care.

**N**o wonder working parents sometimes feel like pioneers wandering in the wilderness. The signposts point every which way. One set of researchers argues that babies who spend more than 20 hours a week in child care may grow up maladjusted. Other experts say the high turnover rate among poorly paid and undertrained child-care workers has created an unstable environment for youngsters who need dependability and consistency. And still others are worried about health issues—the wisdom of putting a lot of small children with limited immunities in such close quarters. Here's a synopsis of the current debate in three major areas of concern.

There's no question that the care of the very youngest children is by far the most controversial area of research. The topic so divides the child-development community that a scholarly journal, Early Childhood Research Quarterly, recently devoted two entire issues to the subject. Nobody is saying that mothers ought to stay home until their kids are ready for college. Besides that, it would be economically impossible; two thirds of all working women are the sole support of their families or are married to men who earn less than $15,000 a year. But as the demographics have changed, psychologists are taking a second look at what happens to babies. In 1987, 52 percent of mothers of children under the age of 1 were working, compared with 32 percent 10 years earlier. Many experts believe that day-care arrangements that might be fine for 3- and 4-year-olds may be damaging to infants.

Much of the dispute centers on the work of Pennsylvania State University psychologist Jay Belsky. He says mounting research indicates that babies less than 1 year old who receive nonmaternal care for more than 20 hours a week are at a greater risk of developing insecure relationships with their mothers; they're also at increased risk of emotional and behavioral problems in later childhood. Youngsters who have weak emotional ties to their mothers are more likely to be aggressive and disobedient as they grow older, Belsky says. Of course, kids whose mothers are home all day can have these problems, too. But Belsky says that mothers who aren't with their kids all day long don't get to know their babies as well as mothers who work part time or not at all. Therefore, working mothers may not be as sensitive to a baby's first attempts at communication. In general, he says, mothers are more attentive to these crucial signals than babysitters. Placing a baby in outside care increases the chance that an infant's needs won't be met, Belsky says. He also argues that working parents have so much stress in their lives that they have little energy left over for their children. It's hard to find the strength for "quality time" with the kids after a 10- or 12-hour day at the office. (It is interesting to note that not many people are promoting the concept of quality time these days.)

Work by other researchers has added weight to Belsky's theories. Wisconsin's Vandell studied the day-care histories of 236 Texas third graders and found that youngsters who had more than 30 hours a week of child care during infancy had poorer peer relationships, were harder to **discipline and had poorer work habits than children who had been in part-time child care or exclusive maternal care. The children most at risk were from the lowest and highest socioeconomic classes, Vandell says, probably because poor youngsters usually get the worst child care and rich parents tend to have high-stress jobs that require long hours away from home. Vandell emphasizes that her results in the Texas study may be more negative than those for the country as a whole because Texas has minimal child-care regulation. Nonetheless, she thinks there's a "serious problem" in infant care.**

**Other experts say there isn't enough information yet to form any definitive conclusions about the long-term effects of infant**

# Who's Minding the Children?

**E**ven with the sharp rise in working mothers, most children are still cared for at home—their own or someone else's.

### Percent of Mothers Working

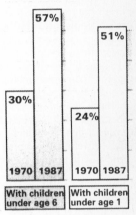

| With children under age 6 | With children under age 1 |
|---|---|
| 1970: 30% — 1987: 57% | 1970: 24% — 1987: 51% |

SOURCE: CHILD CARE INC.

### Day Care
WHO LOOKS AFTER CHILDREN UNDER AGE 5 WHILE THEIR MOTHERS WORK

7.6% In a nursery or school

6.7% By mother at work

14.7% Day-care centers

41.3% In another's home

29.7% In own home

SOURCE: U.S. CENSUS BUREAU

**Day care that might be fine for 3- or 4-year-olds may be damaging to infants**

care. "There is no clear evidence that day care places infants at risk," says Alison Clarke-Stewart, a professor of social ecology at the University of California, Irvine. Clarke-Stewart says that the difference between the emotional attachments of children of working and of nonworking mothers is not as large as Belsky's research indicates. She says parents should be concerned but shouldn't overreact. Instead of pulling kids out of any form of day care, parents might consider choosing part-time work when their children are very young, she says.

For all the controversy over infant care, there's little dispute over the damaging effects of the high turnover rate among caregivers. In all forms of child care, consistency is essential to a child's healthy development. But only the lucky few get it. "Turnover among child-care workers is second only to parking-lot and gas-station attendants," says Marcy Whitebook, director of the National Child Care Staffing Study. "To give you an idea of how bad it is, during our study, we had tiny children coming up to our researchers and asking them, 'Are you my teacher?'"

The just-released study, funded by a consortium of not-for-profit groups, included classroom observations, child assessments and interviews with staff at 227 child-care centers in five cities. The researchers concluded that 41 percent of all child-care workers quit each year, many to seek better-paying jobs. In the past decade, the average day-care-center enrollment has nearly doubled, while the average salaries for child-care workers have decreased 20 percent. Typical annual wages are very low: $9,931 for full-time, year-round employment ($600 less than the 1988 poverty threshold for a family of three). Few child-care workers receive any benefits.

Parents who use other forms of day care should be concerned as well, warns UCLA psychologist Carollee Howes. Paying top dollar for au pairs, nannies and other in-home caregivers doesn't guarantee that they'll stay. Howes conducted two studies of 18- to 24-month-old children who had been cared for in their own homes or in family day-care homes and found that most had already experienced two or three changes in caregivers and some had had as many as six. In her research, Howes found that the more changes children had, the more trouble they had adjusting to first grade.

The solution, most experts agree, is a drastic change in the status, pay and training of child-care workers. Major professional organizations, such as the National Association for the Education of Young Children, have recommended standard accreditation procedures to make child care more of an established profession, for everyone from workers in large for-profit centers to women who only look after youngsters in their neighborhood. But so far, only a small fraction of the country's child-care providers are accredited. Until wide-scale changes take place, Whitebook predicts that "qualified teachers will continue to leave for jobs that offer a living wage." The victims are the millions of children left behind.

When their toddlers come home from day care with a bad case of the sniffles, parents often joke that it's "schoolitis"—the virus that seems to invade classrooms from September until June. But there's more and more evidence that child care may be hazardous to a youngster's health.

A recent report from the Centers for Disease Control found that children who are cared for outside their homes are at increased risk for both minor and major ailments because they are exposed to so many other kids at such a young age. Youngsters who spend their days in group settings are more likely to get colds and flu as well as strep throat, infectious hepatitis and spinal meningitis, among other diseases.

Here again, the state and federal governments aren't doing much to help. A survey released this fall by the American Academy of Pediatrics and the American Public Health Association found that even such basic health standards as immunization and hand washing were not required in child-care facilities in half the states. Inspection was another problem. Without adequate staff, states with health regulations often have difficulty enforcing them, especially in family day-care centers.

Some experts think that even with strict regulation, there would still be health problems in child-care centers, especially among infants. "The problem is that caretakers are changing the diapers of several kids, and it's difficult for them to wash their hands frequently enough [after each diaper]," says Earline Kendall, associate dean of graduate studies in education at Belmont College in Nashville, Tenn. Kendall, who has operated four day-care centers herself, says that very young babies have the most limited immunities and are the most vulnerable to the diseases that can be spread through such contact. The best solution, she thinks, would be more generous leave time so that parents can stay home until their kids are a little older.

Despite the compelling evidence about the dark side of day care, many experts say there's a great reluctance to discuss these problems publicly. "People think if you say anything against day care, you're saying young parents shouldn't work, or if they do work, they're bad parents," says Meryl Frank, who is now a consultant on family and work issues. "For a lot of parents, that's just too scary to think about. But we have to be realistic. We have to acknowledge that good day care may be good for kids, but bad day care is bad for kids."

There is a political battle as well. Belsky, who has become a lightning rod for controversy among child-development professionals, says "people don't want working mothers to feel guilty" because "they're afraid the right wing will use this to say that only mothers can care for babies, so women should stay home." But, he says, parents should use these problems as evidence to press for such changes as paid parental leave, more part-time jobs and higher-quality child care. The guilt and anxiety that seem to be part of every working parent's psyche aren't necessarily bad, Belsky says. Parents who worry are also probably alert to potential problems—and likely to look for solutions.

## Child-Care Checklist

Questions to ask at day-care centers:

■ **What are the educational and training backgrounds of staff members?**

■ **What is the child-staff ratio for each age?** Most experts say it should be no more than 4:1 for infants, 5:1 for 18 months to 2 years, 8:1 for 2 to 3 years, 10:1 for 3 to 4 years and 15:1 for 5 to 6 years.

■ **What are the disciplinary policies?**

■ **Are parents free to visit at any time?**

■ **Are the center's facilities clean and well maintained?**

■ **Are child-safety precautions observed?** Such as heat covers on radiators, childproof safety seals on all electrical outlets?

■ **Are staff members careful about hygiene?** It's important to wash hands between diaper changes in order to avoid spreading diseases.

■ **Are there facilities and staff for taking care of sick children?**

■ **Is there adequate space, indoors and out, for children to play?**

■ **Most important of all, do the children look happy and cared for?** Trust your instincts.

# The Costs of *Not* Providing Quality Early Childhood Programs

## Ellen Galinsky

*Ellen Galinsky served as NAEYC President from 1988 to 1990. She is Co-President of the Families and Work Institute in New York City. A noted authority on early childhood education, her work has been instrumental in shaping the emerging field of work and family issues. She is a prolific author, with publications directed to parents, researchers, the business community, as well as the early childhood field. Her work is widely respected in each of these different arenas.*

The debate in this country has shifted from the issue of whether or not mothers of young children should be employed to a recognition that they are—and will continue to be in the labor force in even greater numbers. Concurrently, there has been a realization that child care responsibilities cannot be placed on families alone, but that both the private and the public sectors have a role in supporting quality early childhood programs. Rather than ask "why" they should be involved, increasingly businesses, governments, and charitable organizations are asking "how" they can help.

In these discussions, decision makers frequently turn to research to guide their efforts. If there is any one clear message to be drawn from the research on child care and early education, it is that the quality of programs has a definite and lasting effect on children's development. This chapter summarizes what is known about the ingredients of quality in early childhood arrangements and their effects on children, their parents, and their teacher-caregivers. In addition, this chapter presents what is known about the cost of *not* providing quality.

## THE EFFECT OF QUALITY ON CHILDREN

### The importance of relationships

*The personal relationship*

The most important ingredient of quality is the relationship between the child and the teacher-caregiver, whether the setting is in a center, a family child care home, or the child's home. This is why NAEYC's accreditation process for early childhood programs places great emphasis on the nature of the interactions between teachers and children. Parents also understand the importance of relationships. Parents report that the kind and quality of the attention their child receives strongly affects their decision in selecting one arrangement over another (Galinsky, 1988).

Children do form attachments to their teacher-caregivers, although Thomas Gamble and Edward Zigler (1986), in a review of this research, remind us that children's attachments to their parents are pre-eminent. Carollee Howes from the University of California at Los Angeles and her colleagues have found that children with a secure attachment to their mothers *and* their teacher-caregiver behave more competently than those with two or more insecure attachments (Howes, Rodning, Galluzzo, & Myers, 1988). Thus, it seems, the cost we could pay for poor relations between the child and the teacher-caregiver is the child's feeling that she or he is just one of the crowd and not a special, unique individual. A good self-concept is one of the foundations of emotional and social well-being. The costs may be very high, especially in terms of children's ability to form healthy relationships with others and enjoy good emotional health.

## 6. REFLECTIONS

### The teaching relationship

No matter what the setting—center, family child care, or the child's home, teacher-caregivers are teaching children every moment, both formally and informally. The way this teaching is done makes a difference in children's development. For example, a study by Deborah Phillips, Kathleen McCartney, and Sandra Scarr (1987) found that when children are talked to, asked questions, and encouraged to express themselves, their social development is enhanced: They are more likely to be considerate. In fact, the children in this study were also rated as more intelligent and task-oriented. The teaching environment was found to be more predictive of the children's achievement than their social class background. Kathleen McCartney (1984), in a re-analysis of this same data set, found that when children were in a verbally stimulating environment, they were more likely to achieve on tests of cognitive abilities and language development.

Early childhood specialists voice concern over situations in which children are either bored or pressured. In a longitudinal study, Deborah Lowe Vandell and her colleagues found that 4-year-olds who attended programs in which they spent time aimlessly wandering around were more likely at 8 years of age to have developmental problems, including less acceptance by peers, less social competence, and poorer conflict resolution skills (Vandell, Henderson, & Wilson, 1988).

Marcy Whitebook, Carollee Howes, and Deborah Phillips, in their landmark National Child Care Staffing Study (1990), found that children were more likely to be engaged in aimless wandering in programs with high rates of staff turnover. This key signal of lower program quality was associated with programs offering lower staff salaries, fewer benefits, and poorer working conditions. These researchers detected immediate negative consequences of poorer program quality. Children in such programs did less well on tests of both social development and language development, critical areas for later achievement.

Just as children do less well when they are bored or wandering aimlessly, David Elkind from Tufts University (1987), has pointed to the potential for problems such as elementary school burnout when preschool children are overly pressured. Thus, the cost we could pay for inadequate teaching relationships in children's early years is great: diminished achievement and poorer social and language skills.

### The disciplinary relationship

There has been a great deal of research indicating that the disciplinary techniques parents use have an impact on the child's subsequent development. These findings can be applied to early childhood programs. Children are more likely to develop self-control and to become more compliant, cooperative, and considerate of others if reasoning is used; if teacher-caregivers explain how a child's behavior affects others; and if problem-solv-

ing skills are taught. Vandell and Powers (1983) found that in higher quality programs, children had many more positive interactions with staff than in lower quality programs. Finkelstein (1982) showed that when teacher-caregivers are trained in behavior management techniques, the frequency of children's aggressive acts is reduced.

Such research counters the societal fear that attendance in group programs itself leads to more aggression in children. The ways that teacher-caregivers (or parents) handle young children's aggression can lead to greater or reduced aggression. The difference lies in understanding how to deal with children's aggression in appropriate ways. Lesser quality programs are more likely to have staff who do not have the knowledge and understanding to deal effectively with young children's normal assertions of prowess and power. The cost that we as a society could pay for children who grow up more aggressive seems high indeed.

### The stability of relationships

With 40% of all center staff and 60% of all in-home providers leaving the field every year, it is no wonder that one 4-year-old recently said to a teacher, "I don't have to listen to you. I was here before you came and I'll still be here when you leave." Other parents report their children resist going to child care because they simply don't know who will care for them that day. According to the research of Mark Cummings from West Virginia University (1986), children have a much easier time separating from their mothers when they are cared for by well-known teacher-caregivers in small groups. Carollee Howes and her colleagues, in their studies of family child care (Howes & Stewart, 1987), found that there was a cost to children who changed arrangements frequently: They were less competent in their interactions with materials and with other children. As previously described, the National Child Care Staffing Study (Whitebook et al., 1990) documented disturbing results for children's social and language development when they were enrolled in programs with high rates of staff turnover. The Staffing Study also painted a disturbing picture of the amount of turnover in programs. Based on initial reports of program directors, the study found a 41% annual turnover rate, comparable to other nationally reported figures. However, the researchers found a 37% turnover rate in just over 6 months, based on the results of follow-up calls.

### The resources of child care

The second aspect of early childhood program quality relates to the program's resources: the group size, adult-child ratio, health and safety considerations, and the professional preparation of teacher-caregivers.

### Group size and staff-child ratio

The federal government funded the National Day Care

Study in the late 1970s to investigate the degree to which the regulated features of child care arrangements had an effect on children's development. One of their most important findings was that the group size made a big difference in program quality. In smaller groups the adults spent more time being with children and less time simply watching them. The children were more verbal, more involved in activities, and less aggressive. Finally, the children in smaller groups made the greatest gains in standardized tests of learning and vocabulary (Ruopp, Travers, Glantz, & Coelen, 1979).

The National Day Care Study did not find staff-child ratio as powerful as group size in predicting development for children 3 to 5 years of age. However, the range they examined was limited. As Deborah Phillips and Carollee Howes point out (1987), "The majority of studies have found that the [adult-child] ratio has a significant effect on adult and child behavior in child care." More recently the National Child Care Staffing Study (Whitebook et al., 1990) found that fewer children per caregiver was associated with more developmentally appropriate activities. Teachers in these groups were more sensitive, less harsh, and less detached when interacting with children. The number of children per adult has obvious consequences for the ability of the caregiver to be responsive to each child. The younger the children and the more dependent they are on adults, the more critical it is that the number of children per adult be limited. The crucial learning from this research is that adult-child ratios and group size must be considered together.

### Health and safety

There has been a great deal of public concern about the transmission of illness in child care. Susan Aronson has been studying the health risks in group programs for the past decade. She has found a clear demarcation between those early childhood programs in which children often become ill and those in which they do not: When adults wash their hands frequently, children are healthier (Aronson, 1987). The cost of children's illness and injury are obvious in health care expenses and missed days of work for their parents.

Children's safety is another critical factor to consider. Children's safety can be improved when providers are knowledgeable and when the environment is hazard reduced. Safety is also enhanced when ratios and group size are limited. Currently 19 states permit ratios of 5 or more infants to each adult (Adams, 1990). These ratios must be questioned not only in terms of their costs on the relationships established between teacher-caregivers and children, but also for their costs in safety. The extra attention afforded by small groups and good ratios helps to prevent minor accidents and injuries. It may be a life-saver in cases of emergency evacuation. The costs of an unsafe arrangement are incalculable when children's lives are literally at stake.

*The costs of an unsafe arrangement are incalculable when children's lives are literally at stake.*

### Teacher-caregiver preparation and training

NAEYC's experience with its accreditation system has documented that developmentally appropriate teaching practices and activities are more likely to occur when staff have a combination of formal education and specific preparation in early childhood education (Bredekamp, 1989). Other research is mixed regarding the specific characteristics of professional preparation that most contribute to program quality. The National Day Care Study (Ruopp et al., 1970) concluded that one of the most important ingredients of quality was the ongoing, relevant training of providers. In programs in which teacher-caregivers had specific early childhood training, the children behaved more positively, were more cooperative, and were more involved in the program. These children also made the greatest gains on standardized tests of learning. The National Child Care Staffing Study (Whitebook et al., 1990) suggested that the formal education of staff was a more potent predictor of program quality than early childhood training alone. While more research is needed to better define the specific relationships between different types and amounts of preparation and quality, the overall message of the importance of specialized knowledge is clear.

In summary, research on the impact of the resources of the child care program reveals a strong connection between group size, staff-child ratios, health and safety, and staff development and children's social, physical, and cognitive well-being.

### Relationships with parents

Numerous studies have been conducted on the long-term effects of early childhood programs, especially model intervention programs and federally funded Head Start programs. One of the most noteworthy findings is that when early childhood programs are effective, they do much more than teach the child. The parents are affected and through this experience become better teachers, motivators, and advocates for their children (Lally, Mangione, & Honig, 1987; Weikart, 1990). This is not happenstance; providing meaningful opportunities for parental involvement has been an integral part of Head Start throughout its 25-year history.

A recent follow-up study of Head Start in Philadelphia (Copple, Cline, & Smith, 1987) is noteworthy in that it reflects typical rather than exemplary programs. In that study, Head Start children were more likely to avoid serious school problems, were less frequently retained, and had better attendance records than their counterparts who did not attend the program. The researchers suggest that the Head Start program may have reduced the helplessness these parents felt in response to the school. Instead of seeing school as a place where their children were doomed, they may have come to see it as a place where their children could hold their own, and where they, as parents, could speak out on behalf of their children's education.

The importance of establishing good working relationships with parents is not universally understood. A recent study conducted by the Families and Work Institute sounds a warning signal about this critical aspect of quality care and education. We found that the parents most likely to have the best parent-teacher relationships were the wealthier, most advantaged parents. Similarly, those least likely to have good relationships—the least advantaged, minority parents—are those who could perhaps use the support the most (Galinsky, Shinn, Phillips, Howes, & Whitebook, 1990).

### Summary of the effects of quality on children

The studies described throughout this chapter have been carefully controlled. The effects of different family backgrounds have been statistically accounted for so that the researchers could determine the impact of quality on children's development. The evidence is resoundingly uniform. The quality of early childhood programs has a strong effect on children's development. Carollee Howes (1990) summarizes her numerous studies on different forms of child care by stating, "Children who entered low quality child care as infants were [the] least task oriented and considerate of others as kindergartners, had the most difficulty with peers as preschoolers, and were distractible, extroverted, and hostile as kindergartners."

## THE EFFECTS OF QUALITY ON EMPLOYED PARENTS

While some of the costs of poor quality for children may not be readily apparent, we do not have to wait to assess the cost of child care problems on employed parents: The repercussions are showing up right now in diminished job performance.

### An inadequate selection

It is difficult for parents to find quality child care. In a survey we conducted with 931 employees at three New Jersey companies (Galinsky, 1988), 46% of the respondents reported that locating quality arrangements was a "major problem"; 48% did not feel they had an adequate selection. Infant care was the most difficult to find—65% indicated that making arrangements for their infants was "difficult" or "very difficult."

A national study conducted by the National Council of Jewish Women (1988) of 1,927 women approximately 5 months after they had given birth found that new mothers who had problems arranging child care were more likely to experience higher levels of stress. In a nationally representative study conducted for *Fortune* magazine (Galinsky & Hughes, 1987), we found that parents who had trouble finding child care were more likely to have higher absenteeism rates.

### Satisfaction

It is well known that it can be difficult for parents to admit that they are dissatisfied with the overall quality of child care even though they may admit displeasure with particular aspects of their arrangements. In the Parent/Teacher Study, conducted in conjunction with the National Child Care Staffing Study, we found that there are two sets of factors that parents use to make judgments about child care. One relates to the quality of the child's experience (the warmth of the teacher-caregiver, the activities, etc.). When parents are dissatisfied with this set of factors they are less likely to be satisfied with their child care arrangement in general. The second set of factors relates to the parents' experience with child care (hours, flexibility of scheduling, cost, location, and parents' opportunity for input). When parents are dissatisfied with these conditions, they are more likely to have higher levels of stress, more work-family conflict, and more stress-related health problems, but there is little effect on their overall satisfaction with the child care (Shinn, Galinsky, & Gulcur, 1990).

These new findings help to explain the seeming contradiction in earlier studies where overall satisfaction is reported at high levels, but considerable concern is expressed about specific factors. Parents voice the most concern with the factors that directly affect them: location, flexibility, and cost (Galinsky, 1988). The one strong exception seems to be those parents who rely on their children to care for themselves or their younger siblings. In a study conducted at Portland State University (Emlen & Koren, 1984), 57% of the sample of more than 8,000 employed parents reported dissatisfaction with latchkey arrangements as compared to 23% using family child care or centers. Taken together, these studies suggest that parents' definition of overall child care satisfaction is primarily influenced by their view of the nature of the child's experience. Parents may be dissatisfied with aspects that affect them, but as long as they feel the child's experience is satisfactory, they are satisfied with the arrangement.

One of the disturbing findings of the Parent/Teacher Study was that parents were quite satisfied with programs deemed low in quality by independent researchers. Parents were more attuned to quality when their children were preschoolers as opposed to infants and toddlers. Unfortunately, parents were more satisfied when there were more children per adult and group sizes were larger. Parents, however, did respond to the quality of the relationship between their child

*Parents' definition of overall satisfaction with child care is primarily influenced by the nature of their child's experience.*

and the teacher-caregiver. When these adults were judged to be more detached, insensitive, or chaotic, parents were less satisfied, lonelier, and missed their child more (Galinsky, Shinn, Phillips, Howes, & Whitebook, 1990). Thus, it seems that while parents are aware of the importance of the teacher-child relationship, they do not know that having fewer children per adult, smaller group sizes, and adequate preparation of the staff make it more likely that the teacher-caregiver will be nurturing and caring as well as able to teach in developmentally appropriate ways.

Parents in this study were very aware of the amount of staff turnover in the center. When the turnover was higher, parents were less satisfied with the program and were less likely to feel that their child benefitted from the experience. These parents also felt less adequate as parents and missed their children more while at work.

When early childhood professionals assess quality, they find a selection process at work that disadvantages the most at-risk parents. For example, Carollee Howes (Howes & Stewart, 1987) found that families who were under the most stress enrolled their children in the lowest quality child care arrangements. This finding led the National Academy of Sciences Panel on Child Care to conclude that such children are in double jeopardy, experiencing stress from their homes and from poorer child care arrangements (Hayes, Palmer, & Zaslow, 1990).

Often the reasons for selecting poorer quality arrangements are economic (Culkin, Helburn, Morris, & Watson, 1990). Sometimes, however, the results may be surprising. For example, the National Child Care Staffing Study (Whitebook et al., 1990) found that children from low-income families were much more likely to be enrolled in nonprofit programs, and children from higher income families were somewhat more likely to be enrolled in nonprofit programs. Children from middle-income families were much more likely to be enrolled in for-profit programs. In this study, auspice (nonprofit or for-profit) was the strongest predictor of quality. As a result, children from middle-income families were found to be enrolled in centers of lower quality than children from either low- or high-income families.

### A patchwork system

Our studies show that parents do not use one arrangement for each child; they piece together a patchwork system. In a study we conducted several years ago, parents at Merck & Co., Inc. reported an average of 1.7

arrangements per child (Galinsky, 1988). A study by Marybeth Shinn and her colleagues (Shinn, Ortiz-Torres, Morris, Simko, & Wong, 1989) from New York University also came up with the same number—1.7. In the *Fortune* magazine study (Galinsky & Hughes, 1987), we found that 38% of the families had to contend with as many as three to four different child care arrangements.

The more arrangements the family has, the more likely they are to fall apart. The issue of child care breakdowns is of great concern because of the high turnover in child care. In the *Fortune* magazine study (Galinsky & Hughes, 1987), we found that 27% of the employed fathers and 24% of the employed mothers had been forced to make two to five special arrangements in the past 3 months because their regular arrangements had fallen apart.

Child care breakdowns are strongly associated with productivity. According to Shinn and her colleagues (Shinn et al., 1989), parents with more breakdowns are more likely to miss work. In the *Fortune* magazine study (Galinsky & Hughes, 1987), we found such parents more likely to come to work late or leave early. In fact, in that study, 72% of all employee tardiness was for family-related reasons.

Parents who face more frequent breakdowns in their child care arrangements report spending more unproductive time at work, according to the *Fortune* magazine study. A study conducted of two New England companies (Burden & Googins, 1987), found that one of every four employed parents said that they worried about their children "always" or "most of the time" while on the job. Such intense reactions to child care problems are expressed by an inability to concentrate on the job and a loss of productivity.

Our research also reveals links between child care breakdown and stress, including stress-related health problems. Parents who had to make more last minute arrangements were more likely to report such symptoms as pains in the back, head, and neck; shortness of breath; heart pounding or racing; as well as eating, drinking, or smoking more than usual (Galinsky, 1988).

It is evident that parents who cannot find quality care, who piece together multiple and tenuous arrangements, who have latchkey children, and who face frequent breakdowns in their child care systems have poorer work attendance, are less able to concentrate on the job, and have more stress-related health problems. Thus, as a nation we are paying the cost of these parents' diminished job performance right now.

### THE EFFECT OF QUALITY ON TEACHER-CAREGIVERS

When we think of the impact of quality child care arrangements, we think of children or perhaps their parents, but seldom of the adults who provide care and education to young children. Although there has been a great deal of research on the working conditions of employees in most fields, there has been a notable absence of such research in the early childhood field until very recently. Perhaps this is related to the common assumption that early childhood teacher-caregivers are motivated by their love and concern for young children, so working conditions don't seem so important.

The staffing shortages that face so many early childhood programs across the country are calling this assumption into question. It has become evident that teacher-caregivers of young children can no longer afford to stay in such a low-paying field and are having to leave their jobs. Consequently, studies are beginning to be done to identify the various predictors of job satisfaction and turnover.

### Job satisfaction
Paula Jorde-Bloom's research (1988) has related various job conditions to the job satisfaction of those working with young children. Among the most salient are job autonomy, relationships with one's supervisor and co-workers, and job clarity. Several studies have found that working in early childhood programs often provides high levels of satisfaction among these variables. For example, teachers in the National Child Care Staffing Study (Whitebook, et al., 1990) reported very high levels of satisfaction with the daily demands of their work. In an Indiana study, Susan Kontos and Andrew Stremmel (1988) found that the majority of child care teachers enjoy their work and want to stay in the field. Likewise, in a study of publicly funded programs in New York City, Bob Granger and Elisabeth Marx (1988) found high levels of job satisfaction among such aspects as working with children, intellectual challenge, and opportunities for creativity.

### Salaries and benefits
While the high levels of intrinsic measures of job satisfaction reported by child care teachers are important, they cannot overcome the harsh realities of inadequate compensation. In a California study by Michael Olenick (1986), staff retention was higher in programs that paid higher wages. These not unexpected findings were confirmed by the National Child Care Staffing Study (Whitebook et al., 1990). Teachers' wages were the most important predictor of turnover, reported on average at 41% annually. This study found an important relationship between salaries and program quality. Programs that met recognized measures of higher quality also paid better wages and provided more benefits. Staff in these programs reported higher levels of job satisfaction and were more sensitive, less harsh, and engaged in more appropriate caregiving with children.

Similar findings were evident in the Granger and Marx study (1988). Teachers in publicly funded child

*The high level of intrinsic job satisfaction in working with young children is important, but cannot overcome the harsh realities of inadequate compensation.*

care and Head Start programs scored significantly lower on several measures of job stability (total years taught, years at current site, and years in current system) than teachers of preschool children in the public school. Demonstrating the relationship between stability and compensation, teachers in programs funded by the public schools received average annual salaries of over $33,000, while those in publicly funded child care and Head Start received annual salaries of just over $19,000. Only a small amount of the disparity was due to differences in education and experience. Granger and Marx estimated that if teachers in the publicly funded child care and Head Start programs were paid according to public school salary schedules, their salaries would have been approximately $31,000 and $27,000 respectively.

In subsequent research, Marx, Zinsser, and Porter (1990) analyzed the impact of 1988 state legislation in New York enacting a one-time child care salary enhancement. Before this legislation was implemented, turnover rates exceeded 30% for teachers and reached 57% for aides and assistants in upstate New York. The $12 million enhancement reached 10,270 full-time equivalent staff, each receiving just over $1,200 on average. Turnover was reduced considerably as a result. In New York City, for example, classroom teachers and supervisory staff had a turnover rate of 42% before enactment. A year following the bill's passage, turnover had dropped to 22%. Staff vacancy rates were also cut in half. Thus, not only are poor salaries linked to higher turnover, but also improved salaries lead to reduced turnover.

When early childhood teacher-caregivers broach the issue of inadequate salaries, it can sound self-serving—professionals trying to aggrandize themselves. Considering the below poverty level wages of those working in most child care and early education programs and the subsequent high rates of staff turnover, the issue must be seen as one of quality. In order to provide quality for children, the early childhood field must be able to attract and retain qualified staff. As described throughout this chapter, children and their families are paying the costs of the lack of quality that results from an insufficient pool of qualified staff.

### WHAT CAN BE DONE

Slowly but surely, families and organizations within both the public and private sectors are recognizing that the costs of not providing quality early childhood

*No one segment of society can solve this nation's child care crisis; all segments of society must join together.*

programs are too high to pay. For example, much time and energy has been devoted to the successful passage of federal child care legislation, accomplished in the fall of 1990 after more than 20 years of effort. A number of promising approaches are also occurring at state and local levels. In addition, there are many private sector initiatives which demonstrate growing understanding of need to address quality.

While the specifics of these different efforts vary, some general principles can be applied to the efforts that show the most promise. As the chapters in this volume describe, there is a complex interplay between quality, affordability, and accessibility. Efforts must be considered in light of their effects on each of these variables.

First and foremost, efforts should be built on the idea that parents must have a choice in selecting the program option that best meets their needs. In order to provide parents with meaningful choices, it is necessary to increase and fortify the existing system of community programs. Issues of supply may be addressed by providing start-up loans or grants to potential programs or providing loans or grants for program expansion. Real choice also depends on parents being able to afford good programs. Low- and moderate-income families especially need assistance to afford the full costs of quality programs, not dependent on the hidden subsidy of inadequate staff compensation.

Efforts are needed to improve the quality of existing services. Improved regulatory standards—and effective enforcement—are essential. State licensing standards should safeguard the protection of children in settings outside their home and promote their development. In many states, rapid growth in the number of programs has outpaced the number of licensing officials. State budgetary cutbacks have in some instances led to fewer licensing officials in spite of the tremendous growth in the total number of centers and family child care homes subject to regulation.

In addition to regulatory approaches, quality can be enhanced by assisting programs and their staff to participate in professional systems of improvement and recognition. Public/private partnerships have been established to assist programs in achieving accreditation by NAEYC's Academy for centers or the National Family Day Care Association for family child care providers. Assistance may also be provided for individuals to gain professional training and credentials such as the Child Development Associate Credential, administered by the Council for Early Childhood Professional Recognition.

No one segment of our society can solve this nation's child care crisis—not the federal government, not states, not employers, and certainly not families. Instead, all segments of society must join together. The federal government must work as a partner with state and local government, business, religious groups, and social service and philanthropic organizations. Years of research knowledge about the ingredients and effects of quality make it evident that we are losing a great deal by not responding to the crisis of inadequate, tenuous, and poor quality care and education for our nation's youngest citizens. If we don't respond now, we will pay even more for our negligence in the future.

## REFERENCES

Adams, G. (1990). *Who knows how safe? The status of state efforts to ensure quality child care.* Washington, DC: Children's Defense Fund.

Aronson, S. (1987). Maintaining health in child care settings. In B.M. Caldwell (Ed.), *Group care for young children: A supplement to parental care.* Proceedings of the 12th Johnson & Johnson Pediatric Round Table (pp. 163–172). Lexington, MA: Lexington Books.

Bredekamp, S. (1989). *Regulating child care quality: Evidence from NAEYC's accreditation system.* Washington, DC: NAEYC.

Burden, D., & Googins, B. (1987, August). *Boston University—Balancing Job and Homelife Study: Summary of results.* Paper presented at the Annual Convention of the American Psychological Association, New York, NY.

Copple, C.E., Cline, M.G., & Smith, A.N. (1987). *Path to the future: Long-term effects of Head Start in the Philadelphia School District.* Washington, DC: U.S. Department of Health and Human Services.

Culkin, M., Helburn, S., Morris, J., & Watson, B. (1990). *Colorado's children: An economic profile of early childhood care and education.* Denver: University of Colorado at Denver, Economics Department.

Cummings, E.M. (1986, April). *Caregiver stability in day care: Continuity vs. daily association.* Paper presented at the International Conference on Infant Studies, Los Angeles.

Elkind, D. (1987). *Miseducation: Preschoolers at risk.* New York: Alfred A. Knopf.

Emlen, A., & Koren, P. (1984). *Hard to find and difficult to manage: The effects of child care on the workplace.* Portland, OR: Regional Institute for Human Services.

Finkelstein, N.W. (1982). Aggression: Is it stimulated by day care? *Young Children, 37*(6), 3–9.

Galinsky, E. (1988, January). *The impact of child care problems on parents on the job and at home.* Paper presented at the Wingspread Conference of Child Care Action Campaign, Racine, WI.

Galinsky, E., & Hughes, D. (1987, August). *The Fortune Magazine child care study.* Paper presented at the Annual Convention of the American Psychological Association, New York, NY.

Galinsky, E., Shinn, M., Phillips, D., Howes, C., & Whitebook, M. (1990). *Parent/teacher relationships.* New York: Families and Work Institute.

Gamble, T.J., & Zigler, E. (1986). Effects of infant day care: Another look at the evidence. *American Journal of Orthopsychiatry, 56*(1), 26–42.

Granger, R.C., & Marx, E. (1988). *Who is teaching? Early childhood teachers in New York City's publicly funded programs.* New York: Bank Street College of Education.

Hayes, C.D., Palmer, J.L., & Zaslow, M.J. (1990). *Who cares for America's children? Child care policy for the 1990s.* Washington, DC: National Academy of Sciences Press.

Howes, C. (1990). Can the age of entry into child care and the

## 6. REFLECTIONS

quality of child care predict behaviors in kindergarten? *Developmental Psychology, 26*(2), 292–303.

Howes, C., Rodning, C., Galluzzo, D.C., & Myers, L. (1988). Attachment and child care: Relationships with mother and caregiver. *Early Childhood Research Quarterly, 3*(4), 403–416.

Howes, C., & Stewart, P. (1987). Child's play with adults, toys, and peers: An examination of family and child care influences. *Developmental Psychology, 23*(3), 423–430.

Jorde-Bloom, P. (1988). *A great place to work: Improving conditions for staff in young children's programs.* Washington, DC: NAEYC.

Kontos, S., & Stremmel, A.J. (1988). Caregivers' perceptions of working conditions in a child care environment. *Early Childhood Research Quarterly, 3*(1), 77–90.

Lally, J.R., Mangione, P.L., & Honig, A.S. (1987). The Syracuse University Family Development Research Program: Long range impact of early intervention on low-income children and their families. San Francisco: Center for Child & Family Studies, Far West Laboratory for Educational Research and Development. [Summary appears in *Zero to Three*, April, 1988, as "More pride, less delinquency: Findings from the ten-year follow-up of the Syracuse Family Development Research Program," newsletter published by the National Center for Clinical Infant Programs, Arlington, VA.]

Marx, E., & Zinsser, C., with T. Porter. (1990). *Raising child care salaries and benefits: An evaluation of the New York state salary enhancement legislation.* New York: Bank Street College and the Center for Public Advocacy Research.

McCartney, K. (1984). The effect of quality of the day care environment upon children's language development. *Developmental Psychology, 20*, 244–260.

National Council of Jewish Women (1988). [Mothers in the workplace]. Unpublished raw data.

Olenick, M. (1986). *The relationship between day care quality and selected social policy variables.* Dissertation submitted to the UCLA School of Education.

Phillips, D.A., & Howes, C. (1987). Indicators of quality in child care: Review of research. In D.A. Phillips (Ed.), *Quality in child care: What does research tell us?* Washington, DC: NAEYC.

Phillips, D., McCartney, K., & Scarr, S. (1987). Child care quality and children's social development. *Developmental Psychology, 23*, 537–543.

Ruopp, R., Travers, J., Glantz, F., & Coelen, C. (1979). *Children at the center: Final report of the National Day Care Study.* Cambridge, MA: Abt Associates.

Shinn, M., Galinsky, E., & Gulcur, L. (1990). The role of child care centers in the lives of parents. New York: Families and Work Institute.

Shinn, M., Galinsky, E., & Gulcur, L. (1990). [The parent/teacher study.] Unpublished raw data.

Shinn, M., Ortiz-Torres, B., Morris, A., Simko, P., & Wong, N. (1989). Promoting the well-being of working parents: Coping, social support, and flexible job schedules. *American Journal of Community Psychology, 17*, 31–55.

Vandell, D.L., Henderson, V.K., & Wilson, K.S. (1988). A longitudinal study of children with varying day care experiences. *Child Development, 59*, 1286–1292.

Vandell, D.L., & Powers, C.P. (1983). Daycare quality and children's free play activities. *American Journal of Orthopsychiatry, 53*(3), 493–500.

Weikart, D.P. (1990, February 26). Testimony at the Subcommittee on Education and Health, Joint Economic Committee, U.S. Congress, Washington, DC.

Whitebook, M., Howes, C., & Phillips, D. (1990). *Who cares? Child care teachers and the quality of care in America. Final report of the National Child Care Staffing Study.* Oakland, CA: Child Care Employee Project.

# Reaching for
# THE YEAR 2000

## Katie Haycock

*Katie Haycock is Vice-President of the Children's Defense Fund, Washington, DC.*

In February 1990, the U.S. Governors and the President adopted a set of ambitious education goals for the year 2000. These six basic goals and 21 related objectives are intended to guide a decade-long effort to ensure that all young Americans are equipped with the knowledge and skills needed to be productive citizens and to maintain America's economic competitiveness.

Most of us, if asked, probably would have come up with a somewhat different list of goals. A different phrase here; perhaps a different word there. At the very least, we would have exercised a little more precision. But on the whole, the goals are a reasonably good statement of national aspirations. And we can all agree that the country will be much better off if we *reach* the goals than if we do not.

Reaching the goals will require significant improvements in a wide range of services for children, including health care, child care and preschool programs. It will also

**Editor's note:** Readers are referred to *State of America's Children* for data cited in this article (Washington, DC: Children's Defense Fund, March 1991).

require a fundamental overhaul of the nation's schools. As we move toward such an overhaul, however, it is worth taking a look at what happened last time around. For this is not, of course, the first U.S. effort to improve public education.

### The "Excellence" Reforms

Over the past seven years, a great deal of energy has been poured into the effort to improve America's public schools. To counteract what David Gardner and his colleagues in *A Nation at Risk* (1983) called a "rising tide of mediocrity," we banded together under the banner of "excellence," replacing lowered expectations with higher ones—both for students and schools. In state after state, we increased graduation requirements, beefed up the curriculum, increased college admissions requirements and insisted on greater accountability for results.

In general, the results of these efforts have been positive. According to most indicators—including standardized achievement tests, advanced course enrollments and college entrance exams—student performance has improved.

But we needed big, across-the-board changes, and we only got small and isolated ones. Dropout rates are still appalling. The college enrollment rate has not changed appreciably since 1967, despite the very real need in a changing

economy for more college-educated workers. Most discouraging of all, the achievement gap separating poor and minority students from other young Americans is still huge. It's as if we were walking—instead of running—to catch up with the train pulling out of the station.

### Economic Imperatives for Change

The U.S. economy is undergoing dramatic changes. Most new jobs being created require workers who can: 1) read, write and compute at high levels; 2) analyze and interpret data, draw conclusions and make decisions and 3) function as a part of a team.

Economists tell us that, to remain competitive in an increasingly tough international marketplace, we must be able to fill all those jobs with motivated, hard-working, highly skilled employees. But employers tell us they are having a tough time. Most report extremely high failure rates (50 to 75 percent) on exams for entry-level workers. Employers often have to provide extensive, on-the-job remedial education even for those who pass. Frustrated, many employers are turning to foreign workers.

If not addressed, the situation will only get worse as the number of young people declines. In the year 2000, there will be 5.4 million fewer 18- to 24-year-olds than in 1980 and millions more senior citi-

From *Childhood Education*, Vol. 67, No. 5, Annual Theme 1991, pp. 276-279. Reprinted by permission of Katie Haycock and the Association for Childhood Education International, 11141 Georgia Avenue, Suite 200, Wheaton, MD. Copyright © 1991 by the Association.

*M*ost discouraging of all, the achievement gap separating poor and minority students from other young Americans is still huge. It's as if we were walking —instead of running—to catch up with the train pulling out of the station.

zens for them to support. This makes each young person even more precious than ever. We simply cannot afford to lose any to unproductive lives.

At the same time as the age group shrinks, a larger portion of that group (more than 1/3) will be minority and poor, the very youngsters with whom we have been least successful in assisting to master the skills they need to become productive citizens. Although these youngsters enter school only slightly behind, the gap separating them from other youngsters accelerates as they progress through the grades.

- By 3rd grade, the average Black and Latino student is already 6 months behind.
- By 6th grade, one year behind.
- By 8th grade, two years behind.
- And by 12th grade—if he or she reaches 12th grade at all—the average Black and Latino youngster performs more than three grade levels below Anglo peers. In many states, as many as half of the minority students drop out.
- But whether they graduate or not, according to the National Assessment for Educational Progress, Black and Latino 17-year-olds have math and English skills about the same as white 13-year-olds; in science, their skills approximate those of white 9-year-olds.
- Not surprisingly, relatively few minority students enter college and still fewer graduate.

As a result, what comes out at the end of the educational system is very different from what went in at the beginning. Those who are prepared by virtue of their education and experience to enter white collar professions are still disproportionately Anglo and from affluent homes. On the other hand, those who are prepared—at best—for the dwindling number of blue collar jobs with decent wages are still disproportionately ethnic and from poor homes.

### Roots of Underachievement

When presented honestly (and they seldom are), data such as these can be discouraging and often overwhelming. They can lead either to a sense of paralysis or to some soul-wrenching questions about whether these kids can really learn.

In a number of schools, however, things are different. Students are being educated in rich and rigorous ways and the results are quite different. Test scores and college acceptance rates are going up; attendance and disciplinary problems are going down. The fact is that minority and poor students *can* achieve at the same high level as anyone else—if they are taught at the highest levels and provided with the help they need to get there.

But far too few minority and poor children are getting this type of challenge. Instead, they often spend their days in boring classrooms, circling *m*'s and *p*'s on dittos for hours on end, doing very

little of anything of any real interest. In fact, although no one likes to talk about this very much because it flies in the face of everything we like to believe about the society, these children get less of everything we believe makes a difference:

- Less in the way of experienced and well-trained teachers
- Less in the way of a rich and well-balanced curriculum
- Less actual instructional time
- Less in the way of well-equipped and well-stocked laboratories and libraries
- Less of what undoubtedly is most important of all—a belief that they can really learn.

How does this happen? It happens primarily in two ways: 1) differences between schools that serve minority children and those that serve other children and 2) differences within schools between high and low tracks.

In the first case, despite what we thought happened in *Brown v. Board of Education*, most minority students in the U.S. are still educated apart from other students. Many of their schools tend to get the least-trained teachers and lowest-level curricular materials. Everything is watered down.

Another practice—grouping and tracking—essentially has the same effect. In general, we herd poor and minority students into low-track classes where we assign them the worst teachers and oldest books and then expect little or nothing from them.

It's hardly surprising, then, that minority and poor students do less well than other students on tests of academic achievement. The fact is that we teach them less.

As if all of this weren't enough, some communities have less, too:

- Less knowledge about how schools work
- Fewer skills to help with homework

- Less flexible time to visit schools
- Fewer resources to pay for educational extras
- And fewer hopes and dreams for children who are all too often overwhelmed by the day-to-day business of survival in today's world.

The combination of these two factors—the "lesses" in schools together with the "lesses" in communities—is simply devastating for poor and minority youngsters. Most are simply nowhere near mastering the knowledge and skills they need to become productive citizens. And how sadly ironic that things should be going from bad to worse just as the economy promises finally to produce the decent jobs that would be capable of permanently lifting people out of poverty.

## Conditions of American Children

Look for a moment at what happens to children in America every day—and think about what these numbers mean for our collective future.

Changing these numbers will require a massive effort from all sectors of society. But no piece of that effort is more important than improving the public schools, especially those that serve minority and poor students, because:

- *no other system* touches all of our children
- *no other system* can equip young people with the skills and knowledge they need to become productive citizens and avoid too-early pregnancy, drug use and other high-risk behaviors
- *no other system* can give our children genuine hope and confidence in a better future.

## So Where Do We Start?

We start, first of all, by remembering one of the chief lessons from past reform efforts: *rising tides do*

---

### Every Day in America

| | |
|---:|---|
| 2,740 | teenagers get pregnant |
| 1,105 | teenagers have abortions |
| 369 | teenagers miscarry |
| 1,293 | teenagers give birth |
| 700 | babies are born with low birthweight |
| 69 | babies die before one month of life |
| 107 | babies die before their first birthday |
| 27 | children die because of poverty |
| 9 | children die from guns |
| 6 | teenagers commit suicide |
| 1,375 | teenagers drop out of high school |
| 1,849 | children are abused |
| 3,288 | children run away from home |
| 2,987 | children see their parents divorced |
| 135,000 | kids arrive at school with a gun. |

(Children's Defense Fund, 1990)

---

*not raise all boats*. Generic, across-the-board reform efforts—efforts that fail to acknowledge that some schools are much further than others from commonly accepted standards of excellence and consequently require more help to get there—are doomed to give us inadequate results.

If we are to close gaps in achieve-ment and graduation rates as called for in the new education goals, we will have to deal head on with the "lesses" in the schools that serve minority and poor children. Instead of watering down what we teach, we must systematically beef it up. Instead of expecting less, we must systematically expect more. Instead of sending in teachers and administrators inadequately prepared for the challenge, we must send in our most able, prepared with strategies for success rather than excuses for failure.

There is, of course, a wide range of strategies to improve achievement and college acceptance rates among minority and poor students. But, there is no magic formula here. Teachers and administrators will have to work together to select the best approach for their school. Four key elements that ought to be included are:

- Reducing unnecessary grouping and tracking
- Making sure all students are educated with a rich and rigorous core curriculum
- Building support systems so students can succeed in higher-level studies
- Communicating regularly with parents on their children's progress and helping them to support their children in school.

*Instead of watering down what we teach, we must systematically beef it up. Instead of expecting less, we must systematically expect more. Instead of sending in teachers and administrators inadequately prepared for the challenge, we must send in our most able, prepared with strategies for success rather than excuses for failure.*

## 6. REFLECTIONS

Schools that attend to these four matters virtually always get improved results.

### Beyond the School Walls

All of these efforts would, of course, be enhanced if society took its children, especially its poor children, more seriously by providing more of the supports they need to arrive at school ready to learn, from prenatal care through Head Start. Educators can play a vital role in bringing the U.S. to its senses by speaking out about children's needs.

One of the most corrosive developments of the 1980s was the propagation of a belief that nothing works—that we can't make a difference, all efforts to ameliorate problems fail, teaching and other forms of public service are an unworthy calling. *We should all withdraw from engagement in public life and lead our lives in ever-smaller circles!*

It is as though the entire nation has been put in one of those spirit-squelching, hope-destroying schools in which we bury so many students. Told that we did not have the ability to perform in public life, we stopped trying. Told that as a nation we could not achieve social reform, we gave up the effort. These teachings poisoned public life and contributed to the widespread despair about mending the nation's social fabric.

The lessons taught in the nation's schoolroom in the 1980s were wrong. The U.S. has made real gains when it paid attention to how we as individuals, as well as collectively through government, can help families and communities.

All of us must let our friends and our political leaders know that some things *do* work. Early investment is cheaper than ignorance, unemployment and dependency, and schools with strong leadership, demanding curricula and caring staff absolutely can raise achievement levels. When we as a society tried, we effected real reductions in infant mortality, low birthweight, childhood illness and school dropouts—and we achieved real increases in achievement, college attendance, health and longevity.

All of this is no mystery, just common sense. We need to learn more. But we also need to discard simple-minded sloganeering and do more of what we know works. You can help that happen by speaking out about what you know works.

### Moving Forward

All of this is a lot of work. Most educators have given their all for children for decades. Somehow, we're going to have to reach inside for that inner strength that will enable us to do still more. Why do I say this? The reason is simple: I have seen the future, and I am scared.

■ I have been to the neonatal intensive wards and watched cocaine babies and other severely low birthweight babies, born to women with no skills and no hope, struggling for life.

■ I have been to the early intervention preschool programs and watched what these youngsters are like as they grow up.

■ I have walked city streets and seen far too many eyes dimmed, far too many dreams shattered.

Is it fair that educators should be the first line of defense—or offense, for that matter—against this kind of a future? No, it is not. If ours were a just society, we would be joined by a veritable army of health care professionals, business leaders, social service workers, political leaders and many, many others. But, at the moment, we are the first line for many youngsters.

All of us are going to have to form an army of our own—an army for children. We're going to have to dig a bit deeper within ourselves for strength until such time as *no* child's needs go unmet. No one is more important to children's future—and the future of the nation—than you are.

### References

Children's Defense Fund. (1990). *Children 1990: A report card.* Washington, DC: Author.

Children's Defense Fund. (1991). *State of America's children.* Washington DC: Author.

National Commission on Excellence in Education. (1983). *A nation at risk.* Washington, DC: Author.

abuse, and neglect, of children, 8
Action for Children's Television (ACT), 119–122
admiration, and self-control, 178
adults: intervention of, in classroom conflict, 172–173; role of, in play, 188; see also, parents; teachers; working mothers
advertising, and children's television, 120–121
affirmative action, and programming for children's television, 121
African Americans, see blacks
after-school programs, and working mothers, 22
age, self-control and, 176
age-appropriate tasks, 117
aggression: and discipline, 238; gender differences in, 62–63, 64; see also, emotions
alcohol abuse, effect of prenatal, on fetus, 12, 13
anxiety: in children, 72; see also, emotions; separation; stress management
A/PLX, see Apple/Polaroid Language Experience Approach
Apple/Polaroid Language Experience Approach, 221–223
art, in stress management, 183
assessment: of cocaine-exposed children, 18; NAEYC's guidelines for developmentally appropriate curriculum and, 86–94; Project Spectrum as alternative to, 135–138; of school readiness, 131–134
at-risk children: early education for, 79; and grade retention, 95, 96, 99
attachment: crack-exposed children and, 17; see also, separation
au pair, child care and, 20
Australia, preschool in, 38–39
authoritative parents, discipline and, 177

behavior modification approach, 114
bibliotherapy: helping children of divorce and, 75; to promote self-control, 178
bilingual children, teaching, 100–104
biological factors, of gender differences, 62–64
birth order, personality effects of, 67–70
blacks, and grade retention, 96
boarder babies, 17
bonding, mother-child, in crack-exposed children, 17
books: and cycle of illiteracy, 72; for helping children of divorce, 75; self-control and, 178
Brazelton, T. Berry: on separation, 59–61; on working parents, 77–81
Bulgaria, preschool in, 37

"Channel One," and advertising for children's television, 120
child care centers, 7, 231; see also, day care
children: effect of substance abuse on, 12–13, 15–18; identification of mild handicaps in preschool, 139–143; neglecting of, 12–14, 24–28; planning of, 206–210; teaching and, of divorce, 74–76; teaching bilingual, 100–104; and television, 119–122
Children's Defense Fund, 27

Children's Television Act of 1990, 122
China, kindergarten in, 47–51
classification, children's use of, 167
climbers, safety of, 202
"CNN Newsroom," and children's television, 120
cocaine, effect of prenatal abuse of, on children, 12, 13, 15–18
cognitive play, 187
commercials, and programming for children's television, 120
communication: and handling classroom conflicts, 172; preschool classroom environment to promote, 145–148
Communication Act of 1934, and children's television, 120, 122
conflict, handling of, in classrooms, 170–173
constructive play, 187
Consumer Product Safety Commission, 201, 204
contagion, 13
cooperative play, 188
crack-exposed children, 12, 13, 15–18
cultural factors, in gender differences, 63, 64–66
curriculum: and developmentally appropriate practice, 8; guidelines of NAEYC for developmentally appropriate, 86–94; science-centered, 217–220

day care: approaches to, and working mothers, 20–23; arguments against school-age, 123–127; effects of, on infants, 227–228; family, homes, 7; long-term effects of, 226–228; poor conditions in, 24–28; see also, child care centers
depression: in children, 78; see also, emotions
developmental and maintenance approach, to bilingual education, 102
developmental kindergarten, and grade retention, 98
developmentally appropriate practice, 8, 112–113, 115; NAEYC's guidelines for, 86–94
discipline, 157, 230; parental methods of teaching, 177–178
divorce: children of, and teachers, 74–76; and working parents, 78, 79–80
dramatic play, 187
dropout rate, and grade retention, 95, 96, 99
dysfunctional families, and teachers, 82

Ecuador, preschool in, 38
Education of Handicapped Act Amendments of 1986, 149
education readiness, national goals for, 132
education reform, and grade retention, 97–98
elaborated plans, 207
elementary school, science-centered curriculum, 217–220
emergent literacy, 112, 196–200
emotions: helping children deal with, 163–164; helping children of divorce deal with, 74–76; see also, aggression; anxiety; depression
encouragement, and self-control, 178
England, preschool in, 37–38

environment: communication and classroom, 145–148; as external control of behavior, 175; Project Spectrum and, 135–138; structuring of time and space in classroom, 105–109
equipment, safety of playground, 201–203
ethics, NAEYC's code of, 6–11
exceptionality, parental reaction to, 150–151
external controls, over behavior, 175

families: cycle of illiteracy in, 71–73; and Head Start, 31, 32, 33; importance of, in early childhood education, 7, 8, 9, and teachers, 82
family day-care homes, 7
Federal Communications Commission (FCC), and children's television, 121, 122
federal government, and regulating day-care programs, 25–26, 27
Federal Trade Commission, and advertising for children's television, 121
fetal alcohol syndrome, 12, 13
FIMAJ, and programming for children's television, 119
firstborn children, effect of birth order on personality of, 68
Fisher-Price, and gender differences in toys, 65
flexible work schedules, and working mothers, 21, 22
free play, of crack-exposed children, 18
functional play, 187

games with rules, and play, 187
gender differences, culture vs. biology in, 62–66
gender-roles, 62, 64
Georgia Kindergarten Assessment Program (GKAP), 133
government, and regulating day-care programs, 25–26, 27
grade retention, evaluation of success of, 95–99
Great Britain, preschool in, 37–38
group planning, 209
guidelines, of NAEYC, for developmentally appropriate curriculum, 86–94

handicapped children, teachers and parents of, 149–151
handicaps, mild, identifying preschool children with, 139–144
Head Start: in bilingual education, 103; report of state of, 29–35
Holmes, C. T., on grade retention, 95–96
homework, and cycle of illiteracy, 72
hormones, sex, and gender differences, 62–64

illiteracy, schools and cycle of, 71–73
imitation, and play, 187
immigrants, and bilingual education, 100–101
individual planning, 209
individuality, of children, 155
Individualized Educational Plan (IEP), and grade retention, 97
Indonesia, preschool in, 38
inductive discipline, 177, 178
infant mortality, 12, 13
infants, effect of day care on, 227–228
in-service training, for teachers, 8
instrumental behavior, and play, 186

integrated thematic approach, to teaching science, 218
interdisciplinary approach, of evaluating for mild handicaps, 140–141
internalized standards of conduct, 175
intimacy, child planning and, 208
invented spellings, development of, 214
Italy, early childhood education in Reggio Emilia, 40–46

kindergarten, 7; in China, 47–51; writing in, and parents, 211–216

language development: and play, 187; and writing development, 212, 213
Language Experience Approach, to teaching writing skills, 221–223
language skills: in childhood, 57, 58; use of Apple/Polaroid Language Experience Approach to teach, 221–223
last-born children, effect of birth order on personality of, 69–70
lead poisoning, 13
learning: and play, 186–190, 192; structuring of time and space for, 105–109
licensing, of child care centers, 7
literacy: emergent, 196–200; see also, illiteracy

maintenance/development approach, to bilingual education, 102
mastering, 116–117
math, 99; and gender differences, 63
maturity, self-control and, 176
merry-go-rounds, safety of playgrounds and, 202–203
Mid-California Science Improvement Program (MCSIP), science-centered curriculum and, 218, 219–220
middle child, effect of birth order on personality of, 68–69
minority students, and America 2000, 238–239
models, adults serving as, for children, 164
Montessori method, 113–114
mother-child bond, crack-exposed children and, 17
mothers, see working mothers
motor development, in children, 57
multidisciplinary approach, of evaluating for mild handicaps, 140
multiple intelligences, Howard Gardner's theory of, 135

National Association for the Education of Young Children (NAEYC), 113, 228, 229; code of ethics of, 6–11; position statement of, on developmentally appropriate practice, 86–94
National Child Care Staffing Study, 28
National Head Start Association (NHSA), 29, 31, 32, 35
National Survey of Playground Equipment in Preschools, 201–205
NELB, see non-English language background
no-fault divorce, and decline in family's standard of living, 78
non-English language background (NELB) children, teaching, 100–104
non-universal domains, David Feldman's theory of development in, 135

North Yemen, preschool in, 36–37
Office of Educational Research and Improvement (OERI), 132, 134
only children, personality of, 68
ownership, and permanency, 192–194

parallel social play situations, 187, 188
parental leave, 20, 23, 226
parents, 111, 112; and birth order of children, 67–70; control of children and, 175–176; and cycle of illiteracy, 71–73; of handicapped children and teachers, 149–151; and Head Start, 32–33; methods of teaching self-discipline of, 176–177; and poor conditions in day-care settings, 24–28; preschool stress management and, 182; in Reggio Emilia, Italy, 41–42; separation and, 59–61; and teachers, 82–83, 231–232; understanding of children's writing in kindergarten and, 211–216; unsupportive, 82–83; working, 77–81, 232–233; see also, working mothers
peer tutoring, as alternative to grade retention, 97
perfunctory plans, 207
permanency, and ownership, 192–194
personality, effect of birth order on, 67–70
photography: of children's play, 194; use of, in Apple/Polaroid Language Experience Approach to teach language, 221–223
physical development, in childhood, 227–228
planning, child, 206–210
play: and child development, 202; and learning, 186–190, 192
play value, and safety on playgrounds, 203
playgrounds, safety of, 201–205
Polaroid Language Experience (PLX), 221–223
portions, and creating environments to promote communication, 147
poverty, children and, 13–14
power-assertive discipline, 177
pregnancy: sexually transmitted diseases and, 13; substance abuse and, 12–13, 15–18
preschool: global impressions of, 36–39; identification of mild handicaps in, 139–144; stress management in, 180–183
proactive discipline techniques, 175
programming, for children's television, 119–122
Project Spectrum, as alternative to assessment, 135–138
project-based teaching, in Reggio Emilia, 42–44
proxy measures, limitations of, to school readiness, 131–132
pseudomaturity, and personality of firstborn children, 68
Public Broadcasting Service (PBS), and children's television, 121
Public Law 99-457, handicapped children, 149

quality of care, in day-care programs, 24–28
quality time, 163

readiness assessment, school, 131–134

reading: and emergent literacy, 112, 196–200; gender differences in, 63
Reggio Emilia, early childhood education in, 40–46
regulations, for day-care programs, 25–26, 27
relaxation, and preschool stress management, 180–183
remedial help, as alternative to grade retention, 97, 98
respect, of children, and child care, 154–159
retention, of students, 95–99
rocking equipment, safety of, 203
role-playing, stress management and, 181–182
routine plans, 207

sabotage, and creating environments to promote communication, 147
SACC, see school-age child care
safety: and child care centers, 24–28, 231; of playgrounds, 201–205
safety standards, for day-care programs, 25–26
salaries, of teachers, 31, 32, 234
school: crack-exposed children and, 17–18; and cycle of literacy, 71
school readiness assessment, 131–134
school-age child care, common arguments against, 123–127
Schroeder, Patricia, 25–26
science-centered curriculum, 217–220
screening, of preschool children for mild handicaps, 139, 143
second language learners, 100–104
second-born children, effect of birth order on personality of, 69
see-saws, safety of playground equipment and, 203
self-control, development of, 174–178
self-discipline, 117–118
self-esteem, children's 8, 78, 79, 80, 161–164, 165–168
separation: T. Berry Brazelton on, 59–61; see also, attachment
setting, child planning and, 208
sex hormones, and gender differences, 62–64
sexually transmitted diseases, in children, 13
shared custody, after divorce, 79
single-parent families, 68, 78, 79, 81
smoking, effect of prenatal, on fetus, 12, 13
social development, and play, 188
social equality, between adults and children, 155–156
social learning, and play, 187
social level of play, 187
socialization, and teaching of self-control, 177–178
sociodramatic play, 187
solitary play, 187, 188
space, structuring of time and, to promote learning, 105–109
specialized training, and care of school-age children, 125
spelling: development of, 213; and emergent literacy, 198–199; see also, writing
stage-appropriate tasks, 117
standards, for day-care programs, 25–26, 27

state governments, and regulating day-care programs, 27
stepfamilies, 80
stereotypes, gender, 63, 66
storybook reading, and emergent literacy, 197
stress: and grade retention, 96; technique for management of, in preschool, 180–183
stress management, in preschool, 180–183
student-teacher ratio, 230–231
substance abuse, effect of prenatal, on children, 12–13, 15–18
supervisors, and working mothers, 22–23
surfacing, of playgrounds, and safety, 203
swings, safety of, 202

teachers, 111; and children of divorce, 74–76; and children's play, 191–195; and discipline, 230; and family illiteracy, 72; identification of mild handicaps in preschool children, 139–144; and parents, 82–83, 158, 231–232; and parents with handicapped children, 149–151; salaries of, 31, 32, 234; stress

management and, 180, 181–182; techniques of teaching self-control of, 178; training of, 112; training of, and science-centered curriculum, 218; working conditions of, 234
teaching: of bilingual children, 100–104; of literacy, 196–200
temperament, self-control and, 176
testosterone, and gender differences, 63–64
tests: and gender differences, 63; of preschool children, for mild handicaps, 139, 140, 141; of school readiness, 31, 132; whole language and standardized, 128–130
time, structuring of space, in classroom, 105–109
tobacco, see smoking
toys: and gender differences, 65; and play, 189
traffic patterns, and play, 189
transdisciplinary approach, of evaluating for mild handicaps, 140, 141
transitional approach, to teaching bilingual students, 102
trust, and self-esteem, 162
tutoring, as alternative to grade retention, 97

two-way approach, to bilingual education, 102–103
unidisciplinary model, of evaluating for mild handicaps, 140
U.S. Communication Act of 1934, and children's television, 120, 122

vague plans, 207
verbal environment, and children's self-esteem, 165–168

whole language tests, as alternative to standardized tests, 128–130
women: unequal pay for, 21; see also, working mothers
word processing, use of, to teach language, 221–223
working mothers, 83, 226, 227, 228; and day-care approaches, 20–23; see also, parents; women
writing: in kindergarten, and parents, 211–216; use of Apple/Polaroid Language Experience Approach to teach, 221–223

Yemen Arab Republic, preschool in, 36–37

# Credits/ Acknowledgments

Cover design by Charles Vitelli

**1. Perspectives**
Facing overview—Elaine M. Ward.

**2. Child Development and Families**
Facing overview—Courtesy of Leslie Holmes Lowlor.

**3. Appropriate Educational Practices**
Facing overview—Courtesy of Leslie Holmes Lowlor.

**4. Guiding Behavior**
Facing overview—Elaine M. Ward.

**5. Curricular Applications**
Facing overview—United Nations photo by Marta Pinter.

**6. Reflections**
Facing overview—United Nations photo by Y. Nagata.

# ANNUAL EDITIONS ARTICLE REVIEW FORM

■ NAME: _____ DATE: _____

■ TITLE AND NUMBER OF ARTICLE: _____

■ BRIEFLY STATE THE MAIN IDEA OF THIS ARTICLE: _____

_____

_____

_____

_____

■ LIST THREE IMPORTANT FACTS THAT THE AUTHOR USES TO SUPPORT THE MAIN IDEA:

_____

_____

_____

_____

_____

■ WHAT INFORMATION OR IDEAS DISCUSSED IN THIS ARTICLE ARE ALSO DISCUSSED IN YOUR TEXTBOOK OR OTHER READING YOU HAVE DONE? LIST THE TEXTBOOK CHAPTERS AND PAGE NUMBERS:

_____

_____

_____

_____

_____

■ LIST ANY EXAMPLES OF BIAS OR FAULTY REASONING THAT YOU FOUND IN THE ARTICLE:

_____

_____

_____

_____

■ LIST ANY NEW TERMS/CONCEPTS THAT WERE DISCUSSED IN THE ARTICLE AND WRITE A SHORT DEFINITION:

_____

_____

_____

_____

*Your instructor may require you to use this Annual Editions Article Review Form in any number of ways:
for articles that are assigned, for extra credit, as a tool to assist in developing assigned papers, or simply
for your own reference. Even if it is not required, we encourage you to photocopy and use this page;
you'll find that reflecting on the articles will greatly enhance the information from your text.

# ANNUAL EDITIONS:
## EARLY CHILDHOOD EDUCATION 92/93
### Article Rating Form

Here is an opportunity for you to have direct input into the next revision of this volume. We would like you to rate each of the 47 articles listed below, using the following scale:

1. **Excellent: should definitely be retained**
2. **Above average: should probably be retained**
3. **Below average: should probably be deleted**
4. **Poor: should definitely be deleted**

Your ratings will play a vital part in the next revision. So please mail this prepaid form to us just as soon as you complete it.
Thanks for your help!

Annual Editions revisions depend on two major opinion sources: one is our Advisory Board, listed in the front of this volume, which works with us in scanning the thousands of articles published in the public press each year; the other is you—the person actually using the book. Please help us and the users of the next edition by completing the prepaid article rating form on this page and returning it to us. Thank you.

| Rating | Article | Rating | Article |
|---|---|---|---|
| | 1. A New Code of Ethics for Early Childhood Educators! | | 26. Tracking Progress Toward the School Readiness Goal |
| | 2. Children in Peril | | 27. Project Spectrum: An Innovative Assessment Alternative |
| | 3. The Shadow Children: Preparing for the Arrival of Crack Babies in School | | 28. Identification of Preschool Children With Mild Handicaps: The Importance of Cooperative Effort |
| | 4. I Couldn't Afford My Job | | |
| | 5. When Parents Accept the Unacceptable | | 29. Preschool Classroom Environments That Promote Communication |
| | 6. Head Start: The Nation's Pride, A Nation's Challenge | | 30. Parental Feelings: The Forgotten Component When Working with Parents of Handicapped Preschool Children |
| | 7. A Global Collage of Impressions: Preschools Abroad | | |
| | 8. Excellent Early Education: A City in Italy Has It | | 31. How Well Do We Respect the Children in Our Care? |
| | 9. A Glimpse of Kindergarten—Chinese Style | | 32. Nurturing Success |
| | | | 33. Children's Self-Esteem: The Verbal Environment |
| | 10. First Year Milestones | | |
| | 11. Easing Separation: A Talk With T. Berry Brazelton, M.D. | | 34. Solving Problems Together |
| | | | 35. The Tasks of Early Childhood: The Development of Self-Control—Part II |
| | 12. Guns and Dolls | | |
| | 13. What Birth Order Means | | 36. A Is for Apple, P Is for Pressure—Preschool Stress Management |
| | 14. How Schools Perpetuate Illiteracy | | |
| | 15. Children of Divorce | | 37. Learning to Play: Playing to Learn |
| | 16. Single-Parent Families: How Bad for the Children? | | 38. "Put Your Name on Your Painting, But . . . the Blocks Go Back on the Shelves" |
| | 17. Where Are the Parents? | | |
| | 18. Guidelines for Appropriate Curriculum Content and Assessment in Programs Serving Children Ages 3 Through 8 | | 39. The State of American Preschool Playgrounds |
| | | | 40. Emergent Literacy: How Young Children Learn to Read and Write |
| | 19. Synthesis of Research on Grade Retention | | |
| | | | 41. The Many Faces of Child Planning |
| | 20. Understanding Bilingual/Bicultural Young Children | | 42. Writing in Kindergarten: Helping Parents Understand the Process |
| | 21. Structure Time & Space to Promote Pursuit of Learning in the Primary Grades | | 43. Science-Centered Curriculum in Elementary School |
| | | | 44. Creating a Reading/Writing Environment |
| | 22. Why Not Academic Preschool? (Part 1) | | 45. The Day Care Generation |
| | 23. What's Missing in Children's TV | | 46. The Costs of *Not* Providing Quality Early Childhood Programs |
| | 24. School-Age Child Care: A Review of Five Common Arguments | | |
| | 25. Tests, Independence, and Whole Language | | 47. Reaching for the Year 2000 |

*(Continued on next page)*

## ABOUT YOU

Name_____ Date_____
Are you a teacher? ☐  Or student? ☐
Your School Name _____
Department _____
Address _____
City _____ State _____ Zip _____
School Telephone # _____

## YOUR COMMENTS ARE IMPORTANT TO US!

Please fill in the following information:

For which course did you use this book? _____
Did you use a text with this Annual Edition?  ☐ yes  ☐ no
The title of the text? _____
What are your general reactions to the Annual Editions concept?


Have you read any particular articles recently that you think should be included in the next edition?


Are there any articles you feel should be replaced in the next edition? Why?


Are there other areas that you feel would utilize an Annual Edition?


May we contact you for editorial input?


May we quote you from above?


**ANNUAL EDITIONS: EARLY CHILDHOOD EDUCATION 92/93**

## BUSINESS REPLY MAIL

First Class          Permit No. 84          Guilford, CT

*Postage will be paid by addressee*

**The Dushkin Publishing Group, Inc.**
**Sluice Dock**
DPG **Guilford, Connecticut 06437**

No Postage
Necessary
if Mailed
in the
United States